THE

LAW OF LITERATURE

REVIEWING

THE LAWS OF LITERARY PROPERTY IN MANUSCRIPTS; BOOKS, LECTURES, DRAMATIC AND MUSICAL COMPOSITIONS; WORKS OF ART, NEWSPAPERS, PERIODICALS, &C.; COPYRIGHT TRANSFERS, AND COPYRIGHT AND PIRACY; LIBEL AND CONTEMPT OF COURT BY LITERARY MATTER, ETC.

WITH AN APPENDIX OF THE AMERICAN, ENGLISH, FRENCH, AND GERMAN STATUTES OF COPYRIGHT

BY

JAMES APPLETON MORGAN, M.A.

OF THE NEW YORK BAR

IN TWO VOLUMES

VOL. I

NEW YORK

JAMES COCKCROFT & COMPANY

1875

Tobitt & Bunce,
Printers and Stereotypers,
131 William Street.

TO

A· W· O

IN LOVE

AND

GRATITUDE.

PREFACE.

FOR thirty-eight years, since Mr. Curtis's scholarly volume, published in 1837, no textual work on the American law of copyright has made its appearance in the United States. And although, since then, the importance of the subject has grown —as it must continue to grow—commensurately and parallel with the growth and importance of literature and the multiplication of books, the department of Copyright does not, even to-day, make a large appearance in our Digests.

The reason why this is so, doubtless lies in the fact that comparatively few Copyright cases, in our courts, get beyond a hearing, in the first instance, at a special term or in chambers—they either proceeding at once therefrom to settlement by the parties themselves, or being abandoned by the pursuers. If the manager of a theater, for example, who has expended large sums to mount a dramatic production upon his stage, should be served—upon the threshold of its production—with a temporary injunction, and an order to show cause why such injunction should not be made final, he will hardly keep his properties unemployed and his actors idle, to carry the case to the Court of Appeals, or to Washington, before presenting his play. If he cannot raise the injunction at special term, the next day, he must settle the difficulty the best way he can; and if he does raise it, the pursuit is generally withdrawn. So, likewise, the publisher of a book, whose first sale is interrupted, is generally very loath to abide the dignified and long-drawn leisure of the Law. As chamber and special term hearings, therefore, are reported but rarely, the great majority of these cases do not get into the volumes of reports, and thence into the Digests. Many of them do not even find their way into the newspapers. But all the more, instead of all the less, does this seem to demonstrate the importance of interests too vital for courts beyond, and which must be settled at first hand, by a single judge; and to prove that there is room for a work like the present.

I am aware that the style I have chosen for this inquiry is an innovation, upon this side of the Atlantic. In the preface to an English work, edited by me, some time ago, I ventured to remark that "there is a wide dissimilarity between the American and the English systems of legal text-writing. While the plan of the American writer has invariably been to consider, in his text, only principles and rules,—connecting them with the cases in which they have been enunciated by foot-note reference,—the English method is to give, in the body of the text, a sort of running history of the cases themselves, their dicta, rulings, and progress—not unfrequently, even, of the argument, objections, and strategy of counsel,—trusting to the detailed and discursive report itself, to develop the principles and rules for which he is seeking. Neither plan is without its excellences, nor quite without its faults. The American undoubtedly produces, from a literary point of view, the more rounded and finished essay. But the student is possibly in danger of being led along by the author's own reasoning or learning, or by his own ideas as to what the law is or ought to be. The English method, though prolix and inartificial, is, at all events, accurate and reliable, since the student is safe to find out, therefrom, exactly what the law is, and what the precedents which courts are likely to follow." At the risk, then, of being "prolix and inartificial," I have, in the following pages, followed the English plan. It is at least a question whether literary merit is any merit at all in a legal work—whether, even, it is not a positive demerit; at all events, if it be accurate and reliable, the lawyer and the student will pardon a lack of unity and style.

There is a vast temptation to the writer of a work upon Literary Property, to allow himself to be led aside by the fascination of the subject; to be dazzled by the great names that glow and sparkle under his pen. The first great case of copyright involved the proprietorship of the assigns of the poet Thompson in his own poems; in its discussion sat Lords Mansfield, De Grey, Aston, Willes, and Yates, and therein Lord Camden delivered his famous argument. Greater than Thompson—Milton, Johnson, Byron, Shelley, Southey, Walter Scott, and Dickens—have been litigants, either personally or through their representatives, in like causes. The History of Clarendon, and the Letters of Chesterfield in England, and—in our own country—the letters of Washington and the Commentaries of Story, have come before the courts for protection; while for the last and most generous encouragement which the British parliament ever extended to its authors, Wordsworth was a petitioner, and Talford a debater.

I have felt the temptation, and have so far yielded, that, in the pages which follow, much that is historical will be found commingled with the technical; but I have tried to remember that I was writing a practical book for a practical profession, and to limit myself to the usefulness of the subject.

A greater or less security in their literary property is now accorded to authors, by the laws of every civilized nation. Both in the United States and England, equity is now prompt to interfere in cases of infringement, while in France (and possibly elsewhere) piracy is a misdemeanor cognizable by the police, and the culprit who steals a poem or a drama, has his case attended to as briskly as his confrère who rifles a pocket, the consequence being, in that happy country, that authors—while they have fewer precedents in their favor than with us—have much more protection. It is remarkable that, of all these civilized nations, the United States is the only one which has not bestowed upon the author a proprietorship over his own productions for at least his own lifetime,—be that lifetime longer or shorter,—but has limited it, absolutely, to a certain term of years. The reason for this policy is not so evident. It is certainly difficult to see the justice of a measure which denies to one's old age the profits of the labor of his earlier years—which, in the noble words of Talford, " Gives a bounty to haste, and informs the laborious student—who would wear away his strength to complete some work which the world will not willingly let die—that the more of his life he devotes to its perfection, the more limited shall be his interest in its fruits." Of a similar provision in the English law—one which, owing to his efforts, has long since disappeared—the sergeant continued: "It stops the progress of remuneration at the moment it is most needed; and when the benignity of nature would extract from her last calamity a means of support and comfort to the survivors—at the moment when his name is invested with the solemn interest of the grave—when his eccentricities or frailties excite a smile or a shrug no longer—when the last seal is set upon his earthly course, and his works assume their place among the classics of his country—your law declares that his works shall become your property, and you requite him by seizing the patrimony of his children." But the time of a wider appreciation and favor to authors is at hand. It is believed that the courts of the United States have gone further than those of any other country in securing to alien authors their common-law rights (such as they happened to be) in their own compositions. It is to be hoped she may yet—in her statutes—be as generous to her own.

I have expressed myself, in the second volume of this work, as unreservedly in favor of an International Copyright, and given some reasons why, as it seems to me, such a measure is demanded, not only by all justice—which scarcely anybody can be found to deny—but by all expediency, as well.

I am very far from wishing to be understood as saying that it is an expediency merely for the authors, or merely for the literature of the country. Years ago, Thomas Hood declared "that America, in the absence of an international Copyright, can never possess a native literature, has been foretold by the second-sighted on either side of the Atlantic."* But that negative prophecy does not appear to be on its way to a fulfillment. It seems to me, rather, that—in a large sense—the interest of the consumers, of the readers—of the people—demand it, and that whatever is the interest of the people, must ultimately and triumphantly prevail. As it stands now, the public—the readers of Great Britain and the United States—are obliged, practically, to pay for the manufacture of a book twice before they can have the opportunity to read it once; a vast and unnecessary burden that is daily making itself felt and realized.

But it is perhaps superfluous to say more. As sure as it is that birds and bards will sing, that authors will write, and that readers will read, until the end of time, so sure is it that one day—come it soon or later—Statutes of Copyright will be as broad as the world.

May 1, 1875,
229 BROADWAY, NEW YORK.

* "Copy Right and Copy Wrong." Letter X. Hood's Choice Works (New York, 1856.) Vol. 1. p. 115. And see a similar remark quoted by Mr. Emerson in his "English Traits." "So long as you (America) deny us (England) copyright, we shall have the teaching of you."—p. 32.

CONTENTS OF VOLUME I.

INTRODUCTORY.

BOOK I.

IN WHAT AND IN WHOM PROPERTY IN LITERARY COMPOSITION MAY EXIST.

CHAPTER I.

OF INNOCENCE.

CHAPTER II.

OF LIBEL.

CHAPTER III.

OF CONTEMPT OF COURT.

CHAPTER IV.

OF ORIGINALITY.

BOOK II.

OF PROPERTY IN LITERARY COMPOSITION BEFORE PUBLICATION.

CHAPTER I.

OF MANUSCRIPTS.

THE

LAW OF LITERATURE.

INTRODUCTORY.

INTELLECTUAL Property—that is, the property existing in Thought, Expression, Sentiment and Language,—in like manner with all other sorts and kinds of property,—must find its origin in Natural Law.

As to what is Natural Law, learned men have differed widely. Some have defined it to be the primal will of the Creator,[1] while others claim that it is nothing more than the tacit consent of mankind.[2] But as to its being the source of this right of property for which we are seeking, all appear to be finally agreed.

2. Property may be defined as anything which is not common to all mankind: which belongs to a less number of individuals than the whole human family, and which may be transmitted and set over at will by its owner or owners, to others, who would, in their turn, become its owners and possessors.

3. This property may exist in whatever is CAPABLE OF OCCUPATION; the surface of the globe, and everything upon it which it is possible to occupy, is, therefore, a

[1] 2 Kent Com. 320.

[2] Grotius Droit de la Guerre (ed. Basle, 1846), liv. 2, ch. 2, § 10, tom. 1. Puffendorf, i. 404; Vat. i. 1.

egitimate subject of property. That surface itself, consisting of solid earth, or rock, or mould, or shifting sands, may be divided up into parcels and become the property of individuals, together with such sheets or portions of water as are included in the boundaries thereof. But the ocean cannot be occupied. No boundaries other than its own can ever be given to it. No limits or marks of proprietorship can ever be fixed or impressed upon its surface. Neither are the air, or the light, or the warmth of the sun, capable of occupation (although the right to enjoy them by means of windows or apertures is often the subject of municipal or personal right or license, just as human life and liberty itself, is sometimes taken or restrained by the law of the land or the policy of States); and so the ocean, the air, the light, the warmth of the sun, can never be the subjects of property.

4. Up to this point, a definition of property has not been either difficult or obscure. When we encounter, however, a claim to a property in ideas, and sentiments, and expressions, clothed in language,—(which appears to be as much the common highway of the thoughts, as the ocean is the common highway of the commerce of nations),—it is necessary to pause and inquire whether that claim can be established under the rule that we have laid down. If it can be, then the right of Literary Property can be easily demonstrated. If it cannot be, then the right must fall.

"Occupancy," says Blackstone,[1] "is the taking possession of those things which before belonged to nobody. This is the true ground and foundation of all property, ... of holding those things in sever-

[1] Com. ii. 257.

alty, which by the law of nature, unqualified by that of society, were common to all mankind. But when once it was agreed that everything capable of ownership should have an owner, natural reason suggested that he who could first declare his intention of appropriating the thing to his own use, and—in consequence of such intention—actually took it into possession, should thereby gain the absolute property of it; according to that rule of the law of nations, recognized by the laws of Rome, *quod nullius est, id ratione naturali occupanti conceditur*."[1] And, after proceeding to examine in detail the various kinds of title by occupancy, the great commentator arrives at the very species of property we are considering, and says:[2] "There is still another species of property which (if it subsists by the common law[3]), being grounded on labor and invention, is more properly reducible to the head of occupancy than any other; since the right of occupancy itself is supposed by Mr. Locke[4] and many others,[5] to be founded on the personal labor of the occupant. And this is the right

[1] Fl. xli. 1, 3. [2] Com. ii. 405.

[3] The doubt expressed by Blackstone, was in deference to the two great literary property discussions in the House of Lords and elsewhere, which at the time this lecture was written, agitated all England, embalmed in the two *causes celebres* of Millar *v.* Taylor and Donaldson *v.* Becket (to which we shall have occasion to make constant reference in these pages), and in the great learning and eminence of the judges therein concerned.

[4] On Govt. part 2, ch. 5. The labor of a man's body, and the work of his hands, we may say are properly his. Whatsoever, then, he removes out of the state that nature hath provided, and left in it, he hath mixed his labor with, and joined to it something that is his own, and thereby makes it his property. But see the force of this reasoning doubted by Christian, note to Blackstone, ii. p. 8.

[5] Bl. Com. ii. 8; Bl. Com. ii. 3–8, 258.

which an author may be supposed to have in his own original literary composition, so that no other person without his leave may publish or make profit of the copies. When a man, by the exertion of his rational powers, has produced an original work, he seems to have clearly a right to dispose of that identical work as he pleases, and any attempt to vary the disposition he has made of it, appears to be an invasion of that right."

What can be more emphatically a man's own than his own ideas? If anything is peculiarly and particularly his, it would seem that these must be. If there is anything in which others cannot, from the nature of things, share, would it not seem to be the creation of a man's own brain? "True," the answer to this might well be, "but to claim a property in anything, you have already stated that you must be able to set bounds to it; to occupy it, to set up distinguishable and proprietary marks. Now, ideas are not capable of visible possession. They have no visible corporeal surface upon which to erect landmarks and limits. Their existence is in the boundless mind of man. They are incapable of acquisition, possession, or enjoyment, save by mental apprehension and mental retention. And once communicated to others, how can you enforce, even if you had been able to subject them to, proprietary rights? How can you force those who receive them from you to forget them as fast as received? You may teach—you may force a man to remember. How will you teach or force him to forget?[1]

[1] When Simonicles offered to instruct Themistocles in an art to improve the memory: "I had rather," replied Themistocles, "be taught how to forget. Things I am most unwilling to remember, these I have no power to forget." Pl. 3.

To this, as we shall see further on, the rejoinder will most likely be, that as soon as the ideas are written down or printed in words, the words become the bounds, and the landmarks, and the warning to trespassers. If they are written upon a manuscript, the manuscript is the author's, and a property in him. If they are printed and published, the purchaser of a copy of the book, though he owns the corporeal thing which he has purchased, has no right to multiply copies of the ideas therein contained, to the injury of the author who wrote it.[1]

5. But conceding even to Blackstone's high authority, that ideas can be the subject of occupancy, a fresh difficulty arises. Admitting the right of a property in every individual in his own thoughts, while they continue and remain locked up in his own brain and in his own mind, does not the author, by imparting those ideas to his neighbors through the medium of the several forms of publication in his power, relinquish his own exclusive occupancy and give them the right (as he certainly does the means) to enter in and possess as tenants in common with himself? How can he expect, after he has induced them to read his sentiments in his book; to hear his opinions as he pronounces them from the rostrum, or to view his conceptions of beauty or of nature, as he spreads them upon canvas before their eyes, that he shall still be alone and single in the possession of his

[1] The questions as to the rights of owners of a manuscript as contradistinguised from the rights of the purchaser of a book, will be treated in their place, further on. It is only necessary to notice here, that while the purchaser of a manuscript is generally supposed to have the right to publish its contents, whether copyrighted or uncopyrighted, the purchaser of a published book if uncopyrighted, may print its contents, but if copyrighted he may not.

own sentiments, opinions, or conceptions? Has he not had his choice between abandoning them, and keeping them to himself? Is it consistent that a man should scatter coins among an eager and scrambling crowd, and at the same moment proclaim, with uplifted voice, that they are his, and a warning to those who touch them? It is the answer to these and the like questions that has been attempted in the following pages.

Without going into the nice and somewhat finical questions[1] suggested by Lord Camden in his famous argument against literary property: without asking whether if, when published, a purchaser can lend his

[1] "When published, can the purchaser lend his book to his friend? Can he let it out for hire, as the circulating libraries do? Can he enter it as common stock in a literary club, as is done in the country? May he transcribe it for charity? Then what part of the work is exempt from this desultory claim? Does it lie in the sentiments, the language and style, or the paper? If in the sentiments or language, no one can translate or abridge them. Locke's Essay might, perhaps, be put into other expressions, or newly methodized, and all the original system and ideas be retained. These questions show how the argument counteracts itself, how the subject of it shifts, and becomes public in one sense, and private in another; and they are all new to the common law, which leaves us perfectly in the dark about their solution."

"And how are the judges, without a rule or guide, to determine them when they arise, whose books and studies afford no more light upon the subject than the common understandings of the parties themselves? What diversity of judgments! what confusion in opinion must they fall into! without a trace or line of law to direct their determination! What a code of law yet remains for their ingenuity to furnish, and could they all agree in it, it would not be law at last, but legislation.

"But it is said that it would be contrary to the ideas of private justice, moral fitness, and public convenience, not to adopt this new system. But who has a right to decide these new cases, if there is no other rule to measure by but moral fitness and equitable right? Not the judges of the common

book to a friend,—can he let it out for hire? can he transcribe it for charity? is there any implied contract between the person who sells, and the person

law, I am sure. Their business is to tell the suitor how the law stands—not how it ought to be; otherwise each judge would have a distinct tribunal in his own breast, the decisions of which would be irregular and uncertain, and various as the minds and tempers of mankind. As it is, we find they do not always agree; but what would it be where the rule of right would always be the private opinion of the judge, as to the moral fitness and convenience of the claim? Caprice, self-interest, vanity, would by turns hold the scale of justice, and the law of property be indeed most vague and arbitrary. That excellent judge, Lord Chief Justice Lee, used always to ask the counsel, after his argument was over, 'Have you any case?' I hope judges will always copy the example, and never pretend to decide upon a claim of property without attending to the old black letter of our law, without founding their judgment upon some solid written authority, preserved in their books, or in judicial records. In this case I know there is none such to be produced."—17 Parl. Hist. 998, 999.

"No man has a right to give an author's thoughts to the world, or to propagate their publication beyond the point to which he has given consent. His reputation is concerned, and he has a right to defend it. This is natural justice, and dictated by reason; consequently, as *Lex est ratio summa, quæ jubet quæ sunt utilia et necessaria et contraria prohibit* (Co. Lit. 319, 6; Jenk. Cent. 117), we may obviously assume that, though copyright as a species of property, was, in a strictly accurate sense, known to the common-law, yet, "the novelty of the question did not bar it of the common-law remedy and protection" (4 Burr. 2345). *Nihil quod est contra rationem est licitum* (Co. Lit. 97, 6). *Son le ley donc chose la ces donc remedie a venir a ceo* (2 Roll. R. 17). *In nova casu, novum remedium apponendum est* (2 Inst. 3). Distinct properties were not adjusted at the same time and by one single act, but by successive degrees, according as either the condition of things or the number and genius of men seemed to require. When once established, the same law which pointed out and settled the line of demarkation commands the observance of everything that may be conductive to the end for which these various boundaries were erected. "*Nequaquam antem omnes res*," says Puffendorf (De Jure nat. et gen., lib. iv., civ., s. 14, s. 6), "*statim ab initio humani generis, aut, ubique, locorum ex*

who buys a printed copy of a book? etc.,—it is apprehended that a clue to the whole difficulty will be found in the simple consideration—founded in the same natural law, or, at least, in (what we have seen has been considered by some to be the same thing) the common consent of mankind—that property is support, income, means of livelihood; that by a man's property he must subsist, and that from it he must produce his living, and the living of those for whom the law has decreed he must provide.

6. For property, again, is capital. One man's capital may be in a certain number of acres or feet of the earth's surface. Another's may be in houses, or ships, or shares of stock, or money. A blacksmith's capital may consist in the strength of his arm; a dancer's, in the lightness of his limbs and feet; a contortionist's, in the suppleness of his joints and frame; a scrivener's, in the nimbleness of his fingers; a musician's, in the acuteness of his ear. Would it not be unjust and a hardship to decree that because the capital of still another citizen was in brains, that therefore he should be deprived of the living which is to be earned by all of these?

Lord Camden, indeed, in the argument [1] to which

definito aliquo præcepto juris naturalis debuerunt proprietatem subire; sed hæc est introducta, prout par mortalium id requirere visa fuit."—Copinger on Copyright, p. 3.

[1] Delivered in the House of Lords, in answer to Lord Mansfield, in Millar *v.* Taylor: "If, then, there be no foundation of right for this perpetuity by the positive laws of the land, it will, I believe, find as little claim to encouragement, upon public principles of sound policy or good sense. If there be anything in the world common to all mankind, science and learning are, in their nature, *publici juris*, and they ought to be as free and general as air or water. They forget their Creator, as well as their fellow-creatures, who wish to monopolize his noblest gifts and greatest benefits Why did we enter into society at all but to enlighten one another's

allusion has been made, disclaimed, with aristocratic bitterness, the idea that any one worthy to write at all, should write for bread. "Glory," he exclaimed,

minds, and improve our faculties for the common welfare of the species? Those great men, those favored mortals, those sublime spirits, who share that ray of divinity which we call genius, are intrusted by Providenee with the delegated power of imparting to their fellow-creatures that instruction which Heaven meant for universal benefit; they must not be niggards to the world, or hoard up for themselves the common stock. We know what was the punishment of him who hid his talent, and Providence has taken care that there shall not be wanting the noblest motives and incentives for men of genius to communicate to the world those truths and discoveries which are nothing if uncommunicated. Knowledge has no value or use for the solitary owner; to be enjoyed, it must be communicated. '*Scire tuum nihil est, nisi te scire hoc sciat alter.*' Glory is the reward of science, and those who deserve it scorn all meaner views. I speak not of the scrib blers for bread, who tease the press with their wretched productions; fourteen years is too long a privilege for their perishable trash. It was not for gain, that Bacon, Newton, Milton, Locke instructed and delighted the world; it would be unworthy such men to traffic with a dirty bookseller for so much a sheet of a letter-press. When the bookseller offered Milton five pounds for his Paradise Lost, he did not reject it and commit his poem to the flames, nor did he accept the miserable pittance as the reward of his labor. He knew that the real price of his work was immortality, and that posterity would pay it. Some authors are as careless about profit as others are rapacious of it; and what a situation would the public be in with regard to literature, if there were no means of compelling a second impression of a useful work to be put forth, or wait till a wife or children are to be provided for by the sale of an edition! All our learning will be locked up in the hands of the Tonsons and the Lintons of the age, who will set what price upon it their avarice chooses to demand, till the public become as much their slaves, as their own hackney compilers are."—17 Parl. Hist. 999, 1000.

Lord Camden, however, seems to have been wrong in his facts. It seems that it was only for an *immediate* payment of five pounds (in those days not such a very inconsiderable sum, either), that Milton sold his copy to Samuel Simmons in 1667. The agreement with Simmons besides entitled him to

"is the reward of science, and those who deserve it, scorn all meaner views." But, unfortunately for Lord Camden, among the class whom he designated as

a payment of five pounds more when thirteen hundred copies should be sold of the first edition; of the like sum after the same number of the second edition; and of another five pounds after the same sale of the third edition. The number of each edition was not to exceed fifteen hundred copies. In two years, Milton appears to have signed a receipt on the 26th of April, 1669, for the second payment. The second edition was not printed till 1674, and Milton did not live to receive his third payment. The third edition was published in 1678; and his widow agreed with Simmons to receive eight pounds for her right, as appears by her receipt, dated December 21, 1680; and she gave him a general release, April 29, 1681. Simmons sold the copyright to one Brabason Aylner for twenty-five pounds, and Aylner sold it in 1633 to the publisher Johnson, who appears to have excited his Lordship's displeasure (Todd's Life of Milton, 193–195. London, 1826.). In commenting on these facts, Mr. Curtis, in his valuable work on Copyright (Boston, 1847, p. 63), remarks with great propriety, "It thus appears that the poet was very careful to assert his full right of property, as he and others understood it at the time, and to make it available to his family. The amount which he chose to receive, compared with the real value of the poem, measured by a modern standard, seems very trifling. But as such rights were estimated then, and considering that the poem gained slowly upon the attention of his own age, it was not a grossly inadequate price. When it had been published fourteen years and upwards, the copyright between one bookseller and another brought only twenty-five pounds. Yet its value could not have been affected by any apprehension at the time of this sale that it was not protected by common law. Such a notion had not then arisen: and long after, viz., in 1739, Lord Hardwicke protected by injunction, the title of Tonson, derived under the assignment made by the poet in 1667. Doubtless Milton did not write his grand poem for money; but we have seen that he supposed the right of exclusive property in authors was acknowledged by the law of his country, and he took pains practically to assert the right in his own case. It seems to me by no means a wild conjecture that he did this for the sake of example, as well as in order to preserve his reputation, by keeping the control of his own poem."

"scribblers for bread," the greatest names in literature, and the profoundest benefactors of their race, have been numbered. The literature of the world has been written in garrets, no doubt; but to a noble mind, the poverty of a man of letters would seem an argument the more, instead of an argument the less, for protecting him in the possession of his own, however small and meager. Lord Camden appears to have been one of those who would have given more abundantly to him that had already, and from him that had not, have taken away even that he had![1]

7. Assuming, then, that the author's means of support is in the employment of the capital which he possesses in his own brain, we purpose devoting the following pages to a consideration of the means by which the law will permit him to make that capital available for the purpose. For it is the policy of the law to encourage every man to provide his own livelihood, and not to become a burden upon his neighbors, or upon the State.[2]

[1] If any author does write "for glory," it probably is the writer of a legal text book, since, it seems, that a law writer is not to be considered an authority in his own lifetime. (Reg. v. Son, 2 Den. C. C. 475; 6 Cox's. C. C. 1; 16 Jur. 746; 14 Eng. Law & Eq. R. 556; 1 Ben. & H. Lead Cas. 400; 3 Bing. 259; Reg. v. Drury, 3 Cox's C. C. 1st Rep. Eng. Com. Law Commissioners.) So, unless he write for purely literary purposes, he may be supposed to speak to posterity alone!

[2] General convenience is a principle of legal judgment. (4 Durn. & E. 243, 245; 1 Taunt. 366; 1 Eden, 230; 1 W. Bl. 166; 3 Barn. & Cr. 156.) *Non solœm quod licet, sed quid est conveniens est considerandum.* (Co. Lit. 66o.) Convenience may be used, "not indeed so as to control the law, but as a guide in doubtful cases, and upon untrodden ground." (King v. St. Catherine's Hall, 4 Durn. & E. 233. Sadgrove v. Kirby, 6 Id. 483.) *Argumentum ab in convenienti plurimum valet in lege.* (Co. Lit. 66a.) The argument of inconvenience is, under

8. The right of property is a right dual in its nature. It is the right of the owner of possessions—first, to use and enjoy the thing possessed, unrestrictedly and indefinitely (subject only to the maxim *sic utere*[2]), and secondly, to prevent and exclude others from the use of it without his license;[3] and this dual right continues in the owner, until he shall voluntarily alienate and part with his possession.

The possessor of literary property[4] enjoys this two-fold right in common with the possessor of each and every other sort of property. Nor will the law attempt any discrimination between his case, and the case of any other owner of chattels. It does, indeed—as seems necessary from the peculiar nature of the thing to be protected—ordain distinct and particular methods to be observed in securing it; but the right

many circumstances, allowed to avail to this extent, that the law will sooner suffer a private mischief than a public inconvenience. *Lex cetius tolerare vœlt privatum damnum quam publicum malum.* (Co. Lit. 152, c., and see Ram's Science of Legal Judgment, pp. 111–117.)

[1] Traites de Legislation (Dumont), 95.

[2] *Sic utere tuo ut alienum non lœdas* (9 Rep. 59; Broom. Log. Max. 328). See, however, this maxim doubted in Bonomi v. Backhouse (27 L. J., N. S.; 388 Q. B).

[3] Austin Jur. iii. 19.

[4] "There is still another species of property which (if it subsists by the common law), being grounded on labor and invention, is more properly reducible to the head of occupancy than any other; since the right of occupancy itself is supposed by Mr. Locke (on Govt., part 2, ch. 5) to be founded on the personal labor of the occupant. And this is the right which an author may be supposed to have in his own original literary composition; so that no other person, without his leave, may publish or make profit out of the copies. When a man, by the exertion of his rational powers, has produced an original work, he seems to have clearly a right to dispose of that identical work as he pleases, and any attempt to vary the disposition he has made of it, appears to be an invasion of that right."—1 Black. Com. p. 405.

to own and to dispose of literary property for value, seems never to have been doubted or denied.

9. The first recorded sale of intellectual property was by Homer, who delivered his Iliad at feasts and celebrations, for his own support; receiving, probably, in those early days, not money, but food and presents.

This right of authors to the profit arising from the sale of their original labor, is of frequent mention by the classic writers. Juvenal, lamenting at the same time the impecuniosity of his craft, and the non-lucrative character of literary fame, alludes to it:

> "Sed, quum fregit subsellia versu
> Esurit, intactum Paridi; Nisi vendat Agave."[1]

So Martial,

> "Sunt quidam, qui me dicunt non esse Poetam
> Sed, que me vendit, bibliopola putat."[2]

So also,

> "Constabit nummis quatuor emta tibi
> Quatuor est nimium; poterit constare duobus
> Et faciet lucrum bibliopola Tryphon."[3]

And again,

> "Exigis, ut donem nostros tibi, Quincte, libellos
> Non habeo, sed habet bibliopola Tryphon.
> Æs dabo pro nugis, et emam tua carmina sanus?
> Non, inquis, faciam tam fatue: nec ego!"[4]

[1] Juvenal, Sat. vii. 86. "But, while the very benches groan under the applause with which his verses are received, he will starve unless he sells to Paris his as yet unpublished Agave."

[2] Martial, Epig. xiv. 194 [192 in Ed. Paris, 1754, and see Id. lib. i. 117 (118)]. "There are some who say that I am not a poet; but the bookseller who sells me, thinks I am."

[3] Martial, Epig. xiii. 3. "The whole multitude of presents contained in this little book will cost you, if you purchase it, four small coins. If four is too much, perhaps you may get it for two; and the bookseller, Trypho, will even then make a profit."

[4] Martial, Epig. iv. 72. "You beg me, Quintus, to present

But the songs of Homer were written only in his memory; while those published works to which Martial and Juvenal allude so much later, were only themselves neatly-copied manuscripts, written upon one side[1] of slips of parchment, and wound upon smooth sticks for preservation.

While literary matter was preserved by such methods as these, copyright acts were unnecessary. It was only when the invention of printing made a multiplication of copies of the author's work practicable and profitable, that statutory forms and observances became necessary. Such statutes coming to aid the unwritten law, in protecting—not a peculiar right—but a peculiar kind of thing possessed.

Literary property is a property in ideas; and the sole right of their author to their use and enjoyment, it was the intent and spirit of the Roman Law,[2] as well as it is of the common and statute law, to recognize not only, but to make absolute and secure.

10. "*Si in chartis membranisse tuis carmen vel historiam, vel orationem Titius scripserit, hujus corporis non Titius sed tu dominus esse videris,*" said the Institutes,[2] and ever since, all arguments in support of the rights of learned men in their works, have been heard, as Lord Kenyon said they always must be heard, "with great favor by men of liberal minds."

To make the laws of recognition of literary prop-

you my works. I have not a copy; but the bookseller, Trypho, has. Am I going to give money for trifles, and buy your verses while in my sober senses? I shall not do anything so ridiculous. Nor shall I."

[1] Hor. Sat. i. 10, 72.

[2] Inst. 2, 1 . . And so by decreeing *to whom* sentiments should belong, the Institutes recognized a property in such sentiments. 27 I. R. 627.

erty available, then, it becomes necessary, from the nature of things, that these ideas should be put into some tangible and material form.[1]

The law can not deal with purely invisible matters. It can enforce, indeed, the subject's right to walk in the public streets, or over the King's highway; but only inasmuch as—though the franchise is immaterial—the street and the highway are material and tangible, so that the law can exercise its jurisdiction over them *in rem*, if necessary, in enforcing that franchise. And so, when an author's ideas are written down upon a substantial substance, or a visible, tangible surface, the law will, from that instant, recognize and protect them, and whether the idea so written down be in the form of a manuscript, a drawing, a book, a plan, or a picture, it will equally decree that its author and originator shall thenceforth deal with it as he pleases, to the exclusion of all others, until he voluntarily parts with his title so to do.

11. It seems, on the other hand, that the law will make no effort to take cognizance of any ownership in ideas not written down, or otherwise embodied in material form.[2] Were the blind father of poetry wandering in our streets to-day, chanting his divine songs,

[1] It is a well known and established maxim, which I apprehend holds as true now as it did two thousand years ago, that nothing can be the object of property which has not a corporeal existence. *Per* YATES, J., in Millar v. Taylor, 4 Burr. 2631.

[2] Among the many intricate and interesting questions which a student of the law of literature can foresee in the future dealing of courts therewith, is the right—if any—of an *ex tempore* speaker (for instance) to restrain the publication of his efforts. Such protection would be, indeed, but a step in advance of the present position of courts, which have latterly, as will been further on in these pages, gone to great lengths to protect authors in their properties.

the law could not secure any by-stander who had listened to them, from chanting them over again himself, for hire. Nay, more, it has been held that the law will not protect ideas or sentiments, even after they have once been written down, from being carried and conveyed—so that they be not carried and conveyed in some material form—to the use of others not their proprietors. Thus, it has been said that the law will not interfere to prevent an author's ideas from being transported in the memory of one who has heard them repeated; should their author, or another, have announced or repeated them in conversation or by natural speech.[1] It is not that the right of the individual to his own thoughts or conceptions is not the same in one case as in the other : the difference would appear to arise solely from the impossibility of protection, for the law is a practical science, and recognizes no right which it cannot enforce or protect. For it is one of its maxims that *ubi jus ubi remedium.*[2]

12. The twofold right of an author to his literary property,[3] consisting, 1. in his right to publish, and 2. in his right to enjoy, we have said is the same as his right to any other possible possession. There is, however, one difference; from grounds of public policy, which is the supremest law, it would appear that the right to enjoy has been limited by the statute as to duration and time.[4]

[1] Coleman v. Wathen, 5 T. R. 245. Wallack v. Williams, Sp. T. N. Y. Sup. Court, 1867 (unreported, but see *post* chapter on Dramatic Copyright); Palmer v. De Witt, 7 Amer. 480; 47 N. Y. 532.

[2] Broom. Leg. Max. 180.

[3] Copyright is not of a simple, but a complex nature, involving two conditions: one of publication, the other of exclusion. Prince Albert v. Strange, 2 DeG. & Sm. 674.

[4] *Vide* chapter on Copyright. Subject to certain copy-

For it would seem that, just as the owner of lands and houses pays to the state a certain percentage of their value, as his contribution to the wealth and power of the government whose protection he enjoys; so is it but fitting that after the author shall have enriched himself from the store of his own culture and thought, that culture and thought should pass into the general fund of the culture of the commonwealth and enrich the stores of art and learning of his mother land, to which, as the Greek poet said, he owes the whole honor of his rearing.[1]

For the writings of an author belong to the history of his race—to the history of the thought and culture and speculation of his country; and even though his own self-love or vanity might lead him to suppress what to his maturer judgment appears crude or feeble, or though time or circumstance may have led him to alter his views and opinions,[2] neither his contemporaries nor posterity will be interested other than in his work as a part of those common intellectual stores which they have inherited as citizens of the same soil.

right, deemed sufficient to encourage genius and learning, a published book is the heritage of the public, and can not be taken from them by the author himself. Letters on Literary Copyright, Hotten, p. 114.

[1] Euripides.

"Glory is the reward of science, and those who deserve it scorn all meaner views. . . . It was not for gain that Bacon, Newton, Milton, and Locke instructed and delighted the world. When the bookseller offered Milton five pounds for his Paradise Lost, he did not reject it and commit his poem to the flames, nor did he accept the miserable pittance as the reward of his labor; he knew that the real price of his work was immortality, and that posterity would pay it."—Lord Camden's Argument against Literary Property.

[2] See the case of Southey v. Sherwood, 2 Meriv. 434, where the poet sought to restrain the publication of one of his

13. In the examination of this right to literary property as affected or controlled by this public policy of limitation, it appears convenient to inquire first, in what and in whom the ownership of literary matter may exist at all, and, having settled that, to proceed to observe the simple division of the subject into—

I. Property in literary composition before publication; and

II. Property in literary composition after publication.

With the single exception which obtains in the case of literary productions whose sole value would seem to arise from the power of their author to prevent their appearance in print,—(as, for instance, lectures, plays, songs, &c.),—it will be found that the right to such property before and up to publication, mainly exists by common law; and that, upon and after publication there arises by virtue of statute, a new

earliest manuscripts upon the ground that his own opinions and tastes had changed since preparing it. And see Mr. Hotten's fourth letter to Earl Stanhope, "Lord Macauley and the Pirates," in which he concludes: "Lord Eldon, for example, in the case of Gee v. Pritchard, 'repudiated, and that most distinctly, any notion of interference by the court of chancery with a publication, simply because it might wound feelings,' and as Mr. Phillips says (Law of Copyright, p. 36): 'It seems abundantly clear that except upon the ground of property or of breach of contract or trust, an English court of law or equity will not give relief in the case of an unauthorized publication.' The reason of this, of course, is, that private feelings, however commendable in individuals, ought not to be permitted to interfere with public rights. With so many motives for suppression and modification of by-gone speeches, as every active statesman must experience in later years, it is indeed intelligible enough why so few of such publications are issued. It might even be argued that the author of such speeches is himself the worst person to be allowed to revise them, for the reason that the motives for tampering with their historical truth and accuracy are presumptively stronger in him than in any other person."

form of right, which, while neither extinguishing nor impairing the right *in rem* of the author in the unpublished book or manuscript, operates, when invoked, to protect his title in the sentiments, ideas, and expressions which they contain, in their circulation beyond his manual reach, after they have been given to the world.

The right by statute is called COPYRIGHT.

14. Statutes of copyright do not grant monopolies; they are only protectory legislation against trespass on the rights of authors. "Not that," as a layman[1] has well said, "writers are a more important body than many others, but because it gives the state more trouble to keep thieves off their productions than off those of other skilled laborers; and also because it

[1] It was held, formerly, in Millar v. Taylor (in R. B. Pasch, 1759), that an exclusive and permanent copyright, in authors, existed by the common law; but afterwards, in Donaldson v. Becket (before the House of Lords, 22d Feb., 1774), it was held to exist only by statute and during the statutory period (1 Bl. Com. 405, *vid.* Jeffreys v. Boosey, 44 L. Cas. 815; 3 C. L. R. 625; 1 Jur. N. S. 615; 24 L. J. Exch. 81). The right and property of an author or a composer of any work, whether of literature, art, or science, in such work, unpublished or kept for his private use or pleasure, entitle him to withhold the same altogether, or so far as he may please, from the knowledge of others, and the court of chancery will interfere to prevent the invasion of this right by the publication of a catalogue containing a description of such work (Prince Albert v. Strange, 1 Mac. & I. 25; 1 H. & S. 1; 13 Jur. 109; 18 L. J. Chanc. 120; *vid.* also, Broom. Leg. Max. 326).

The property of an author in an unpublished work exists independently of the statute (Southey v. Sherwood, 2 Mer. 435; S. P. Tonson v. Collins, 1 W. Bl. 301; Palmer v. De Witt, 7 Amer. 480; 47 N. Y. 532).

The right to own his (an author's) property is from common law; the right to multiply copies is conferred by statute. . . . The right of property in literary matter has never been and never can be impaired by the passage of copyright laws (Palmer v. DeWitt, 9 Amer. 480; 47 N. Y. 532).

needs a superior intelligence to see that ideas and woven words can be made property, and that they must be, or else their authors outlawed, degraded, and starved, and the community suffer in the end."[1]

[1] Mr. Charles Reade—"The Eighth Commandment," p. 7.

BOOK I.

IN WHAT AND IN WHOM PROPERTY IN LITERARY COMPOSITION MAY EXIST.

CHAPTER I.

OF INNOCENCE.

15. THE great exception which arises to this right of property which we have been considering, is that it will not be protected by law, in things not innocent in their nature.

It is a cardinal principle of the common law that *nihil quod est inconveniens est licitum*,[1] or, as Lord Truro stated it, "No subject can lawfully do that which has a tendency to be injurious to the public good, which may be termed, as it sometimes has been, 'the policy of the law,'"[2] and therefore the law, ever solicitous for the moral as well as the physical safety of its subjects, will refuse its protection to a vicious, immoral, or otherwise harmful publication.

16. It seems particularly fitting that the author

[1] Co. Lit. 66 *a;* 97, 178 *a;* 258, 6; Broom Leg. Max. 328. This doctrine certainly needs some qualification, and a qualification, perhaps, receives from that learned writer (Coke) when he says: "*Quod est inconveniens non permissum est in lege.* An argument *ab inconvenienti* is forcible in law. *Argumentum ab inconvenienti est validum in lege, quia lex non permittet aliquod inconveniens.*" Id.; and see Ram's Science of Legal Judgment, Am. ed., p. 114, *ante*, p. 11, note 2.

[2] Egerton v. Brownlow (4 H. L. Cas. 196).

should regard with careful circumspection this policy and doctrine of the law. On its part that law has given him the power of speaking to an audience bounded only by the limits of the language itself; and, at the same time, of retaining his hold upon the words and thoughts which have floated so far beyond him. It asks on his part, in return, that he use not this vast power and influence to the injury and harm of his fellow-citizens.

By common law, then, there can be no literary property in compositions which are not innocent in their nature, and the first test, to be applied to the literary or scientific matter in inquiring whether or not it can be the subject of ownership is, is it innocent?

17. The discrimination between lawful and unlawful publications in respect to innocence, has never been made a statutory one. None of the English or American copyright statutes expressly enact anything of the sort, or make any allusion whatever to the moral character of the subject-matter of a book. But over and above them the doctrine of public policy and of common law prevails; and the courts of the land have power over works injurious or dangerous to the public good, after their copyright, as well as before; over the registered and copyrighted volume, as well as over the written manuscript. And this is one case, at least, in which statutes have not interfered with the conditions of literary ownership at common law.[1]

[1] The element of innocence is peculiar to common-law countries. Its consideration does not enter into the copyright jurisprudence of France. All works in that country are equal before the law, without reference to their character (Renouard Droits des Auteurs, tom. 2, p. 94). And yet, in no country is the censorship of the press so watchful and exacting, and nowhere does the punishment for seditious or *quasi* seditious utterance in print meet such swift and rigorous punishment as in France.

This doctrine of innocence is mainly a negative one, however, and its enforcement by courts will be mainly in the negative form of a refusal to recognize, and not of an absolute sequestration or condemnation of the improper composition. In the case, as we shall presently see, of works so bestial and obscene that there can be no possible doubt in the mind of a decent person as to their disgusting nature, the police regulation of the community will itself take cognizance to suppress and destroy; but such proceedings are statutory, and will not detain us here. Such matter cannot well be literary, and therefore cannot claim treatment in these pages.

18. Owing to this negative nature of its supervision, it may, and doubtless often does happen, that Equity stands by with folded hands and silently regards the publication of injurious and non-innocent matter, mischievous in its tendencies and dangerous to the public morals and the public peace. So, too, a man might build a nuisance upon his land, or circulate representations or statements which might induce two of his neighbors to quarrel. In either case the law might be blind and silent as to the irregularity from the necessity of the case, or the impossibility of interference, or in pursuance of a policy above the individual. But it would be very rash and unsafe to conclude from its silence that it would interfere positively to protect the wrong-doer in his wrong.

The effect of the attitude of courts of equity to matters of this nature is to throw the burden of proof—where the burden ought always to be, in cases of denial of any right of property presumably established by law—upon the party intruding; in this case, upon the party defending the piracy or denying his liability for the piracy of a composition. It is for him to establish clearly that, notwithstanding a *prima facie* title by copyright in the complainant, there is no title in him, in reality, by reason of the dangerous character or tendencies of the book.

"The soundness of this general principle," says Mr. Justice STORY,[1] can hardly admit of question. The chief embarrassment and difficulty lie in the application of it to particular cases. If a court of equity, under color of its general authority, is to enter upon all the moral, theological, metaphysical, and political inquiries which in the past times have given rise to so many controversies, and in the future may well be supposed to provoke many heated discussions; and if it is to decide dogmatically upon the character and bearing of such discussions, and the rights of authors growing out of them; it is obvious that an absolute power is conferred over the subject of literary property, which may sap the very foundations on which it rests; and retard, if not entirely suppress, the means of arriving at physical as well as at metaphysical truths. Thus, for example, a judge who should happen to believe that the immateriality of the soul, as well as its immortality, was a doctrine clearly revealed in the scriptures (a point upon which very learned and pious minds have been greatly divided), would deem any work anti-christian which should profess to deny that point, and would refuse an injunction to protect it. So, while a judge who should be a Trinitarian, might most conscientiously decide against granting an injunction in favor of our author, enforcing Unitarian views, while another judge of opposite opinions might not hesitate to grant it."

Great care is, therefore, to be observed in the application of this rule of the law. "In equity," says

[1] 2 Eq. Jur. § 936, n. 2.

Curtis,[1] "The sounder rule would be to refuse no injunction when the book is not illegal 'upon the face of it.'" "And we think that both law and equity in this country would require the mischievous and harmful character of a book to be proved with unmistakable clearness, before they would refuse to interfere in cases of piracy or infringement. The burden of such proof will always be upon the infringer, and he cannot be relieved of it by any disposition on the part of the court to apply its own private opinions, doctrines, beliefs, or standards, to the publication before it." *Prima facie*, the copyright confers title, and the burden is on the other side to show clearly that, notwithstanding the copy, there is an intrinsic defect in the title.[2]

19. It is submitted, however, that this principle is to be applied only to published works. An immoral or dangerous manuscript in the hands of its author is not an instrument of evil to the state, and dangerous to its morals or its peace,[3] and its character cannot be pleaded as against the right of its owner to be protected in its possession. Where the famous Dr. Priestly brought an action for the loss of certain manuscripts, by the riotous proceedings of a mob at Birmingham, although it was alleged (but not proved) that the contents of these manuscripts were injurious to the government of the state, the court appears to have virtually held that the plaintiff was seeking damages only for what might have been a source of

[1] Curtis on Copyright, p. 165.

[2] Id., p. 166. And generally upon this subject see Am. Quarterly Review, April 1822; 6 Petersdorff's Abridg. 560, 561.

[3] Curtis on Copyright, p. 160. Southey v. Sherwood, 2 Meriv. 434. And see Dr. Priestly's Case, cited in Wolcott v. Walker, 7 Ves. 1, and Shortt. L. L. p. 4.

profit to him, like any other property. However, there is a difficulty in this case which the traditional reports do not help us in solving. It would seem that the owner of matter libellous to an individual, at least, will only be protected in his ownership by law, to the extent in which the matter contains innocent ingredients. So in the case where an artist exhibited to the public, for money, a picture, called "Beauty and the Beast," but which appeared to be a scandalous libel upon a gentleman and his wife, the defendant having destroyed the picture by cutting it in pieces, and plaintiff having brought suit thereupon for damages, Lord Ellenborough instructed the jury to award the plaintiff merely the value of the canvas and paint of the picture, and to disregard any other value which it might possess.[1]

20. Any public libel is a seditious publication, and, therefore, not innocent, and not entitled to the protection of courts. So a libel upon public justice, said Lord Ellenborough in Hine v. Dale.[2] "If the

[1] Wolcott Du Bost v. Beresford, 2 Camp. 511.

[2] Hine v. Dale, 2 Camp. 27 (note), was an action for pirating the words of a song called "Abraham Newland," published on a single sheet of paper. It appeared that the song, though pretending to be a panegyric upon money, was in reality a libel upon the administration of British justice, and its object and tendency, not to satirize folly, but to excite the people against the law, as was supposed to be apparent from a single verse:

"The world is inclined
To think justice blind;
Yet what of all that,
She will blink like a bat,
At the sight of friend Abraham Newland.
Oh, Abraham Newland, magical Abraham Newland!
Though justice 'tis known,
Can see through a stone,
She can't see through Abraham Newland!"

composition appeared upon the face of it to be a libel, so gross as to affect the public morals, I should advise the jury to give no damages. I know the court of chancery on such an occasion would grant no injunction.[1]

21. The rule in England is uniform, that the law will not class as innocent, works "contrary to religion and truth,"[2] and a court of equity refused an injunction to restrain infringement of the copyright of a work as to which it appeared doubtful as to whether it did or did "not intend to impugn the doctrine of the Scriptures."[3] But it does not seem probable that courts in the United States would carry the doctrine to this extent.

The test as to whether or not a work is innocent, was held by Lord Eldon to be "the possibility of making it the foundation of a successful action at law."[4] "If the doctrine," said his lordship, "of Chief Justice Eyre[5] is right,—and I think it is,—

[1] The author or publisher of a work of a libelous or of an immoral tendency can have no property in it. Stockdale v. Onwhyn, 7 D. & R. 625; 5 B. & C. 173; 2 C. & P. 163. No action can be maintained for pirating a work which professes to be an account of the amours of a courtesan; and it is no answer to the objection that the party is also a wrong-doer in publishing it, and that he ought not therefore to set up its immorality.—*Id.*

[2] Fisher's Digest of English Patent, Trademark, and Copyright Cases, art. Copyright.

[3] Lawrence v. Smith, Jacob. 471.

[4] Southey v. Sherwood, 1 Meriv. 437.

[5] In the case of Dr. Priestly (cited Walcott v. Walker, 7 Ves. 1), on the trial of an action brought by him against a hundred, to recover damages sustained by him in consequence of the riotous proceedings of a mob at Birmingham, amongst other property alleged by him to be destroyed, he asked for compensation for certain unpublished MSS. It was alleged, in defense, that the plaintiff was in the habit of publishing works injurious to the government of the state

that publications may be of such a nature that the author can maintain no action at law, it is not the business of this court, even upon the submission in the answer (defendants had admitted the piracy of one edition) to decree either an injunction or an account of the profit of works of such a nature, that the author can maintain no action at law for the invasion of that which he calls his property, but which the policy of the law will not suffer him to consider his property. If this publication is an innocent one, I apprehend that I am authorized by decided cases to say, that—whether the author did or did not intend to make a profit by its publication—he has a right to an injunction to prevent any other person from publishing it." "If, on the other hand, this is not an innocent publication, in such a sense that an action would not lie in case of its having been published by the author and subsequently pirated, I apprehend that this court will not grant an injunction." And the same learned judge observes elsewhere:[1] "This court interferes by injunction; but not in cases where an action cannot be maintained."

22. And not only will equity refuse protection to such works of harmful and immoral tendency, but it will go further, and decline to take any cognizance of them whatever, treating them precisely as if they did not exist. So, when one pirates and prints a book which should never have been printed at all, no protection will be given from, or action for, the piracy.[2]

but no evidence was produced to that effect. The lord chief justice observed that, if such evidence had been produced, he should have held it fit to be received as against the claim made by the plaintiff.

[1] Lawrence v. Smith, 1 Jacob. 472.

[2] Walcott v. Walker, 7 Ves. 1; Southey v. Sherwood, 2

The effect of chancery refusing an injunction, may be, indeed, to render still more unlimited the piracy; but, although such would probably be the case, it is clear that chancery is powerless in the matter.[1] "For," said Lord Eldon, "this court has no jurisdiction in matters of crime."[2] It has been said that, if

Meriv. 435; Clark v. Freeman, 11 Beav. 117, 119; and *vid.* remarks of Cairns, J., in Maxwell v. Hogg, L. R., 2 Ch., app. 310; 16 L. T. N. S. 130; 36 L. J., 438 Ch.; and of Malin, V. C., in Springhead Spinning Co. v. Riley, L. R., 6 Eq. 561; 19 L. T. N. S. 65; 37 L. J., 889 Ch.

[1] Lawrence v. Smith, Jacob, 471.

[2] Lord Chancellor Macclesfield, in Burnett v. Chetwood (cited from MS. in note to Southey v. Sherwood, 2 Meriv. 438), seems to have taken a different view of the province of courts of equity in dealing with books of this character, holding "that the court of chancery had a superintendence over all books, and might, in a summary way, restrain the printing or publishing of any that contained reflections on religion or morality," and granting an injunction to restrain the publication of the translations of two Latin works, "Archæologia Philosophica," and "De Statu Mortuorum et Resurgentium," written by Dr. Burnett, on the sole ground that "inasmuch as the book contained to his (the chancellor's) knowledge (he having read it in his study) strange notions, intended to be concealed from the vulgar in the Latin language—in which language it could not do much hurt, the learned being better able to judge of it—it was proper to grant an injunction to the printing and publishing it in English." Lord Ellenborough, in dealing with the case of a libelous picture, in Du Bost v. Beresford, 2 Camp. 511, said that, "upon an application to the lord chancellor, he would have granted an injunction against its exhibition." This dictum of Lord Ellenborough seems to have excited the editor of Howell's State Trials, who says (vol. xx., p. 799): "I have been informed, by very high authority, that the promulgation of this doctrine, relating to the lord chancellor's injunction, excited great astonishment in the minds of all the practitioners in the courts of equity; and I had apprehended that this must have happened, since, I believe, there is not to be found in the books any decision or any dictum posterior to the days of the star chamber, from which such doctrine can be deduced, either directly, or by inference or analogy; unless, indeed, we are

the injunction be refused, it has the effect of increasing the number of copies. The answer to that is, I have nothing to do with it as a crime. The question relates only to a civil right of property. If the one party has that right, the other must not invade it; if he has not that right, the court cannot give him the consequences that belong to it.

In the much quoted case of Southey v. Sherwood,[1] where the poet Southey sought to restrain the publication of his poem, "Wat Tyler," which had lain for twenty-three years in manuscript in the printer's hands, until he himself had forgotten its existence, the same rule prevailed, and the poem being held of too libelous a nature to merit protection, an injunction was refused.[2]

23. There seems, however, to be one exception, if it be an exception, to this rule: and that is, if it appears that the publication will tend to the destruction

to except the proceedings of Lord Ellenborough's predecessors—Scroggs, and his associates—in the case of Henry Care, in which case '*ordinatum est quod. liber intitulat,*' The Weekly Packet of Advice from Rome, or the History of Popery, '*non ulterius imprimatur vel publicatum per aliquam personam quamcunque.*'" The editor might have found another precedent for what so surprised him, in Burnett v. Chetwood, cited *ante.*

[1] 2 Meriv. 435.

[2] To the same effect was the ruling in Stockdale v. Onwhyn (7 D. & R. 625). In that case an action was brought in the court of king's bench, in 1826, to protect a certain volume, entitled, "Memoirs of Harriet Wilson," which, on examination, appeared to be a history of the life and amours of a courtesan, containing anecdotes either libeling or ridiculing the various persons with whom she professed to have communication. "The ground of this action," said Holroyd, J., "if any, must be that the defendant has worked an injury to the plaintiff's exclusive right of publishing the book in question. Now, it is criminal in him to publish such a book. Then he has no right to publish it; and having no right, he has sustained no injury, and has no ground of action."

or deterioration of other property, courts of equity will for the protection of such other property, take jurisdiction to restrain the publication.[1]

Neither will equity regard as innocent, and interfere to protect obscene books, or theatrical exhibitions, immoral and prurient in their character, even if copyrighted according to the prescribed formula.[2] And so where a spectacle styled the "Black Rook" was shown unmistakably to be an infringement upon a previously composed spectacle, "The Black Crook," it appearing that the latter was a notoriously immoral and prurient production, equity refused its protection.

So it will be seen further on, when we come to treat of personal libels by newspapers, and their right to comment upon matters of public interest, that the law will not regard as innocent an undue haste to publish or to comment upon charges made against a citizen before they are proved, though the editors or newspaper proprietors will be allowed every opportunity to show an absence of malice or a misinformation as to the authority of the proceeding.[3]

And so also a publication in a suit reflecting on a court engaged in trying a suit, or upon the witnesses, parties, or jurors, will be construed as non-innocent, or, as this particular form of non-innocence is called, "a contempt of court."[4]

[1] Springfield Spinning Co. v. Riley, L. R. 551; 19 L. T. N. S. 64; 37 L. J., 889 Ch.

[2] Martinetti v. Maguire, Deady's R. 216. See this case treated *supra* in the chapter on dramatic copyright.

[3] Ackerman v. Jones, 37 N. Y. Sup. Ct. (J. & S.) 42.

[4] Hollingsworth v. Duane, Wall. 77, 102; Bronson's Case, 12 Johns. (N. Y.) 460; S. P. Respublica v. Passmore, 3 Yeates (Pa.), 408; Same v. Oswald, 1 Dal. 319. But see *Exp.* Hickey, 12 Miss. (4 Sm. & M.) 751; Stuart v. People, 4 Ill. (3 Scam.) 395; Matter of Bergh, 16 Abb. Pr. N. S. *post*, "Contempt of court."

24. In England, works "subversive of religious truth," "hostile to natural and revealed religion," or "impugning the doctrine of the immateriality of the soul," have been declared to be the reverse of innocent.[1] To the latter extent it is hardly to be expected that the law of innocence would be carried in this country, where the largest liberty of thought and expression is supposed to obtain.

25. "To say religion is a cheat," said the court in one case,[2] "is to desolve all those obligations whereby civil societies are preserved. Christianity is parcel of the laws of England, and therefore, to reproach the

[1] The cases of Lawrence v. Smith (7 Jacob. 471), and of Murray v. Benlow (cited in Shortt L. Lit., p. 8), exhibit the extent to which the question of innocence in a work may be carried. In the former case, Lord Eldon dissolved an injunction to hinder the publication of a pirated edition of certain "Lectures on Physiology, Zoology, and the Natural History of Man," on the ground that the lectures could not be the subject of copyright, as they contained several passages hostile to natural and revealed religion, impugning the doctrines of the immateriality and immortality of the soul. "Looking," said he, "at the general tenor of the work, and at many particular parts of it; recollecting that the immortality of the soul is one of the doctrines of Scripture; considering that the law does not protect those who contradict the Scriptures; and entertaining a doubt—I think a rational doubt—whether this book does not violate that law, I cannot continue the injunction. The plaintiff may bring an action, and when that is decided he may apply again." In Murray v. Benlow (February, 1822), the same lord chancellor refused to enjoin the publication of a pirated edition of Lord Byron's "Cain," on the ground of a doubt whether the poem was not intended to bring into discredit that portion of Scripture to which it relates. In 1823, again, Leach, V. C., dissolved an injunction to prevent publication of pirated portions of Lord Byron's "Don Juan," on similar grounds.

[2] 1 Rex v. Taylor, Vent. 293; 3 Keb. Rep. 607; *vid.* 4 Bl. Com. 287. This view of the matter is put broadly by Michaelis, quoted 2 Stark. (2nd edit.) 131. He says: "On God's account, then, punishments for blasphemies are not necessary; but

Christian religion is to speak in subversion of the law."[1]

26. With regard to absolute blasphemy, however, the case is different, and the law in this country, equally with the English, recognizes blasphemy as an offense; not only against good manners and good morals, but against the public weal as well.

"Whether the principle," says Bishop,[2] "upon which this doctrine rests, is that they (blasphemy and profane swearing) tend to undermine Christianity, which is a part of our law,[3] or that they disturb the peace and corrupt the morals of the community, is a question not fully settled. Perhaps we may even take another view, namely, that reverence toward God and religion—Christianity being our form of religion—is essential to man, who is injured in his nature and being, when this reverence is impaired; or, still another view, that these offenses so shock his purer and higher sensibilities as to create an injury to him against which he needs protection, precisely as against an assault. Probably these several considerations,

perhaps they are necessary for the sake of our neighbor, who, if he believes in a God, or holds his religion, whether true or false, to be true, always feels himself extremely scandalized by them. Nor is it only blasphemy against the true God that ought to be punished; but even that against false gods, supposed saints, and fictitious religion, whenever they happen to be the gods, saints, and religion of the people." Shortt. L. Lit. 298.

[1] *Vid.* Patterson's Case, 1 Brown, 627.

[2] 1 Crim. Law, vol. ii., § 87.

[3] Blackstone (4 Com. 287) describes the offense of blasphemy as consisting in a denial of the being or providence of the Almighty; or in contumelious reproaches of our Lord and Saviour, Christ; or in profane scoffing at the holy Scripture, or exposing it to contempt and ridicule, for Christianity is part of the laws of England. *Vid.*, also, Rex v. Taylor, 2 Vent. 293; 3 Kebl. R. 607.

and some others also, may each be deemed to enter more or less into the policy of the law."

27. The English law against blasphemy is very severe, and the makers and publishers of works construed to be blasphemous in their nature, are criminally dealt with.[1]

[1] In Rex v. Woolsten (Str. 834), relating to a book designed to show that the Christian miracles were not to be taken in a literal but an allegorical sense, the court would not suffer it to be debated whether to write against Christianity in general was not an offense punishable in the temporal courts at common law. They laid stress on the word "general," and stated that they did not intend to include disputes between learned men upon particular controverted points. Raymond, Ch. J., in delivering the judgment of the court, said: "I would have it taken notice of that we do not meddle with any differences of opinion, and that we interpose only where the very root of Christianity itself is struck at," which the court considered to be done in the book in question.

In Rex v. Williams, the defendant was convicted of having published a blasphemous libel, called "Paine's Age of Reason," which denied the authority of the Old and New Testaments, asserted that reason was the only guide by which the conduct of men ought to be directed, and ridiculed the prophets, Jesus Christ, his disciples, and the Scriptures. Ashurst, J., in that case remarked that, "although the Almighty did not require the aid of human tribunals to vindicate his precepts, it was nevertheless fit to show our abhorrence of such wicked doctrines, which were not only an offense against God, but against all law and government, from their direct tendency to dissolve all the bonds and obligations of civil society. It was upon this ground that the Christian religion constituted part of the law of the land. But if the name of our Redeemer was suffered to be traduced, and his holy religion treated with contempt, the solemnity of an oath, on which the due administration of justice depended, would be destroyed, and the law be stripped of one of its principal sanctions—the dread of future punishment;" which seems to be a very concise statement of the reason and policy of the law on this subject.

It is a blasphemous libel to represent by a published writing that Jesus Christ is an impostor, the Christian religion a mere fable, and those who believe in it infidels to God (Rex v.

"With us, however, the law is more tolerant," said Kent, J., in the case of The People v. Ruggles.[1] 'After conviction we must intend that the words

Eaton, 31 Howell's St. Tr. 927. Eaton was sentenced, by Lord Ellenborough, to be imprisoned for eighteen months in Newgate, and to stand in the pillory between the hours of twelve and two, once within a month), or that Jesus Christ was an impostor, a murderer, and a fanatic (Rex v. Waddington, 1 B. & C. 26). It has been held to be a blasphemous libel to publish anything which tends to question or cast disgrace upon the Old Testament alone; for (as was said in Reg. v. Hetherington, 5 Jur. 529) the Old Testament is so connected with the New, that a reflection on the one is a reflection on the other also.

Vid., also, 17 D. & R. 629; Poplett v. Stockdale, Ry. & M. 337.

In addition to the doctrines of the common law relating to blasphemous libels, there are some express enactments of the legislature on the subject. Several of the old statutory provisions have been repealed, but the following still remain in force:

1 Edw. 6, ch. 1, enacts that persons reviling the sacrament of the Lord's Supper by contemptuous words or otherwise, shall be punished by fine and imprisonment.

1 Eliz. ch. 2, enacts that if any minister shall speak anything in derogation of the book of Common Prayer, he shall, if not beneficed, be imprisoned one year for the first offense, and for life for the second; and if he be beneficed, shall for the first offense be imprisoned six months, and forfeit a year's value of his benefice; for the second, shall be deprived and suffer one year's imprisonment; and for the third, shall in like manner be deprived and suffer imprisonment for life. And that if any person whatsoever shall in plays, songs, or other open words, speak anything in derogation, depraving, or despising of the said book, &c., he shall forfeit for the first offense, one hundred marks; for the second, four hundred; and for the third, shall forfeit all his goods and chattels, and suffer imprisonment for life.

The most important of the statutes now in force is the 9 & 10 Will. III., ch. 32. It enacts that if any person educated in or having made profession of the Christian religion, shall by writing, printing, teaching, or advised speaking, deny any

[1] 8 Johns. 292.

were uttered in a wanton manner, and, as they evidently import, with a wicked and malicious disposition, and not in a serious discussion upon any controverted point in religion. The language was blasphemous, not only in a popular, but in a legal sense; for blasphemy, according to the most precise definitions, consists in maliciously reviling God or

one of the persons of the holy Trinity to be God (repealed by 53 Geo. III., ch. 160, § 2, "so far as the same relates to persons denying as therein mentioned respecting the holy Trinity"), or assert or maintain that there are more gods than one, or deny the Christian religion to be true, or the holy Scriptures to be of divine authority, he shall, upon the first offense, be rendered incapable to hold any office or place of trust; and for the second, be rendered incapable of bringing any action, being guardian, executor, legatee, or purchaser of lands, and shall suffer imprisonment without bail for three years. But the person convicted for a first offense is to be discharged from all penalties and disabilities for that offense, if he renounce his error in open court within four months after conviction. Information of an offense against the act must be given within four days after it has been committed, and the prosecution must be within three months after such information.

There is no recorded instance of a prosecution under this act.

This statute has not altered the common law on the subject of blasphemous libels, but has only introduced certain peculiar disabilities cumulative upon the penalties previously inflicted by the common law (Rex. v. Carlisle, 3 B. & Ald. 161; Rex. v. Williams, 26 How. St. Tr. 656; 2 Str. 884), for it is a general rule that, where an offense is already punishable by a common-law proceeding, a statute providing a particular punishment for it does not exclude the common-law punishment, but only supplies an alternative or a cumulative one (Rex v. Robinson, 1 Burr. 799).

Neither, it seems, does the 53 Geo. III., ch. 160, alter the common-law doctrine as to blasphemous libels; it only removes the penalties imposed by 9 & 10 Will. III., ch. 32, upon persons denying the Trinity, and extends to them the benefit of the Toleration Act of 1 Will. & M., sess. 1, ch. 18.—Shortt, L. Lit. 301, 302.

religion, and this was reviling Christianity through its author. The jury have passed upon the intent or *quo animo*, and if those words spoken, in any case, will amount to a misdemeanor the indictment is good. . . . . The free, equal, and undisturbed enjoyment of religious opinion, whatever it may be, and free and decent discussions on any religious subject, are granted and secured; but to revile, with malicious and blasphemous contempt, the religion professed by almost the whole community, is an abuse of that right."[1]

[1] In Rex v. Waddington (1 B. & C. 26), where the libel stated that Jesus Christ was an impostor, and a murderer in principle, and a fanatic—the defendant, in moving for a new trial, urged that the lord chief justice had misdirected the jury by stating that any publication in which the divinity of Jesus Christ was denied was an unlawful libel; and he argued that, since the 53 Geo. III., ch. 160, the denying one of the persons of the Trinity to be God was no offense, and consequently that a publication in support of such a position was not a libel. The court of king's bench unanimously refused a rule for a new trial, and held that the publication was a blasphemous libel. Best, J., said: "The 53 Geo. III., ch. 160, has made no alteration in the common law relative to libel. If, previous to the passing of that statute, it would have been a libel to deny, in any printed work, the divinity of the second person in the Trinity, the same publication would be a libel now. The 53 Geo. III., ch. 160, as its title expresses, is an act to relieve persons, who impugn the doctrine of the Trinity, from certain penalties. If we look at the body of the act, to see from what penalties such persons are relieved, we find that they are the penalties from which the 1 Will. & M., sess. 1, ch. 18, exempted all Protestant Dissenters, except such as denied the Trinity, and the penalties or disabilities which the 9 & 10 Will. III., ch. 32, imposed on those who denied the Trinity. The 1 Will. & M., sess. 1, ch. 18, is, as it has been usually called, an act of toleration, or one which allows Dissenters to worship God in the mode that is agreeable to their religious opinions, and exempts them from punishment for non-attendance at the Established Church, and non-conformity to its rights. The legislature, in passing that act, only thought

The rule was laid down, as follows, by Duncan, J., in Updegarth v. Commonwealth:[1] "No author or printer who fairly and conscientiously promulgates opinions with whose truth he is impressed, for the benefit of others, is answerable as a criminal. A malicious and mischievous intention is, in such a case, the broad boundary between right and wrong; it is to be collected from the offensive levity, scurrilous and opprobrious language, and other circumstances, whether the act of the party was malicious."

of easing the consciences of Dissenters, and not of allowing them to attempt to weaken the faith of the members of the Church."

From the fact that a particular form of the Christian religion is established here by law, this consequence follows: that a person may, without being liable to prosecution for it, attack Judaism, or Mohammedanism, or even any sect of the Christian religion, except the established religion of the country; and the only reason, says Alderson, B. (Reg. v. Gathercole, 2 Lewin, 254), why the latter is in a different situation from the others is, "because it is the form established by law, and is therefore a part of the constitution of the country. In like manner, and for the same reason, any general attack on Christianity is the subject of criminal prosecution, because Christianity is the established religion of the country" (*vid.*, also, Cowan v. Milbourn, 16 L. T. N. S. 290; 36 Q. J. 124; L. Rep., 2 Ex. 233).

How far, then, is liberty of discussion allowed on questions relating to the fundamental doctrines of religion? or, is the expression of all views adverse to those now received, prohibited and punishable? Would the law now make no distinction in favor of the fair and temperate expression of opinions sincerely entertained? It is by no means easy to give an answer, for there is no reported English case in which the question has been fairly raised and broadly dealt with.

Malice is a necessary ingredient in the crime; and were it not that our law implies malice wherever anything unlawful is done willfully or intentionally, whatever the motive which prompted the action, this consideration might help us to a conclusion. As the law stands, it throws no light upon the subject.—Shortt, L. Lit. 302–304.

[1] 11 Serg. & R. 394.

"Still," says Bishop,[1] in commenting on the above, "one who should utter words or sentiments calculated, according to common judgment, to corrupt the public morals, or to shock the sensibilities of mankind in a Christian community, would, doubtless, not be permitted to excuse himself under the plea of conscientious conviction."

28. The doctrine that Christianity is parcel of the common law, began with the Dome-Book of Alfred, which sets forth at once, as the law of the realm, the ten commandments, accompanied by many Mosaic precepts. After quoting the canons of the apostolical council at Jerusalem, Alfred cites the injunction, "As ye would that men should do unto you, do ye also to them;" adding, "from this one doom, a man may remember that he judge every one righteously: he need heed no other doom book."[2] Lord Coke affirmed it, and Blackstone[3] and Lord Mansfield asserted it after him.[4] But in the United States,

[1] Crim. Law, 93. The proposed criminal code of the State of New York, art. 31, extracting a definition from existing common-law decisions, describes blasphemy as consisting in "wantonly uttering or publishing words, casting contumacious reproach or profane ridicule upon God, Jesus Christ, the Holy Ghost, the holy Scriptures, or the Christian religion;" and art. 32 adds: "If it appears, beyond reasonable doubt, that the words complained of were used in the course of serious discussion, and with intent to make known or recommend opinions entertained by the accused, such words are not blasphemy."

[2] Blackstone quotes the Dome-Book as extant so late as the reign of Edward IV.

[3] 4 Bl. Com. 63.

[4] See also Rex v. Taylor, Vent. 293; 3 Keble, 621; Tremayne's Pleas of the Crown, 226; East P. C., ch. 1, § 33; Rex v. Carlisle, 3 B. & Ald. 161; Rex v. Alwood, Cro. Jac. 421; Rex v. Williams, 26 Howell St. Tr. 654; Rex v. White, Leach, 430; Rex v. Webster, Fitzg. 64; 2 Str. 834; Reg. v. Gathercole, 2 Lewin C. C. 237; Reg. v. Hetherington, 5 Jur.

unless, perhaps, we except the colony of New England, which resolved at a "general court, October 25th, 1639, ... the worde of God shall be the onely rule to be attended vnto in ordering the affayres of government in this plantatio," no statute has expressly re-enacted the principle, though that it is part of the spirit of the written, as well as of the common law of this country we think, we shall be able to show.

29. In The People v. Ruggles,[1] Kent, J., declared that "blasphemy against God, and contumelious reproaches and profane ridicule of Christ or the holy scriptures, are offenses punishable at the common law, whether uttered by words or writings. . . . Such offenses have always been considered independent of any religious establishment or the rights of the church," continued the chancellor, "and why should not the language contained in the indictment be still an offense with us? There is nothing in our manners or institutions which has prevented the application or the necessity of this part of the common law. We stand equally in need now as formerly of all that moral discipline, and of those principles of virtue which help to bind society together. The people of this state, in common with the people of this country, profess the general doctrines of Christianity,

529, Q. B.; Rex v. Paine, 1 East P. C. 5; Bish. Cr. Law, §§ 945, 947; 2 Id. § 87; Holt on Libel, 32; Mence on Libel, i. 303.

[1] 3 Johns. 291. In this case it was held that wantonly, wickedly, and maliciously uttering the following words: "Jesus Christ was a bastard, and his mother must be a whore," was a public offense, punishable by the common law of the State of New York. See Emlyn's preface to the State Trials, 8; Whitlock's Speech, 2 State Trials, 273; Rex v. Woolston, Str. 834; Fitz. 64; Taylor's Case, 1 Vent. 293; 3 Keb. 607.

as the rule of their faith and practice; and to scandalize the author of these doctrines, is not only, in a religious point of view, extremely impious, but, even in respect to the obligations due to society, is a gross violation of decency and good order. Nothing could be more offensive to the virtuous part of the community, or more injurious to the tender morals of the young, than to declare such profanity lawful. It would go to confound all distinction between things sacred and profane; for, to use the words of one of the greatest oracles of common wisdom, 'Profane scoffing doth by little and little, deface the reverence for religion,'[1] things which corrupt moral sentiment, as obscene actions, prints, and words, . . . have upon the same principle been held indictable, and shall we form an exception in these particulars to the rest of the civilized world? No government among any of the polished nations of antiquity, and none of the institutions of modern Europe (a single and monitory case excepted) ever hazarded such a bold experiment upon the solidity of public morals, as to permit, with impunity and under the sanction of their tribunals, the general religion of the community to be openly insulted and defamed. The very idea of jurisprudence, with the ancient law-givers and philosophers, embraced the religion of the country, *jurisprudentia est divinarum atque humanarum rerum notitia*."[2]

30. The principle as laid down on this high authority undoubtedly is, that while in the United States every shade of religious belief is protected, yet the spirit of the law will not permit, upon grounds of public policy, that Christianity should be scandalized openly

[1] Lord Bacon's Works, ii., 291, 503.

[2] Dig. 61, 10, 2; Civ. De Legibus, 62, *passim*.

and wantonly. For the Christian religion is one whose influence upon the public peace and security, and upon good order and commercial and municipal prosperity, is marked and salutary. One of its prime injunctions is a perfect allegiance and obedience to the state, and the only instance in history in which a premium upon its neglect not only, but upon its open and wanton insult and abuse, was followed by that carnival of blood and anarchy at which the world has not yet ceased to shudder—the first French Revolution. The morals and the manners of good society have come to be very deeply imbedded in religion, and while the law of the United States takes to itself no scrutiny as to things spiritual, prescribes no creed, and holds no theory of a life beyond the present, it will not discourage man in the belief of a religion which teaches morality, sobriety, patriotism and obedience to the law of the land. Nor can it be doubted that the same protection would be extended to any body of believers. And a man who should intrude upon a community of worshippers of any creed, and openly and wantonly attack their tenets, would undoubtedly be punished. Nearly every state in the Union has its statute making the Christian sabbath a day of rest from business cares and pursuits; which protect public worshippers from disturbance, and many go further and make profane swearing a misdemeanor.[1] And this, we may be assured, not from any wish to dictate to the conscience of the citizen, but to encourage order and to promote the public peace. To this extent it may well be said that Christianity is parcel of our common law.

The statutes of the United States certainly do not

[1] Laws of N Y. 2 R. S. (5th ed.), vol. ii., pp. 935, 936, 937.

discourage morality. "I suppose," says Deady, J.,[1] "that it is both proper and constitutional for congress so to legislate as to encourage virtue and to discourage immorality. Congress in exercising its powers to establish a uniform rule of naturalization,[2] has always discriminated in favor of morality, by providing that on the hearing of the application for citizenship, the applicant must prove that for five years prior to such application he has behaved as a man of good moral character."[3]

And the learned judge might have added that the same spirit is indicated by congress, in the statutes which enact, that any person who, within the jurisdiction of the United States, "sells, or lends, or gives away, or in any manner exhibits, or offers to sell, or to lend, or to give away, or in any manner to exhibit, or otherwise publishes or offers to publish in any manner, or has in his possession for any such purpose, any obscene book, pamphlet, paper, writing, advertisement, circular, print, picture, material, or any cast, instrument, or other article of an immoral nature, or any drug or medicine . . . . . . or who causes to be written or printed any card, circular, book, pamphlet, advertisement, or notice of any kind, stating when, where, how, or of whom, or by what means" . . . such articles may be purchased, or who "manufactures, draws, or prints, or in anywise makes any of such articles, shall be imprisoned at hard labor in the penitentiary for not less than six months nor more than five years for each offense, or fined not less than one hundred dollars, nor more than two thousand dollars, &c.,[4] and further by

[1] Martinelli v. Maguire, 1 Deady, 216.

[2] Con. Art. 1, § 8, subd. 4.

[3] 2 Stat. 154.

[4] Revision of 1873–74, § 5389.

imposing a fine and imprisonment upon the aiding or abetting by any of its officers of the use of the general post office for circulating any obscene or indecent publications, representations, or articles of indecent or immoral use or tendency;[1] and prohibiting by the like penalties the importation[2] and deposit in the mail[3] of such and similar matter.

And, again, in every court of justice in the land oaths are administered upon the holy scriptures; either by kissing, or laying the hand upon the gospels or upon some other portion (as in the case of Hebrews). Are we not, then, at liberty to conclude that words, writings, and actions, which would tend to undermine the authority and vilify the sanctity of those pages, would attack the regard for the sacredness of an oath, without which no legal formality is complete, and so strike at the very root of our jurisprudence? Such acts, words, and writings it seems to us, are, and must be, inconsistent with public peace, order, and safety.

In so far, then, as Christianity in its popular sense, as contradistinguished from barbarism or heathenism,—in so far and in such sense as the United States is reckoned among Christian rather than among the heathen nations of the globe—we submit that Christianity is "parcel of our common law."

"Christianity, as it has been asserted, is now in a modified sense the religion of this state" (New York), said Duer, J.[4] "It is so, as a part of that common law

[1] Revision of 1873-74, § 1785; 3 March, 1873, ch. 258, § 4, vol. 17, p. 599.

[2] Id., §§ 2941, 2942.

[3] Id., § 3893.

[4] Andrew v. N. Y. Bible, &c., Society, 4 Sandf. 156; and see People v. Ruggles, 8 Johns. 290.

which our ancestors introduced, and we have retained the maxim that Christianity is part and parcel of the common law, has been frequently repeated by judges and text writers, but few have chosen to examine its truth or attempt to explain its meaning. We have, however, the high authority of Lord Mansfield and of his successor,[1] for stating as its true and only sense, that the law will not permit the essential truths of revealed religion to be ridiculed and reviled. In other words, that blasphemy is an indictible offense at common law. The truth of the maxim, in this very partial and limited sense, may be admitted. But if we attempt to extend its application, we shall find ourselves obliged to confess that it is unmeaning and untrue. If Christianity is a municipal law in the proper sense of the term, as it must be if a part of the common law, every person is liable to be punished by the civil law who refuses to embrace its doctrines and follow its precepts; and if it must be conceded that in this sense the maxim is untrue, it ceases to be intelligible. Since a law without a sanction is an absurdity to logic and a nullity in fact."

In concluding our examination of whether and to what extent "Christianity is parcel of the common law of the United States," we cannot do better than adopt and make our own the words of Chancellor Kent in the case we have been considering,[2] believing that what he finds in this case and in the contemplation of the constitution of the state of New York, will be found to be within the spirit of the unwritten law of the nation at large.

The free, equal, and undisturbed enjoyment of

[1] Lord Campbell. Judge Duer here refers to Campbell's Lives of Chief Justices, vol. 2, p. 513.

[2] People v. Ruggles, 8 Johns. 291.

religious opinion, whatever it may be, and free and decent discussions on any religious subject, is granted and secured; but to revile with malicious and blasphemous contempt, the religion professed by almost the whole community, is an abuse of that right. . . . . We are not to be restrained from animadversion upon offenses against public decency, merely because there may be barbarous nations whose sense of shame would not be affected by what we should consider the most audacious outrages upon decorum. It is sufficient that the common-law checks upon words and actions dangerous to the public welfare apply to our case, and are suited to the condition of this and every other people whose manners are refined, and whose morals have been elevated and inspired with a more enlarged benevolence by means of the Christian religion.[1]

31. The policy of the law is not to forcibly prevent one from owning property not innocent in its nature, but to refuse to encourage, by its protection, the circulation of that property. The law will not break open a man's private house and forcibly capture and destroy an obscene picture which he may happen to own; but if he keep a collection of obscene pictures for the purposes of trade, from which he sells to persons of depraved tastes, he is violating the laws of the United States, and the law will break up his

[1] The doctrine, however, has not commanded the full assent of many learned minds. It was disputed by Jefferson (letter to Cartwright, 9 Am. Jurist; Life and Letters of Joseph Story, vol. i., pp. 430–434; vol. ii., pp. 8, 462–464), and by Webster and Sergeant (see their arguments in the Girard Will Case). See, generally, as to the doctrine, Lindenmuller v. The People, 33 Barb. 548; Bedford Charity, 2 Swans. 527; Da Costa v. Paz, 2 Swans. 420 *n.*; Att'y-Gen'l v. Pearson, 3 Mer. 399; Andrew v. N. Y. Bible & Prayer Book Soc., 4 Sandf. 157.

business, seize his collection, and proceed to punish him by fine and imprisonment. There is a provision in the United States postal laws which forbids the circulation of such wares through the mails, and, besides making the property liable to confiscation, renders the party circulating the injurious matter liable to indictment.

So, again, while the law will not break open a man's doors and seize an obscene manuscript, known to be in his possession, it will not encourage him to print and circulate the contents of that manuscript. Neither, perhaps, will the law regard as innocent a picture not harmful in itself which its owner pretends to have been produced by a spiritual or supernatural process. In 1869, one William H. Mumler, in the city of New York, publicly advertised to the effect that he would take photographs which should not only be life-like representations of the sitter, but should contain in shadow the ghostly form of some departed friend or relative of the sitter, as it alleged that friend or relative was really beside him, only unseen to the carnal eye. The gist of the fraud here was, evidently, not the taking of the picture, or the production of the chemical or mechanical effect of a shadow upon the camera; nor perhaps the assertion that an actual spiritual presence accompanied the sitter (for that there are or are not spiritual presences about us continually, is a matter of fact concerning which men cannot reason from any data known to the law, and hence it cannot hear the opinion of experts upon the subject, nor form any conclusions of its own), but, it is submitted, the pretense that the operator and his camera were different from other operators and cameras, inasmuch as they had a connection with the spirit world. It was for obtaining money under false pretenses, therefore, that the prosecution by the people against Mumler proceeded.[1]

[1] As the only case of the kind which is known to have arisen, it is remarkable that "The People v. Mumler" should never have been reported—the only record of it extant being the argument of Mr. Elbridge T. Gerry, for the People, from which we draw the facts as follows:

The prisoner, William H. Mumler, stood charged by the People—First: With having, by false pretenses, defrauded one Joseph H. Tooker out of, and of having obtained from him the sum of ten dollars, lawful money. Second: Of having, by means of gross frauds and cheats, practiced habitually upon the public for the purpose and with the result of obtaining sums of money from credulous persons. Third: With stealing, taking, and carrying away by trick or device, the sum aforesaid from said Tooker, and other similar sums from other persons.

The facts upon which the charge of false pretenses was based, were—

First: A statement made by the prisoner "that he was a spiritual medium; that he produced spirit likenesses; that no other person could take such wonderful pictures; that the pictures were not the result of a trick or deception;" coupled with the exhibition of a picture with a faint outline of another form than that of the sitter, and a further assertion by the prisoner "that he (Tooker) would come to recognize the face as that of some relative or friend." Second: A previous payment of two dollars, by Tooker, on the strength of a previous similar statement made by one Guay, who acted as agent for the prisoner; and a subsequent payment by him of eight dollars on the strength of the prisoner's statement, and on the furnishing of certain photographs purporting to be of spirit forms, and on receiving a printed book containing an additional statement by the prisoner, over his signature, and designed to further induce a belief that the indistinct form on the picture was not produced by mechanical or natural means. Third: A discovery by Tooker, after parting with his money, that the photographs were ordinary photographs, and that all the forms on them were produced by mechanical means.

Mumler's answer alleged:

I. That there is no trick, fraud, or deception in what are called spirit pictures by the accused.

II. That in order to produce those pictures, nothing more is done or used by him than by ordinary photographers in

32. In one of the latest English cases involving this doctrine of non-innocence, the question arose

producing their pictures, than mere resting his hand on the camera.

III. That the spirit-pictures coming or abstaining from coming is in no respect subject to his control or volition.

IV. That the process of taking them has been again and again carefully scrutinized and watched in its every step by men of intelligence, and by those skilled in the art of photography, whereby it has been ascertained, beyond doubt, that there is no deception or fraud about it.

V. That there has been produced, on the same plate with the picture of a living person, the picture or ghost-like image of persons who have died, which have been recognized as likenesses of such persons by those who knew them in life.

VI. That this has been done in cases where there was no likeness or picture in existence of such deceased person, and whom the operator had never seen or heard of.

VII. That it is now some twelve or fourteen years since these spirit-pictures were first heard of in this country; that within the last four or five years the taking of these pictures has been publicly heard of and known in Boston, and there frequently investigated with the utmost care and scrutiny; and that, simultaneously with their production in New York, they have been produced in Paris, and in Poughkeepsie, Waterville, and Buffalo, in this State.

VIII. That in the various attempts to imitate these pictures, and which some photographers claim are the same thing, there are essential points of difference, plainly to be discovered by the practical or the discerning eye, and which distinguish the genuine from the false, and which cannot be produced by the imitator.

IX. That the accused does not know and never has pretended to know by what power or process, other than that of producing an ordinary photograph, these spirit-pictures are produced. That he has often solicited and obtained the closest scrutiny by men more capable than himself of understanding the process, and he is now at all times ready and willing to have his work scrutinized and watched in the most critical manner. And to that end he invites an investigation by a delegation of the most expert and experienced photographers in town, and pledges himself to afford the fullest opportunity therefor.

X. That there are a great many intelligent men and women, who, after a careful investigation, are firm believers that the

whether a breach of contract to let rooms for the purpose of delivering lectures could be justified on

pictures are truly likenesses of the spirits of the departed, and that he and such believers are of opinion that the taking of these pictures is a new feature in photography, yet in its infancy, surely but gradually and slowly progressing to greater perfection in the future, requiring for such perfection time and a scientific knowledge of the power that is operating.

William P. Slee, who watched the camera during Mumler's operations, testified that he looked into the camera, and observed that Mumler kept his hand on it while the process was going on, and that he put the cloth over his head before he put the slide in with the plate. He proved exhibits Nos. 1 to 9 for the People, and admitted they could all be done by mechanical means.

William Guay, a partner of Mumler's, proved that a great many persons called to have their photographs taken with these "spirit" forms, and paid their money for that purpose; admitted that the ghost might have been produced by means within the camera; that Mrs. Mumler was always present on these occasions; and that he was allotted by Mumler "to stay on the second floor to carry on the business on systematic rules and principles generally."

Hon. John W. Edmonds, ex-judge of the N. Y. supreme court, and all during his life a firm believer in and advocate of spiritualism, testified that he went to this gallery of Mumler's on a preconcerted notice. He knew nothing of photography; that he paid ten dollars for the first, and five dollars for the second sitting, and went away satisfied; but said, "I do not say that they (the shadowy forms alleged) are produced by spiritual means."

William Gurney, a photographer, testified that he saw Mumler have his hand on the camera, but could not discover the trick; that he has been a photographer for twenty-eight years; and that it was not possible to produce such an object except from outside the instrument.

Mr. Snodgrass—or *alias* James R. Gilmore, *alias* "Edmund Kirke"—testified that he called on the prisoner; that he sat twice, but the pictures were not distinct. Rockwood, a photographer of large experience, testified that he had produced similar "ghosts" in different ways; and that although not exactly a "spiritual" process, there was certainly something remarkable about it.

the ground that the lectures to be delivered were of a blasphemous and illegal nature, some of them being

Elmer Terry testified that he went there expressly to get a picture of the spirit of a deceased friend. He paid his money in advance, on the statement that he would be furnished with such a picture, and he paid afterwards when he thought he had it. He recognized the "spirit" of a four-year-old boy, who died twenty years ago, and he recognized the picture of Miss Frances Catlin, whose portrait he had seen only four days before this photograph was taken.

Jacob Kingsland testified that he recognized the likeness of Miss Catlin, but could not speak positively of the children.

Paul Bremond testified that he was a believer in "spirits," and was so fifteen years ago, when he used to hear the voices, and that he recognized the "ghosts" that Mumler photographed as likenesses of the departed. He particularly recognized "Elizabeth Trapp."

David A. Hopkins testified that he paid his money and watched the prisoner. He went to Mumler for a "spirit" photograph, and identified one of the "ghosts" as that of a lady deceased.

William W. Silver testified that he was a believer in the supernatural; that Mumler closed the slide on every occasion when a spirit appeared; and that he watched Mumler's process without detecting any trick.

Mrs. Luthera C. Reeves testified that she went with her nephew, Mr. Welling; sat for a portrait; that she identified a "spirit" apparition thereupon as her son, by the length of his ears!

Samuel R. Fanshawe testified that he went there and saw Mrs. Mumler, and announced that he was a skeptic. After having notified them in advance that he meant to find out the trick, he sat for a picture, upon which the shadowy forms appeared, and recognized the ghosts of his mother and son, although they were so indistinct that it was almost impossible to recognize any shade at all.

Charles F. Livermore testified that he sat five times, and a ghostly picture, which he recognized as his wife's picture, finally appeared. Three different pictures were produced by him in evidence.

Mrs. Ann F. Ingalls recognized in a photograph her mother, son, and brother, all of whom died long before.

A pamphlet issued by Mumler was produced and read in evidence, as follows:

advertised as follows: "The Character and Teachings of Christ: the former defective, the latter misleading:

"My object in placing this little pamphlet before the public, is to give to those who have not heard, a few of the incidents and investigations on the advent of this new and beautiful phase of spiritual manifestations. It is now some eight years since I commenced to take these remarkable pictures; and thousands, embracing as they do scientific men, photographers, judges, lawyers, doctors, ministers, and in fact all grades of society, can bear testimony to the truthful likeness of their spirit friends they have received through my mediumistic power. What joy to the troubled heart! What balm to the aching breast! What peace and comfort to the weary soul! to know that our friends who have passed away can return and give us unmistakable evidence of a life hereafter—that they are with us, and seize with avidity every opportunity to make themselves known; but alas! in many instances, that old door of sectarianism has closed against them, and prevents their entering once more the portals of their loved ones and be identified. But, thank God, the old door is fast going to decay; it begins to squeak on its rusty and time-worn hinges; its panels are penetrated by the worm-holes of many ages, through which the bright, effulgent rays of the spiritual sun begin to shine; and in a short time it will totter and tumble to the earth. Boston has been the field of my labors, most of the time, since I commenced taking these wonderful pictures, where I have been visited by people from all parts of the Union; but at the earnest solicitation of many friends, I have concluded to make a tour through the principal cities of the United States, that all may avail themselves of this opportunity to obtain a likeness of their loved ones. I am often asked, 'Are there no other mediums for this phase of spiritual manifestations?' I answer, there are a number, now, in the United States and Europe, that are taking them with more or less success, and there are hundreds of photographers who have taken what I call an approximation to the spirit form. If they will but look carefully at some of their cards or negatives, they will see a semi-indefinite form. To those who find these forms on their negatives, no matter how vague or indistinct, let me assure you that you are capable of becoming a medium for this beautiful manifestation, if you will but give the proper time and attention to your own development. Let me entreat you to persevere, throw aside all skepticism, sit as often as you can with some good medium for development, and I hope the time is not far distant when I

The Bible shown to be no more inspired than any other book," &c.; the court of exchequer, without any reference to the motives which prompted the delivery of the lectures, held that a publication of the doctrines stated in the advertisements referred to, was blasphemy, and, therefore, the breach of contract was justifiable.[1] An indictment setting forth certain passages from the poem of "Queen Mab," and a passage in prose from the notes thereto; a work described in the indictment as a "scandalous, impious, profane, and malicious libel of and concerning the Christian religion, and of and concerning the holy scriptures, and of and concerning almighty God, in which were contained certain passages charged as blasphemous;" Sergeant (afterwards Mr. Justice) Talfourd, himself a poet, addressed the jury for the defense, in a noble speech, in which he asked, whether it could be blasphemy in the publisher to present to the world, or rather to the calm, the laborious, the patient searchers after wisdom and beauty, who alone would peruse the volume, the awful mistakes, the mighty struggles, the strange depressions, and the imperfect victories of such a spirit as Shelley's, because the picture has some passages of frightful gloom? "In the wise and just dispensations of providence," said the accomplished advocate, in a passage which we may be excused for quoting, "great powers are often found associated with

shall have hundreds of co-workers in this beautiful spirit photography. Yours, truly,

"WM. H. MUMLER."

Mr. Gerry appeared for the prosecution; but the defendant, Mumler, was ultimately discharged, upon other grounds than those taken by the learned counsel.

---

[1] Cowan v. Milbourn, L. R., 2 Eq. 230; 36 L. J. 124; 16 L. T. N. S. 230.

weakness or with sorrow; but when these are not blended with the intellectual greatness they countervail, but merely affect the personal fortunes of their possessors, as when a sanguine temperament leads into vicious excesses, there is no more propriety in unveiling the truth, because it is truth, than in exhibiting the details of some physical disease. But when the greatness of the poet's intellect contains within itself the elements of tumult and disorder; when the appreciation of the genius in all its divine relations and all its human lapses depends on a view of the entire picture, must it be withheld? It is not sinful elysium, full of lascivious blandishments, but a heaving chaos of mighty elements, that the publisher of the early productions of Shelley unveils. In such a case, the more awful the alienation, the more pregnant with good will be the lesson. Shall this life, fevered with beauty, restless with inspiration, be hidden? or, wanting its first blind but gigantic efforts, be falsely because partially revealed? If to trace back the stream of genius, from its greatest and most unearthly breadth to its remotest fountain, is one of the most interesting and instructive objects of philosophic research; shall we—when we have followed that of Shelley through its majestic windings, beneath the solemn gloom of 'The Cenci,' through the glory-tinged expanses of 'The Revolt of Islam,' amidst the dream-like haziness of 'Prometheus'—be forbidden to ascend with painful steps its narrowing course to its farthest spring, because black rocks may encircle the spot whence it rushes into day, and demon shapes, frightful but powerless for harm, may gleam and frown on us beside it?" It was urged also that the poem of "Queen Mab" was presented with the distinct statement that Shelley himself, in mature life, departed from its offensive dogmas; that it was accompanied by his own letter, in which he expresses his wish for its suppression; that, therefore, it was not given as containing his deliberate assertions, but only as a feature in the development of his intellectual character. Was it not "antidote enough to the poison of a pretended atheism, that the poet, who is supposed to-day to deny Deity, finds Deity in all things?"

Lord Denman, however, told the jury that he and they "were bound to take the law as it had been handed down to them. The only question for their consideration was, whether, in their opinion, the work, which had been made the subject of prosecution, deserved the imputations that were cast upon it by the indictment, and whether the publisher had sent it forth deliberately into the world, knowing its character to be such. The purpose of the passage cited in 'Queen Mab' was, he thought, to cast reproach and insult upon what, in christian minds, were the peculiar objects of veneration; it was not, however, sufficient that mere passages of an offensive character should exist in a work, in order to render the publication of it an act of criminality; it must appear that no condemnation of such passages appeared in the context. It had been said that the extraordinary poem in question was the production of a mere youth. Were the lines indicted calculated to shock the feelings of any christian reader? Were their points of offense explained, or was their virus neutralized by any remarks in the margin, by any note of explanation or apology? If not, they were libels on God, and indictable."[1]

[1] The jury returned a verdict of guilty; but the prosecutor abandoned all further proceedings on payment of his costs.

Still another class of works esteemed not innocent at common law were publications seditiously libelous

Rex v. Moxon, 2 Mod. State Trials, 362. Blackburn, J., alluding to this case in Reg. v. Hicklin (L. Rep., 3 Q. B. 374), says: "I hope I may not be understood to agree with what the jury found, that the publication of 'Queen Mab' was sufficient to make it an indictable offense." For Lord Lyndhurst's view of the prosecution, see Debates in the House of Lords, for 13th July, 1857. The prosecutor was Hetherington, who had, a short time before, been found guilty of publishing certain libels on the Old Testament (see Reg. v. Hetherington, 5 Jur. 529), and his object in instituting the prosecution against Mr. Moxon is not very clear. His counsel concluded his opening speech by expressing the satisfaction he should feel if the result of the trial were to establish that no publication on religion should be a subject for prosecutions in future (2 Mod. State Trials, 365); but Mr. Moxon's counsel treated the prosecution as one prompted solely by an indiscriminate desire, on the part of the prosecutor, of retaliating on some other person the punishment which he had himself suffered. And Blackburn, J., says of it: "I believe, as everybody knows, that it was a prosecution instituted merely for the purpose of vexation and annoyance" (Reg. v. Hicklin, L. Rep. 3 Q. B. 374; S. C. 37 L. J. 89, M. C.; 18 L. T. N. S. 395, *nom.* Reg. v. The Recorder of Wolverhampton. See also Patterson's Case, 1 Brown, 627).

. . . .

Blasphemous publications are punishable either by indictment at common law or by criminal information. Persons convicted were formerly compelled to stand in the pillory, besides suffering other punishments. The act of 56 Geo. III., ch. 138, which abolished the punishment of the pillory in most cases, provides (sect. 2) that the court may, in all cases where it was formerly used, pass such sentence of fine or imprisonment, or of both, in lieu of the sentence of pillory, as to it shall seem most proper.

The punishment by banishment was abolished by 11 Geo. IV. & 1 Will. IV., ch. 73, § 1.

The Scotch law is not different from the English law on the subject of blasphemous libels. An act of 6 Geo. IV., ch. 47, after reciting the expediency of making the crime punishable in the same manner as if committed in England, enacted that any person convicted of blasphemy shall be liable to be punished only by fine or imprisonment, or both, at the discretion of the court; and that if any person, after being so con-

of the sovereign's royal person, of the parliament, or the constitution.

While the spirit of the law was to encourage a certain latitude of political discussion, or the disputations of learned men upon matters and shades of religious belief, it could not justify a wanton and gratuitous attack upon christianity in general,[1] or upon the king, the government, or the constitution in general. And so any man might, and still may

victed, shall offend a second time and be convicted, he may be adjudged, at the discretion of the court, either to suffer the punishment of fine or imprisonment, or both, or to be banished from the United Kingdom, and all other parts of the sovereign's dominions, for such term of years as the court in which such conviction shall take place shall order; and in case the person, so adjudged to be banished, shall not depart from the United Kingdom within thirty days after the pronouncing of such sentence, for the purpose of going into banishment, he may be conveyed to such parts out of the dominions of the sovereign, as the sovereign, by advice of the privy council, may direct. If the person sentenced to be banished, after the end of forty days from the time the sentence has been pronounced, is at large within any part of the United Kingdom, or any other part of the sovereign's dominions, without some lawful cause, before the expiration of the term for which the offender has been adjudged to be banished, every such offender being so at large and being thereof convicted, shall be transported to such place as the sovereign shall appoint, for any term not exceeding fourteen years. This statute still remains in force, with the exception of the provisions as to punishment by banishment, which are repealed by 7 Will. IV. & 1 Vict., ch. 5. Before the repeal of the acts of 1661, ch. 21, and 1695, ch. 11, by the 53 Geo. III., ch. 160, § 3, blasphemy was punishable, for the first offense, by public atonement in sackcloth to the parish where the scandal was committed; for the second offense, by payment of a fine of a year's rent of his real estate, and a twentieth part of his personal effects, and by imprisonment till the offender should again make satisfaction to the parish; for the third offense, with death.—Shortt, L. Lit., pp. 302–311.

[1] Rex. v. Waddington, 1 B. & C. 126.

fearlessly advance new doctrines of politics, religion, or morals, providing he does so with proper respect to the government of his country.

The old law of seditious libel contemplated, first, words spoken against the sovereign personally; second, libels on the administration; and, third, libels on the constitution generally. Libels upon parliament were ordinarily regarded as analogous to contempts, and will be hereafter treated;[1] but it may not be uninteresting to the student of the law of literature to follow briefly the progress of letters as hampered by the divine right of kings and the sacredness of the state.

That law on the subject of words spoken or written against the sovereign personally has undergone considerable alteration in more recent times. An Act of 3 Edw. 1, c. 34, provides "that from henceforth none be so hardy to tell or publish any false news or tales whereby discord, or occasion of discord or slander may grow between the king and his people, or the great men of this realm." Section 1 of 6 Anne, c. 7, made it high treason for any person maliciously, advisedly, and directly, by writing or printing, to maintain and affirm that the then sovereign was not the lawful and rightful queen of the realm, or that the pretender had any right or title to the crown, or that any other person or persons has or have any right or title to the same, otherwise than according to the bill of rights, the act of settlement, and the acts for the union of England and Scotland; or that the kings or queens of the realm, with and by the authority of parliament, were not able to make laws and statutes of sufficient force and validity to limit and bind the crown, and the descent, limitation,

[1] *Post*, chapter on contempt of court.

inheritance, and government thereof. Words spoken against the king were, before the time of Charles I., held to be treasonable. To accuse the king of having committed murder,[1] or to say that a king *de facto* and not *de jure* was the rightful king,[2] was held to amount to high treason.[3] But in the case of Hugh Pine,[4] who was accused of having spoken several disparaging words concerning the king (Charles I.), the judges resolved "that the speaking of the words before mentioned, though they were as wicked as might be, were not treason; that, unless it were by some particular statute, no words will be treason."

To charge the king with a personal vice was held by the judges, upon debate of Peacham's case, not to be treason.[5] In that case the accused, a clergyman, was found guilty of treason, in the reign of Charles I., for certain passages in a sermon found in his study, which was never preached or intended to be preached. Many of the judges, however, were of opinion that this was not treason, and the prisoner was not executed.[6] In the case of Algernon Sidney, an unpublished paper, forming part of a theoretical work on government, found in his house, was given in evidence against him, and the Chief Justice (Jefferies) in his charge to the jury, insinuated that the doctrines contained in the paper were treasonable in themselves without reference to other evidence.[7]

[1] Juliana Quick's Case, 21 Hen. VI.
[2] Germaine's Case, 2 Edw. IV.
[3] Challercome's Case, cited Cro. Car. 125.
[4] Cro. Car. 117, 126.
[5] Ib. 126.
[6] First Discourse of High Treason, ch. 1, 199.
[7] 9 St. Tr. 889, 893.

The judgment in Sidney's case was reversed by act of parliament in 1689.

Though neither words spoken, nor an unpublished writing, was held in England to amount to an overt act of treason, to make good an indictment of compassing the death of the sovereign, under 25 Edw. 3, c. 2, yet a writing which imports such a compassing, if it be published, will amount to an overt act of treason under that statute.[1]

Apart from statute, all contempts against the sovereign's person or government, are, according to the text-books, very highly criminal, and punishable with fine and imprisonment, by the discretion of the judges, upon consideration of all the circumstances of the case. Under this head is ranked contemptuously speaking of the sovereign, as by cursing him, &c., or giving out that he wants wisdom, valor, or steadiness; or in general, doing anything which may lessen him in the esteem of his subjects, weaken his government, or raise jealousies between him and his people. Stating or insinuating that he acts from partial or corrupt motives, or with an intention to favor or oppress any individual, or class of men, would be a seditious libel; but not the imputation of honest error without moral blame.[2]

It is a criminal libel to publish falsely of the sovereign, as of any other person, that he is insane.[3]

In a leading case on the subject of seditious libels in England, defendants were printer and proprietor of a newspaper. The libel for the publication of which the criminal information was filed was the following: "What a crowd of blessings rush upon one's mind

[1] Williams' Case, 2 Roll. Rep. 88; 2 Inst. 12.
[2] Rex v. Lambert, 2 Camp. 402.
[3] Rex v. Harvey, 2 B. & C. 257.

that might be bestowed upon the country in the event of a total change of system! Of all monarchs, indeed, since the Revolution, the successor of George the Third will have the finest opportunity of becoming nobly popular."[1]

In 1729, an information was filed against John Clerk, charging him with printing and publishing an infamous libel called "Mist's Weekly Journal," wherein the king's title to the crown was openly struck at, his legitimacy called in question, and the persons of several of the royal family scandalously traduced under borrowed names; by representing the late king (George I.) under the name of Merewits, his present majesty under that of Esreff, the queen under that of Sultana; and at the same time drawing a beautiful character of the Pretender by the name of the Young Sophi, and setting forth the tyranny and subjection all Englishmen lay under, by representing them under the name of the Persians. The charge against the defendant was for maliciously and traitorously printing off one of these papers in particular; but the jury found the defendant guilty.[2]

A similar information was filed against a compositor named Knell, one of the two servants of Mist, for printing and publishing the same work. The evidence being that the defendant and his fellow-servant set up the type, and that one took one column of it downward and the other the other column upward, the chief justice directed the jury to acquit the defendant as to the publication; but, if they believed the evidence, to find him guilty of the printing; and the jury did so. An old bed-ridden woman was also indicted for publishing the same libel, she having kept a pamphlet

[1] Rex v. Lambert, 2 Camp. 398

[2] Barnardiston's Rep. 304.

shop at which the libel was sold, the shop being shown to be a mile distant from the house in which she had for a long time lain bed-ridden.[1]

In 1763, an information was filed against John Wilkes, for printing and publishing a certain malicious, seditious, and scandalous libel, intituled "The North Briton," number 45, tending to vilify and traduce the king and his government, to impeach and disparage his veracity and honor, and to represent and make it to be believed that his majesty's most gracious speech delivered from his throne to the parliament, on the 19th day of April, 1763, contained many falsities and gross impositions upon the public, and that his majesty had suffered the honor of his crown to be sunk and prostrated, and the interests of his subjects and allies to be treacherously betrayed; and also to render the king and his government contemptible and odious, and to excite tumults, commotions, and insurrections; and to violate and disturb the public tranquillity, good order, and peace of the kingdom. He was found guilty, and sentenced to be fined and imprisoned. George Kearsley was convicted of printing and publishing, and John Williams of publishing the same number of "The North Briton."[2]

In 1848 parliament made it treason to publish or utter such seditious writings or language as would incite the people to disaffection and rebellion.[3]

Everybody may, with impunity, criticise the conduct of the government, provided he does it fairly and honestly; but imputations of corrupt motives in the administration of affairs, or other writings calculated

[1] Rex v. Nutt, Id. 306. The attorney-general consented to withdraw a juror.

[2] Dig. L. T. 69, K. B. MSS.

[3] 11 & 12 Vict., ch. 12.

to alienate the affections of the people by bringing the government into disesteem,[1] or likely to excite sedition, whether such be the writer's intention or not, come within the denomination of seditious libels, and are punished as such.

"It is certain," says Hawkins,[2] "that it is a very high aggravation of a libel that it tends to scandalize the government by reflecting on those who are entrusted with the administration of public affairs, which doth not only endanger the public peace, as all other libels do, by stirring up the parties immediately concerned in it to acts of revenge, but also has a direct tendency to breed in the people a dislike of their governors, and incline them to faction and sedition."

"It has been observed," said Lord Ellenborough,[3] "that it is the right of the British subject to exhibit the folly or imbecility of the members of the government. . . . If, in so doing, individual feelings are violated, there the line of introduction begins, and the offense becomes the subject of penal legislation."

"A writer," says Fitzgerald, J.,[4] "may criticise or censure the conduct of the servants of the crown or the acts of the government; he can do it freely and liberally, but it must be without malignity, and not imputing corrupt or malicious motives. With the same motives a writer may freely criticise the proceedings of courts of justice and of individual judges —nay, he is invited to do so, and to do so in a free and fair and liberal spirit. The law does not seek to put any narrow construction on the expressions used

[1] Rex v. Burdett, 4 B. & Ald. 131; Rex v. Cobbett, 29 How. St. Tr. 49.

[2] P. C., Book 1, ch. 28., "Libels," § 7.

[3] Rex v. Cobbett, *ubi supra.*

[4] Cox. Crim. Cas. 49.

and only interferes when, plainly and deliberately, the limits are passed of frank and candid and honest discussion. . . . . There is no sedition in censuring the servants of the crown, or in just criticism on the administration of the law, or in seeking redress of grievances, or in the fair discussion of all party questions."

Many cases have been decided under this head of the law of libel, but no finer test of what constitutes the offense can be deduced from them than that the plain intrinsic tendency of the particular publication to produce public disorder, and the malicious intention of its author must be considered.

In Rex v. Tutchin,[1] the defendant was charged with having falsely, seditiously, and scandalously written, composed, and published a certain false, malicious, seditious, and scandalous libel, intituled "The Observator." The information set forth several passages from "The Observator," some of which lamented the sad state of the country owing to the influence of French gold on those who had the conduct of affairs; while others complained of the mismanagement of the navy, attributing ignorance and incapacity to those who had the management of it. It having been contended on behalf of the defendant that the publications could not be libels, because they did not reflect upon particular persons, Lord Holt, C. J., said to the jury: "This is a very strange doctrine, to say it is not a libel reflecting on the government, endeavoring to possess the people that the government is maladministered by corrupt persons that are employed in such or such stations either in the navy or army. To say that corrupt officers are appointed to administer affairs, is certainly a

[1] 14 St. Tr. 1095.

reflection on the government. If people should not be called to account for possessing the people with an ill opinion of the government, no government can subsist; for it is very necessary for all governments that the people should have a good opinion of it. And nothing can be worse to any government than to endeavor to procure animosities as to the mismanagement of it; this has been always looked upon as a crime, and no government can be safe without it be punished. Now you are to consider whether these words I have read to you do not tend to beget an ill opinion of the administration of the government."

Richard Francklin was tried and convicted in 1731 for printing and publishing in "The Craftsman" a seditious libel, intituled "A Letter from the Hague,"[1] wickedly, maliciously, and seditiously contriving and intending to disturb and disquiet the public peace and tranquillity of the kingdom, and to bring the treaty of peace into contempt and disgrace, and also to detract, scandalize, traduce, and vilify the administration of his majesty's present government of this kingdom and his principal officers and ministers of state, and to represent his said officers and ministers of state as persons of no integrity and ability, and as enemies to the public good of this kingdom, and to cause it to be believed that his majesty by the advice of his said principal officers and ministers intended to break and violate the said treaty last mentioned, &c. "Even a private man's character," said Lord Raymond, C. J., "is not to be scandalized, either directly or indirectly, because there are remedies appointed by the law in case he has injured any person, without maliciously scandalizing him in his character; and

[1] 9 St. Tr. 626.

much less is a magistrate's, minister of state, or other public person's character to be stained, either directly or indirectly, because the law hath pointed out another remedy than publishing libels, if they have injured any person, either in a public or private capacity. And the law always punishes libels, even among private persons, because they flow from malice and tend to create disturbance, quarrels, and revenge between them, their families and kindred, and disturb the public peace; and the law reckons it a greater offense when the libel is pointed at persons in a public capacity, as it is a reproach to the government to have corrupt magistrates, &c., substituted by his majesty, and tends to sow sedition and disturb the peace of the kingdom." And his Lordship refused to allow the admission of any evidence to prove that the matters charged in the libels were true.

In 1777 an information was filed against John Horne, charging that the defendant wickedly, maliciously, and seditiously intending, devising, and contriving to stir up and excite discontents and seditions amongst his majesty's subjects, and to alienate and withdraw the affection, fidelity, and allegiance of his majesty's subjects from his said majesty, and to insinuate and cause it to be believed that divers of his majesty's innocent and deserving subjects had been inhumanly murdered by his said majesty's troops in the province, colony, or plantation of the Massachusetts Bay, in New England, in America, belonging to the crown of Great Britain, and unlawfully and wickedly to seduce and encourage his said majesty's subjects in the said province, colony, or plantation to resist and oppose his majesty's government, &c., did wickedly, maliciously, and seditiously write and publish a certain false, wicked, malicious, scandalous, and seditious libel of and concerning his said majesty's government and the employment of his troops. The information was tried before the Earl of Mansfield by a special jury, and the defendant was found guilty and sentenced to pay a fine of £200 to the king, to be imprisoned for twelve months and until the fine should be paid, and to find sureties for his good behavior for three years.[1]

In 1804 an information was filed against William Cobbett, for a libel upon the administration of the Irish government, and upon the public conduct and charac ter of the lord-lieutenant and lord-chancellor of Ire land. The libel was contained in a letter signed "Juverna," published in "The Weekly Register," and the information charged that the defendant, unlawfully and maliciously devising and intending to move and incite the liege subjects of the king to hatred and dislike of his majesty's administration and government of this kingdom, and to insinuate and cause it to be believed that the people of that part of the United Kingdom of Great Britain and Ireland called Ireland were oppressed, aggrieved, and injured by our said lord the king's government of the said part of the United Kingdom, and to traduce, defame, and vilify the persons employed by our said lord the king, in the administration of the government of the said part of the said United Kingdom, &c., did unlawfully and mali ciously print and publish the said libel. Mr. Cobbett was not the author, but only the publisher of the letter.

An information was filed in 1811 against John Hunt and John Leigh Hunt for printing and publishing in "The Examiner" a libel tending to create disaffection in the army.[2]

[1] 11 St. Tr. 651; Cowp. Rep. 676.
[2] 31 How. St. Tr. 408.

In 1820 an information was filed against Sir Francis Burdett, for writing and publishing a certain scandalous, malicious, and seditious libel of and concerning the government of this realm, and of and concerning the troops of our lord the king, unlawfully and maliciously devising and intending to raise and excite discontent, disaffection, and sedition among the liege subjects of the king, and among the soldiers of our said lord the king, and to move and excite the liege subjects of our said lord the king to hatred and dislike of the government of this realm, and to insinuate and cause it to be believed by the liege subjects of our said lord the king that divers of the liege subjects of our said lord the king had been inhumanly cut down, maimed, and killed by certain troops of our said lord the king at Loughborough, in the county of Leicester, on the 16th of August, 1819; the libel being contained in an address to the electors of Westminster.[1] Best, J., told the jury that if the address was published with the intention alleged in the information, such intention was to be collected from the paper itself; unless the import of the paper were explained by the mode of publication or any other circumstances, the paper was a libel. The jury found the defendant guilty.

A body of police having dispersed an assembly of people at Birmingham, an indictment for seditious libel was preferred against the writer and publisher of certain resolutions agreed to by a body called the General Convention, condemning the act of the police as "a wanton, flagrant, and unjust outrage upon the people of Birmingham by a bloodthirsty and unconstitutional force from London, acting under the authority of men who, when out of office, sanc-

[1] 4 B. & Ald. 95.

tioned and took part in the meetings of the people, and now, when they share in the public plunder, seek to keep the people in social slavery and political degradation;" asserting that the people of Birmingham were "the best judges of their own right to meet in the 'Bullring' or elsewhere, have their own feelings to consult respecting the outrage given, and are the best judges of their own power and resources to obtain justice;" and that the arrest of a particular individual "affords another convincing proof of the absence of all justice in England, and clearly shows that there is no security for life, liberty, or property, till the people have some control over the laws they are called upon to obey."[1]

"With respect to the intent of the defendant," said the learned judge, "a man must be taken to intend the natural consequences of what he has done; and if this paper has a direct tendency to cause unlawful meetings and disturbances, and to lead to a violation of the laws, that is sufficient to bring it within the terms of this indictment, and it is a seditious libel.

"If it be the highest crime known to our laws to attempt to subvert by force the constitution and state, it is certainly a crime, though of inferior magnitude, yet of great enormity, to endeavor to despoil it of its best support—the veneration, esteem, and affection of the people. It is, therefore, a maxim of the law of England, flowing by natural consequence and easy deduction from the great principle of self-defense, to consider as libels and misdemeanors every species of attack by speaking or writing, the object of which is wantonly to defame or indecorously to calumniate that economy, order, and constitution of

[1] Rex v. Collins; Rex v. Lovett, 9 Car. & P. 456.

things which make up the general system of the law and government of the country."[1]

"That to accomplish treasonable purposes, and to delude the weak, the unwary, and the ignorant, no means can be more effectual than a seditious press. With such machinery the preachers of sedition can sow widecast those poisonous doctrines, which, if unchecked, culminate in insurrection and rebellion. . . . . Words may be of a seditious character, but they might arise from sudden heat, be heard only by a few, create no lasting impression, and differ in malignity and permanent effect from writings."

Criticism on any part of the constitution, made with a view to bring about improvements in it, are not interdicted; but attacks calculated to promote insurrection, and circulate discontent, to degrade and vilify the constitution, to asperse its justice and anywise impair the exercise of its functions, are termed seditious libels, and punished as such.

The state of the country and of the public mind when the publication takes place are material to be considered in determining whether the libel was published with a seditious intention.

A particular passage in a work may constitute a seditious libel; but although the jury are to form their judgment upon the particular passage charged as such, they may compare it with the whole book, and see how it is qualified by it. So with regard to newspaper articles: the jury are to consider, not isolated passages, but the whole of the articles complained of.

Whether a newspaper article is original or not, may, however, be a material consideration in

[1] 11 Cox Crim. Cas. 46.

determining the intention with which it was published.

Williams, a barrister of the Middle Temple, was, in the seventeenth year of James I., indicted, convicted, and executed for high treason, in writing two books, the one called "Balaam's Ass," and the other called "Speculum Regale," in which he predicted that the king would die in the year 1621.[1]

One Brewster was indicted and convicted in the 15th Chas. II., for printing and publishing a libel called "The Phœnix, or the Solemn League and Covenant," in which it was declared that a king abusing his power to the overthrow of religion, laws, and liberties, may be controlled and opposed; and if he sets himself to overthrow all these by arms, then they who have the power, as the estates of the land, may and ought to resist by arms.[2]

In the 29th Chas. II. an information was filed against one Harrison, charging that he, maliciously and traitorously intending to stir up sedition and to create a disturbance between the king and his people, had published, uttered, and proclaimed of and concerning the government and rule of England, and of and concerning the traitors who adjudged King Charles I. to death, that the government of the kingdom consists of three estates, and that if a rebellion should happen in the kingdom, unless that rebellion was against the three estates, it was no rebellion. The court, supposing that the words did tend to set on foot that position upon which the war levied in 1641 by the two Houses against the king, was grounded, were much displeased that the counsel for the defendant would pretend to defend

[1] 2 Roll. Rep. 88.

[2] Rex v. Brewster, Dig. L. L. 76.

them, or to put any tolerable sense upon them, and gave judgment for the king.[1]

In the 5th Anne, Dr. Brown was convicted, on an information, of having published a libel, entitled "Mercurius Politicus," reflecting on the state and constitution, as settled at the Revolution, which he represented as the "destruction of the laws of England."[2]

A treatise on hereditary right, by Bedford, was held to be a libel, though it contained no reflection upon any part of the then government, in the 12th Anne.

An information was filed in 1754 against Richard Nutt, for printing and publishing a certain false, wicked, scandalous, seditious, and malicious libel, entitled "The London Evening Post," tending to represent this kingdom as in a miserable and wretched state and condition, and with a view to traduce the "late happy revolution," and to suggest that it was an unjustifiable and unconstitutional proceeding; and also to dispute and call in question the settlement and limitation of the succession of the crown of this realm in the present most illustrious family; and to represent the same as illegal and unwarrantable, and to make it be believed that the said late most happy revolution and the settlement of the crown of this realm as now by law established, had been attended with fatal and pernicious consequences to the subjects of this realm. He was found guilty, and sentenced to the pillory, a fine of five hundred pounds, and imprisonment in the King's Bench for two years.

Dr. John Shebbeare was convicted in 1758 of

[1] Rex v. Harrison, 3 Keb. 842; Vent. 324.
[2] Rex v. Brown, 11 Mod. 86.

printing and publishing a certain false, wicked, scandalous, seditious, and malicious libel, entitled: "A sixth letter to the people of England, on the progress of national ruin, in which it is shown that the present grandeur of France and the calamities of this nation are owing to the influence of Hanover on the councils of England;" tending to traduce the Revolution, and to represent it as the foundation of all those imaginary evils and calamities which the defendant would falsely insinuate the subjects of this kingdom did labor under; and also to asperse the memory of King William III. and of King George I.; and to represent the public measures which were taken and pursued during the course of their respective reigns as wicked, corrupt, and fatal measures to this kingdom; and also to asperse, scandalize, and vilify the late king and his administration of the government of this kingdom; and to make it thought that the public affairs of this kingdom were in a most unhappy and declining state; and that the subjects of this kingdom were unnecessarily and most intolerably loaded and oppressed with taxes, debts, and subsidies; and also to insinuate that the late king had no concern for the people of England, nor any regard for the interest, honor, or welfare of this kingdom, but that the treasure and riches of this kingdom were misapplied, wasted, and dissipated in support of the electorate of Hanover and his German dominions.[1]

Thomas Paine was convicted in 1792 upon an information charging him with being the author and publisher of a seditious libel, the tendency of which was "to traduce and vilify the late happy Revolution, the settlement of the crown and regal government, as by law established, and also the bill of rights, the leg-

[1] Rex v. Shebbeare, Hil. Term, 31 Geo. II., K. B. MSS.

islature, government, laws, and parliament of this kingdom."[1]

John Cuthell, a bookseller, was found guilty in 1799, of publishing a seditious libel written by the Rev. G. Wakefield, but, on filing an affidavit that he had no knowledge whatever of the contents or nature of the book, he was discharged on payment or a fine of thirty marks.[2]

33. For many years the history of the English law is a history of the censorship of the press, exercised by the Star Chamber, and, in a less degree, by statutes and by courts ever since.[3]

"On the abolition," says Shortt,[4] "of the Star Chamber, in 1641, the Long Parliament assumed to itself the jurisdiction exercised by that court, in matters relating to the press, and passed many severe ordinances in restraint of printing. The restraints of the press were continued after the Restoration by the Licensing Act of 13 & 14 Car. 2, c. 33 ("An act for preventing the frequent abuses in printing seditious, treasonable, and unlicensed books and pamphlets, and for regulating of printing and printing presses"). This act interdicted the printing of pamphlets and books except in London, York, and the Universities; limited the number of master printers to twenty; regulated the number of their presses and apprentices; appointed licensers, and imposed severe penalties on offenders

[1] Rex v. Paine, 32 Geo. III., K. B. MSS. The defendant, not appearing to receive the judgment of the court, was outlawed.

[2] Rex v. Cuthell, 27 St. Tr. 642.

[3] The foregoing account of the common-law decisions as to seditious libel, is epitomized from Mr. Shortt's work, pp. 322–344.

[4] Law Lit., p. 319. In 1680, when the licensing act had ceased,

against its provisions, and many cruel and ingenious punishments were inflicted under it. It continued in force till 1679, and in 1685 was revived (by 1 Jac. 2, c. 17) for seven years. In 1692 it was continued (by 4 Will. & M. c. 24) until the end of the session of 1693, when its operation ceased, notwithstanding several attempts to revive it.[1] The liberty of the press dates from that year.

for a time, to operate, the opinion of the judges on the subject of unlicensed printing was expressed by Chief Justice Scroggs, in the following manner. At the trial of Benjamin Harris, a bookseller, for the publication of a libel entitled, "An Appeal from the Country to the City, for the Preservation of his Majesty's Person, Liberty, Property, and the Protestant Religion," the chief justice said: "It is not long since that all the judges met by the king's command—as they did some time before, too—and they both times declared unanimously that all persons that do write or print or sell any pamphlet that is either scandalous to public or private persons, such books may be seized, and the person punished by law; that all books which are scandalous to the government may be seized, and all persons so exposing them may be punished; and, further, that all writers of news, though not scandalous, seditious, or reflective upon the government or the State, yet if they are writers (as there are few others) of false news, they are indictable and punishable upon that account" (7 St. Tr. 929).

[1] "While the abbey was hanging with black for the funeral of the queen, the Commons came to a vote which, at the time, attracted little attention, which produced no excitement, which has been left unnoticed by voluminous annalists, and of which the history can be but imperfectly traced in the archives of Parliament, but which has done more for liberty and for civilization than the great charter or the bill of rights. Early in the session a select committee had been appointed to ascertain what temporary statutes were about to expire, and to consider which of those statutes it might be expedient to continue. The report was made; and all the recommendations contained in that report were adopted, with one exception. Among the laws which the committee advised the House to renew was the law which subjected the press to a censorship. The question was put 'that the House do agree with the committee in the

"The liberty of the press, when rightly understood," says Blackstone,[1] "consists in laying no previous restraints upon publications, not in freedom from censure for criminal matter when published."[2]

That liberty in the United States is practically unlimited and absolute. Such a thing as a prosecution for seditious libel, at least so far as our knowledge goes, is, and always appears to have been, utterly unknown. The right of the government, however, to restrain or punish utterances calculated to diminish its power or weaken its authority, cannot be supposed, from the fact of its never having been asserted (except, perhaps, in time of war, when arrests were made by force of martial law and as a military measure[3]) not to exist. Not only does such right inhere in the government by virtue of the common law, but an act of congress of July 14, 1798, makes it an indictable offense to libel the government, congress, or president of the United States.

34. It is apprehended, as we have said already, that the prevention of injurious publications in this country will be directed rather to their sale when published, than to a forbidding of their publication, and so would fall under the police jurisdiction of the states themselves, rather than under the copyright jurisdiction of congress. There can be no property,

resolution that the act entitled an act for preventing abuses in printing seditious, treasonable, and unlicensed pamphlets, and for regulating of printing and printing presses, be continued.' The Speaker pronounced that the 'noes' had it; and the 'ayes' did not think fit to divide" (Macaulay, Hist. of Eng., vol. 4, p. 540). As to the reasons which induced Parliament to discontinue the licensing act, see p. 541 of the volume last referred to.

[1] 4 Com. (Steph.) 346.

[2] *Vid.* Hallam Const. Hist., vol 3, p. 227 (ed. 1832).

[3] *e. g.*, the case of Vallandigham, 1863.

either literary or otherwise, in such matter. No action at law would lie for its recovery if withheld, or if lost by a carrier—and we have already seen that it is a misdemeanor to deposit it in the post-office. Statutes forbidding the sale of such productions will probably be found in most if not all of the states; but even in their absence, the dealing in this class of publications would be indictable,[1] for the circulating of obscene matter to deprave and corrupt the public morals, is, indeed, as Lord Campbell characterized it, "an abominable offense,"[2] and the jurisdiction of such offenses having come down from the star chamber through the ecclesiastical courts,[3] has finally settled upon the civil courts as the custodians of the morals of the realm[4] or commonwealth.

In treating of obscenity the law encounted a difficulty at the very outset. It was difficult to draw a

[1] "Preserving and keeping in one's possession" obscene works for the purpose of selling them, is not an indictable offense. But "obtaining and procuring" them for that purpose is an indictable misdemeanor at common law (Sugdale's Case, 1 Dears. C. C. 64). "And this because"—said Campbell, Ch. J., in that case—"the plaintiff in error may have had the pictures in his possession with an innocent intention; and there is no act shown to be done which can be considered as the first step in the prosecution of a misdemeanor. . . . . Procuring is an overt act, an unlawful step taken in pursuance of the abominable offense of circulating obscene prints to deprave and corrupt the public morals.

[2] Ibid.

[3] Hill's Case, 2 Str. 790; Dig. L. L. 60.

[4] Rex v. Curl, 2 Str. 789. One of the members of the court, when this case first came before it—Fortesque, J.—was of opinion that the offense (of having published a base and obscure libel, entitled, "Venus in the Cloister, or the Nun in her Smock"), though great, was not punishable by law (Ib. 790). The court, however, upheld the temporal jurisdiction, and Curl was pilloried for his offense. Since this decision, the temporal character of the offense has not been doubted.—Shortt, L. L. 312.

line between works wholly and designedly obscene and those obscene only in portions. The question arose how large or how small a portion of a work must be worthy and moral in its character to make it proper to be promiscuously circulated. The labors of the great masters of art, and the writings of the fathers and masters of poetry and the drama, might readily be brought under a too general and comprehensive definition, and thus works good in themselves, and standard and elevating in their nature, might be interdicted; while, under a more specific and narrower one, compositions designedly vicious and corrupting in all their tendencies might avoid the injunction of the law.[1]

35. Again, a work written with the laudable intention of reforming abuses, and to expose errors, may be, from the very nature of the abuses and errors sought to be reformed, liable to the charge of obscenity.

It is indeed a delicate question, and one that jurists, legislators, and sociologists have constantly encountered. The offense is rank, but it would seem as if any attempt to abate it became, almost at the outset, ranker than the offense itself. It is an offense of which the world has not yet learned even to speak, without danger to the very interests it strives to protect.

[1] Hill's Case, 2 Str. 790. The defendant, in this case, was indicted for publishing some poems of Lord Rochester's. In 1857, pending the passage of a bill in the English House of Lords, relating to obscene productions, Lord Lyndhurst pointed out this difficulty. "The magistrate," said he, "must also be satisfied that the case is a proper one for a prosecution; so that if indecent passages were taken out of such authors as Dryden or Pope, he would say: 'Although these are very indecent passages, and ought never to have been inserted in these works, yet this is not a case for a prosecution' (Parliamentary Debates, July 13, 1857), and accordingly the words, 'proper to be prosecuted as such' (obscene), were inserted."—Rex v. Hicklin, L. Rep. 32, B. 371.

In a recent case,[1] the test of obscenity was said to be "whether the tendency of the matter charged as obscenity is to deprave and corrupt those whose minds are open to such immoral influences, and into whose hands a publication of the sort may fall."

This latter was a case where a pamphlet, called "The Confessional Unmasked; professing to show the depravity of the Romish priesthood, the iniquity of the confessional, and the questions put to females in confession"—containing extracts in Latin, with translations of the same, from various writers, half the pamphlet relating to controversial matters, and the other half being grossly obscene as relating to impure and filthy acts, words, and deeds—was circulated by the appellant, a member of "The Protestant Electoral Union," not for profit or gain, but for the purpose of exposing what he deemed to be the errors of the Church of Rome, and particularly the immorality of the confessional; the pamphlet, in fact, containing a preface and notes condemnatory of the tenets and principles of the writers cited from.

The court of queen's bench held that the justices were right in ordering a number of copies of the pamphlet to be seized in the appellant's house, and destroyed as obscene books under the law.

"I take it," said Cockburn, Ch. J., "that, apart from the ulterior object which the publisher of this work had in view, the work itself is, in every sense of the term, an obscene publication, and that consequently, as the law of England does not allow of any obscene publication, such publication is indictable. We have it, therefore, that the publication itself is a breach of the law. But then it is said for the appel-

[1] Rex v. Hicklin, L. Rep. 32, B. 371; 18 L. T. N. S. 398; 36 L. J. 9; 8 M. C.

lant: 'Yes, but his purpose was not to deprave the public mind; his purpose was to expose the errors of the Roman Catholic religion, especially in the matter of the confessional.' Be it so. The question then presents itself in this simple form: May you commit an offense against the law, in order that thereby you may effect some ulterior object which you have in view, which may be an honest and even a laudable one? My answer is, emphatically, no. The law says you shall not publish an obscene work. An obscene work is here published; and a work, the obscenity of which is so clear and decided, that it is impossible to suppose that the man who published it must not have known and seen that the effect upon the minds of many of those into whose hands it would come, would be of a mischievous and demoralizing character. .... I think the old sound and honest maxim, that you shall not do evil that good may come, is applicable in law as well as in morals; and here we have a certain and positive evil produced for the purpose of effecting an uncertain, remote, and very doubtful good. I think, therefore, the case for the order is made out; and although I quite concur in thinking that the motive of the parties who published this work, however mistaken, was an honest one, yet I cannot suppose but what they had that intention which constitutes the criminality of the act; at any rate, that they knew perfectly well that this work must have the tendency which, in point of law, makes it an obscene publication, namely, the tendency to corrupt the minds and morals of those into whose hands it might come. The mischief of it, I think, cannot be exaggerated. But it is not upon that I take my stand in the judgment I pronounce. I am of opinion, as the learned recorder has found, that this is an obscene publication. I hold that where a man publishes a work manifestly obscene, he must be taken to have had the intention which is implied from that act; and that, as soon as you have an illegal act thus established, *quoad* the intention and *quoad* the act, it does not lie in the mouth of the man who does it, to say, 'Well, I was breaking the law, but I was breaking it for some wholesome aud salutary purpose.' The law does not allow that. You must abide by the law, and if you would accomplish your object, you must do it in a legal manner, or let it alone; you must not do it in a manner which is illegal."

36. We apprehend the rule will be in general somewhat as follows: Standard works of great literary value, like the plays of Shakespeare, Jonson, Beaumont and Fletcher, Congreve or Wycherley, the poems of Chaucer, Dryden, or Byron, or the prose fiction of DeFoe, Smollett, or Fielding, manifestly will not be construed to be obscene productions, although, whether designedly, or by the fault, the fashions, and follies of the days when they were composed, all the works of these writers contain passages which are in these times—without question, perhaps—grossly immoral and obscene. It is not upon such episodes that their immortality rests; such passages are the tares which grow with the wheat, which are to be forgiven for the sake of the sublime, or brilliant, or epigrammatic character of the composition, ascribing them only to the manners of his times and to the humanity of the author. Neither will we prosecute the successful editors and publishers of these works, nor class the works themselves as falling under the interdiction of the law.

37. If, however, an editor or publisher should undertake and publish a volume of selections from the above or like authors, which should contain ex-

clusively their obscene passages and nothing else, so that every passage or sentiment of literary or epigrammatic merit which has made those writers famous should be carefully banished, and only the grossly sensuous or filthy thoughts and sentiments included; such a volume—we think it cannot be doubted—would be clearly an obscene publication. A publication might be even made grossly obscene by culling passages wholly from the sacred scriptures, which passages, standing alone and unrelieved by their natural context, might constitute a work indictable by law.[1] It might be objected that such a work would harm nobody; but, on the other hand, there might be many persons ignorant enough to suppose that the lofty authority of the source attached itself to garbled extracts isolated therefrom.[2]

38. The circulation of grossly obscene and filthy engravings, prints, cuts, photographs, or pictures of any kind, is generally prohibited by statute, whether by passing through the mails, or by selling and vending, or exposing or procuring them to be so sold or vended. And even if it were not, we think, undoubtedly, that an authority to check such offenses *contra bones mores* exists by common law in all the courts of criminal jurisdiction. Undoubtedly no copyright[3] or other property can exist in such productions, for the law will not protect in one form what it punishes in another.

39. With regard to photographs, prints, or engravings, the of the works old masters, antiques and classical fragments, a more careful discrimination might be necessary. There must be here, as in the case of the stan-

[1] Matter of Train, N. Y. General Sessions, 1873.

[2] Ibid.

[3] Du Bois v. Beresford, 2 Camp. 511; 4 Bl. Com. (Steph.) 545; Fores v. Johnes, 4 Esp. 97.

dard writers, a careful discrimination between what is merely sensual and suggestive (from which, perhaps, equity might withhold its protection) and that which is grossly obscene and filthy, the circulation of which the law might follow with punishment.[1]

40. There is another character of publications which the law will not consider as innocent, namely, those which in their pretensions, titles, or advertisements, deceive, or are calculated to deceive, the public.

In such cases the publisher of the matter will be held to obtain, or as seeking to obtain money under false pretenses, not only in the publication of the work, but every time a single copy is sold. And he cannot, therefore, have any copyright in the publication nor any standing in court to ask protection in the possession of what he has no right to possess.[2]

This rule was laid down in Wright v. Tallis, by Tindal, C. J., and as carrying the principle, perhaps, to its limit, it may be well to examine that case somewhat in detail. The declaration alleged that before and at the time of committing the grievances, &c., there was a subsisting copyright in a certain book entitled, "Evening Devotions; or the worship of God in spirit and in truth, for every day in the year," from the German, by C. C. Sturm, author of the "Morning Devotions"; and that the plaintiff was the proprietor of such copy-

[1] Thus the paintings of "Leda and the Swan," and "Io and Jupiter," in the Royal Museum at Berlin, and the innumerable Danaes, and other renderings of classical fictions, while assuredly not modest in their tone, could scarcely be called obscene. The selection of paintings from the "chamber of the nymphs," in Pompeii, and the bronzes and statuary from that city, preserved in the secret chamber of the Royal Museum at Naples, however, are unquestionably obscene, and seem to illustrate the distinction endeavored to be indicated above.

[2] Wright v. Tallis, 1 C. B. Rep. 893.

right, and had printed divers, to wit, twenty thousand copies of the said book, to his own great profit and advantage. The defendant, however, was enabled to establish in defense, that the book in question was procured by the complainant to be written by one Robert Huish, and was not a translation from the German of C. C. Sturm, whose works were well known and highly valued. And, on demurrer, it was held that the work, being a palpable attempt to deceive the public, no copyright could exist therein, and the plaintiff could not maintain his action for piracy. The learned chief justice, however, was careful to discriminate between this case and the others examined in this chapter, saying: "The cases in which a copyright has been held not to subject where the work is subversive of good order, morality, or religion, do not, indeed, bear directly on the case before us; but they have this analogy with the present inquiry, that they prove that the rule which denies the existence of copyright in those cases, is a rule established for the benefit and protection of the public, and we think the best protection that the law can afford to the public against such a fraud as that laid open by this plea, is to make the practice of it unprofitable to its author."

The case of Lord Byron v. Johnston[1] is a peculiar one. In that case an injunction was continued by Lord Eldon, restraining the defendant from publishing a poem as the work of Lord Byron, who was then abroad, on an affidavit of Lord Byron's agents of circumstances rendering it highly probable that it was not his work, and the defendant declining to swear that he believed it was.

41. There may be, and are, however, innumerable

[1] 2 Meriv. 29. (See this case, and Harte v. De Witt, treated *post*, in the chapter on Piracy.)

cases of misrepresentation in the authorship of literary productions, which are entirely innocent, harmless, and permissible, as not only deceiving nobody, but adding—as a sort of coup d'eclat—to the interest or the success of the work. Notable instances of the like are frequent in literature, and should be carefully discriminated from the rule just laid down.

As where the author of a fiction, for instance, pretends to be the editor of a manuscript that he has discovered in a hidden spot—in an old garret or chest of drawers, or in a cave or the trunk of a tree. Or where the fiction holds itself out to be a translation, as did Walpole's Castle of Otranto; or where the form of letters, passing between imaginary correspondents, or of statements or affidavits made by them is chosen; or where the author's name is concealed under a fanciful or invented nom de plume. There is no serious design, in any one of these cases, to deceive the purchaser, or to make gain or profit from him on the false representation. The purchaser probably would not have been deterred from purchasing at the same price, had he known or been informed, by the bookseller, that the name of the author was assumed, and not genuine; or had known that the work was original, and not translated.[1]

If Chatterton had invoked the protection of a

[1] Wright v. Tallis, 1 C. B. Rep. 893. There is no more common device of authors than this—certainly none more harmless, or, we may add, delightful. (See the interesting treatise of M. Delepierre: "Supercheries Litteraires, Pastiches, Suppositions d'auteur, dans les Lettres et dans les Arts. Londres: N. Trubner et cie. 1872;" and also, "Questions de Litterature Legale,"—Ch. Nodier; "Pastiches et Imitations, Libres du style de quelques Ecrevains de 17[me] et du 18[me] Siecles,"—L. Chatelaine; "Reflexions sur le Style Original,"—Marquis de Roure; and "Supercheries Litteraires," by Querard.

court of equity for a copyright in his published works, who could doubt that it would have been extended him, since the antique and the literary charm of the work was his, to whomsoever among imaginary beings he chose to assign it. Imagine a purchaser, of that day, bringing back a volume of the "Rowlie Poems" to his bookseller, and asking a return of his money, on the ground that it was not a transcription from old manuscripts of the monk, Thomas Rowlie, but the original work of a boy—one Thomas Chatterton; or the "Tales of a Grandfather," because they were written by Walter Scott, and not by Jedediah Cleishbotham; or "Knickerbocker's History of New York," because there was no such man as Deidrich Knickerbocker, but that the whole was a burlesque and absurdity, proceeding from the brain of one Washington Irving!

42. By the common law, there is still another class of works not innocent. It was laid down by Lord Ellenborough, in the trial of Jean Peltier for a libel upon Napoleon Bonaparte, first consul of the French republic, in 1803,[1] that any publication which tends to degrade, revile, and defame persons in considerable situations of power and dignity in foreign countries, may be taken to be and treated as a seditious libel, particularly where it has a tendency to interrupt pacific relations between the two countries.[2] If the publication contains a plain and manifest incitement and persuasion, addressed to others, to assassinate and destroy the persons of such magistrates, as its tendency is to interrupt the public peace, the libel becomes subversive of government, and assumes

[1] Rex v. Peltier, 28 Howell's St. Tr., 617; and London, M Peltier, 1803.

[2] The same appears to be the law in Scotland—*vid.* Borthwick's Law of Libel, pp. 74, 75.

a still more criminal complexion. It is difficult to conceive of such a case occurring in the United States. It would certainly be an interesting spectacle, if a foreign power should complain of a libel through the press of a government which permits herself, her own rulers, statesmen, and machinery of state, to be criticised, characterized, caricatured, and maligned, without limit and without protest. Still, it has not been thought inappropriate, in this connection, to examine the few instances in which this kind of publication has been condemned.

The information, in 1808, against Jean Peltier, was for publishing matter defamatory of the first consul of France—a country with whom England was then at peace—and containing passages inciting to his assassination.[1]

[1] Two of these passages were as follows:

"De la France, ô honte éternelle!
César, au bord du Rubicon,
A contre lui, dans sa querelle,
Le Sénat, Pompée, et Caton;
Et, dans les plaines de Pharsale,
Si la fortune est inégale—
S'il te faut céder aux destins;
Rome, dans ce revers funeste—
Pour te venger, au moins il reste
Un poignard aux derniers Romains."

. . . .

"Il est proclamé chef et consul pour la vie! . .
Pour moi, loin qu'à son sort je porte quelqu' envie,
Qu'il nomme, j'y consens, son digne successeur,
Sur le pavois porté qu'on l'elise Empereur!
Enfin, et Romulus nous rappelle la chose,
Je fais vœu—dés demain qu'il ait l'apothéose. Amen."

"Oh! eternal disgrace of France! Cæsar, on the banks of the Rubicon, has against him, in his quarrel, the Senate, Pompey, and Cato; and in the plains of Pharsalia, if fortune is unequal—if you must yield to the destinies, Rome, in this sad reverse—at least there remains to avenge you a poniard among the last Romans." "He is proclaimed chief and

Lord Ellenborough, having called the attention of the jury to these passages, said that it appeared to him that their aim and tendency was to degrade and vilify, to render odious and contemptible, the person of the first consul in the estimation of the people of England as well as France, and likewise to excite to his assassination and destruction. "That appearing to be the immediate and direct tendency of these publications, I cannot," said his lordship, "in the correct discharge of my duty, do otherwise than state, that they are, in point of law, libels. And in the correct discharge of your duty, I am sure no memory of past or expectation of future injury, will warp you from the straight and even course of justice; but your verdict will mark with reprobation all projects of assassination and murder. Consider, likewise, how dangerous projects of this sort may be, if not discountenanced and discouraged in this country. They may be retaliated on the head of all those whose safety is most dear to us."

Anterior to this, however, in 1764, an information had been filed against one D'Eon de Beaumont, a Frenchman, for a libel upon the then French ambassador, Count de Guerchy. The libel principally consisted of some angry reflections on the public conduct of the ambassador, charging him with ignorance in his special capacity, and of having used stratagem to supplant and depreciate the defendant at the court of

consul for life. As for me, far from envying his lot, let him name—I consent to it—his worthy successor. Carried on the shield, let him be elected! Finally (and Romulus recalls the thing to mind), I wish that on the morrow he may have his apotheosis. Amen." Palm of Nuremburg was court-martialed and sentenced to be shot, at Brenau, in 1807, for writing some echo verses on Napoleon I. And very poor ones they were, too; poor enough to have let the author crawl away—one would think.—Morgan's Macaronic Poetry, p. 98.

Versailles. After the defendant had been found guilty, Lord Mansfield observed to the Prussian and other foreign ambassadors then attending the court, that the law of England paid a high regard to the function of ambassadors, and would equally protect them from all insults, as well on their reputation as their persons or property.[1]

Lord George Gordon was convicted, in 1787, of publishing, in a newspaper known as "The Public Advertiser," certain false, scandalous, malicious, and defamatory libels on the queen of France, Marie Antoinette, and on the French ambassador in London, imputing to the former, tyranny and oppression, and charging the latter with being the tool employed in carrying them on;[2] and in 1799, John Vint, George Ross, and John Parry, were tried upon an information for publishing, in "The Courier" newspaper, the following libel upon the emperor Paul I., of Russia: "The emperor of Russia is rendering himself obnoxious to his subjects by various acts of tyranny, and ridiculous in the eyes of Europe by his inconsistency. He has now passed an edict prohibiting the exportation of timber, deals, &c. In consequence of that ill-

[1] Rex v. D'Eon, W. Black. Rep. 501, 517; Dig. L. L. 74, 75.

[2] 22 Howell's St. Tr. 175. For the above libel Lord George Gordon was sentenced to two years' imprisonment in Newgate (to be computed from the expiration of a three years imprisonment to which he was sentenced on the same day for a former libel, which has been noticed), and to a fine of £500; and at the expiration of his term of imprisonment, to find sureties for his good behavior for the space of fourteen years, himself in £10,000, and two sureties in £2,500. On the 18th of January, 1793, he was brought into court for the purpose of being admitted to bail; but being unable to provide the requisite security, he was remanded to prison, where he remained until his death on the 1st of November, 1793.—Shortt, p. 381.

timed law, upwards of one hundred sail of vessels are likely to return to this kingdom without freights." Lord Kenyon, Ch. J., told the jury that such a publication, holding up the sovereign of Russia as a tyrant, and ridiculous over Europe, might tend to his calling for satisfaction, as for a national affront, if it passed unreprobated by our government, and in our courts of justice.[1]

43. To recapitulate, then: Works not innocent in their nature—although they come into court and pray it—cannot receive the recognition of the law which will give no damages for their piracy, and consequently no protection, through equity, against such piracy. Works that, in addition to being not innocent, are absolutely and undeniably vicious, monstrous, and corrupting, by being either outrageously blasphemous, or filthy and obscene, will, as we have already seen, fall under the attention of the law without soliciting it, and be positively and criminally dealt with by the municipal or local authorities—they, and their authors and publishers and circulators.

44. There remain, still, two other classes of productions, namely, matters libelous (properly so called) of the individual, which are proceeded against both civilly and criminally, and matters contemptuous of courts of justice. These we propose to consider in a separate chapter.

[1] 27 Howell's St. Tr. 627, 643. The defendants were all found guilty, and the proprietor of the paper was sentenced to six months' imprisonment, to pay a fine of £100, and to give security for his good behavior for five years, himself in £500, and two sureties in £250 each. The printer and the publisher were sentenced to one month's imprisonment.—Ib.

CHAPTER II.

OF LIBEL.

45. It appears then, that the law, in return for the protection it extends to authors, requires that they shall not use their liberty to the hurt of the subject: and that the literary matter in which their rights are secured shall be—to begin with—Innocent. We have seen, so far, that this innocence must exist: I. in the Intention (*i.e.*, that it shall not prejudice or imperil the morals of the community), and II. in Representation (*i.e.*, that it shall not harmfully deceive the public as to its genuineness or its value).

There is besides a third class of publications so directly, absolutely, and often maliciously harmful, that the law will not merely express its disapprobation by withholding its protection from them, but will interfere directly to shield the party injured, and to punish the utterers and publishers; whether that party be an individual, the state, or the community at large.

This class consists of publications Libelous; and the wrong which they commit is known as libel.

To the Roman law of libel, as applied to literature, Horace makes allusion in one of his satires:

> Quinetiam lex
> Pœnaque lata, malo quæ nollet carmine quenquam
> Describi. Vertere modum formidine fustis.[1]

---

[1] Hor. Sat. ii. "Moreover, it is an extensive law and punishment which will not permit a person to be described in dog-

The Institutes of Justinian defined a libeler to be "one who shall, to the infamy of another, write, compose, or publish a book, song, or fable, or maliciously procure any of those acts to be done;" and a distinction was very early taken in the Roman law, between slander spoken and written. The *injuria verbalis* was deemed a much lower degree of injury than the *malum carmen* and *famosus libellus.*

This distinction has survived the civil law, and is the one observed to-day;[1] slander being a defamation conveyed by speech, and libel a defamation conveyed by writing or effigy.[2] It follows, therefore, that what

gerel verse. To change the style for fear of a club!" The punishment at Rome, for slander, by means of defamatory verses (*si quis aliquem publice defamisset, eique adversos bonos moros convicium feicisset vel carmen famosum in eum condidisset*), was, beating with a club. Tiberias ordered one whom he had befriended, and who afterwards wrote defamatory verses against him, to be thrown from the Tarpeian rock (Dio. lvii., 22). There was no action for ingratitude among the Romans, as with the Persians; for, says Seneca, all the courts at Rome would scarcely have been sufficient for trying them.

There was something superstitious in the horror with which the Icelanders regarded a libel; and no offense among them was more surely or bloodily avenged than the publication of satirical verses, or the setting up of a "Nid"—that is, an insulting or indecent figure, or a horse's head on a pole on the lands of another. (See "The Story of Burnt Njal; or, Life in Iceland at the End of the Tenth Century." By George W. Dasent, D.C.S.) The Russian people "feel corporeal punishment less sensibly than a verbal insult. This idea has a religious foundation. A good Christian cannot admit that the punishment of fustigation, which has been inflicted on the Saviour of humanity, can be for a man a stain of infamy. He believes that a verbal insult affects the immortal part of man; whereas, a blow only produces suffering in the least noble part of his being" (Essai sur l'Histoire de la Civilization en Russie. Par Nicolas de Gerebtzoff. Paris, 1858, vol. ii., p. 575. Westminster Review, January, 1864—Art. Russia).

[1] Holt on Libel, p. 21.

[2] So, suspending a lamp before the plaintiff's house, intimat-

may be slanderous only, when spoken or uttered so as to reach the ear, upon being so published as to reach the eye, becomes libellous. These two wrongs are so intermixed that a knowledge of one is necessary to an understanding of the other, and we have, therefore, treated them together in this chapter. To one bearing the above simple distinction in view, no confusion can possibly arise from such a method, which, unless we presented a separate treatise upon each, appears to be unavoidable. It is to be noticed that while libel is, besides being actionable, an indictable offense,[1] slander is not criminally cognizable, the party injured being left to his civil remedy, which, as will be seen, is ample, and all that he could desire.[2]

The word defamation, when occurring in this chapter, is to be taken in its ordinary popular signification of matter tending to injure one's good name, character, or occupation[3]: and not as intending any allusion to the technical and now obsolete crime of defamation, which was an ecclesiastical offense, cognizable only in the ecclesiastical courts,[4] such as laying violent hands on a clerk, or the like.

Satire is a form of speech, which is sometimes,

ing that it was a house of ill-fame, is a libel (Jefferies v. Duncombe, 2 Camp. 3; 11 East, 226).

[1] Bailey v. Dean, 5 Barb. 297.

[2] Except in cases of high treason; and we have seen (*ante*, p. 76) that, in the United States, in time of war, individuals may be proceeded against for words spoken, which tend to weaken the authority of government. In the reign of queen Anne, words reflecting on a magistrate in the discharge of his duties, as such, were held indictable; but on account of their seditious character as against the government, rather than as an offense against the individual (Reg. v. Langley, 2 Lo. Raym. 1060; Holt L. 654).

[3] Blackstone, adopted by Webster.

[4] Abolished by statutes 18 & 19 Vict., ch. 12.

perhaps, permitted to approach the verge of libel, but which, nevertheless, is to be carefully distinguished from it: "For," as said Pope, "there is not in the world a greater error than that into which fools are apt to fall into, and knaves with good reason, to encourage; the mistaking of a satirist for a libeler."[1] And in "Joseph Andrews,"[2] Fielding says: "The distinction between the satirist and the libeler is, that the one speaks of the species, the other of the individual; the one holds the glass to thousands in their closets, that they may contemplate the deformity, and thereby endeavor to reduce it, and thus, by private mortification, avoid public shame. Thus the satirist privately corrects the fault, like a parent, while the libeler mangles the individual like an executioner;" which perhaps is sufficiently exact to be adopted as the legal distinction.

46. We have alluded, further on, to the difficulties experienced in defining the word "libel." A similar difficulty did not seem to occur in the case of slander, that wrong being defined closely by common law. It consisted in the imputation of: 1. Some temporal offense for which the party might be indicted and punished in the temporal courts. 2. An existing contagious disorder, tending to exclude the party from society. 3. An unfitness to perform an office or employment of profit, or want of integrity in an office of honor. 4. Words prejudicing a person in his lu-

[1] Pope. Anon. Satires and Epistles. Advertisement. Other forms of speech were formerly brought under the scrutiny of the law. Thus, scolding often repeated, to the disturbance of a neighborhood, was indictable (Reg. v. Foxby, 6 Mod. 145). And so profanity, calumny, and perjury, are forms of offenses by words. As to brawling, see Stephen's Ecclesiastical Statutes, p. 336; Jacob's Law Dict., tit. Cuckinstool.

[2] Vol. ii., p. 5.

crative profession, calling, or trade. 5. Any untrue words occasioning actual damage.[1] It is only with this slander when written down, and thereby constituted a libel, that the author is concerned, in preparing his labors for publication.

47. The punishment for injuries done by means of words has at different times varied in severity. Pascal "charges the Jesuits of his day with sanctioning killing for slander, particularly for slander of one in

[1] Hilliard on Torts, ch. 7, § 3. The word slander, in former times, appears to have been synonymous with accused. "But because some are wrongfully slandered (accused), king Henry I. ordained that none should be arrested or imprisoned for a slander (accusation) of mortal offense, before he was thereof indicted by the oaths of honest men before those who had authority to take such indictments" (Mirror of Justices, ch. 11, § 22). "In this same year the mysseles (lepers) thorowoute Cristendom were slaundered that they had made covenant with Sarasenes for to poison all Christen men" (Capgrave's Chronicle of England, p. 186).

In an address by the dean and chapter of Aberdeen, to Bishop Gordon, dated January 5, 1558, is the following:

"*Imprimis*, that my lord bishop cause the kirkmen within his diocie to reform themselves in all their slanderous manner of living, and to remove their open concubines, as well great as small. *Secundo*, that his lordship will be so good as to show edificative example—in special, in removing and discharging himself of the company of the gentlewoman by whom he is greatly slandered; without the which be done, diverse that are partners say they cannot accept counsel and correction of him which will not correct himself," &c., &c.—Reg. Aberd. 61.

If any slanderously charge another with any false crime (Ridley's Civil Law, 31); and in the statute (3 Edw. I., ch. 34), none are to publish false news whereby slander may grow between the king and his people (Townshend on Libel and Slander, p. 60, note).

"I would not . . . .
Have you so slander any moment's leisure
As to give words or talk with the Lord Hamlet."
(Hamlet, i. 3.)

religious orders, but they held that the killing should be secret, and not open, to create scandal."[1] And in the "Ethica Christiana,"[2] published in 1789, "*cum permissu superiorum*" we read that a Christian may, to prevent a "*contumelia gravis certo provisa* . . . . *aut calumnia*" . . . murder the "*injusti aggresoris aut calumniatoris.*" "The necessity," says Borthwick,[3] "of protecting character by law could not obtrude itself till society had begun to assume a complicated form. The earlier days were distinguished by an undiplomatic coarseness of language. Henry III. (A. D. 1248) spoke of the aldermen of London as "London boors;" applied a like epithet to the Bishop of Ely, and dismissed Bishop Aymer by telling him to "go to the devil."[4] And the action for words, given by the common law, has necessarily varied its penalties with the customs and habits of men. At the present day: upon the theory that a man's reputation has a pecuniary value to him, the penalty inflicted by the law will be—principally, in the form of a mulcting in damages; or—in the case of a libel calculated to interfere with and provoke a breach of the public peace—a fine and not immoderate imprisonment.

48. There is but a single known example in history, of a libel being deliberately chosen as a means of promoting the public interest and weal. It seems that, in the eleventh century, there existed in Denmark a species of libel called "Bersöglisvisur," or free-speaking song. We are told that when king Magnus gave dissatisfaction to his subjects, a meeting was held, at which lots were drawn to see which of those

[1] Pascal's Provincial Letters, xiii.

[2] By Father Slattler. Paragraphs 1889, 1891, 1892.

[3] On Libel, p. 1.

[4] Townshend on Libel and Slander, p. 98.

assembled should address one of these songs to the king.[1]

49. The first difficulty which confronts us in dealing with the subject of this chapter, arises at the outset, as to a definition. As is the case with most words (as Dean Trench has pointed out), the tendency of the word "libel" has been to retrograde, and—from signifying something indifferent or trifling—come to mean a thing actually bad.

The first meaning of "libellus" or "libel" is evidently "a little book." At Rome the cards of the races, with the colors of the horses, were called *libelli*;[2] it was only the *libellus famosus* that signified "a little book giving an ill name."[3]

And in an early act of parliament[4] the word seems to be used in the sense of a book or pamphlet. The act reads: "That what person so ever shall make, write, print, publish, sell, or utter any book, pamphlet, treatise, ballad, libel, or sheet of news whatsoever, or cause so to be done, except the same be licensed by both or either house of parliament," &c.; the word cannot here mean a defamatory publication, as it is not to be supposed the parliament would, in any case, license a defamatory publication. Its present use, however, is in the sense in which we shall now proceed to its definition. Perhaps there is no single word in the language, in whose interpretation so many attempts have been made, and which is so generally conceded to be impossible of exhaustive and sententious definition. As the philosopher said of another

[1] "Det Norske Folkes Historie," Christiania, 1852–5; "Den Danske Erobring of England og Normandict," Copenhagen, 1863; "North British Review," Nov., 1863.

[2] Hor. ii., iv.

[3] Ainsworth.

[4] Of September 30, 1647.

matter, "these things do not sum themselves up in single sentences."[1] The nearest approach to a sententious definition seems to be found in Wasson v. Walter,[2] where the plaintiff, a barrister, defined it as "defa-

[1] Cousin, when asked to state, in a single sentence, the spirit of German philosophy.

[2] L. R., iv. Q. B. 93. It is to be observed that no correct, no logical definition of a libel has ever been given (George on Libel, 14). A noted peculiarity of the law of libel is its vagueness and uncertainty (Encyc. Brit., *voce* Libel). It is indeed in the very nature of the subject (the law of libel) that it is extremely difficult to clear it of those popular conceits, and of that vagueness of generality, which adhere to it as a question of political discussion (Holt on Libel, preface).

It is a subject to which I have paid considerable attention; but, I must freely own, without any success whatever. I hold it to be hardly possible to define libels by which guilt may be incurred as tending to a breach of the peace, to other proceedings of a violent nature, ... and to a variety of other heads. . . . . Any definitions that I have ever seen given had one or other of two faults, ... they were either so vague as not to specify or define anything, or . . . . they were only rendered particular and definite by omitting some species of libel . . . . which ought to have been comprehended. . . . . I have never yet seen, or been able myself to hit upon, anything like a definition of libel . . . . which possessed the requisites of a definition; and I cannot help thinking that the difficulty is not accidental, but essentially inherent in the nature of the subject. . . . . The Latin of libel is not *libellus*, but *libellus famosus*. . . . . Libel then means, in its original, not "little book," but "a defamatory little book." . . . . Libel is an offense of a somewhat vague description, but sufficiently known in law, and, perhaps, as well defined as assaults and some others; and I do not believe, from all the experience I have had, that in practice any considerable difficulty is felt on account of its indistinctness (Lord Lyndhurst's Report of House of Lords on Defamation and Libel, July, 1843).

A bad word in circulation—*Vox semel emissa nunquam revertit.* Obl. 4.

A libel is a malicious publication, tending to the disrepute of an individual, the breach of the peace, the seditious violation of the good order of government (Capel Loft's Essay on Libels, edit. 1785, p. 6).

mation without legal excuse;" while Jeremy Bentham appears to have defined it, simply as "anything

A libel is any published defamation (American Encyclopedia—Libel).

It is not infamous matter or words which make a libel; for, if a man speak such words, unless they are written, he is not guilty of the making of a libel; writing is of the essence of a libel (Ld. Raym. 416). The words most nearly synonymous to the word libeling, are defaming, disparaging, aspersing, slandering (George on Libel, pp. 35, 36, 41).

A libel is a contumely or reproach, published to the defamation of the government, of a magistrate, or of a private person (Comyn's Digest).

Everything written of another, holding him up to scorn and ridicule, and calculated to provoke a breach of the peace, is a libel (Torrance v. Hurst, Walker, 403; Newbraugh v. Curry, Wright, 47; White v. Nicholls, 3 How. U. S. 266; Armentrout v. Moranda, 8 Blackf. 426; Dexter v. Spear, 4 Mason, 115).

Defamatory words, written and published (Maunder).

A libel has been usually treated of as scandal, written or expressed by symbols. Libel may be said to be a technical word, deriving its meaning rather from its use than its etymology (Russell's Crimes, edit. 1819, p. 308).

In a strict sense it is taken for a malicious defamation, expressed either in printing or writing; in a larger sense, the notion of libel may be applied to any defamation whatsoever, expressed either by signs or pictures, as by affixing up a gallows at a man's door, or by painting him in a shameful and ignominious manner (Hawkins' Pl. Cr.).

Libel, a criminous report of any man cast abroad, or otherwise unlawfully published in writing; but then, for difference sake, it is called an infamous libel—*famosus libellus* (Minshœi: A Guide into the Tongues, &c. London, 1627).

Written or printed slanders are libels (Bouvier).

Libel, a word which has many different meanings, but is chiefly known in this country as the name of a department of the law, which, from incidental circumstances, has come to include the naturally distinct heads of written slander, sedition, and outrage against religion (Encyc. Brit.—Libel).

Everything, therefore, written of another, which holds him up to scorn and ridicule, that might reasonably—that is, according to our natural passions—be considered as provoking him to a breach of the peace, is a libel (Holt, Libel, 215, 233). This agrees with his (Holt's) two preceding defini-

of which one thinks proper to complain." But these, as will be seen, are neither exhaustive nor exclusive of the subject.

tions, and with the common acceptation of the term libel, by making it essential that the subject or object of the attack should be some person or persons; but it disagrees with them, by introducing the tendency to provoke a breach of the peace. It follows that, if this be a correct definition, the other two must be defective; because, in one of them, the tendency, or, as is there said, the intent, to provoke is required only in cases where the object of the slander is a deceased person, and in that from Lord Coke it is wholly omitted. On the other hand, if the two former definitions be correct, the third must necessarily be inaccurate; for an accurate definition is one which neither omits what is essential, nor admits what is superfluous. . . . . And it is to be further observed that the third definition disagrees with the two former, and the common acceptation of the term libel, not only by introducing the intent or the tendency to provoke, but by leaving out the falsehood and malice. For libel, in common acceptation, signifies written slander; and the term slander, and all its synonyms, as defamation, detraction, calumny—even without the epithets malicious and injurious—imply falsehood and malice (Mence's Law of Libel, vol. 1, p. 120; Law Times, Rep. N. S. 604; Townshend on Slander and Libel, p. 74).

A censorious or ridiculing writing, picture, or sign, made with a mischievous and malicious intent towards government, magistrates, or individuals (*per* Hamilton, arg. People v. Crosswell, 3 Johns. C. 354; Steele v. Southwick, 9 Johns. 214; Cooper v. Greeley, 1 Den. 347).

A libel is a malicious publication in printing, writing, signs, or pictures, imputing to another something which has a tendency to injure his reputation; to disgrace or to degrade him in society, and lower him in the esteem and the opinion of the world; or to bring him into public hatred, contempt, or ridicule (State v. Jeandell, 5 Harring. [Del.] 475).

A malicious publication expressed either in printing or writing, or by signs and pictures, tending either to blacken the memory of one dead, or the reputation of one who is alive, and expose him to public hatred, contempt, or ridicule (Commonwealth v. Clapp, 4 Mass. 163, 168; *per* Ch. J. Parsons, Root v. King, 7 Cow. 613).

A libel is a censorious or ridiculing writing, picture, or

"The greater portion of all law business," says the late Dr. Lieber, in his admirable and invaluable treatise on "Civil Liberty," "arises from the impossibility of giving an absolute definition of things not absolute in themselves."[1] Without, however, attempting one that shall be exhaustive, and referring the student to the notes, where the attempts of various authorities have been quoted, we may state, generally, that a libel is any slanderous publication in writing or printing, or expressed by signs,[2] pictures, effigies, or other fixed representation to the eye, tending to asperse the repu-

sign, made with a mischievous intent (The State v. Farley, 4 M'Cord, 317).

That tends to injure one's reputation in the common estimation of mankind, to throw contumely or reflect shame and disgrace upon him, or hold him up as an object of hatred, scorn, ridicule, and contempt, although it imputes no crime liable to be punished with infamy, or to prejudice him in his employment (1 Hilliard on Torts, ch. 7, § 13).

We define slander and libel as wrongs occasioned by language or effigy; that is to say, slander is a wrong occasioned by speech, and libel is a wrong occasioned by writing or effigy (Townshend on Slander and Libel, p. 770).

[1] "Nothing," says Dean Trench, "is harder than a definition. While, on the one hand, there is, for the most part, no easier task than to detect a fault or a flaw in the definition of those who have gone before us, nothing, on the other hand, is more difficult than to propose one of our own which shall not also present a vulnerable side."

[2] A definition, in order to satisfy the requisites of a good logical definition, ought not only to be sufficiently precise, so that it should take in nothing except what was intended to be specified, but also sufficiently comprehensive to omit nothing which ought to be included. I have never yet seen, nor been able, myself, to hit upon anything like a definition of libel, or even of sedition, which possessed those requisites of a definition; and I cannot help thinking that the difficulty is not accidental, but essentially inherent in the nature of the subject-matter (Lord Lyndhurst; and see Burrill's Law Dict., *voce* Definition, and 2 Wooddes. Lect. 196).

tation of the living, or the memory of the dead,[1] that is published without lawful justification or excuse,[2] whatever the intention of the publisher may be.[3]

[1] Broom. Leg Max. The full definition of a libel includes defamation by signs (Fray v. Fray, 17 C. B. N. S. 603 [112 E. C. L. R.]; Cox v. Lee, L. R. 4, Ex. 284; Walker v. Brogden, 19 C. B. N. S. 65 [115 E. C. L. R.]).

Vid. Civil Code of the state of New York, § 29.

The intention of the writer or publisher of the defamatory matter is wholly immaterial, except so far as it may affect the amount of damages which a jury will award. "Everything printed or written," says Parke, B., "which reflects on the character of another, and is published without lawful justification or excuse, is a libel, whatever the intention may have been" (Bayliss v. Lawrence, 11 A. & El. 924).

A judge who, in an action of libel, left it to the jury to say whether the defendant intended by his publication to injure the plaintiff, was held to have wrongly directed them. "If the tendency of the publication," said Littledale, J., "was injurious to the plaintiff, then the law will presume that the defendant, by publishing it, intended to produce that injury which it was calculated to effect. If it had that tendency, there can be no doubt it was a libel." "The judge," said Lord Tenterden, Ch. J., "ought not to have left it as a question to the jury whether the defendant intended to injure the plaintiff; for every man must be presumed to intend the natural and ordinary consequences of his own act" (Haire v. Wilson, 9 B. & C. 643; Darby v. Ouseley, 1 H. & N. 9; 25 L. J. 230 Ex.; Fisher v. Clement, 10 B. & C. 472; Dubost v. Beresford, 2 Camp. N. P. C. 511).

Bacon's Abrdt., tit. Libel. "In a larger sense, the notion of a libel may be applied to any defamation whatever, as by fixing a gallows against a man's door, or by painting him in a shameful and obnoxious manner" (Pleas of the Crown, 8th ed., 542). "So where an artist, whose sitter had refused to pay for a portrait of himself, added asses' ears to the head, and exposed it to public view, it was held libel" (Mazzara's Case, N. Y. Sessions, 1817).

[2] Gathercole v. Miall, 15 M. & W. 321; Digby v. Thompson, 4 B. & Ald. 821 (24 E. C. L. R.); Bloodworth v. Gray, 8 Scott N. R. 9; Pemberton v. Calls, 10 Q. B. 461 (59 E. C. L. R.).

[3] O'Brien v. Clement, 15 M. & W. 437; O'Brien v. Bryant, 15 M. & W. 168; Darby v. Ouseley, 1 H. & N. 1.

50. Not only will the common law restrain the dissemination of such libellous matter by injunction, and allow to the party injured his action for damages sustained by reason thereof, but it may, and often does, also proceed criminally against the offender, for his offense against the state.[1]

Sampson was careful to inquire the law, before he committed himself:

"Abram.—Do you bite your thumb at us, sir?

"Sampson.—Is the law on our side if I say—ay?

"Gregory.—No.

"Sampson.—No, sir; I do not bite my thumb at you, sir, but I bite my thumb."[2]

And it is well that the writer should clearly comprehend the law and the definition of slander, before he sends his manuscript to his publisher. For libel is slander written or printed; and while the law sometimes hesitates to find premeditation and malice in the spoken word, it cannot forbear to recognize deliberation in the work printed and published and given to the world.[3]

[1] The action for slander was one of the inferior actions of which the early English courts of Piepoudre had jurisdiction (Jacobs' Law Dict., tit. Court of Piepoudres). Slander is not, like libel, an indictable offense (Bailey v. Dean, 5 Barb. 297). Nor is a single precedent of any criminal proceeding for unwritten imputations upon the characters of individuals, to be found, except in cases of high treason, ... and it must have been as constituting rather an offense against the government, than an injury to the individual, and being, therefore, seditious, that words reflecting on a magistrate in the immediate execution of his office were for the first time in the reign of Queen Anne held to be indictable (Reg. v. Langley, 2 Ld. Raym. 1060; Holt R. 654). But I am not aware that Mr. Starkie has adverted to this case, or to the doctrine which is laid down in it (1 Mence on Libel, 90).

[2] Romeo & Juliet, i. 1.

[3] It seems to have generally been—though perhaps questioned in later cases (see remarks of Mansfield, Ch. J., in

51. "There is nothing in nature," said a learned judge,[1] "but may be an instrument of mischief," and any vehicle in which thought may be expressed, if that thought be defamatory of an individual, may become a means of injury, and, therefore, libelous. Thus, words spoken, written,[2] printed, marked, or formed with pen or pencil, graver, stylus, or set up in type, or formed in or with any material or pigment, as lead,[3] chalk, ink, paint, or on any surface or substance such as parchment, paper, cloth, wood, or any metal, such as copper or steel, or on stone, or on a wall, or post, or tree, may become libelous. And so, too, may be any picture, statue, or any gesture, sound,[4] such as ringing bells, firing guns, beating drums, clapping hands, hooting,[5] or sign, which it is possible for human ingenuity to conceive of or express.[6]

The conceiving of a thought injurious to one's neighbor, the law cannot reach. The act of commu-

Thorley v. Lord Kerry, 4 Taunt. 364, and of Best, Ch. J., in Tuam v. Robinson, 5 Bing. 51; Holt's Law of Libel, p. 75; Penal Code of N. Y., § 309; Fisher v. Clement, 10 B. & C. 472)—the policy of the law to regard with much greater leniency slanderous and defamatory words spoken in the heat of passion, than slanderous and defamatory words which are written down in black and white; for the writing of such words implies deliberation and malice in the writer.

[1] Pratt, Ch. J., in Chapman v. Pickersgill; 2 Wils. 145.

[2] Sanderson v. Jackson, 2 Bos. & Pul. 238; Henshaw v. Foster, Pick. 318.

[3] Geary v. Physic, 5 B. & C. 238; Classon v. Bailey, 2 Johns. 484.

[4] Austin v. Culpepper, Skin. 123; Show. 314.

[5] Martin v. Nutkin, 2 P. Wms. 266; Soltan v. De Held, 2 Sim. N. S. 133; 16 Jur. 326; First Bap. Ch. v. Sch. R. R. Co., 5 Barb. 79; Tarleton v. McGawley, Peake's Cas. 205; Moshier v. Utica & Sch. R. R. Co., 8 Barb. 427; Cole v. Fisher, 11 Mass. 137; Loubz v. Hafner, 1 Dev. 185; Gregory v. Brunswick, 6 M. & G. 953; Trustees, &c., v. Utica, &c., 6 Barb. 313; Davidson v. Isham, 1 Stock. 186.

[6] Bouvier's Law Dict., title, Effigy.

nicating that thought, however, by any of the above means, the law can reach, and will punish.

On the trial of Algernon Sidney, the prisoner inquired, "And is writing an act?" to which Lord Jeffries replied: "Yes, it is *agere*."[1] So any representation, even if that representation be conveyed in the exercise of one's legitimate duty and calling, if its effect be to raise a presumption or create an impression injurious to another's reputation in his business or social relation, if the impression be erroneous in fact, will be defamatory and actionable. So where a banker, having sufficient funds in hand belonging to his customer, dishonors that customer's check, he is liable to an action for damages.[2] And where a notary protested a note for non-payment, without having previously presented the note to and demanded payment of the maker, he was held liable in an action for the damage thereby occasioned to the reputation of the maker.[3] Or any act otherwise legitimate or permissible under the circumstances, which happens to convey an erroneous impression as to the business or social standing of another. So where defendants, by causing plaintiff's goods to be seized on an unfounded claim for debt, occasioned his customers to think him insolvent,[4] and in trespass for breaking and entering plaintiff's dwelling, upon false charge of having stolen property concealed therein, *per quod* she was injured in her credit, it was held that the jury might give damages as aggravated by the false charge.[5]

[1] Townshend on Slander and Libel, p. 58; *Scribere est agere.* People v. Rathbun, 1 Wend. 509, 540; Robinson v. Marchant, 7 Q. B. 918; and see Marzetti v. Williams, 1 B. & A. 415.

[2] Robinson v. Merchant, 7 Q. B. 918; and see Marzetti v. Williams, 1 B. & A. 415.

[3] Townshend on Slander and Libel, p. 58.

[4] Brewer v. Day, 11 M. & W. 625.

[5] Bracegirdle v. Oxford, 2 Maule & Selw. 77. (See Jeffries

These are all acts which tend to raise scandal . . . by which one is affronted in public[1] as to his business standing. The law will also protect social standing. So where a woman, "maliciously intending to marry the plaintiff, did often affirm that she was sole and unmarried, and importuned *et strenue inquisivit* the plaintiff to marry her; to which affirmation he gave credit, and married her, when *in acto* she was wife of the defendant, so that the plaintiff was much troubled in mind, and put to great charges, and damnified in his reputation," an action against the woman and her real husband was held to lie.[2]

Words occasioning any particular loss by prefer-

v. Duncombe, 11 East, 226; Spall v. Massey, 2 Stark. Cas. 559.) Perhaps the most ingenious method by which a legitimate and ordinary transaction was ever employed to communicate a libel, is that mentioned by Hazlitt, in his "Essay on Wills" (see "London Quarterly Review," October, 1860): "A wealthy nobleman hit upon a still more culpable device for securing posthumous ignominy. He gave one lady of rank a legacy, 'by way of compensation for injury he feared he had done her fair fame'; a large sum to the daughter of another, a married woman, 'from a strong conviction that he was the father'; and so on, through half a dozen more items of the sort, each leveled at the reputation of some one from whom he had suffered a repulse—the whole being nullified (without being erased) by a codicil." A court of probate, however, would probably order the omission of such offensive matter from the record (Re Honywood, Law Rep. II., Prob. & Div. 251; Re Wartnaby, 1 Rob. Ecc. 423; Curtis v. Curtis, 3 Add. 33; Marsh v. Marsh, 1 Sw. & Tr. 528). And an attorney's bill may be so worded as to be libelous: Where defendant delivered a bill headed, "Relative to your defalcations," which phrase was repeated in several parts of the bill; in an action for libel thereby, it was claimed that the bill, having been delivered under a judge's order, was a legal proceeding, and privileged, but it was ruled otherwise, and plaintiff had a verdict (Bruton v. Downes, 1 Fost. & F. 668).

[1] Jacob's Law Dict., tit. Scandal.

[2] Beaumont v. Reeve, 8 Adol. & Ell. 483; 1 Siderfin, 375.

ment in marriage,[1] or service,[2] or by disinheritance,[3] will be especially actionable.[4] Formerly the condition in life of the person spoken of, materially affected the construction, and words concerning "great men of the realm" were actionable, which would not have been, if published concerning private persons. Such words constituted *scandalum magnatum*. In the United States no such distinction of persons exists.[5]

[1] But where the plaintiff alleged that in consequence of the words he (the plaintiff) refused to marry his betrothed, and so he lost his marriage—it was held that, under the circumstances, no special damage was shown (Carter v. Smith, Vin. abr. Act. for Words, D. a. 12; Reston v. Pomfreicht, Cro. Eliz. 639; Shepherd v. Wakeman, Sid. 79; Anon., Mar. 2, Wicks v. Shepherd, Cro. Car. 155; Nelson v. Stapz, Cro. Jac. 422; Southold v. Johnston, Cro. Car. 269; Moody v. Baker, 5 Cow. 351.

[2] Swadling v. Tarpley, app. to Townshend on Slander and Libel, 2d ed.; Knight v. Gibbs, 3 Nev. & M. 461; 1 Adol. & L. 43.

[3] See, however, a case where the plaintiff alleged that, by reason of the publication, he had incurred the ill-will of his mother-in-law, who had previously promised him £100, and it was held that no cause of action was shown (Harris v. Porter, Curt. 1).

Where plaintiff alleged that she was a single woman, and chaste, and that her mother meant to give her £150, and her brother £100, and that, by reason of the defendant's charging her with incontinence, they did not give her these sums, it was doubted if the action was maintainable (Bracebridge v. Watson, Lily. Ent. 61; and see Townshend on Slander and Libel, §§ 198–205).

[4] Or which occasion any particular damage (Introduction to the Law Relative to Trials at *Nisi Prius*. By a Learned Judge [Lord Bathurst]. Vol. I., p. 3).

[5] Townshend on Slander and Libel, § 138; Barrington on Penal Statutes; 3 Reeve's Hist. of the Common Law. (See note to § 182). *Secundem gradum dignitatis*, &c., was the rule of the Roman law, and is the rule in Scotland and France (Borthwick on Libel, 176, 177 n., Inst. Lib. IV., tit. 4; Code Criminel, tit. 111, art. 1; Black. Com., bk. iii. ch. 7, § 5; Selwy's N. P. 1155.

No man has a prerogative right to the protection[1] of his standing, but all must show damage thereto alike.

52. It is the tendency of a law, however simple in its spirit and nature, and however easily recognized its principles and rules, to become, through long and constant interpretation, complex and unwieldy. In no case is this more thoroughly exemplified than in the law of slander and libel, or as it might be very properly styled, "the law of words." Starting with the simple rule, which we shall have occasion many times to reiterate in this chapter, that a man's reputation for a general fitness to move in the society to which his birth, or fortune, or manners, or education may entitle him, or for skill, reliability, knowledge, or proficiency in his profession (if a professional man), or for capital and resources in his business (if, for instance, a banker or merchant), or for chastity, sobriety, and good moral character (if a clergyman),[2] or for experience in any of these walks of life, is his property as much as his estates, or his family, or his chattels: that law has become in time so embarrassed and overburdened, with interpretation and illustration, as to be cumbersome, awkward, and troublesome almost beyond expression.

53. From the necessities of its nature and existence, the law lets no reported case perish from its memory, but keeps each one as a precedent; meanwhile, the world moves. New civilizations engraft themselves upon the old. New standards of conduct and intercourse arise. Religion, politics, social and municipal regulations, the mutations of art and

[1] See Townshend on Slander and Libel, §§ 391–417.

[2] But see Gallevey v. Marshall, 9 Ex. 294; Breeze v. Sarls, 23 Up. Can. Q. B. 94, which appear to hold that continence and chastity may not be a *sine qua non* to the standing of a minister of the gospel.

traffic, all combine to render what was proper, improper; and what was lawful, infamous. With all this change the law advances. While she clings to what she has said, she never fetters herself by her own utterances to do wrong or injustice,[1] and so if we were to attempt to draw the law of libel from the books of cases, we should, after an almost interminable and laborious investigation, be forced to the conclusion that every case was "a law unto itself." This confusion will be found to arise from three great causes: first, from the delicate nature of the thing to be protected; secondly, from the mutations of society and the dilemma of courts, who, clinging to the maxim of *stare decisis*,—let the decision stand,—and striving ing, as they are bound to do, rather to reconcile than to overrule, find themselves, while obliged to recognize the precedent, obliged, as well, to do justice between man and man; and thirdly, from the wonderfully rapid changes in the meaning of words and phrases, which imposes upon courts the necessity of being not only expounders of the law, of society, of religion, of trade, of domestic relations, and of all human contracts, but actually of grammar, rhetoric, philology, and of the exact significances of dialect, patois, argots, and vernacular speech. It is not impossible to imagine, that from these complications may have arisen the difficulties experienced in defining the term "libel," to which allusion has been made.

Reputation is only a bubble at best, and often the

[1] To accommodate the law to the altered state of society is laid down as one of the obligations of judges (Dwarris on Statutes, 792; Raun's Legal Judgment, 22). The rule *stare decisis* is one of the most sacred of the law (Per Buller, J., 1 East, 495; Ram's Legal Judgment, 234). But while it is dangerous to depart from it, the rule will generally be that given in the text. Id. 197, 202, 231, 234, 235, 413, 423.

over-sensitive party who fancies himself libeled, is put in the position of him—as the old maxim hath it—"*qui excusat*, and—at the same time—*accusat*," for, as Iago says in the play, "You have lost no reputation at all, unless you repute yourself such a loser."[1]

54. This *jus et norma loquendi* of which courts will take judicial cognizance, impose upon it a finer discrimination than may, perhaps, be looked for in so ponderous a digest as the law of libel. It was held in some of the older cases that "adjective words," or "words spoken adjectively," would not be actionable, but Lord Coke expressed himself as of the opinion that "sometimes adjectives will maintain an action;"[2] (the distinction possibly being that words imputing mere inclination or intention are not actionable, but only those imputing an act.[3]) So, again: a distinction was made between the conjunctions "and" and "for": thus, to say "thou art a thief, for thou hast stolen" (such a thing, as a tree, which could not be felony), and the saying, "thou art a thief, and hast stolen" such a thing—in the former case, the subsequent words show the reason of calling the plaintiff a thief, and that no felonious imputation was meant; but in the latter, the action lies for calling him a thief; and the addition, "thou hast stolen," is another distinct sentence by itself, and not the reason of the former speech, nor any diminution thereof.

[1] Othello, ii. 3.

[2] 4 Coke, 19. And see Killick v. Barnes, 2 Bullst. 138; Ld. Raym. 236; Gulford's Case, 2 Rolle R. 71; Ward v. Thorne, Cro. Eliz. 171; Booth v. Leach, Lev. 90; Selby v. Carryer, 2 Bullst. 260; Vin. Abr. Act for Words, 1 a. 4.

[3] Townshend on Slander & Libel, § 165; 3 Id. § 186; Cro. Jac. 114; Bull. N. P. 5; Hob. 77, 106; Cro. Eliz. 857; Browl. 2; Godb. 241; Hard. 7; All. 31; Sty. 66; 1 Starkie on Slander, 99. This distinction was questioned by Holt, Ch. J.,

In one case[1] it is said that to call a man "cuckold" is not an ecclesiastical slander, but to call him "wittol" is, for "wittol" imports his knowledge and consent; but as it readily appears, these decisions are more curious than valuable at the present day.

55. The profession of the law, then, more than any other possible profession, necessitates a wide and vastly liberal education; and while the physician studies chemistry and medicine, the engineer mechanics, and the writer philology; the lawyer, who does not study all of these, if not in bulk at the outset, at least more or less in the course of his experience at the bar, will be a practitioner of very little value to his clients.

One who will examine thoroughly the law of libel, as laid down in the books, cannot fail to be impressed with the vast and incredible number of words and phrases which, in the course of six hundred years, courts have been called upon to interpret, either by taking judicial cognizance of their meaning, and pronouncing them to be "English": or by summoning testimony and hearing argument, thereupon fixing their meaning definitely and beyond dispute.

The utter inadequacy, therefore, of a single chapter to satisfactorily treat of "the law of words," will be readily appreciated. A library would be adequate to the task: nor is such a task necessary to our purpose. One who would sit down, patiently, to com-

Baker v. Pierce, 6 Mod, 23, where it is said *and* and *for* have the same meaning. And see Lewis v. Acton, Yelv. 34; Vin. Abr. Act for Words, P. a. 2.

[1] Smith v. Wood, 2 Salk. 692. A cuckold was a man whose wife was false to his bed (Swift). A wittol was a man who knew of his wife's infidelity, and submitted to it—a tame cuckold (Shakespeare). "Wittol-cuckold. The devil himself hath not such a name" (Merry Wives of Windsor, ii. 2).

pile a dictionary, drawn from the reports since the Year Books, of words passed upon by courts, would find, at the close of his labors, that his unabridged folios were, after all, more curious than valuable; teeming, indeed, with whimsicalities, but of very little practical value. What will be attempted in this chapter is, therefore, to proceed, by means of comment and illustration, to spread before the writer who would produce a work that shall be entitled to a copyright at the hands of the law—and to the protection of the law for that copyright after it shall have been secured—the general body of the law, regulating the doing of injury by the use of words.

56. The law, then, regards a man's reputation as a sort of capital to be employed by him in earning his living, and as a resource for enjoying the social intercourse of his peers. In the enjoyment of his good name, therefore, the law will protect him. "Men's reputations," said Lord Bacon, "are tender things, and ought to be like Christ's coat, without seam,[1] . . . who can see worse days than he that, yet living, doth follow the funeral of his reputation?" But, in order to protect this reputation (the law, being as we have seen, a practical science, recognizing nothing which it cannot guard and protect[2]), it is necessary that what some have called "a fiction"[3] should be raised: namely,

[1] Charge against Lumsden.

[2] *Ante*, p. 15.

[3] Townshend on Slander and Libel, p. 105. "I am not certain," says Lord Kames, "that in England any verbal injury is actionable, except such as may be attended with pecuniary loss or damage. If not, we in Scotland are more delicate. Scandal, or any imputation upon a man's good name, may be sued before the commissaries, even when the scandal is of such a nature that it cannot be the occasion of any pecuniary loss. It is sufficient to say, I am hurt in my character" (Historical Law Tracts, p. 225).

that the value of a man's reputation can be estimated in dollars and cents. Pecuniary damages, therefore, becomes the gist of the civil action for libel and slander.

The Roman law made personal contumely and insult the essence of the offense of slander: thus a most essential and characteristic distinction between the law of England and that of Rome, and of those countries which have adopted the civil law, arises: . . . "For the law of England has from very distant times considered the temporal injury to a man's estate, and not the contumely or insult of the agent as the ground of compelling reparation in damages."[1] "There must be some certain or probable temporal loss or damage, to make words actionable."[2] "The principle on which this species of action (action for saying orally plaintiff, an innkeeper, was a bankrupt) is, that the slander has the effect of producing temporal damage to the party complaining." To maintain the action there must be injury to the plaintiff.[3]

"Reputation or fame is under the protection of the law, because all persons have an interest in their good name, and scandal and defamation are injurious to it, though defamatory words are not actionable otherwise than as they are a damage to the estate of the person injured."[4] Reputation is property.[5]

57. It was laid down in Onslow v. Horne,[6] "that words are actionable when spoken of one in an office

[1] Starkie on Slander, Am. ed., vii.

[2] Onslow v. Horne, 3 Wils. 177; Holt v. Scholefield, 6 T R. 691.

[3] Whittaker v. Bradley, 7 D. & R. 649.

[4] Maitland v. Goldney, 2 East, 426; Lowe v. Harwood, Cro Car. 140 S. C.; Palmer, 520; Ley, 82.

[5] Townshend on Slander and Libel, 104; 2 Wood's Inst. 927; Foulger v. Newcomb, 2 L. R. Ex. 330.

[6] Dixon v. Holden, 7 L. R. Eq. 492.

of profit, which may probably occasion the loss of his office, or when spoken of persons touching their respective professions, trades, and business, and do or may probably tend to their damage;" or, again:[1] "if the words may be of probable ill consequence to a person in a trade, a profession, or an office."

The rule, as thus expressed, is, according to Bayley, B., objectionable, the words "probably" and "probable" being too indefinite and loose, and—unless considered as equivalent to "having a natural tendency to," and confined within the limits of showing the want of some necessary qualification, or some misconduct in the office—not warranted by the authorities. "Every authority," he says, "which I have been able to find, either shows the want of some general requisite, as honesty, capacity, fidelity, &c., or connects the imputation with the plaintiff's office, trade, or business."[2]

The law is the same in the case of imputations made against a member of any of the professions, having a tendency to injure him in respect thereof, whether the imputation be want of integrity or want of ability, unless, indeed, it be held that want of integrity cannot injure him in his business, or profession.[3] And, as with one holding an office, so with one practicing or exercising any lawful profession, occupation, trade, or business, however humble.[4] It was once held

[1] W. Black. 753.

[2] Lumby v. Allday, 1 Cr. & Jer. 305.

[3] Pecuniary damage is the gist of the actions of libel or of slander (Townshend on Libel and Slander, ch. iv.—"Gist of the action").

[4] Bellamy v. Burch, 16 M. & W. 590; Sellars v. Killew, 7 Dowl. & R. 121; 4 B. & C. 55; Morris v. Langdale, 2 Bos. & Pul. 284; Whitaker v. Bradley, 7 D. & R. 649; S. C., Whittington v. Gladwin, 5 B. & C. 180; 2 Car. & P. 146; Gates v. Bowker, 8 Vt. (3 Wash.) 23; Ostrom v. Calkins, 5 Wend. 264; Carpenter v. Dennis, 3 Sandf. 305; Jones v. Joice, Vin. Abr.

that "a tinker or a peddler was a rogue by statute,"[1] but the rule has disappeared, and every man has a right to earn his bread by honest labor.[2] So it is actionable to accuse an auctioneer of dishonesty,[3] or a merchant with swindling,[4] or to insinuate that he is[5] or was[6] a bankrupt, or that he is "in trouble" in such a way as to effect his commercial standing;[7] or that his cheques were dishonored,[8] or that a banker has suspended.[9]

And an action will lie for saying of a schoolmaster, "He has no knowledge in grammar or in the Latin tongue, nor knows how to educate his scholars in the Latin tongue" (with an allegation of loss of scholars[10]), or "put not your son to him, for he will come away as very a dunce[11] as he went;" or, of a shoemaker, that

Act. for Words, U. a 7; Southam v. Allen, Raym. 231; Alexander v. Angle, 1 Cr. & J. 143; 1 Starkie on Slander, 128; Cooke on Defam. 21; Terry v. Hooper, Lev. 115; Rex v. Ld. Cochrane, 3 Maule & S. 10; Sinclair v. Charles Phillipe, 2 B. & P. 363; Morris v. Langdale, 2 Bos. & Pul. 284.

[1] Cockaine v. Hopkins, 2 Lev. 214.

[2] Thomas v. Jackson, 3 Bing. 104; 10 Moore, 425; Odiorne v. Bacon, 6 Cush. 185; Gay v. Horner, 13 Pick. 535; Ludwell v. Hole, 2 Ld. Raym. 1417; Davis v. Miller, 2 Strange, 1169; Obaugh v. Finn, 4 Pike, 110; Boydell v. Jones, 4 M. & W. 446; 7 Dowl. (P. C.) 210; Baboneau v. Farrell, 15 C. B. 360; Bryant v. Loxton, 11 Moore, 344; Davis v. Davis, 1 Nott & McCord, 290; Chipman v. Cook, 2 Tyler, 456; Rush v. Cavenaugh, 2 Barr. 187; Brown v. Mims, 2 Rep. Con. Ct. 235; Foot v. Brown, 8 Johns. 64; Riggs v. Deniston, 3 Johns. Cas. 198; Sempsey v. Levy, 2 Jur. 776; Fowles v. Bowen, 30 N. Y. 24; Greenfield's Case, Mar. 82; 1 Vin. Abr. 465, pl. 19.

[3] Ramsdale v. Greenacre, 1 F. & F. 61; Bryant v. Loxton, 11 Moore, 344.

[4] Herr v. Bamburg, 10 How. Pr. 128.

[5] Stanley v. Obarton, Cro. Eliz. 268.

[6] Hull v. Smith, 1 M. & S. 287.

[7] Sewall v. Catlin, 3 Wend. 291.

[8] Rollin v. Steward, 14 C. B. 595.

[9] Semble, in Foster v. Lawson, 3 Bing. 452

[10] London v. Eastgate, 2 Roll. R. 72.

[11] Hetley, 71.

he is a "cobbler;"[1] or of a watchmaker that he "does not know how to make a good watch;"[2] and so it was held actionable to say of a bishop that he is bankrupt[3] or a wicked man,[4] or to charge a clergyman with having come into his pulpit in a towering passion;[5] or with having, by personal invectives from the pulpit against a young lady of spotless reputation, caused a misunderstanding in his congregation;[6] that he preaches lies in the pulpit;[7] he made a seditious sermon,[8] he hath two wives,[9] he is a drunkard,[10] or incontinent,[11] or guilty of incest,[12] or he has a bastard,[13] or he is a perjured priest,[14] or that he has desecrated his church;[15] but in all cases there must appear to be some special damage; the law will not give a remedy for mere sensitive or outraged feeling.[16]

[1] 1 Mod 19; Vin. Abr. Act for Words (Va.), 16.

[2] Redman v. Pyne, 1 Mod. 19.

[3] Holt on Libel, 233, note. This appears to be an exception to the general principle, for that a bishop were bankrupt would not injure him in his calling, as if he were a banker; but the word "bankrupt" appears always to have been a word of reproach; Hull v. Smith, 1 M. & S. 287.

"Bas.—Why dost thou whet thy knife so earnestly?
"Shy.—To cut the forfeiture from that bankrupt there."
(Merchant of Venice, iv. 1.)

[4] Holt on Libel. Id.

[5] Walker v. Brogden, 19 C. B. N. 3, 65.

[6] Edwards v. Bell, 8 Moore, 467.

[7] Drake v. Drake, Sty. 363; Crandel v. Walden, 3 Lev. 17.

[8] Phillips v. Badley, 4 Rep. 19 (*a*).

[9] Nicholson v. Lynes, Cro. Eliz. 94.

[10] McMillan v. Birch, 1 Binn, 178; Chaddock v. Briggs, 13 Mass. 248.

[11] Demarest v. Haring, 6 Cow. (N. Y.) 76; but see Gallewey v. Marshall, 9 Ex. 294.

[12] Staers v. Gardner, 6 Up. Can. Q. B. R. O. S. 512.

[13] Payne v. Beaumorris, Lev. 248.

[14] Hogg. v. Vaughan, Sty. 6.

[15] Kelly v. Sherlock, L. R. 1, Q. B. 686.

[16] Terwilliger v. Wands, 17 N. Y. 54; Wilson v. Goit, 17

58. There was an old maxim, born of the star chamber, and of the days when men were punished for libels contained in sealed letters, that "the greater the truth the greater the libel." That maxim, as it has been said, "disappeared very reluctantly from the statute books."[1] Prior to the statute of Anne in 1706, there is no record of a plea of truth in an action for slander or libel,[2] though, until 1835, the truth was admitted in mitigation under the general issue of not guilty.[3] But it is now generally conceded that in civil actions the truth of the alleged libel is a defense.[4]

N. Y. 442; Alsop v. Alsop, 5 Hurl. & Nor. 534; Bedell v. Powell, 13 Barb. 183. These decisions overrule Brandt v. Towsley, 13 Wend. 253; Fuller v. Fenner, 16 Barb. 333; Olmstead v. Brown, 12 Barb. 657; Underhill v. Welton, 32 Verm. (3 Shaw) 40.

[1] "I am quite clear that the truth ought not to be made decisive (as a defense) either in civil or criminal proceedings; for cases may be put where the truth, instead of being a justi fication, would not even be any mitigation; nay, where it would be an aggravation (Lord Brougham, Evidence, Rep. of House of Lords on Libel, &c., July, 1843); and in the same report see the opinions of other lawyers and judges to the same effect; and see 2 Kent's Com. 25; Borthwick on Libel 252; 29 Parl. Hist. 575; Preliminary Discourse to Starkie on Slander, xliv.

[2] Townshend on Slander and Libel, § 211.

[3] Ib.

[4] Townshend on Slander and Libel, § 73; 1 Starkie on Libel, 9; Maitland v. Goldney, 2 East, 426; Perry v. Mann, 1 Rhode Island, 263; Root v. King, 7 Cow. 613, and 4 Wend. 113; 1 Stark. on Sland. 229; Lake v. Hutton, Hob. 253; I'Anson v. Stuart, 1 T. R. 748; Underwood v. Parkes, Str. 1200; Manning v. Clement, 7 Bing. 367; 2 Greenl. Ev. § 424; Andrews v. Van Deuser, 11 Johns. 38; Van Ankin v. Westfall, 14 Johns. 233; Shephard v. Merrill, 13 Johns. 475; Snyder v. Andrews, 6 Barb. 23; Wagner v. Holbrunner, 7 Gill, 296; Smith v. Smith, 8 Ired. 29; Kelly v. Dillon, 5 Porter [Ind.], 426; Else v. Evans, Anthon N. P. 23; Burns v. Webb, 1 Tyler, 17; Samuel v. Bond, Litt. Sel. Cas. 158; Treat v. Browning, 4 Conn. 408; Bisbey v. Shaw, 12 N. Y. 67; Sheahan v. Collins,

The truth of an alleged libel is a complete defense to an action therefor,[1] "not," said Littleton, "because it negatives the charged malice, for a person may wrongfully or maliciously utter slanderous matter, though true (and thereby subject himself to an indictment), but because it shows that the plaintiff is not entitled to recover damages; for the law will not permit a man to recover damages in respect of an injury to a character which he either does not or ought not to possess.[2]

If the libel be false, however, it will be no justification that the writer believed *bona fide* in its truth, though the fact may be taken in mitigation of damages.[3]

59. The question of variance is one which properly arises in considering the pleadings in an action for libel, or the proof upon the trial. The purposes of this chapter are to consider the means of avoiding, rather than of conducting a lawsuit upon the subject; but its scope might well include a few illustrations of what will and what will not justify certain spoken and written statements.

In the case of Spencer v. Southwick,[4] the declaration charged that, by hypocritical cant, etc., plaintiff

20 Ill. 325; Haws v. Stanford, 4 Sneed, 520; Arrington v. Jones. 9 Port. 139; Douge v. Pearce, 13 Ala. 127; Kay v. Fredrigal, 3 Barr, 221; Thompson v. Bowers, 1 Doug. 321; Taylor v. Robinson, 29 Maine [16 Shep.], 323; Teagle v. Deboy, 8 Blackf. 134; Wagstaff v. Ashton, 1 Harring. 503; Bodwell v. Swan, 3 Pick. 376; Alderman v. French, 1 Pick. 1; Updegrove v. Zimmerman, 13 Penn. 619; Scott v. McKinnish, 15 Ala. 662; Eagan v. Gantt, 1 McMullan, 468; Rumsey v. Webb, 1 Car. & M. 104; Sidgreaves v. Myatt, 22 Ala. 617).

[1] Bl. Com. 342 *vid.* Borthwick 190–195.

[2] McPherson v. Daniel, 10 B. & C. 272, *vid.* Anon, 11 Mod. 99; Cockayne v. Hodgkisson, 5 C. & P. 548; Weaver v. Lloyd, 2 B. & C. 678; Tighe v. Cooker, 7 El. & B. 639; Beggs v. Great Eastern Ry. Co. 18 L. T. N. S. 482.

[3] Campbell v. Spottiswoode, 8 B. & S. 769, 8 L. T. N. S. 201; 32 L. J. 185; Reade v. Sweetzer, 6 Abb. (Pr.) N. S. p. 9 (note)

[4] 11 Johns. 573, reversing 10 Johns. 259.

and his associates effected the incorporation of the Manhattan Bank, in the city of New York, in which plaintiff was interested to the extent of several thousand dollars; that plaintiff, as a member of the senate, advocated the bill entitled "an act for supplying the city of New York with pure and wholesome water," knowing that it contained a clause authorizing the company to carry on banking business, and that the other members of the legislature were ignorant of that fact, &c. It was held in justification that the plaintiff was a senator on 2nd April, 1798; that such a law was passed: that—at the time of passing said law (1st April, 1798)—plaintiff, as senator, advocated the bill, knowing at the time that it contained such clause, &c.; and that a large majority of the members of the legislature were ignorant of that fact, &c.; and that, at the time and place first above mentioned, plaintiff held, and was owner of a large portion of the stock created by the said law, to wit, five thousand dollars.

A charge of stealing a pot and waiter, is not justified by proof of stealing a waistcoat pattern.[1] Nor of stealing a dollar from A., by proof of stealing a dollar from B.[2] Proof of a forgery amounting to $80 is not a justification of a charge of forgery to the amount of $250.[3] Nor is a charge that the plaintiff carried on smuggling as a business, justified by proof of a single act of smuggling;[4] nor of smuggling during the war by showing a smuggling before the war.[5] A charge that plaintiff, a counsellor-at-law, had

[1] Eastland v. Caldwell, 2 Bibb. 21.
[2] Self v. Gardner, 15 Miss 480.
[3] Stiles v. Comstock, 9 How. Pr. 44.
[4] Andrews v. Van Deuzer, 11 Johns. 38.
[5] Id.

offered himself as a witness to divulge secrets of his client, is not justified by the fact that, in a private conversation out of court, the plaintiff disclosed a secret of his client, nor by the fact that plaintiff offered himself as a witness to divulge matters not privileged, communicated to him by his client;[1] or that an attorney had been struck from the rolls, by showing that he was suspended for two years.[2] A charge that a minister of the gospel has asserted that the blood of Christ had no more to do with our salvation than the blood of a hog, is not justified by the fact that plaintiff had denied the divinity of Christ and the doctrine of the atonement; and asserted that Christ was a creature, a perfect man, but that there was no more virtue in his blood than that of any creature.[3] A charge that a diplomatic minister had traitorously betrayed the secrets of his own government, is not justified by the fact that the plaintiff disclosed the instructions given to him as such minister, although coupled with the fact that he was censured by his government for making such disclosures.[4] The charge must be accurate in all its details; thus, where the libel charged that the plaintiff had been tried for murder in a duel, and that "he spent nearly the whole of the night preceding the duel in practicing pistol firing," held, that, to justify, it must be shown not only that the plaintiff had been tried for murder, but that he spent nearly the whole of the night preceding the duel in practicing pistol firing.[5] And a charge of stealing "hogs" is not justified by proof that plaintiff stole one "hog."[6]

[1] Riggs v. Denniston, 3 John. Cas. 198.
[2] Blake v. Stevens, 4 Fost & F. 432.
[3] Skinner v. Grant, 12 Vt. 456.
[4] Ginet v. Mitchell, 7 Johns. 120.
[5] Clarkson v. Lawson, 6 Bing. 206, 587.
[6] Swan v. Rary, 3 Blackf. 298. And see generally as to

"I recollect," said Crompton, J.,[1] "being satisfied, early in my professional life, that I could justify calling a man a 'rugged Russian bear,' by showing that his manners were rough." But when the charge is that a plaintiff "bolted" it is not a justification to show that he "quitted,"[2] and the charge must be directly met and not argumentatively or by inference.[3]

what will or will not justify an injurious statement. Fidler v. Delavan, 20 Wend. 57; Riggs v. Denniston, 3 Johns. Cas. 198; McNally v. Oldham, 16 Ir. Com. Law, 298; 8 Law Times, N. S. 604; Sanford v. Gaddis, 13 Ill. 329; Clarke v. Taylor, 4 Bing. N. C. 654; Wilson v. Nations, 5 Yerg. 211; Morrison v. Harmer, 3 Bing. N. C. 758; 5 S. C. 410; Edwards v. Bell, 1 Bing. 403; Moore v. Terrell, 1 N. & M. 559; Cooper v. Lawson, 1 Per. & D. 15; Clark v. Taylor, 2 Bing. N. C. 654; Morrison v. Harmer, 3 Bing. N. C. 759; 5 Scott, 410; Barrows v. Carpenter, 1 Cliff, 204; Cook v. Tribune Asso. 5 Bl. C. C. 352.

[1] Tighe v. Cooper, 21 Jur. 716; 7 Ell. & Bl. 619.

[2] O'Brien v. Bryant, 16 M. & W. 168; 4 D. & L. 341; 16 Law Jour. Rep. 77, Ex. And see Wachter v. Quenzer, 29 N. Y. 547; Ede v. Scott, 7 Ir. L. R. N. S. 607; Watkin v. Hall, Law Rep. III. Q. B. 396.

[3] Fidler v. Delavan, 20 Wend. 57; Mountney v. Watton, 2 B. & Ad. 673; Weaver v. Lloyd, 2 B. & C. 678; 4 D. & R. 230; Bissell v. Cornell, 24 Wend. 354; Stillwell v. Barter, 19 Wend. 478; Torrey v. Field, 10 Vt. 353; Crump v. Adney, 1 Cr. & M. 362; Burford v. Wible, 32 Penn. 95; Wilson v. Beighler, 4 Iowa, 427; Van Derveer v. Sutphin, 5 Ohio N. S. 293; Morrow v. McGaver, 1 Ir. C. L. 569; Powers v. Skinner, 1 Wend. 451; Cooper v. Barber, 24 Wend. 105; McKinly v. Rob. 20 Johns. 351; Skinner v. Grant, 12 Vt. 466; Gregory v. Atkins, 42 Id. 237; Ormsby v. Douglass, 2 Abb. Pr. 407; 37 N. Y. 377. Fero v. Ruscoe, 4 N. Y. 165; Wakley v. Cooke, 4 Exch. 511; Odiorne v. Bacon, 6 Cush. 185; Holton v. Muzzy, 30 Vt. 365; Ricke v. Stanley, 6 Blackf. 169; Sharp v. Stephenson, 12 Ired. 348; Walters v. Smoot, 11 Ired. 315; Pallet u. Sargent, 36 N. H. 496; Randall v. Holsenbake, 3 Hill, So. Car. 175; Ridley v. Perry, 4 Shepl. 21; Smithies v. Harrison, 1 Ld. Raym. 727; Talmadge v. Baker, 22 Wis. 624; Stow v. Converse, 4 Conn. 17; Torrey v. Field, 10 Vt. 353; Andrews v. Van Deuzer, 11 Johns. 38; Smith v. Buckecker, 4 Rawle, 295.

60. And if the libelous words impute a felony, it will be no justification of the libel to prove facts sufficient to raise a suspicion merely.[1]

61. If any material part of the defamatory matter fails to be proved, the publication is a libel.[2]

[1] Where the declaration stated that the defendant, intending to cause it to be believed that the plaintiff was guilty of feloniously stealing a horse, published a libel concerning him, which was headed "Horse-stealer," and alleged that the plaintiff had been taken up, on suspicion of having stolen a horse, by a constable who was informed that "such a character" was at a certain public-house; the libel then going on to state the circumstances of suspicion against the plaintiff, and alleging finally that having obtained permission to go out of the constable's sight, he had made his escape, but was retaken and confined in jail for examination; innuendo that the plaintiff was guily of stealing a horse: it was held that a plea setting out the several circumstances related in the libel, and justifying all the parts of it, except the words "Horse-stealer," was not a sufficient justification of the libel—Mountney v. Walton, 2 B. & Ad. 673. *Vid.* also Chalmers v. Shackell, 6 C. & P. 475.

Compare, however, a case where the alleged libel, contained in a letter addressed to a person who employed the plaintiff as cashier, was, "I conceive there is nothing too base for him to be guilty of;" a plea alleging that the plaintiff signed and delivered to the defendant an I. O. U., and afterwards, on having sight thereof, falsely and fraudulently asserted that the signature was not his, and averring that the alleged libel was written and published solely in reference to this transaction, was held to be a sufficient justification. Tighe v. Cooper, 7 E. & B. 639, 26 L. J. 215 Q. B.

[2] Thus, if a libel imputes to a person that he has been guilty of murder in killing his opponent in a duel, and alleges further that the duel was supposed to have been fought under circumstances revolting to the ordinary notions of honor (it being suggested that the plaintiff had spent the whole of the night preceding the duel in practicing pistol firing), it is not a sufficient defense to prove merely that the plaintiff had killed his antagonist, and had been tried for murder and acquitted. "When an action is brought for a libel," said Maule, J., in this case, "to make a good plea to the whole charge, the defendant must justify everything that the libel contains which

62. Nor is it a justification of a libel that it is only a repetition of one already and previously published.

In the Earl of Northampton case, in the star chamber,[1] A. D. 1613, it was laid down that it would be a defense to an action for words, to show that the defendant repeated them, and that they were not original with him. The rule was allowed to stand in this condition until in 1769. Lord Kenyon, in a case before him,[2] added the qualification that, to justify the publication, the defendant must, at the time thereof, have mentioned the name of the previous publisher, and that it would not be sufficient to mention it for the first time in his plea. In 1805, this was further qualified[3] by asserting that, if the prior publisher had retracted the slander to the knowledge of the defendant, the latter would not be excused by mentioning his authority.

In this country, in certain States, the mention of the authority was never considered a defense, but only

is injurious to the plaintiff. If the libel charges the commission of several crimes, or the commission of a crime in a particular manner, the plea must justify the charge as to the number of crimes, or the manner of committing the crime. If the crime is charged with circumstances of aggravation as here, the plea is clearly bad if it omit to justify that. . . . If the libel had imputed murder *simpliciter*, it would have been enough to show in the plea that the plaintiff had committed murder. But if the libel goes further, and states something besides, which is injurious to the plaintiff's character, it is clear upon every principle of the law of libel, that that must be justified as well as the rest, or the defense fails." Helsham v. Blackwood, 11 C. B. 128, 20 L. J. 187 C. P. *Vide* also Clarkson v. Lawson, 6 Bing. 266; Clark v. Taylor, 2 Bing. N. C. 654; 3 Scott, 95.

[1] 2 Rep. 132; Moore, 821. See Crawford v. Middleton, 1 Lev. 82.

[2] Davis v. Lewis, 7 T. R. 17.

[3] In Woodnoth v. Meadows, 5 East, 463.

as going in mitigation[1] or as rebutting an inference of malice;[2] while in others it has been held to be a justification.[3]

But giving the name of an authority appears never to have been considered a justification of a libel,[4] even though the first publisher were the plaintiff himself.[5]

[1] As in Connecticut, Leister v. Smith, 2 Root, 24. But see Austin v. Hanchett, Id. 148; Treat v. Browning, 4 Conn. 408. In Pennsylvania, Kennedy v. Gregory, 1 Ben. 90, (n). New Jersey, Cook v. Barkley, 1 Penn. N. J. R. 169. Mississippi, Jarnigan v. Fleming, 43 Mis. 711.

[2] Benns v. McCorcle, 2 P. A. Brown, 79; Hirsh v. Ringwalt, 3 Yeates, 508.

[3] Abrams v. Smith, 8 Blackf. 95; Haynes v. Leland, 29 Me. 233; Jones v. Chapman, 5 Blackf. 88; Crane v. Douglass, 2 Id. 85. See generally, Mapes v. Weeks, 4 Wend. 659; Austin v. Hanchett, 2 Root, 148; Skinner v. Grant, 12 Vt. 456; Scott v. Peebles, 2 Sme. & M. 546; Gilman v. Lowell, 1 Amer. Mead. Cas. 202, n.; 2 Greenl. Ev. § 424, n.; Cummerford v. McAvoy, 15 Ill. 311; Johnston v. Lance, 7 Iredell, 448; Kelly v. Dillon, 5 Ind. (Porter), 426; Trabue v. Mayo, 3 Dana, 138; Robinson v. Harvey, 5 Monr. 519; Parker v. McQueen, 8 B. Monr. 16. Miller v. Kerr, 2 McCord, 285; Church v. Bridgeman, 6 Miss. 190. And see Easterwood v. Quin, 2 Brevard, 64; Smith v. Stewart, 5 Barr. 372; Sexton v. Todd, Wright (Ohio), 317; Haine v. Welling, 7 Ham. 253; Farr v. Roscoe, 9 Mich. 353; Brooks v. Bryan, Wright, 760.

[4] Runkle v. Meyers, 3 Yeates, 518; Dole v. Lyon, 10 Johns. 447; Larkins v. Tarter, 3 Sneed, 681; Miles v. Spencer, 1 Holt, N. P. 533; Lewis v. Walter, 4 B. & Ald. 605; Chevalier v. Brush, Anthon's Law Student, 186; Mapes v. Weeks, 4 Wend. 659; Inman v. Foster, 8 Id. 602; Hotchkiss v. Oliphant, 2 Hill, 510. And see Johnston v. Laud, 7 Iredell, 448; Dole v. Lyon, 10 Johns. 447; Clarkson v. McCarty, 5 Blackf. 574; Moberly v. Preston, 8 Mis. 462; Romayne v. Duane, 3 Wash. C. C. 246; State v. Butman, 15 La. An. 166; McGregor v. Thwaites, 3 B. & C. 24; 4 D. & R. 695; De Crespigny v. Wellesly, 5 Bing. 392; Bennett v. Bennett, 6 C. & P. 588; Fidman v. Linslie, 10 Exch. 63; Saus v. Joerris, 14 Wis. 663; Cook v. Ward, 6 Bing. 409; Abshire v. Cline, 3 Ind. 115.

[5] Abshire v. Cline, 3 Ind. 115; Cook v. Ward, 6 Bing. 409.

63. A defamatory publication, true in part and false in part, will be held libelous as to the part which is false.[1]

So where the libel alleged that the plaintiff, a proctor, had been suspended from practice three times for extortion, a plea in justification which alleged only one suspension, was held bad. It was urged on behalf of the defendant in this case, that it was sufficient if the sting and substance of the libel were answered by the plea, and that the discredit attaching to a single suspension from office, was not substantially aggravated by a repetion of similar reproof; but the court did not agree that a man's character would not fall into lower discredit by the imputation of repeated offenses, than by the imputation of one only; and held that the plea fell within that class which, professing to justify the whole of the libel, in effect justifying only a part, are therefore bad.[2]

[1] Mountney v. Walton, 2 B. & Ad. 673. *Vid.* also Chalmers v. Shackell, 6 C. & P. 475.

[2] Shortt, L. Lit., p. 393; Campbell v. Spottiswoode, 3 B. & S. 769.

And where the libel consisted of a paragraph published in a newspaper, stating, in substance, that the plaintiff was a confederate of blacklegs; that he had sought admission into a yacht club; that he gave an entertainment in the expectation of being elected, but was blackballed, and the next morning bolted, and some of the tradesmen of the town had to lament the fashionable character of his entertainment—a plea of justification, which, after alleging facts to show that the plaintiff was the confederate of persons who had been guilty of cheating at cards, and the facts of his giving an entertainment, and being blackballed, &c., stated "that on the following morning he quitted the town and neighborhood, leaving divers of the tradesmen, to whom he owed money, unpaid," was held bad, because the quitting might be innocent and without any intention to defraud. "The libel, as stated in the declaration," said Parke, B., "imputes to the plaintiff a fraudulent evasion of his creditors, he being unable to pay them. The plea does

64. But on the other hand, if the truth of the substantial imputation contained in the libel be proved, the justification need not extend also to every epithet or term of general abuse which may be found in the description or statement of the imputation, and which contains no ground of charge substantially distinct in its nature or character, from that which forms the main charge or gist of the libel.[1]

not meet that; for the plaintiff might be unable to pay without being guilty of fraud, as imputed by the word 'bolting,' used in the libel. That expression charged the plaintiff with going away suddenly from Plymouth, leaving debts unpaid, and under such circumstances that the creditors could not find him, and therefore means more than the mere 'quitting,' which is stated in the plea. That would be an innocent departure, and consistent with proof that he went out of town for a day, but afterwards returned and paid his debts" (O'Brien v. Bryant, 16 M. & W. 168).

See also Wadsworth v. Bentley (23 L. J. 3 Q. B.), where the declaration in an action of slander alleged that the defendant spoke of the plaintiff, in the way of his trade, the words, "He cheated me"; "He is a thief, and robbed me of £100"; and contained an averment of special damage, and the defendant pleaded a former judgment recovered for the same grievances. The record of the previous action showed the slanderous words to have been: "That thief is a villain, a scoundrel, and a rascal, and I can prove him a thief at any moment"; and it neither alleged that the words were spoken of the plaintiff in the way of his trade, nor contained an averment of special damage. This was held to be no bar to the action. "I cannot think," said Crompton, J., "that the cause of action in that record, which contains words charging the plaintiff with felony, is the same cause of action as that in the present declaration, which imputes a charge against the plaintiff as a trader."

[1] Morrison v. Harmer, 3 Bing. N. C. 76; 4 Scott, 933. So, in an action for libeling the plaintiffs in their business of sellers of medicine, by publishing that the defendants claimed "the merit of having crushed the self-styled hygeist system of wholesale poisoning, since they commenced exposing the homicidal tricks of those impudent and ignorant scamps who had the audacity to pretend to cure all diseases with one kind

65. "Our laws," said the court in a late case,[1] "allow a man to speak the truth, even if it be done ma-

of pill;" and that "several of the rot-gut rascals had been convicted of manslaughter, and fined and imprisoned for killing people with enormous doses of their universal vegetable boluses," &c.; the defendants pleaded a justification of the libel on the ground of truth, but did not justify the expressions "scamps" and "rascals;" and they proved at the trial that two persons had died in consequence of taking large quantities of the plaintiff's pills, and that the parties who had administered the pills were tried, convicted, and imprisoned for manslaughter. The defense, after verdict, was held sufficient, though the plea contained no justification of the expressions "scamps" and "rascals," and though it had not been proved that the defendants had "completely crushed the self-styled hygeist system of wholesale poisoning."

As to the objection grounded on the non-justification of the words "scamps" and "rascals," the court said: "It must be admitted that if these terms of invective and reproach contain any ground of charge or imputation against the plaintiffs, substantially distinct in its nature or character from that which forms the main charge or gist of the libel, and the truth of which has been justified by the plea, the consequence contended for on the part of the plaintiffs would justly follow, for the plea upon that supposition would not contain an answer to so much of the declaration as by the commencement of the plea it expressly undertakes to justify. The main charge against the plaintiffs in the libel is, that they were the compounders and sellers of pills of a poisonous and deleterious nature; and the main and principal allegation in the plea of justification is, 'that the pills sold by the plaintiffs, when administered and taken in the doses and quantities suggested and recommended by them, were of a highly dangerous, deadly, and poisonous nature, and in the highest degree injurious to the stomachs and bowels of persons using and taking the same.' The question therefore

---

[1] Baum v. Clause, 5 Hill, 199, and see Foss v. Hildreth, 9 Allen, 76.

By the Code Napoleon, in cases of libel, the defendant was not allowed to adduce proof of his asseverations. This law was repeated by the National Assembly in 1781, but only so far as libels against Government functionaries are concerned. A writer libeling a private person is still denied the privilege of proving that his libel is truth.

liciously." "But that truth" (says Mr. Townshend, in his valuable essay), "which is admitted as a defense, is the truth of the defamatory matter, in substance and in fact; and in the sense in which it was used, and was intended to be understood. If A. says of X. that he is a thief, and C. publishes that A. said X. was a thief, in a certain sense C. would publish the truth, but not in the sense which would constitute a defense; C.'s publication would, in fact, be but a repetition of A.'s words, which, as we have seen, would not be a defense. The truth, which in such a case would amount to a defense, would be that X. was a thief. Again: if A., speaking ironically, says of X. that he is an honest man, meaning and conveying the idea that X. is a dishonest man, it would not be a justification of these

is, whether the terms of abuse which have been above referred to, carry the matter any further than this, the main charge. The words themselves, in their vulgar use, convey no other meaning than that of general reproach and invective; and we can only discover whether they have any particular meaning in this libel by referring to the context of the libel and to the allegations on the record. As to the word 'scamps,' the plaintiffs themselves have given the meaning to it; for they allege in their declaration that it is intended to be applied to them 'in the way of their aforesaid trade, business, and occupation;' that is, as vendors of the pills, the making and selling of which by the plaintiffs is the main imputation against them. And the word 'rascals' is associated with an epithet or adjunct which appears to confine its general abusive quality to a description and designation of the persons who have been occupied in administering the pills spoken of in the libel, of whom two have been convicted of manslaughter. We cannot, therefore, understand these words, however offensive, as containing any charge different and distinct from that of which the truth has been justified in the first plea; and we are not aware of any authority by which it is determined that the justification of the truth of the substantial imputation contained in a libel is not sufficient, unless it extends also to every epithet or term of general abuse which may be found in the description or statement of such imputation."

words to allege that it was true X. was an honest man; but, to constitute a defense, the allegation required would be, that it was true X. was a dishonest man."[1]

66. A mere belief in the truth of the matter published, however honestly that belief may be entertained, will not, of itself, constitute any defense.[2] The question of belief, it is evident, will mainly present itself in considering the intent with which a publication is made, as to whether that intent be or be not malicious; and the principles which will govern courts are most safely drawn from the reported cases.

The question as to how far a belief in the truth of statements made, relieves the publisher from the re-

[1] Essay upon Slander and Libel, 7 § 211.

[2] Townshend on Slander and Libel, § 216. A defendant can not justify a charge of theft by showing that he has just grounds for believing the plaintiff dishonest. (Woodruff v. Richardson, 20 Conn. 238.) The publication in a newspaper of rumors is not justified, but may be mitigated, by the fact that such rumors existed. (Skinner v. Powers, 1 Wend. 451, § 411, *post.*) In mitigation of damages, in an action for libel, defendant was allowed to show that he copied the statement from another newspaper (Saunders v. Mills, 6 Bing. 213; 3 M. & P. 520). And that he had omitted many of its parts reflecting on the plaintiff (Creevy v. Carr, 7 C. & P. 64. And see Darbey v. Ousely, 1 Hurl & N. 1; Campbell v. Spottiswoode, 3 Best & Smith, 769; 8 Law Times Rep. N. S. 201; and see Moore v. Stevenson, 27 Conn. 14; Woodruff v. Richardson, 20 Conn. 238; Fry v. Bennett, 3 Bosw. 200; Smart v. Blanchard, 42 N. Hamp. 137; Kerr v. Force, 3 Cr. C. C. 8; Watson v. Moore, 2 Cush. 133; Hotchkiss v. Porter, 30 Conn. 314; Gilmer v. Ewbank, 13 Ill. 271; Duncan v. Brown, 15 B. Monr. 186; Grimes v. Coyle, 6 Monr. 301; Huson v. Dale, 19 Mich. 35; Farr v. Rusco, 9 Mich. 353; Long v. Brougher, 5 Watts, 399; Smith v. Luckecker, 4 Rawle, 295; Powell v. Plunkett, Cro. Car. 52; Moyer v. Pine, 4 Mich. 409; Hutt. 13; Bridg. 62; Brownlow, 2; Holt v. Parsons, 23 Tex. 9).

[3] As—it is submitted—will also the nice and accurate questions as to what will constitute publication of a libel. See Townshend on Slander and Libel p. 78, *et seq.*

sponsibility for making them; a question intricate in itself, but rendered still more involved by considerations as to how far the persons to whom the statements are uttered, believe in the truth, we are forced to admit, after all the years during which the law has been engaged in its discussion, must be solved anew with and according to the circumstances of each recurring case.[1] The law has never been able to lay down an infallible or invariable rule. While an action of slander would perhaps be influenced by the fact that the slanderous words were not credited by any one hearing them—the main question will nevertheless be—the intent of the person speaking them.

Nor is it necessary to be finical as to the exact legal meaning of the word intent. The law generally will construe it in its popular sense of intention, motive, animus. As to the word malice, however, there may be a legal significance, not recognized in the popular definition; though Daly, Ch. J., in a late case seemed to hold that there was none. "I apprehend," said he, "that there is no ground for distinguishing between the legal and the popular sense of the word, and that it means, in its legal sense, exactly what it means in its popular sense, namely, a mischievous design or intent to do an injury to an individual, or to the public."[2] The law presumes, from the act, an intent to bring about its consequences; "to denominate this intent malice, or malice in law, when it may have arisen from a good motive, the defendant believing what he alleges to be true, is to employ the word malice in a

[1] Knight v. Gibbs, 3 Nev. & M. 467; 1 Adol. & El. 43; Gillett v. Bullivant, 7 L T. 490; Wilson v. Galt, 17 N. Y. 445.

[2] Viele v. Gray, 10 Abb. Pr. R. 5; 18 How Pr. R. 550.

sense neither justified by its etymology, its ordinary meaning, nor its previous legal signification."[1]

But a difference is made by Sir Thomas Moore between *malitia* and *malevolentia*.[2]

However honestly the party who publishes a libel believes it to be true, if it is untrue in fact, the law implies malice, unless the occasion justifies the act; and whether the occasion justifies the act, is a question of law for the court.[3]

No suspicion, however strong, will justify a man in aspersing his neighbor,[4] nor can a defendant show that the aspersion had been for years generally credited,[5] or that a near relative (*e.g.* a sister) of the plaintiff believed her guilty.[6] Common fame even will not justify an extra judicial charge.[7] Though a *bona fide* belief in the truth of statements made will sometimes be allowed to mitigate damages.[8] Recantation also is sometimes allowed to go in mitigation of damages.[9]

[1] In Viele v. Gray, 10 Abb. Pr. 5; 18 How. Pr. 550.

[2] 17 Howell's St. Tr. 43, 63. (See also his remarks upon the introduction of the words *Falso et malitiose* into indictments for libel [1 Id. 30; 6 Id. 1113]).

[3] Darby v. Ouseley, 1 Hurl & N. 1.

[4] Powell v. Plunkett, Cro. Car. 52; Moyer v. Pine, 4 Mich. 409.

[5] Long v. Brougher, 5 Watts, 437.

[6] Smith v. Buckecker, 4 Rawle, 295.

[7] Hutt, 13; Brownlow, 2; Bridg. 62.

[8] Farr v. Rusco, 9 Mich. 353; Huson v. Dale, 19 Mich. 35, overruling Thompson v. Bowers, 1 Douglass, 321.

[9] Perret v. New Orleans Times Newspaper, 25 La. An. 170. (See this question discussed *post*, in chapter on newspapers.)

"In Dicas v. Lawson" (Id.), says Alderson, B., "I directed the jury to look to the whole of the publication, to see whether it was calculated to injure the plaintiff's character. The publication there complained of, was the report of a trial in which there were strong observations on the character of the plaintiff, but in which the plaintiff had recovered a verdict for £30. It was said that the report was libelous, because it set

It was formerly the policy of the law to construe all words *in mitiori sensu*.[1] The old judges abounded in such maxims as "where words are ambiguous, so as they may be expounded in good or ill part, no action lies, for they shall be expounded in the best sense."[2] "The law strains not to hurt but to heal."[3] 'Where words are indifferent and discouraged the action of slander by all sorts of evasions, and the like."[4]

67. But the rule, *mitiori sensu*, was held by Lord Ellenborough[5] in 1807, to have been long superseded, and courts will now construe words in the

forth the charge made on the trial against the plaintiff. I left it to the jury to say whether, taking the whole of the publication together, they thought it likely to depreciate his character. The jury thought not; and on application for a new trial, this court (exchequer) approved of my direction."

[1] King v. Bagg. Cro. Jac. 331; Holland v. Stoner, Id. 315.

[2] Anon. Cro. Eliz. 672.

[3] Coote v. Gilbert Hob, 77 pl. 100.

[4] Per Gibson, J., Bash v. Sommer, 20 Pa. St. 159. See Harrison v. Thornborough, 10 Mod. 196. "We will not give more favor unto actions on the case for words than of necessity we ought to do, where the words are not apparently scandalous, these actions being now too frequent." (Coke, C. J., Crofts v. Brown, 3 Bulst. 167.) In Aslop v. Aslop (5 Hurl. & N. 534), the court says actions for slander are not to be encouraged; nor is the spirit wanting in the later decisions in this country; see Bennett v. Williamson (4 Sandf. 67), where it is said: "The law of libel ought to be considered and is in its spirit a benevolent and salutary provision for the peace and security of the community, but it can not redress every injury sustained by a breach of morals or of good manners. We may not approve of the taste of publications such as is set forth in the declaration in this case. We may lament the existence of a disposition to make private character too much the subject of comment and abuse without having it in our power through the instrumentality of the law to arrest the evil;" and in Dollaway v. Turrell (26 Wend. 397), the action for libel is designated as a sordid action.

[5] Roberts v. Camden, 9 East, 96; Cf. Woolnoth v. Meadows, 5 East. 463; Somers v. House, Holt Rep. 39.

plain and popular sense in which the rest of the world naturally understands them.[1] The language will be equally libelous if grammatical or ungrammatical;[2] whether positive or insinuating;[3] whether mispelled,[4] ironical,[5] figurative,[6] or allegorical, or if expressed in the form of a question.

68. Truth being a defense, it follows that a greater or less degree of truth in the alleged libel, may be pleaded in mitigation of damages. Thus, it would be a mitigation of the offense, to show such facts as establish a ground of suspicion, not amounting to actual proof of the charge,[7] or as tend to a proof of the charge, although falling short of it.[8] Not only

[1] Button v. Hayward, 8 Mod. 24; Rex v. Horne, 2 Cowp. 672; Rex v. Watson, 2 T. R. 206; Fisher v. Clement, 10 B. & C. 472; Roberts v. Camden, 9 East, 93; Wakley v. Healey, 7 Com. B. 591; Ogden v. Riley, 2 Green, 186; Duncan v. Brown, 15 B. Monr. 186; Fallenstein v. Boothe, 13 Mo. R. 427; Demarest v. Haring, 6 Cow. 76; Pike v. Van Wormer, 6 How. Pr. R. 99; Backus v. Richardson, 5 Johns. 476; Gibson, J., Bash v. Sommer, 20 Penn. St. R. 159; Harrison v. Thornborough, 10 Mod. 196; Le Fance v. Malcomson, 1 H. L. Cas. 664.

[2] Shortt, L. Lit. 385.

[3] Rex v. Edgar, 2 Sess. Cas. 29; 5 Bac. Abr. tit. Libel, 199.

[4] Hob. 215; 11 Mod. 86; Boydell v. Jones, 4 M. & W. 446.

[5] Hoar v. Silverlock, 12 Q. B. 624, 632; Woodgate v. Rideout, 4 F. & F. 202.

[6] Guthercole's Case, 2 Lew. C. C. 255; Cf. Hunt v. Thimblethorpe, Moo. 418; 1 Vin. Ab. 429; Earl of Northampton's Case, 12 Rep. 134; Delany v. Jones, 4 Esp. C. 191; Woolnoth v. Meadows, 5 East, 463; Hemming v. Power, 10 M. & W. 564.

[7] Wagner v. Holbrunner, 7 Gill, 296. That is, a suspicion of the truth; for if the matter is false, no suspicion, however strong, will avail, as will be presently seen.

[8] Snyder v. Andrews, 6 Barb. 43; Scott v. McKinnish, 15 Ala. 662; Bisbey v. Shaw, 12 N. Y. 67. Evidence of general bad character may be admitted under the general issue (Smith

against actual words, but against implications and innuendoes, it behoves the writer to guard. It is not at all unfrequent, that one uttering words innocent in themselves, might be able, by implication, to make them really injurious, and against this innuendo, as well as against the words themselves, the law will protect the citizen. As, for instance, where the defendant wrote in a letter: "I have reason to suppose that many of the flowers of which I have been robbed, are growing upon your premises" (thereby meaning that the plaintiff had been guilty of larceny, and had stolen from the defendant certain plants, roots, and flowers of the defendant, and had unlawfully disposed of them to P., and unlawfully placed them in P.'s garden). The previous part of the letter stated that the plaintiff, whom P. had taken into his employ as a gardener, had been in the defendant's employ in the same capacity, and had been discharged for dishonesty; held, on error,

v. Smith, 8 Ired. 29; Taylor v. Richardson, 29 Maine, 323). An action of slander for charging a man with having the venereal disease, and, with that disease upon him, contracting marriage, and communicating that disease to his wife, cannot be maintained, if the plaintiff immediately after his marriage had the disease in fact, even by proof that his wife, whom he married without knowing that she had the disease, communicated it to him (Golderman v. Stearns, 7 Gray, 181). In slander for calling plaintiff a whore, the words were laid to have been spoken in 1842; plea, that plaintiff, while unmarried, in 1834, had carnal connection with one A. Replication, that plaintiff, at the time mentioned in the plea, was betrothed to said A.; that afterwards she was lawfully married to him; that she lived with him a virtuous life until August, 1836, when he died; and that she had ever since continued to live in innocent and virtuous widowhood. Held, on general demurrer, that the replication was insufficient (Alcorn v. Hooker, 7 Blackf. 58). Where the charge is of a crime of which the plaintiff was convicted, it is no answer to a plea of the truth of the charge, that the plaintiff was pardoned (Baum v. Clause, 5 Hill, 196; Townshend on Slander and Libel, note, p. 328).

that the innuendo was not too large. Of course, the innuendo, like the word, or act, or effigy, must be construed by the circumstances of each particular case, but against it the writer will do well to guard.

69. The word "innuendo," in its legal sense, signifies something which avers the intendment or meaning of language published.[1] That is to say: that, while ordinarily, as we have seen, words will be construed

[1] And as to innuendo generally, and example, see Gardner v. Williams, 2 Cr. M. & R. 78; 3 Dowl. Pra. Cas. 796; 1 M. & W. 245; Rex v. Horne, 2 Cowper, 688; Reg. v. Virrier, 4 Per. & D. 161; 1 Stark. Sland. 418; Rex v. Greepe, 2 Salk. 513; 1 Ld. Raym. 256; 12 Mod. 139; 1 Saund. 243; Van Vechten v. Hopkins, 5 Johns. 220; McClaughry v. Wetmore, 6 Id. 83; Thomas v. Croswell, 1 Id. 271; Weed v. Bibbins, 32 Barb. 315; Parham v. Nethersole, Yelv. 21; Cramer v. Noonan, 4 Wis. 231; Stevens v. Handley, Wright (Ohio), 123. Where the charge was that plaintiff was a "bunter," without any innuendo to explain the meaning of that term, the court on the trial refused to receive evidence of the meaning, and plaintiff was nonsuited (Rawlings v. Norbury, 1 Fost. & F. 174; Worth v. Butler, 7 Blackf. 251; Watson v. Nicholas, 6 Humph. 174). The office of the innuendo is to explain doubtful words or phrases, and annex to them their proper meaning. It can not extend their sense beyond their usual and natural import, unless something is put upon the record by way of introductory matter with which they can be connected. In such case, words which are equivocal or ambiguous, or fall short, in their natural sense, of importing any libelous charge, may have fixed to them a meaning, certain and defamatory, extending beyond their ordinary import (Beardley v. Tappan, 1 Blatchf. C. C. 588). And to the like effect, see Dorsey v. Whipps, 8 Gill, 457; Nichols v. Packard, 16 Vt. 83; Patterson v. Edwards, 2 Gilman, 720; Andrews v. Woodmansee, 15 Wend. 232; Taylor v. Kneeland, 1 Douglass, 67; Gosling v. Morgan, 32 Penn. St. R. 273; State v. Henderson, 1 Richardson, 179; Caverley v. Caverley, 3 Up. Can. Rep. 338, O. S.; Van Vechten v. Hopkins, 5 Johns. 211; Caldwell v. Abbey, Hardin, 529; McCuen v. Ludlam, 2 Harr. 12; Beswick v. Chappel, 8 Monr. 486; Penaway v. Coyne, Chand. (Wis.) 214; Vaughan v. Havens, 8 Johns. 109; Gompertz v. Levy, 1 Perr. & Dav. 214; Dodge v. Lacey, 2 Carter (Ind.) 212.

by courts in the plain and popular sense in which the rest of the world naturally understand them,[1] in that natural and ordinary meaning and acceptation which the world gives them. However general the language of a defamatory publication may be, if its application

"An innuendo means nothing more than the words '*id est*,' '*scilicet*,' or 'meaning,' or 'aforesaid,' as explanatory of a matter sufficiently expressed before. It is in the nature of a *prædict*. It may serve for an explanation, to point a meaning where there is precedent matter, expressed or necessarily understood or known, but never to establish a new charge. It may apply what is already expressed, but cannot add to, nor enlarge, nor change, the sense of the previous words. If the words before the innuendo do not sound in slander, no meaning produced by the innuendo will make the action maintainable, for it is not the nature of an innuendo to beget an action. An innuendo helps nothing, unless the words precedent have a violent presumption of the innuendo. The business of an innuendo is, by a reference to preceding matter to fix more precisely the meaning. The office of an innuendo is to explain, not to extend, what has gone before; and it cannot enlarge the meaning of words, unless it be connected with some matter of fact expressly averred." The innuendo "is only a link to attach together facts already known to the court" (Townshend on Slander and Libel, p. 527).

[1] Roberts v. Camden, 7 East, 93; Tenterden, Ch. J., Harvey v. French, 1 Cr. & M. 11; Bonyon v. Trotter, Sty. 231; Woolnoth v. Meadows, 5 East, 463; Spencer v. Southwick, 11 Johns. 579; Pratt, Ch. J., Button v. Heyward, 8 Mod. 24; Fallenstein v. Boothe, 13 Mis. 427; Ogden v. Riley, 2 Green, 186; Duncan v. Brown, 15 B. Monr. 186; Hancock v. Stephens, 11 Humph. 507; their most obvious meaning, Hogg v. Wilson, 1 N. & M. 216; or Thirman v. Mathews, 1 Stew. 384; Hogg v. Dorrah, 2 Port. 212; Dorland v. Patterson, 23 Wend. 422; Butterfield v. Buffam, 9 N. Hamp. 156; McGowan v. Manifee, 7 Monr. 314; Demarest v. Haring, 6 Cow. 76; Truman v. Taylor, 4 Iowa, 424; Wright v. Paige, 36 Barb. 438; S. C., on appeal, 3 Trans. App. 134; 1 Starkie on Slander, 60; Pike v. Van Wormer, 6 How. Pr. R. 99; Dias v. Short, 16 Id. 322; Walrath v. Nellis, 17 Id. 72; Hughley v. Hughley, 2 Bailey, 592; Tuttle v. Bishop, 30 Conn. 80; Carroll v. White, 33 Barb. 618; Somers v. House, Holt, 39.

to a particular individual or individuals can be generally recognized or perceived, it is a libel on him or them. It is not necessary that its object be described in any express form of words, but only so that it is known whom they are, "and if those who must be acquainted with the circumstances connected with the party described, may also come to the same conclusion, and may have no doubt that the writer of the libel intended to mean those individuals; it would be opening a very wide door to defamation, if parties suffering all the inconvenience of being libeled, were not permitted to have that protection which the law affords. If they are so described that they are known to all their neighbors as being the parties alluded to; and if they are able to prove, to the satisfaction of a jury, that the party writing the libel did intend to allude to them, it would be unfortunate to find the law in a state which would prevent the party being protected against such libels." "Whether a man," said Lord Campbell, "is called by one name, or whether he is called by another, or whether he is described by a pretended description of a class to which he is known to belong, if those who look on know well who is aimed at, the very same injury is inflicted; the very same thing is in fact done, as would be done if his name and Christian name were ten times repeated."[1]

Neither is the rule as to malice an inflexible one. When malice is said to be the gist of an action for libel, the legal import of the word must be borne in mind.

"Malice," said Lord Campbell,[2] "in the legal acceptation of the word, is not confined to personal spite

[1] Le Fann v. Malcomson, 1 H. L. Cas. 664.

[2] In Ferguson v. Earl of Kinnoul, 9 Cl. & Fin. 32.

against individuals, but consists in a conscious violation of the law to the prejudice of another." "Malice," says another learned Judge,[1] "in common acceptation, means ill-will against a person; but in its legal sense it means a wrongful act done intentionally, without just cause or excuse. If I give a perfect stranger a blow likely to produce death, I do it of malice, because I do it intentionally, and without just cause or excuse. If I maim cattle without knowing whose they are; if I poison a fishery without knowing the owner, I do it of malice, because it is a wrongful act, and done intentionally. If I am arraigned of felony, and wilfully stand mute, I am said to do it of malice, because it is intentional, and without just cause or excuse. And if I traduce a man, whether I know him or not, and whether I intend to do him an injury or not, I apprehend the law considers it as done of malice, because it is wrongful and intentional. It equally works an injury, whether I meant to produce an injury or not, and if I had no legal excuse for the slander, why is he not to have a remedy against me for the injury it produces?" "If a person writes defamatory matter of another," says Bramwell, B.,[2] "however honestly he may believe it to be true, if it be in fact untrue, the law implies malice." And "the law implies malice from the publication of a libel, except where the occasion justifies the publication." And a man may wilfully publish a mischievous libel without intent to injure the party, and may yet be responsible.[3]

By the Scotch law, it is not necessary, in the case of a civil action for libel, that malice should be either proved or presumed; but it is necessary in the case of

[1] Bayley, J., in Bromage v. Prosser, 4 B. & C. 255.
[2] Darby v. Ousley, 1 H. & N. 9; 25 L. J. 330, Ex.
[3] Bayliss v. Lawrence, 11 A. & El. 924.

a criminal proceeding. "In general," says Hume, "the criminal is herein distinguished from the civil process; that to warrant the inflicting of any punishment the *animus injuriandi*, or special malice of the act, must be shown; whereas mere petulance or indiscretion may be the just ground of an award for the reparation of damage, though the parties are not even known to each other, if the things said are naturally and in themselves of an injurious tendency."

The whole publication, however, is to be looked at; and if the jury think that the effect of one part of it, which if taken alone would be injurious to the plaintiff's character, is removed by the other part of it, they should find for the defendant.[1] The jury will take the whole together and say whether the result of the whole is calculated to injure the plaintiff's character; if, in one part of the publication, something disreputable to the plaintiff is stated, but is removed by the conclusion, the bane and antidote must be taken together.[2]

This presumption of malice can sometimes be overturned by proof of belief, such as we have already considered. Evidence of recantation of a libel, also, will be evidence to overburden such presumption.

"Malice: the doing any act without a just cause."[3] Malice in its legal sense always excludes a just cause.[4] It is a technical expression, and means the absence of any excuse;[5] and is implied in every [wrongful] act for which there is no legal justification, excuse, or extenuation.[6] Malice is the deliberate disregard of the

[1] Chalmers v. Payne, 2 C. M. & R. 156; 5 Tyrw. 66.
[2] Id.
[3] Chitty Genl. Pr. 46.
[4] Jones v. Given, Gill. Cas. 185.
[5] Penn v. Lewis, Add. 282.
[6] Penn v. Honeyman, Id. 149; Bromage v. Prosser, 4 B. &

rights of others;[1] the doing of any act injurious to another without just cause.[2]

In criminal law and general practice, malice signifies a wickedness of purpose; a spiteful or malevolent design against another; a settled purpose to injure or destroy another. Any formed or evil disposition or design of doing mischief.[3] General wickedness of heart; inhuman or reckless disregard of the lives or safety of others; as when one coolly discharges a gun, or throws any dangerous missile among a multitude of people, or strikes, even upon provocation, with a weapon that must produce death.[4] Deliberate disregard of the rights of others, as when one carries on the trade of melting tallow, to the annoyance of the neighboring dwellings.[5] All these will constitute malice.

Malice, again, will be either express, or implied from the circumstances given to the jury. Or, it has again been divided into legal malice or malice in law, and actual malice or malice in fact. This latter distinction, however, is not in the malice itself, but rather in the evidence by which it is established. "If the charge complained of is injurious, and no justifiable motive for making it is apparent, malice is inferred from the falsity of the charge. The law,

C. 247; 1 Russ. Cr. 483; 1 Starkie on Libel, 3, 213; Bouvier's Law Dict. tit. Malice. See York's Case, 9 Metc. 93; Darry v. People, 10 N. Y. 122; Mitchell v. Jenkins, 5 B. & A. 500; Hilliard on Torts, ch. vii. § 106.

[1] Per Abbott, Ch. J., 3 B. & C. 584.

[2] Id. And see Townshend on Slander & Libel, notes to pp. 122, *et seq.*, where numerous definitions of malice are collected.

[3] Hale's P. C. 455; 2 Stra. 766; 4 Bl. Com. 198; 2 Roll. R. 461.

[4] 4 Bl. Com. 199.

[5] 3 B. & C. 584.

in such cases, does not impute malice not appearing in fact, but presumes a malicious motive for making a false and injurious charge, if no innocent motive appears. If, from the circumstances, however, the defendant may be reasonably supposed to have had a worthy motive for making the charge, the law ceases to infer malice from the mere falsity of the charge, and requires from the plaintiff other proof of its existence. It is actual malice in either case, only the proof is different."[1] "The jury may infer malice from want of probable cause, but they are not bound to make this inference. And if malice is deduced from want of probable cause, it is as much malice in fact, within the meaning of the law, as though shown or deduced from any other fact or facts."[2]

70. The various decisions upon the subject of defamation may seem finical, over-nice, and even ludicrous to the layman; and many, perhaps a majority of them, may be such as would no longer govern. But the principles controlling them are still law, and it is matter of marvel that in the reported cases the old judges were able to look beyond the annoyance of the petty, trivial, and absurd details which encumbered them, and lay down rules with a reasoning so clear and forcible, that from their conclusions, even to-day, there can be no escape.

71. Words which sound in disability only, are not actionable, unless spoken of one who gains his livelihood by that thing, profession, or business wherein the words disable him.[3] "An action," it has been said,

[1] Selden, J., Lewis v. Chapman, 16 N. Y. 372.

[2] Smith v. Howard, 28. Iowa, 51. And see the brief of Nicholas Hill, in Darry v. People, 10 N. Y. 123, which cites a large number of authorities.

[3] Bill v. Neal, 1 Lev. 52. *Vid.* How v. Prin, Holt, 652; 3 Salk. 694.

"lies for speaking scandalous words of any man of any trade or profession, be it never so base, if they are spoken with reference to his profession."[1] Thus: it has been held actionable to say of a servant in husbandry and bailiff, "Thou art a cozening knave, and hast cozened thy master of a bushel of barley;"[2] or of a tradesman, "Thou art a rogue, and thou hast cheated me of several pounds;"[3] of a person carrying on the business of a butcher, that she had used false weights in her trade;[4] of a cornseller, "You are a rogue and a swindling rascal; you delivered me one hundred bushels of oats, worse by sixpence a bushel, than I bargained for;"[5] of an auctioneer and appraiser, employed by the defendant to value certain goods, "He is a damned rascal; he has cheated me out of a hundred pounds on the valuation;"[6] of an asphalte manufacturer, "The old materials have been relaid by your company in the asphalte work executed in front of the ordinance office, and I have seen the work done;" innuendo, that the plaintiff "had been guilty of dishonesty in the conduct of his said trade, by laying down again the old asphalte materials which had before been used at the entrance of the said ordinance office instead of new asphalte, according to his contract;"[7] or of a certificated master mariner, that "during his stay at N. he was frequently drunk, and in that state had to be carried to his boat to reach his vessel, &c."[8] So it was held slanderous to say of a

[1] Terry v. Hooper, Lev. 115.
[2] Seaman v. Bigg, Cro. Car. 480.
[3] Surman v. Shelleto, Burr. 1688.
[4] Griffith v. Lewis, 7 Q. B. 61.
[5] Thomas v. Jackson, 3 Bing. 104.
[6] Bryant v. Loxton, 4 Moore, 344.
[7] Baboneau v. Farrell, 13 C. B. 360.
[8] Irwin v. Brandwood, 2 H. & C. 960; 9 L. T. N. S. 772; 33

gamekeeper that he had trapped foxes; the declaration stating that it was his duty as such gamekeeper not to kill foxes, and that he was employed on the terms of his not doing so, as the defendant knew.[1] Any unfounded imputation against a person who is in the enjoyment of an office, either public or private, whether of honor, profit, or trust, which imports a charge of unfitness to administer the duties of that office, is actionable.[2]

Thus, it is slanderous to say of a lawyer, "He is a dunce, and will get little by the law;"[3] or "Thou art no lawyer; thou canst not draw a lease; thou hast that degree without desert; they are fools that come to thee for law,"[4] or "Thou art a false knave, a cozening knave, and hast got all that thou hast by cozenage; and thou hast cozened all those that have dealt with thee;"[5] or that "he is no lawyer,"[6] or that he is a "common barrator;"[7] or if one say to a counsel, "Thou didst disclose my counsel;" or to a counsel or attorney, "Thou didst deliver my evidence to my adversary;"[8] or to style him in a tone of irony—an "honest lawyer."[9]

But it has been held to be not actionable to charge one in a business or profession to have exhibited, in some particular case, bad management or unskillful

L. J. 257, Ex. *Vid.* Coxhead v. Richards, 2 C. V. 569; 15 L. J. 278, C. P.; Harwood v. Green, 2 C. & P. 141.

[1] Foulger v. Newcome, L. Rep. 2 Ex. 327; 16 L. T. N. S. 596; 36 L. J. 169, Ex.

[2] See Butler N. P. 45.

[3] Peard v. Jones, Cro. Cas. 382.

[4] Bankes v. Allen, Roll. Abr. 54.

[5] Jankins v. Smith, Cro. Jac. 586. *Vid.* also Berckley's Case, 4 Rep. 16.

[6] Day v. Buller, 3 Wils. 59.

[7] Taylor v. Starkey, Cro. Car. 192.

[8] Per Anderson and Grammond, JJ.; Wright v. Moorhouse, Bro. Eliz. 358. *Vid.* Brown v. Kennedy, 43 L. J. 342, ch. 342.

[9] Boydell v. Jones, 4 M. & W. 446; 7 Dowl. P. C. 210.

treatment.[1] Thus: for saying of an attorney in a particular suit, "he knows nothing about the suit; he will lead you on until he has undone you," no action lies.[2] It seems, however, that it would be actionable to charge such ignorance or unskillfulnes as would infer gross ignorance and unskillfulness in all cases.[3]

It is not easy to see the distinction between the case of the attorney and of the physician, on whom it was held libelous to say, "he was the death of J. P.[4]" J. P.'s case being a particular case, the distinction is somewhat finical and might not always be servilely followed.[5]

"It is actionable to call a counselor a "daffodowndilly," if there be an averment that the words signify an ambidexter;[6] or to say of an attorney that he hath no more law than Master Cheyny's bull, even although Master Cheyny actually had no bull, for if that be the case, as Keeling, Ch. J., observed, 'the scandal is the greater.'[7] It is quite clear that to say that a lawyer 'hath no more law than a goose,' is actionable;[8] and the reporter adds a query whether it be not actionable to say a lawyer 'hath no more law than the man in the moon.'" In another case, it was held actionable to say of an attorney that "he is no more a lawyer than the devil."[9] But it is not actionable to say of a lawyer that he kept back his bill fifteen years, until his client was dead.[10] Very few clients, probably, would

[1] Garr. v Selden, 6 Barb. 416; Camp v. Martin, 23 Conn. 86; Southee v. Denny, 1 Ex. 196.

[2] Foot v. Brown, 8 Johns. 64.

[3] Townshend on Slander & Libel, § 194.

[4] Maires v. Thornton, 8 Term R. 303.

[5] And see Cawdrey v. Telley, Godb. 441.

[6] Pearce's Case, 1 Roll. Abr. 55, pl. 17.

[7] Baker v. Morfue, Sid. 327.

[8] Id.

[9] Day v. Buller, 3 Wils. 59.

[10] Reeves v. Templar, 2 Jur. Exc. 137.

be deterred from employing an attorney on that account. It is not slanderous to say that a clergyman "is a remarkably bad preacher;"[1] but it would be, to say of a church warden, "thou art a cheating knave, and hast cheated the parish of forty pounds;"[2] or of a town clerk, "he has taken forty shillings for a bribe;"[3] or of a constable, "he is not worthy the office of a constable, for he and his company, the last time he was constable, stole five of my swine and ate them."[4] An imputation of insanity to a governess would be actionable,[5] but to say of an alderman that "when he put on his gown Satan enters into it,[6] or to charge a member of Parliament with insincerity,"[7] would not be actionable.

Words of general or doubtful signification, standing alone, are not slanderous; and no action will lie for speaking the words "rogue," "rascal," "scoundrel," "swindler," or "blackleg," unless special damage can be proved. It seems, however, it would be otherwise if they were published.[8]

To say of a trader that he is "A sorry, pitiful fellow, and a rogue; he compounded his debts at five

[1] Gathercole v. Miall, 15 M. & W. 344.

[2] Strode v. Holmes, Sly. 338; 1 Vin. Abr. 468; Woodruff v. Wooley, Id. 463.

[3] Yelv. 142; 1 Vin. Abr. 463. *Vid.* 1 Roll. Abr. 56.

[4] Cro. Eliz. 861; 1 Vin. Abr. 464.

[5] Morgan v. Lingen, 8 L. T. N. S. 800.

[6] 2 Starkie on Slander, 314.

[7] Onslow v. Horne, 2 W. Black. 750.

[8] Anon. Lofft, 322; Dyer v. Morris, 4 Miss. 214; Lt. Anson v. Smith, 1 Tr. 748; Hayes v. Mitchell, 7 Blackf. 117. But if those words were written and published, I doubt not an action would lie (Gould, J., in Villers v. Monsley, 2 Wils. 403; Barnett v. Allen, 3 H. & N. 376; 27 L. J. 412, Ex.; Richardson v. Allen, 2 Chit. 657; Saville v. Jardine, 2 H. Bl. 331).

shillings in the pound;"[1] or, "If he does not come and make terms with me, I will make a bankrupt of him, and ruin him;"[2] of a brewer, "I will bet £5 to £1 that Mr. J. was in a sponging house for debt within the last fortnight, and I can produce the man who locked him up; the man told me so himself," &c.;[3] of a dyer, that "He is a bankrupt knave, and is not worth three half-pence;"[4] of a tailor, "I heard you were run away;"[5] of a husbandman, "He owes more money than he is worth; he is run away and is broke;"[6] of a carpenter, "He is broken and run away, and will never return again;"[7] and even in cases where an expectation or opinion only was expressed, as "I believe all is not well with Daniel Vivian: there are many merchants who have lately failed, and I expect no otherwise of Daniel Vivian."[8]

It was held actionable to say of an upholsterer, "You are a soldier; I saw you in your red coat doing duty; your word is not to be taken"—it having been a common practice for tradesmen to protect

[1] Stanton v. Smith, Ld. Raym. 1480. See case of a pawnbroker, Holt, 652.

[2] Brown v. Smith, 13 C. B. 596; 22 L. J. 151, C. P.

[3] Jones v. Littler, 1 M. & W. 423.

[4] Squire v. Johns, Cro. Jac. 585.

[5] Davis v. Lewis, 1 T. R. 17.

[6] Dobson v. Thornistone, 3 Mod. 112.

[7] Chapman v. Lampshire, 3 Mod. 155. In this case it was argued for the defendant that the plaintiff might be broken, and yet be as good a carpenter as before. "But," said the chief justice, "the credit which the plaintiff has in the world may be the means to support his skill, for he may not have an opportunity to show his workmanship without those materials with which he is intrusted."

[8] 3 Salk. 326; Raym. 207. *Vid.* Harrison v. Thornborough, 10 Mod. 196.

themselves against their creditors by a counterfeit enlisting.[1]

In one case, where it was said of a merchant, "He came a broken merchant from Hamburgh," the court[2] held that an action would lie, the charge being of having been "once broken, *Et qui semel malus semper presumitur esse malus eodem genere*, or at least may have an inclination thereto; and it being alleged to be spoken *falso et malitiosè*, and to scandalize him in his profession, it is a great cause of discrediting and impairing him in his trade; whereas their credit is the principal means of their gain."[3]

And it is libelous to impute untruly to any person, pecuniary embarrassment and inability to purchase a certain property without the aid of a loan from a third party; even although it be, at the same time, stated that the loan was afterwards honorably repaid.[4]

72. Defamatory attacks on persons in the way of their trade, profession, or calling must be distinguished from hostile criticisms, fairly and temperately expressed, on such of their works and performances as appeal to the public; for such criticisms, however severely they may condemn or effectually turn into ridicule the works of authors, painters, architects, actors, &c., or even the advertisements or handbills of a tradesman, may be justifiable, though not in all respects accurate; whereas publications which have for their object the private injury of the person attacked can only be justified by their substantial truth.

It is slanderous to remark of a physician that he

[1] Arne v. Johnson, 10 Mod. 111.

[2] Shortt, L. Litt. 406 (note).

[3] Leycroft v. Dunker, Cro. Car. 317.

[4] Cox v. Lee, L. Rep. 4, Ex. 284; 38 L. J. 219, Ex.; 21 L. T. N. S. 1, 8.

"killed six children in one year:"[1] "Thou art a drunken fool and an ass:" "Thou wert never a scholar, and are not worthy to speak to a scholar, and that I will prove and justify;"[2] or of a surgeon and accoucher, "I wonder you had him to attend you. Do you know him? He is not an apothecary; he has not passed any examination; he's a bad character; none of the medical men here meet him. Several have died that he has attended, and there have been inquests held on them;"[3] or of an apothecary, "It is a world of blood he has to answer for in this town, through his ignorance; he did kill a woman and two children at ——; he did kill —— at ——; he was the death of ——; he has killed his patient with his physic;"[4] or, of a midwife, "She is an ignorant woman and of small practice, and very unfortunate in her way; there are few that she goes to but lie desperately ill, or die under her hands;"[5] or, that "many have perished for her want of skill."[6]

There is no law, however, against calling an innkeeper "a caterpillar;"[7] neither is it actionable to say of a justice, "He is a logger-headed, a slouch-headed and a bursen-bellied hound;"[8] or, "He is a fool, an ass, a beetle-headed justice,"[9] or, "He is a debauched man,

[1] Carrol v. White, 33 Barb. 615.

[2] Cawdrey v. Highley, Cro. Car. 270; 1 Roll. Abr. 54.

[3] Southee v. Denny, 1 Exch. 196. But it was held to be no libel to publish in a medical journal of a physician that he had met homœopathists in consultation, though it was alleged that, in the opinion of the profession, meeting homœopathists in consultation was improper, and against etiquette (Clay v. Roberts, 8 L. T. N. S. 397; 9 Jur. N. S. 580; 11 W. R. 649).

[4] Tulty v. Alewin, 11 Mod. 221. *Vid.* also Edsall v. Russel, 4 M. & W. 1090.

[5] Wharton v. Brook, 1 Vent. 21.

[6] Flower's Case, Cro. Car. 211.

[7] Vin. Abr. Act. for Words, V. a. 34.

[8] 1 Keb. 629.

[9] Bill v. Neal, 1 Lev. 52.

and unfit to be a justice;"[1] or, "He is a base, rascally villain, and is neither nobleman, knight, nor gentleman, but a most villainous rascal, and by unjust means doth most villainously take other men's rights from them, and keeps a company of thieves and traitors to do mischief, and giveth them nothing for their labor, but base blue liveries;"[2] or, "He is half-eared;"[3] or, "He is a blackguard;" "There is a combined company here to cheat strangers, and Squire Van Tassel has a hand in it. I don't see why he did not tell me the execution had not been returned in time, so that I could sue the constable;"[4] or, "Squire Oakley is a damned rogue;"[5] so, to publish orally of a justice "He is a blood-sucker and seeketh after blood; if a man will give him a couple of capons he will take them;"[6] or, "You robbed the poor and are worse than a highwayman;" is not actionable. It does not follow, however that one might write down all this, even of a justice,[7] with impunity from an action for libel.

"Because," said Lord Holt,[8] "it is not a slander to call a justice of the peace blockhead, ass, &c., for

[1] Hammond v. Kingsmill, 7 Jac. 1.

[2] Hollis v. Briscow, Cro. Jac. 58.

[3] Markham v. Bridges, Cro. Car. 223. The justices, however, have some decisions in their favor: *e. g.*, it is actionable to say of a justice that he was a "Jacobite" (How v. Prin, Holt, 652; 3 Poulk, 694). "He is a rascal, a villain, and a liar" (Kerler v. Osgood, 1 Vent. 50). "He is not fit to be a justice of the peace" (Ib.). "When thou wert justice thou wert a bribing justice" (Aston v. Blagrave, Str. 617; Prudham v. Tucker, Yelv. 153; Herle v. Osgood, 1 Vent. 50). "He covereth and hideth felonies, and is not worthy to be a justice of the peace" (Stuckley v. Bulhead, 4 Rep. 16).

[4] Van Tassel v. Capron, 1 Den. 250.

[5] Oakley v. Farrington, 1 Johns. 129.

[6] Palmer v. Edwards, Rep. Cas. Prac. in C. B, 160.

[7] Hillard v. Constable, Mo. 418.

[8] How v Prin, Holt, 652.

which action lies, since he is not thereby accused of any corruption in his employment, nor any ill design or principle; and it was not his fault that he was a blockhead, for he cannot be otherwise than his Maker made him; but if he had been a wise man, and wicked principles were charged on him when he had them not, an action would have lain, for, though a man cannot be wiser, he may be honester than he is." "If a person," he continues, "be in a place of profit, and he is accused of insufficiency, he shall have remedy by action; 'tis otherwise if he be only in a place of honor; though, even there, if he is charged with ill principles, and as disaffected to the government, he shall have an action for such scandal to his reputation." To say of a judge that he was a corrupt judge,[1] or that a particular sentence delivered by him was corrupt,[2] is actionable. In Waldin v. Mitchell,[3] it was said that, where a man had been in an office of trust, to say that he behaved himself corruptly in it, as it imported great scandal, so it might prevent his coming into that or the like office again, and therefore was actionable.[4] But the authority of the two latter cases is much weakened by what DeGray, C. J., says in Onslow v. Horne,[5] "I know of no case where ever an action for words was grounded upon eventual damages which may possibly happen to a man in a future situation, notwithstanding what the Chief Justice throws out in 2 Vent. 266. . . . . I think the Chief Justice went too far." There

[1] Birchley's Case, 4 Rep. 16.

[2] Cæsar v. Carseny, Cro. Eliz. 305.

[3] 2 Vent. 306.

[4] Cramer v. Riggs, 17 Wend. 209; and see 7 Id. 204; Wilson v. Noonan, 23 Wis. 231; Littlejohn v. Greeley, 13 Abb. Pr. 41; Walden v. Mitchell, 2 Vent. 266.

[5] 3 Wils. 188; and see Hellard v. Constable, Mo. 418; 2 Palmer v. Edwards, Rep. Cas. Prac. in C. B. 160.

is no doubt, however, that an action of libel would lie, if such an imputation as the above were written or printed and published.

73. Language falsely imputing to one in office any malfeasance or want of integrity—such as would impair public confidence in him,[1] or with want of capacity for the duties of the office he holds,[2] or with having committed a breach of the public trust is actionable[3]—the language must clearly appear to affect him in his office. In the cases just cited, however much the personal character of the justice was aspersed, nothing was alluded to which would make him less useful as a justice; neither would it be actionable to declare that he had tried a case that was not within his jurisdiction.[4]

But if the charge be that he made the office of clerk of his court a matter of private negotiation,[5] or that he procured one to take false oaths;[6] or if it consist of words that necessarily imply corruption generally,[7] it would be actionable *per se*.[8] Charges that a judge took a bribe,[9] or is false,[10] or is forsworn, and not fit to sit upon a bench;[11] that he has acted unjustly in

[1] Lansing v. Carpenter, 9 Wis. 340.

[2] Townshend on Slander and Libel, § 196; Robbins v. Treadway, 2 J. J. Marsh. 540.

[3] Kinney v. Nash, 3 N. Y. 177, and cases cited.

[4] Oram v. Franklin, 6 Blackf. 42; but see Carter v. Andrews, 16 Pick. 1; Stone v. Clark, 21 Pick. 51.

[5] Robbins v. Treadway, 2 J. J. Marsh. 540.

[6] Chetwind v. Meeston, Cro. Jac. 308.

[7] Chaddock v. Briggs, 13 Mass. 253; Chipman v. Cook, 2 Tyler, 456; Aston v. Blagrave, 1 Strange, 617; 2 Ld. Raym. 1369; Kent v. Pocock, 2 Str. 1168.

[8] Townshend on Slander and Libel, § 196.

[9] Lindsey v. Smith, 7 Johns. 360; Colton's Case, Mo. 695.

[10] Wright v. Moorhouse, Cro. Eliz. 358.

[11] Carn v. Osgood, 1 Levinz, 280; S. C., Kerle v. Osgood, 1 Vent. 50; and see Pepper v. Gay, 2 Lutw. 1288; Stuckley v. Bulhead, 4 Rep. 16 a, 19 a; Lassels v. Lassels, Mo. 401; Hollis

his office,[1] or that he is partial,[2] or half-eared, and will hear but one side, or that he cannot hear of one ear,[3] or that he perverted justice,[4] or made use of his office to worry one out of his estate,[5] or to say that "he did seek my life, and offered ten shillings to the under-sheriff to impanel a jury that might find me guilty,"[6] would be actionable.

74. Words imputing an attempt to commit a felony, as "He sought to murder me, and I can prove it;"[7] or a hiring or solicitation of another to commit a crime, are actionable.[8]

The charge of a crime, in the vulgar language, is sufficient to ground an action. It is not necessary that the words should impute the crime in the technical terms known to the law; all that is requisite being, that the intention to charge the plaintiff with its commission, should plainly appear.[9]

Whether defamatory words are uttered or printed, the ordinary sense of them is to be taken to be the meaning of the person who uses them. However, if anything can be shown to have taken place which

v. Briscoe, Cro. Jac. 58; Burton v. Tokin, Cro. Jac. 143; Beamond v. Hastings, Cro. Jac. 240.

[1] Isham v. York, Cro. Car. 14.

[2] Kemp v. Housgoe, Cro. Jac. 90.

[3] Masham v. Bridges, Cro. Car. 223, and Alleston v. Moor, Het. 167.

[4] Delaware v. Pawlet, Mo. 409.

[5] Newton v. Stubbs, 3 Mod. 71.

[6] Bleverhassett v. Baspoole, Cro. Eliz. 313.

[7] Cro. Eliz. 308; Lewknor v. Cruchley, Cro. Car. 140.

[8] Tibbott v. Haynes, Cro. Eliz. 191; 4 Coke, 16; Cro. Eliz. 747; Lady Cockaine's Case, Cro. Eliz. 49; Id. 710.

[9] See Coleman v. Goodwin, 2 B. & Cr. 285, note; and Francis v. Roose, 3 M. & W. 191. See also Hankinson v. Bilby, 16 M. & W. 442; Woolnoth v. Meadows, 5 East, 463; Cf. Sweetapple v. Jesse, 5 B. & Ald. 31; see also Hob. 126; Cro. Eliz. 250, 496; 1 Roll. Abr. 74; and 4 Rep. 13.

may give a peculiar character to the expressions used, evidence of it may be given.[1]

Where slanderous words complained of—"Thou art a thievish rogue, for thou hast stolen my faggots" —were spoken by the defendant's wife, who, as a married woman, could not have possessed the property in the faggots, the court held the words to be actionable—understanding them, according to c mmon intendment—to mean a charge of having stolen her husband's faggots.[2]

On the same footing as an imputation of an indictable offense, stands the imputation of being, at the time the imputation is made, afflicted with an infectious or contagious disease, which would cause the person who had it to be shunned by society, such as leprosy, or the *lues venerea*.[3]

In the case of words spoken which would not otherwise be actionable, but which become so when they are, without justification, spoken of a person in respect of his profession, office, trade, or calling (provided it be not an unlawful one), and have a tendency to injure him in respect thereof, the law implies "actionable damage" without proof of any:[4] *à for-*

[1] See *per* Pollock, C.B., Daines v. Hartley, 3 Exch. 200; 18 L. J. 81, Ex.; and cf. Hankinson v. Bilby, *ubi supra;* Tempest v. Chambers, 1 Stark. 68; Tomlinson v. Brittlebank 4 B. & Ad. 630; Harvey v. French, 1 C. & M. 17; Thompson v. Bernard, 1 Camp. 48; Christie v. Powell, Peake's Cas. 4; 4 Rep. 13.

[2] Stamp v. White, Cro. Jac. 600. See also Charnel's Case, Cro. Eliz. 279. The doctrine as to repugnancy, laid down in 7 Bac. Abr. 296, 1 Roll. Abr. 74, cannot now be considered law (see sect. 61 of the C. L. P. A., 1852).

[3] 7 Bac. Abr. 266; Holt. 653; Cro. Eliz. 214, 289, 648; Cro. Jac. 144, 430; 1 Vin. Abr. 488; Carslake v. Mapledorum, 2 T. R. 473; Str. 1189; Bloodworth v. Gray, 7 M. & G. 334.

[4] Foulger v. Newcomb, L. Rep., 2 Ex. 330; 16 L. T. N. S. 596; 36 L. J. Ex 169

tiori, if the injurious imputation is conveyed by writing or printing, the defamation being, in this case, punishable criminally as well as by action. So, also, in the case of any unfounded imputation against a person who is in the enjoyment of an office, either public or private, whether of honor, profit, or trust; which imports a charge of unfitness to administer the duties of that office, is a libel.[1]

If the office is merely one of honor—as that of justice of the peace—the oral imputation, according to the old authorities,[2] must be of want of integrity, or charge a criminal breach of duty: an allegation of incompetency or want of ability is not, of itself, sufficient to ground an action of slander.

It by no means follows, however, that in any of the cases mentioned, if the words had been written down, they would not be actionable as libelous.

The following additional cases, where words have been held to be slanderous, although no special damage was alleged, may be rapidly glanced at. Saying that the plaintiff had done an act for which the defendant could transport him:[3] saying, "If you had your deserts, you had been hanged before now:"[4] saying that the plaintiff had murdered his first wife by administering improper medicines to her for a certain complaint,[5] using the words, "I am thoroughly convinced that you (the plaintiff) are guilty (innuendo of the death of D.), and rather than you should go without a hangman, I will hang you:"[6] saying that the

[1] *Vid.* Buller, N. P. 4, 5.

[2] Bill v. Neal, 1 Lev. 52; How v. Prin, 652; 3 Saulk. 694.

[3] Curtis v. Curtis, 10 Bing. 477.

[4] Cro. Eliz. 62.

[5] Ford v. Primrose, 5 D. & R. 287.

[6] Peake v. Oldham, Cowp. 275, 2 W. Bl. 960; and see Button v. Hayward, 8 Mod. 24.

plaintiff was "a returned convict:"[1] that he had been "in gaol and tried for his life, and would have been hanged had it not been for L., for breaking open the granary of farmer A., and stealing his bacon:"[2] that he had been "in gaol, and burnt in the hand for coining;"[3] though in none of the three last mentioned cases was there any imputation of present or future liability to punishment; imputing bigamy to the plaintiff's wife,[4] saying either that the plaintiff or his wife kept a bawdy house;[5] saying any of the following things: "You robbed me, for I found the thing you have done it with."[6] "He (the plaintiff) is a thief, and robbed me of my bricks;"[7] "He robbed J. W.;"[8] "You are a rogue, and broke open a house at Oxford;"[9] "You are a rogue, and I will prove you a rogue, for you forged my name;"[10] charging the plaintiff with having committed embezzlement,[11] or receiving goods, knowing them to be stolen,[12] calling him a "pickpocket,"[13] "or

[1] Fowler v. Dowdney, 2 M. & Rob. 119.

[2] Carpenter v. Tarrant, Rep. Temp. Hardwicke, 339.

[3] Gainford v. Tuke, Cro. Jac. 536.

[4] Heming v. Power, 10 M. & W. 564; Delaney v. Jones, 4 Esp. 191.

[5] Cro. Eliz. 643; 1 Roll. Ab. 44; 1 Buls. 138; 7 C. B. N. S. 114.

[6] Rowcliffe v. Edmonds, 7 M. & W. 12; 4 Jur. 684.

[7] Slowman v. Dutton, 10 Bing. 402. See also Baker v. Pierce, Ld. Raym. 959; Holt, 654; 6 Mod. 23; Cro. Jac. 687.

[8] Tomlinson v. Brittlebank, 4 Barn. & A. 630; 1 N. & M. 455.

[9] Jones v. Herne, 2 Wils. 87.

[10] See Williams v. Stott, 3 Tyr. 688; 1 C. & M. 675.

[11] Alfred v. Farlow, 8 Q. B. 854; 15 L. J. 260, Q. B. See Briggs' Case, God. 157.

[12] Stebbing v. Warner, 11 Mod. 255; overruling 3 Salk. 326.

[13] Holt v. Scholefield, 6 T. R. 691. See also Ceeley v. Hoskins, Cro. Car. 509; Roberts v Camden, 9 East, 93.

accusing him of subornation of perjury;"[1] saying of the plaintiff, who was one of four Commissioners appointed by the Court of Chancery to examine witnesses and hear and determine a suit, "Sir G. M. (the plaintiff) is a corrupt man, and hath taken bribes of R. K." (one of the parties to the suit); "R. K. hath set Sir G. M. on horseback, with his bribes to pervert justice and equity,"[2] bribery having been an offense at common law punishable by indictment or information; saying at a Parliamentary election of the plaintiff, who was one of the candidates, "These guineas are Mr. B.'s (the plaintiff's) money, and were given me to vote for him; he has bought my vote, and he shall have it."[3]

To accuse a person of having committed fornication was also held to be actionable, whilst the statute making that a temporal offense was in force;[4] and so, it seems, was saying, "Thou art a witch and a sorcerer," whilst the statutes against witchcraft remained in operation.[5]

The law is the same if the imputation be made, not directly, but by means of words of suspicion, as (with reference to a crime of arson), "I cannot imagine who should do it but S.;"[6] or, "I do not doubt but within two days to arrest H. for suspicion of

[1] Harris v. Dixon, Cro. Jac. 158.

[2] Moor v. Foster, Cro. Jac. 65.

[3] Bendish v. Lindsay, 11 Mod. 194. See Purdy v. Stacey, Burr. 2699.

[4] Mo. 142; 1 Vin. Abr. 435. See also Smith v. Wisdome, Cro. Eliz. 348.

[5] Hext v. Yeomans, 4 Rep. 15; Poph. 210; 3 Bulst. 262.

[6] Web v. Poor, Cro. Eliz. 569. According to the old authorities, if the charge be of killing a person who is not really dead, an action cannot be maintained. See Snag v. Gee, 4 Rep. 16; Talbot v. Case, Cro. Eliz. 823; 1 Vent. 117.

felony;"[1] or, "I will call him in question for poisoning my aunt, and I make no doubt to prove it;"[2] or by repeating a story heard from another, as "A woman told me that she heard some one say that M., his wife, had poisoned G., her first husband, &c.;"[3] and though it should be only in alternative words, as that "either the plaintiff or somebody else" committed the offense;[4] or that A. or B. did it,"[5] or that a plaintiff was perjured.[6]

To say "Thou art as very a thief as any in Warwick goal," no thief then being in the goal, would not be actionable, but if a thief is in the goal at the time, the words would be actionable.[7] To call a man a "frozen snake" is slanderous, "For," says Coleridge, J.,[8] "we ought to attribute to a jury an acquaintance with ordinary terms and allusions, whether historical, figurative, or parabolical. If an expression, originally allegorical, has passed into such common use that it ceases to be figurative, and has obtained a signification almost literal, we must understand it as it is used. The term "frozen snake," has an application very generally known, which is calculated to bring into contempt a person against whom it is directed. If, therefore, a publication imputes to a person that his friends, who have been assisting him, have realized in him the fable of the frozen snake, it is for a jury to say whether these words do not convey an imputation of ingratitude to friends and benefactors, and if they do, they are action-

[1] Harrison v. Thornborough, 10 Mod. 196.
[2] Wiseman v. Wiseman, Cro. Jac. 107.
[3] Anon. 2 Sid. 21.
[4] Rogers v. Gravat, Cro. Eliz. 571.
[5] See Cro. Eliz. 645; Mo. 408.
[6] Somers v. House, Holt's Rep. 39.
[7] Fenn v. Dixe, Jo. 444, pl. 5.
[8] Hoare v. Silverlock, 12 Q. B. 624.

able." Similarly "lame duck,"[1] as applied to a broker; "black sheep,"[2] as applied to an attorney; "dirty slut,"[3] as applied to a school-mistress; and "hermaphrodite,"[4] as applied to a woman, are equally slanderous.

It is sometimes slanderous merely to repeat what one says of himself. A man is entitled to his own opinion of himself, and yet his neighbors may not repeat it. It is no defense to an action for libel to show that a ludicrous narrative in a newspaper concerning the plaintiff, was only a repetition of a story told by the plaintiff of himself; "for there is a great difference between a man's telling a ludicrous story of himself, to a circle of his own acquaintance, and a publication of it to all the world through the medium of a newspaper."[5] But while one may not use words tending to injure a man in his business reputation, it does not seem to be always scandalous to speak disparagingly of his wares.[6]

Calling a woman by lewd name, and thereby questioning her chastity, was formerly not actionable, except in the cities of London or Bristol, because of the custom which obtained there, to "cart" women of that description.[7] Neither, formerly, was it slanderous to say

[1] Morris v. Langdale, 2 B. & P. 284; Robinson v. Marchant, 72 B. 918.

[2] Barnet v. Allen, 3 H. & N. 381.

[3] Wilson v. Runyon, Wright, 651.

[4] Malone v. Stewart, 15 Ohio, 315. But it seems this was not slanderous in England in 1656. (*Vid.* Weatherhead v. Armitage, 2 Leving, 233.)

[5] Cook v. Ward, 6 Bing. 409, 415. And see Abshire v. Cline, 3 Ind. 115.

[6] Fenn v. Dixe, Jo. 444, pl. 5. And see *post*, as to libels of things.

[7] Robertson v. Powell, 2 Selw. N. P. 1224; Alsop v. Alsop, 5 Hurl. & N. 534; Power v. Shaw, 1 Wils. 62. "The common law is not very tender of women in respect to defamation. This is probably for the reason that women themselves are

of a spinster that she "was *enciente*," or that she had had a child, unless she was about to be married, and loses her marriage in consequence, or suffers other pecuniary damage.[1]

always uttering slanders, and are practically as irresponsible as children for the consequences" (Albany Law Journal, Feb. 21, 1874). By the Scotch law, however, the oral imputation of unchastity to a woman is actionable without proof of special damage (Borthwick's Law of Libel, p. 185); and such is the law in the state of New York. As to the charge of unchastity generally, see Ranger v. Goodrich, 17 Wis. 78; Rogers v. Lacey, 23 Ind. 507; Frisbie v. Fowler, 2 Conn. 707; 1811, McGee v. Wilson, Litt. Sel. Cas. 187; Smalley v. Anderson, 2 Monr. 56; Spencer v. M'Masters, 16 Ill. 405; Moberly v. Preston, 8 Mis. 462; Stieber v. Wensel, 19 Mis. 513; Malone v. Stewart, 15 Ohio, 319; Wilson v. Robbins, Wright, 40; Wilson v. Runyan, Id. 351; Sexton v. Todd, Id. 317; Terry v. Bright, 4 Md. 430; Sidgreaves v. Myatt, 22 Ala. 617; Berry v. Carter, 4 Stew. & Port. 387; Shields v. Cunningham, 1 Blackf. 86; Worth v. Butler, 7 Id. 251; Rodeburg v. Hollingsworth, 6 Ind. 639; Linck v. Kelley, 25 Ind. 278; Blinkenstaff v. Perrin, 27 Ind. 527; McBrayer v. Hill, 4 Ired. 136; Snow v. Witcher, 9 Id. 346; Watts v. Greenlee, 2 Dev. 115; Freeman v. Price, 2 Bailey, 115; Beardsley v. Bridgman, 17 Iowa, 290; Cleveland v. Detweiler, 18 Id. 299; Cox v. Bunker, Morris, 369; Dailey v. Reynolds, 4 G. Greene, 354; Freeman v. Taylor, 4 Iowa, 424; Smith v. Silence, Id. 321; Byron v. Elmes, 2 Salk. 693; W. v. L., 2 Nev. & M. 204; Eliot v. Ailsbury, 2 Bibb, 473; Keiler v. Lessford, 2 Cr. C. C. 190; Falkner v. Cooper, Carth. 55; Cavel v. Birket, Sid. 438; *contra*, Hicks v. Hollingshead, Cro. Car. 261; Buys v. Gillespie, 2 Johns. 115; Smalley v. Anderson, 2 Monr. 56; Rickett v. Stanley, 6 Blackf. 169; Joralemon v. Pomeroy, 2 N. Jersey, 271; Dailey v. Reynolds, 4 Greene, 354; Woodbury v. Thompson, 3 N. Hamp. 194; Stanfield v. Boyer, 6 Har. & J. 248; *contra*, Miller v. Parish, 8 Pick. 384; Walton v. Singleton, 7 S. & R. 449; Heard on Libel, p. 46; Ayre v. Craven, 2 Adol. & El. 2; 4 Nev. & M. 220; Evans v. Gwyn, 5 Q. B. 844; Lucas v. Nichols, 7 Jones' Law, No. Ca. 32; Brooker v. Coffin, 5 Johns. 188; Adecock v. Marsh, 8 ed. 360; Underhill v. Welton, 32 Verm. 40; Guard v. Risk, 11 Ind. 156.

[1] Davis v. Gardner, 4 Co. 166, p. 11.

Charging a woman with having a venereal disease is actionable, because it causes her to be shunned,[1] but charging her with having had such a disorder is not actionable, because it is no reason why her company should be avoided.[2] But to imply incontinence to a woman who held a copyhold *dum castra vixerit* is actionable.[3]

An action will lie for charging a person with being a returned convict.[4]

[1] Williams v. Holdridge, 22 Barb. 376.

[2] Eastlake v. Mapledoran, 2 T. R. 473; Bloodworth v. Gray 8 Scott, N. R. 9.

[3] Boys v. Boys, Sid. 214.

See also Robertson v. Powell, 2 Selw. N. P. 124, and Davis v. Gardiner, 4 Co. 16, 6, p. 11.

"Falstaff.—Go to—you are a woman—go!

"Dame Quickly.—Who, I? I defy thee. I was never called so in mine own house before!"

[4] Fowler v. Gardiner, Q. M. & Rob. 118. A writer in the "Albany Law Journal" (Feb. 21, 1874), discusses the inconsistency—as he says—of the law of defamation. Referring to Villiers v. Mansley, 2 Wils. 403, where it was held libelous to publish of a man "that he stank of brimstone, and had the itch," he says: "Now why this distinction between the convict and the man with the itch? The convict is not contagious; having once been apprehended, he cannot be caught again; and wherein, therefore, is the immorality of the latter charge greater than that of the former? The law tries to get around this by saying that slander 'is always for the loss of character, and not the danger of punishment' (Van Ankin v. Westfall, 11 Johns. 233). But is it, really? If it is, why make words charging a felony actionable, in themselves, while others, although imputing as deep moral degradation, are not? Old Coke had a more plausible explanation. Commend us to the ancients for ingenious injustice. He said: 'There is this difference of scandal in the past tense, when it touches the mind and when it touches the body. If it be a scandal to the mind and affections—as perjury, felony, &c.—then the mind that remains is slandered; but if it be of an accidental infirmity or disease of the body, it is otherwise, for none now will forbear his company, though he had the plague in times past' (Smith's Case, Noy. 127). We fear Coke was and is practically right;

So far we have been considering what spoken words will be deemed slanderous; and we have seen that the law will construe them strictly by the inquiry as to what damage they have done to, and what loss, positive or prospective, may have been sustained by the person against whom they are spoken.

But when the slanderous words come to be written down in black and white, the matter becomes more serious. The law will no longer construe them by the question of mere damage, but will hold the fact of their being written to be *prima facie* proof of the deliberation and malicious motive of their perpetrator.

The slander, upon publication, becomes libel, and an offense, not only against the party libeled, but against the public peace.

75. When merely oral, they might have been measured by their source, or by the audience to whom they were addressed.[1] Once written they may pass, no

'none now will forbear his company though he had' any disgraceful disease 'in times past.'" But we think, if the learned gentleman will look again, he may possibly discover that the law is quite consistent in the matter—the charge of the itch, being written, and so libel; while the charge of having been a convict, was spoken, or slander, which may have constituted the difference.

[1] In the old reporters we find many cases in which the culture and degree of intelligence of the auditors in whose presence an alleged slander was uttered, was taken into the account in construing whether it was slander or not (Kennedy v. Gifford, 19 Wend. 296; Ausman v. Veal, 10 Ind. 355; Fen v. Dixe, Jo. 444, pl. 5). This famous case of Tom Fenn's beer, it seems to me, is open to criticism. The defendant said: "I will give my mare a peck of malt, and lead her to the water and let her drink, and she shall piss as good beer as any Tom Fenn brews." This was held not to be actionable, because it is i possble that the words should be true in any man's understanding. But if to say of a lawyer that "he hath no more law than Master Cheyny's bull," and Cheyny hath no bull, i actionable, because equivalent to saying that he is no

one knows whither; he who was their source can no longer control them; "for who," says the philosopher "can recall the written word?" and it is equally impossible to know where they may find their audience. All publications are libelous which hold a man up to such scorn and ridicule as might reasonably be supposed to be liable to provoke him to a breach of the peace.[1] "In a libel," says Best, C.J.,[2] "any tendency to bring a party into contempt or ridicule is actionable; and, in general, any charge of immoral conduct although in matters not punishable by law."[3]

"If any man," says Wilmot, C.J.,[4] "deliberately or maliciously publishes anything in writing concerning another which makes him ridiculous, or tends to hinder mankind from associating or having intercourse with him, an action well lies against such publisher." "Scandalous matter is not necessary to make a libel; 'tis enough if the defendant induces an ill opinion to be had of the plaintiff, or makes him contemptible and ridiculous."[5] "In case upon a libel, it is sufficient, if

lawyer (1 Siderfin, 327), are not the words uttered of Tom Fenn actionable, because equivalent to saying that his beer is all water? It seems to us to be the poorest compliment possible to Mr. Fenn's beer.

Although something depends upon the intelligence of the hearer, the same does not seem to be true of the person making the charge. Thus, where one said of a jeweler, "He is a cozening knave in selling me a sapphire for a diamond," it was held actionable. It would seem that one who does not know a sapphire from a diamond is indeed stone-blind (Albany Law Journal, February 28, 1874).

[1] Holt L. L. 213; Parmiter v. Coupland, 6 M. & W. 108.

[2] Archbishop of Tuam v. Robeson, 5 Bing. 21.

[3] Clement v. Chivis, 9 B. & C. 172; Churchill v. Hunt, 1 Chit. 480.

[4] Villiers v. Monsley, 2 Wils. 403.

[5] Cropp v. Tinley, 3 Salk. 226.

the matter be reflecting, as to paint a man playing at cudgels with his wife."[1]

Nor will one be permitted to slander or libel his neighbor by way of joke. It is no defense to say that the defamatory matter was uttered in jest, and not in earnest, and that the utterer did not expect to be believed.[2] It is related of Sergeant (afterward Lord Chancellor) Maynard, however, that, he having once brought a suit for slander against a man who said "that a client gave the sergeant a basket of pippins, and that each pippin had a gold piece for a core;—and then the other side came to him and gave him a roasting pig, within which, in place of dressing were fifty broad gold pieces more,"—although the sergeant had a verdict in his favor, judgment was arrested in consequence of the actionable words being discovered to be "the burden of an old story," which "used to be told of Noy and all the cock lawyers of the west, and had been repeated by the defendant of Maynard, the reigning cock, as mere merriment over ale, without intent to slander."[3]

But drunkenness although not, from policy, a de-

[1] Per Holt, J., 11 Mod. 99. See also People v. Croswell, 3 Johns. Ch. 337, 354; State v. Southwick, 9 Id. 214; Cooper v. Greeley, 1 Duer, 347; Root v. King, 7 Cowp. 613.

[2] Hatch v. Potter, 7 Ill. (2 Gilm.) 725; McKee v. Ingalls, 5 Ill. (4 Scam.) 30; Long v. Eakle, 4 Md. 454; Donohue v. Hayes, Hayes, J. Ex. 265. And see Hawkins, Pl. C. 356, § 13; 2 Stark. Ev. 464; Wood's Civil Law, 247; Holt on Libel, 230, 291; Moore, 627; 9 Coke, 59.

[3] Campbell's Lives of the Lord Chancellors, Mallory's edition, vol. iv. ch. civ. 433; Life of Guilford, i. 235. When the suit was tried before Lord Chief Justice North, when the story of the pippins came out, "those were golden pippins," quoth the judge; and when the pig was mentioned, "that's good sauce to a pig," quoth the judge. See Percy Anecdotes, "The Bar."

fense[1] would probably be matter in mitigation.[2] Olivia uttered very good law when she said "there is no slander in an allowed fool,"[3] for fools and madmen are tacitly exempted from all laws.[4]

76. The writing will not lose its libelous character although disguised in bad spelling,[5] initials[6] hieroglyphics,[7] bad grammar;[8] or because constructed in the form of an allegory,[9] an anagram,[10] or a rebus,[11] or a caricature,[12] because the persons it libels are designated by fictitious names,[13] or by the locality in which a class of

[1] McKee v. Ingalls, 4 Scam. 30; Reid v. Harper, 25 Iowa, 87.

[2] Howell v. Howell, 10 Ired. 84; Isley v. Lovejoy, 8 Blackf. 462; Gates v. Meredith, 7 Ind. 440.

[3] Twelfth Night, i. 5. "*Oli.*—There's no slander in an allow'd fool, though he do nothing but rail."

[4] Townshend on Slander & Libel, 434; City of London v. Vanacker, Carthew, 483; Horner v. Marshall, 5 Munf. 466; Bryant v. Jackson, 6 Humpf. 199; Yeates v. Reed, 4 Blackf. 463; Dickinson v. Barber, 9 Mass. 225. Perhaps delirium tremens, which is a species of insanity, would be a defense, if one wrote a libel while laboring under an attack of that distemper. (Maconnehey v. State, 5 Ohio, N. S. 77; O'Brien v. People, 48 Barb. 275.)

[5] Rex v. Edgar, 2 Sess. Cas. 29, Pl. 33.

[6] Holt on Libel, 235; Read v. Huggonson, Salk. 470.

[7] Townshend on Slander & Libel, § 133, note.

[8] Cornelius v. Van Slyck, 21 Wend. 70; Borthwick on Libel, 142.

[9] Holt on Libel, 245.

[10] Id.

[11] Id.

[12] Mezzaro's Case, 2 City Hall Recorder, 113; Du Borst v. Beresford, 2 Camp. 812· 1 Wood's Inst. 445; Holt on Libel, 244.

[13] Ryckman v. Delavan, 25 Wend. 186; Mix v. Woodward, 12 Conn. 262; State v. Jeaudell, 32 Penn. St. 475. So that the libel is brought home (Van Vechten v. Hopkins, 5 Johns. 211; Gibson v. Williams, 4 Wend. 320; Morgan v. Livingston, 2 Rich. 573; Miller v. Butler, 6 Cush. 71; Leonard v. Allen, 11 Id. 241; McLaughlin v. Russell, 17 Ohio, 475; Good-

persons to which the person libeled belongs, reside, or congregate;[1] or by the order to which he belongs.[2] "Common sense is not to be deemed a stranger to legal process, but as very influential in ascertaining the force and effect of words and sentences which, although technical, are to receive a sensible construction," said Parker, Ch. J. "All the libelers of the kingdom now know," said Lord Hardwicke, so far back as 1742, "that printing initial letters will not serve their turn, for that objection has been long got over."[3]

On the same footing as written or printed libels, stand those which are published by means of pictures, prints, or caricatures; and it is as libelous to paint a man with a fool's cap and bells, or with horns, or asses' ears, as it is to openly call him by the names that those signs imply.[4]

So, too, where an indictment was demurred to on the ground that, by reason of its bad spelling, it was unintelligible, and wanted a meaning. The libel as set out in the indictment was as follows: "Here is there cockels in this place (meaning cuckolds), we now (meaning know) them well, he (meaning Lambert) is a nave (meaning knave), he cheats and rongs (meaning wrongs) the county, and is the cur of a son of a whore;" the indictment was held good, Raymond, Ch. J., saying: "The present libel is plain to all men and easily to be understood, and it would be hard that

rich v. Davis, 11 Metc. 473; Goodrich v. Stone, Id. 486; Allensworth v. Coleman, 5 Dana, 315; White v. Sayward, 33 Me. 322; Smaley v. Stark, 9 Ind. 386).

[1] Ryckman v. Delavan, 25 Wend. 186; Le Faun v. Malcomson, 1 H. L. C. 637.

[2] Harrison v. Bevington, 8 C. & P. 807; Morchtand v. Cadell, 4 Paton, 385.

[3] Commonwealth v. Runnels, 10 Mass. 518.

[4] Mezzaro's Case, *ubi supra.*

a court of justice must not understand it is badly spelt, when all the world besides make no scruple to find the signification of the words."[1]

In a case where a great portion of the libel consisted of insinuations by means of questions, Alderson, B., directed the jury that "if a man insinuates a fact in asking a question, meaning thereby to assert it, it is the same thing as if he asserted it in terms." The libel in that case containing the following passage, "We should be glad to know how many popish priests enter the nunneries at Scorton and Darlington each week? and also how many infants are born in them every year, and what becomes of them? whether the holy fathers bring them up or not, or whether the innocents are murdered out of hand or not?" The learned judge told the jury that if they thought that the defendant, by asking the questions, "meant to insinuate and to state that infants are born in the nunnery at Scorton, and that holy fathers bring them up or murder the innocents," then it was a libel on those persons.[2] And said Cowen, J.,[3] "one cannot protect himself from an action by the mere grammatical construction of the phrase."

In a case *De Libellis Famosis*,[4] it was held, that a "*famosus libellus sine scriptis* may be *picturis*; as, to paint the party in any shameful and ignominious manner." "In case upon a libel," says Holt, Ch.

[1] Rex v. Edgar, 2 Sess. Cas. 29; 5 Bac. Abr. tit. Libel, 199.

[2] Gathercole's Case, 2 Lew. C. C. 255; Hunt v. Thimblethorpe, Moo. 418; 1 Vin. Abr. 429; Earl of Northampton's Case, 12 Rep. 134; Delany v. Jones, 4 Esp. C. 191; Woolnoth v. Meadows, 5 East, 463; Hemming v. Power, 10 M. & W. 564; Le Fanu v. Malcomson, 1 H. L. Cas. 664.

[3] Cornelius v. Van Slyck, 21 Wend. 70.

[4] 5 Cok. 125.

J.,[1] "it is sufficient if the matter be reflecting: as to paint a man playing at cudgels with his wife."[2] Lord Ellenborough, Ch. J., said of a libelous picture of a gentleman and his lady, which was entitled "La Belle et la Bête," that the person who exhibited it in public was "both civilly and criminally liable for having exhibited it."[3]

So a libel may be expressed by fixing a gallows or other reproachful or ignominious signs at a person's door, or elsewhere;[4] or, in general, by any insinuation upon him appealing to the eye of the community in which he lives.[5]

[1] Anon. 11 Mod. 99.

[2] According to Blackstone (in a statement omitted in the later editions of his "Commentaries"), in the case of signs or pictures it seems necessary to show not only the import and application of the scandal, but also "that some special damage has followed;" and he gives as a reason—that "otherwise it cannot appear that such libel by picture was understood to be leveled at the plaintiff, or that it was attended with any actionable consequences" (see 3 Com. 126). There appears to be no authority whatever for the proposition that, in the case of signs or pictures, special damage must be shown to have followed from the publication; and there is as little force in the reason assigned for making a distinction between libelous signs or pictures and written or printed libels; for the former tell their tale, in general, even more unmistakably than the latter (Shortt, L. Litt. 389).

[3] Du Bost v. Beresford, 2 Camp. 511. See also Austin v. Culpepper, 2 Show. 314; Skin. 123, where the defendant was held liable in an action for having forged an order of the court of chancery defamatory of the plaintiff, and drawn, on the bottom of it, the picture of a pillory, with the words subscribed, "For Sir J. Austin and his witnesses by him suborned" (Ib. Shortt, L. Lit. 390).

[4] 5 Coke, 125.

[5] See Jeffreys v. Dunscombe, 11 East, 226, where a lamp was set up in front of the plaintiff's house, and kept burning in the daytime, in order to defame him as the keeper of a bawdy-house; or by the custom known as "riding Skimmington." See Cropp v. Tilney, 3 Salk. 225, 226, and Bolton v.

77. It has been held libelous to publish of a protestant archbishop that he had attempted to convert a Roman Catholic priest (against whom a charge of seduction had been made), by offers of money and preferment;[1] of a person seeking charity that she preferred unworthy claims or squanders money in printing circulars;[2] or of the overseer of a parish that he paid paupers their weekly allowance in orders for flour upon a particular tradesman,[3] or to placard of an overseer that he advocated low rates when out of office, but high rates when in office, and that the defendant would not trust him with five shillings of his property.[4]

In another case where an action was held maintainable, the important part of the libel was, "I sincerely pity the man" (meaning the plaintiff) "that can so far forget what is due, not only to himself, but to others, who, under the cloak of religious and spiritual reform, hypocritically and with the grossest impurity, deals out his malice, uncharitableness, and falsehoods."[5]

It has also been held libelous to publish of any man that he has been guilty of gross misconduct, and insulted females in a barefaced manner.[6] The individual libeled in this case was a coachman, but the publication was not held libelous, because published of him in that capacity, the court considering it only necessary to inquire whether the publication in ques-

Dean, referred to by the court in Austin v. Culpepper, 2 Show. 314.

[1] Archbishop of Tuam v. Robeson, 5 Bing. 21.

[2] Hoare v. Silverlock, 12 Q. B. 624.

[3] Woodward v. Downing, 2 M. & Ry. 74.

[4] Cheese v. Scales, 10 M. & W. 488; cf. Warman v. Hine, 1 Jac. 820.

[5] Thorley v. Lord Kerry, 4 Taunt. 355.

[6] Chement v. Chivis, 9 B. & C. 192.

tion held up the plaintiff to public hatred, contempt, or ridicule; the imputation was a very serious and contumelious one, clearly calculated to bring the plaintiff into contempt by some persons, and hatred by others, and, therefore, according to established rule, the publication was libelous.

The publication in a newspaper, of a papagraph stating that, although the plaintiff was aware of the death of a lady occasioned by his furious and careless driving, he nevertheless, on the very evening of the catastrophe, attended a public ball, was held actionable.[1]

A publication alleging that a person has for years, without cause, systematically done everything to annoy another, and had unnecessarily dragged that other into the court of chancery and put him to great expense,[2] or that the plaintiff was ungrateful,[3] or of one who had been an attorney that when practicing, he had been guilty of "sharp practice,"[4] "cozener,"[5] "tan-money."[6] And courts have hesitated to take judicial notice of the meaning of the word "swindle,"[7] or that "hooked" is sometimes used to mean "stole,"[8] or "goose-house" to mean "brothel."[9] The word "wool-comber," however, does not need an innuendo to show it means one who buys wool to work with.[10] "Truck-

[1] Churchill v. Hunt, 1 Chitt. 480.

[2] Fray v. Fray, 17 C. B. N. S. 603; 34 L. J.; 45 C. P.

[3] Cox v. Lee, L. Rep. 4 Ex. 284; 21 L. T. N. S. 178; 38 L. J. 219 Ex.; Hoare v. Silverlock, 12 C. B. 624; 17 L. J. 306. Q. B.

[4] Digby v. Thompson, 4 B. & Ald. 821.

[5] Walcot v. Hind, Hutt. 14.

[6] Day v. Robinson, 1 Ad. & El. 554.

[7] L'Anson v. Stewart, 17 R. 748; but see Forrest v. Hanson, 1 Cro. Car. C. 63.

[8] Hays v. Mitchell, 7 Blackf. 117.

[9] Dyer v Morris, 4 Mis. 214.

[10] Anon., Lofft 322.

master," a word said not to be found in any dictionary, was used without an innuendo; it was left to jury to decide if used in libelous sense.[1]

The court, however, will inform itself of the meaning of words peculiar to a certain place.[2] And a defendant will be allowed to show what he meant by the words used,[3] or explanatory circumstances of time and place, known to both parties at the time the words were said, from which the court will construe the intent or malice of the speech.[4]

[1] Homer v. Taunton, 5 Hurl. &. Nor. 661.

[2] Parke, B., McGregor v. Gregory, 2 Dowl. N. S. 769; 11 M. & W. 287; Com. Dig. Act. for Defam. C.; Rolle Abr. 86; Hobart, 126; Pearce's Case, Cro. Car. 382; McGregor v. Gregory, 2 Dowl. N. S. 769.

[3] Tighe v. Cooper, 7 Ell. & Bl. 639; 4 Co. 14; Cro. Jac. 90; Kinnersly v. Cooper, Cro. Eliz. 168; Brittridge's Case, 4 Co. 18; Abrams v. Smith, 8 Blackf. 95; Coles v. Haviland, Cro Eliz. 250; Miles v. Van Horn, 17 Ind. 245; Rodeburgh v. Hollingsworth, 6 Ind. 339; Vin. Abr. Act. for Words, L. b. 7; Dimmock v. Fawset, Cro. Car. 393, pl. 5; Vin. Abr. Act. for Words, L. b. 6; Id. 4, 7.

[4] Explanatory circumstances known to both parties, speaker and hearer, are to be taken into the account as part of the words (Dorland v. Patterson, 23 Wend. 422; citing Andrews v. Woodmansee, 15 Id. 232; Miller v. Maxwell, 16 Id. 9; Heming v. Power, 10 M. & W. 569; Hankinson v. Bilby, 2 Car. & Kir. 440; 16 M. & W. 446; Perry v. Mann, 1 R. I. 263; Dole v. Rensselear, 3 Johns. Cas. 458; Aldrich v. Brown, 11 Wend. 596; Trabue v. Mays, 3 Dana, 138; Emery v. Miller, 1 Denio, 208; Thompson v. Bernard, 1 Camp. 48; Shecut v. McDowel, Const. Rep. 35; Christie v. Cowell, Peake, 4; Pegram v. Styron, 1 Bailey, 595; Beardsley v. Tappan, 1 Blatch. C. C. Rep. 588; Cooper v. Perry, Dudley, 247; Ceeley v. Hoskins, Cro. Car. 509; Norton v. Ladd, 5 N. H. 203; Stevens v. Handley, Wright, 123; Williams v. Cowley, 18 Ala. 206; Hays v. Mitchell, 7 Blackf. 117; Harrison v. Findlay, 23 Ind. 265; Robinson v. Keyser, 2 Foster (N. H.), 323; 2 Starkie on Slander, 85; Penfold v. Westcote, 2 N. R. 325; Christie v. Cowell, Peake's Cas. 4; Sel. N. P. 1250; Bissel v. Cornell, 24 Wend. 354; Watson v. Nicholas, 6 Humph. 174.

Again: the condition of things, as well as the meaning of words, may, in course of time, alter; and of the mutations in language courts will take judicial notice.[1]

For instance, in the time of Charles II., it was held actionable to say of a man that he was a papist, or that he went to mass,[2] while in the United States it has been held actionable to call one a "mulatto."[3] Though in the course of time the word "mulatto," may come to be no more a word of reproach than the word "papist" is to-day.

78. Nor will a libel be any the less actionable, if the defamatory imputation is made by reference or comparison—direct or indirect—to some character in history or fiction, or to some animal which suggests an injurious idea.

Thus, it was held a libel to publish, in a newspaper, of the plaintiff—who was an applicant for assistance from a charitable society—that her warmest friends, in giving up the advocacy of her claims, stated that they had realized the fable of the "Frozen Snake."[4] To an objection, grounded on the absence of an innuendo in the declaration, explaining the meaning of the allusion to the "Frozen Snake," Coleridge, J., replied:

[1] Holt on Libel, 43; Borthwick on Libel, 142; Harrison v. Thornborough, 10 Mod. 196; Beardsley v. Dibblee, 1 Kerr, 246; Vanada's Heirs v. Hopkins, 1 Marshall Ken. R. 287; Gibson, J., Bash v. Sommer, 20 Penn. St. R. 159; Pollock, C. B., Tozer v. Mashford, 6 Ex. 539; Beardsley v. Dibblee, 1 Kerr, 260; Foster v. Small, 3 Whart. 143; Bloss v. Tobey, 2 Pick. 320. Carth. 55; Holt, Ch. J., Baker v. Pierce, 6 Mod. 23.

[2] Row v. Clargis, Ld. Raym. 482; 2 Salk. 696; Walden v. Mitchell, 2 Ventr. 265; Cutler v. Friend, 2 Show. 140. But held otherwise in the reign of King James (Ireland v. Smith 2 Brown, 166).

[3] King v. Wood, 1 N. & M. (So. Car.) 184; Eden v. Legare, 1 Bay, 171; Atkinson v. Hartley, 1 McCord, 203; contra, Barrett v. Jarvis, 1 Hamm. 83, note.

[4] Hoare v. Silverlock, 12 C. B. 624; 17 L. J. 306 Q. B.

"The jury and court, in such a case as this, are in an odd predicament, if they alone of all persons are not to understand the allusion complained of. Suppose the libel had said that the plaintiff acted like Judas; must the history of Judas have been given and referred to by innuendo? We ought to attribute to a court and jury an acquaintance with ordinary terms and allusions, whether historical or figurative, or parabolical. If an expression originally allegorical, has passed into such common use that it ceases to be figurative, and has obtained a signification almost literal, we must understand it as it is used. Half of our language is founded upon allegorical allusion: "Vinegar is used in describing a bad temper; even the word 'sour' is figurative. We must understand such terms according to the sense which has become familiar." "Nothing is easier," said Erle, J., "than to bring persons into contempt by allusion to names well known in history, or by mention of animals to which certain ideas are attached; and I may take judicial notice that the words 'Frozen Snake' have an application very generally known indeed, which application is likely to bring into contempt a person against whom it is directed."[1]

See also a case where part of the libel consisted in a comparison of the conduct of the plaintiff, an attorney, in reference to a particular case, with that of the firm of Quirk, Gammon, and Snap, in the novel of "Ten Thousand a Year."[2]

So where a newspaper copied a libelous paragraph from another newspaper, and added the word "fudge" at the end of it, Lord Lyndhurst, C.B., on the trial of an action of libel against the publisher, left it to the

[1] Hoare v. Silverlock, 12 Ad. & El. N. S. 624.

[2] Woodgate v. Ridout, 4 F. & F. 206.

jury to say with what motive the paragraph was copied, and what was meant by the addition of the word "fudge;" if that word were added only for the purpose of making an argument at a future day, it would not take away the effect of the libel.[1] And, accordingly, courts will take judicial cognizance of the meaning of words and idioms in the vernacular language,[2] and no innuendo will be necessary to point out their meaning. But otherwise as to expressions which have not become idiomatic, such as "milk your purse,"[3] "bogus peddler,"[4] "shooting out of a leather gun."[5]

79. But absurd and ridiculous and preposterous charges that are impossible, and in the truth of which no rational person will believe, will not be held libelous. As, for instance, to charge that a woman had a litter of pups by a dog.[6] Though the court will undoubtedly take into consideration the discrimination or common sense of the persons to whom the scandalous matter was communicated,[7] or their peculiar relations to or dealings with the person slandered;[8] as, for in-

[1] Hunt v. Algar, 6 C. & P. 245.

[2] 1 Greenl. Ev. § 5; 6 Vin. Ab. 491, Pl. 6, 7, 8; Tit. Court C.; Hoyle v. Cornwallis, 1 Stra. 387; Page v. Faucet, Cro. El. 227; Harvey v. Brand., 2 Salk. 626; Elam v. Badger, 23 Ill. 498; Forbes v. King, 1 Dowl. P. C. 672; Hoare v. Silverlock, 12 Adol. & Ell. N. S. 624; Homer v. Taunton, 5 Hurl. & Nor. 661; Edgar v. McCutchen, 9 Missouri, 768; Ashley v. Billington, Carth. 231; Vin. Abr. Act. for Words, S. a. 12.

[3] King v. Lake, 2 Ventr. 18.

[4] Pike v. Van Wormer, 6 How. Pr. 101; 5 Id. 175; and see Forbes v. King, 1 Dowl. 672.

[5] Harman v. Delaney, 2 Stra. 898.

[6] Kennedy v. Gifford, 19 Wend. 296. This statement, however, was held to be libelous, upon other grounds. And see Fen. v. Dixe, Jo. 444, pl. 5; Harper v. Delph., 3 Ind. 225.

[7] Id.

[8] Wyatt v. Gore, Holt, 299; Ward v. Smith, 6 Bing. 749; Keene v. Ruff, 1 Clarke (Iowa), 482; Schenck v. Schenck, 1

stance, if they be spoken in a foreign tongue, it must be shown that the audience understood the foreign tongue.[1]

80. Not only the living but the dead can be subjects of libel. Although the person defamed be dead, the libel is, nevertheless, punishable; for it stirs up others of the same family, blood, or society, to revenge and to break the peace.[2] The chief cause for which the law so severely punishes all libels is, says Hawkins,[3] the direct tendency of them to a breach of public peace, by provoking the parties injured, and their friends and families to acts of revenge, which it would be impossible to restrain by the severest laws, were there no redress from public justice for injuries of this kind, which of all others are most sensibly felt. And so histories, biographies, or memoirs, published at long intervals after the death of their subjects, might be so scandalous and prurient as to be actionable;[4] but, in such cases, the intent to libel must be proved.[5]

It was held libelous to publish an obituary notice, as follows: "On Saturday evening died of the small-pox at his house in Grosvenor Square, Sir Charles Gaunter Nicoll, Knight of the Most Honorable Order of the

Spencer, 208; Wenman v. Ash, 13 Com. B. 836; and see Mills v. Monday, Lev. 112; De La Croix v. Thevenot, 2 Stark. C. 63.

[1] Amann v. Damm, 8 Com. B. N. S. 597. But where words are spoken in German, in a German county, it will be presumed they were understood (Bechtell v. Shaler, Wright, 107; and see 1 W. Saund. 242, n. 1; Keene v. Ruff, 1 Clarke [Iowa], 482; Danvers Abr. 146, pl. 1, 2; 2 Starkie on Slander, 52; Fleetwood v. Curley, Hob. 267; Viner's Abr., tit. Actions for Words, A. b.; 2 Stark. Ev. 844; Holt on Libel, 245; Cro. Eliz. 496, pl. 16).

[2] P. C. Book 1, c. 28.

[3] Co. 5, 124, C.

[4] See a query as to the somewhat celebrated Greville Memoirs, Albany Law Journal, March 13, 1875.

[5] Rex v. Topham, 4 T. R. 126.

Bath, and representative in Parliament for the town of Peterborough. He was blessed with an ample fortune, which he enjoyed in a manner that rendered him, in early years of life, a truly valuable husband and friend. He could not be called a friend to his country, for he changed his principles for a red ribbon, and voted for that pernicious project, the excise."[1]

In the case, however, of libels on the dead, the intention of the person publishing must be shown to have been malevolent; for, to say that the conduct of a dead person can at no time be canvassed—to hold that, even after ages are passed, the conduct of bad men cannot be contrasted with the good—would, in the words of Lord Kenyon,[2] be to exclude the most useful part of history; "and, therefore," said that learned judge, "it must be allowed that such publications may be made fairly and honestly. But let this be done whenever it may, whether soon or late after the death of the party, if it be done with a malevolent purpose, to vilify the memory of the deceased, and with a view to injure his posterity, as in Rex v. Critchley, then it comes within the rule stated by Hawkins; then it is done with a design to break the peace, and then it becomes illegal."[3] And so, again, it

[1] Rex v. Critchley, cited 4 T. R. 129.

[2] Rex v Topham, 4 T. R. 129.

[3] Id. For the reasons thus stated by Lord Kenyon, the court of king's bench, in 1791, held bad, after a verdict of guilty, an indictment charging the defendant that he, "wickedly and maliciously contriving and intending to injure, defame, disgrace, and vilify the memory, reputation, and character of George Nassau Clavering, Earl Cowper, then deceased, and to cause it to be believed that the said earl in his lifetime was a person of a vicious and depraved mind and disposition, and destitute of filial duty and affection, and of all honorable and virtuous sentiments and inclinations, and that the said earl had

would be libelous to publish an obituary notice of one whom the author knew to be alive.[1]

81. Not only persons, but things, fall under the protection of the law of words. Properly speaking, perhaps, a thing has no rights to be invaded, and no claims to any particular duties from persons. But for all that, it may be quite possible to injure a person, by speaking disrespectfully of a thing.

"I am far from saying," said Chief Justice Cockburn,[2] "if a man falsely and maliciously makes a statement disparaging an article which another manufactures or vends (although in so doing he casts no imputation on his personal or professional character), and

led a wicked and profligate course of life, and had addicted himself to the practice and use of the most criminal and unmanly vices and debaucheries, &c., wickedly, maliciously, and unlawfully did print and publish, and cause to be printed and published, in a certain newspaper called 'The World,' a certain false, scandalous, and malicious libel of and concerning the said Earl Cowper, &c., to the great disgrace and scandal of the memory, reputation, and character of the said Earl Cowper; in contempt, &c.; to the evil example, &c., and against the peace, &c." The court made absolute a rule to arrest the judgment, because the indictment did not allege that the libel had been published with an intent to create any ill blood, or to throw any scandal on the family and posterity of Lord Cowper, or to induce them to break the peace in vindicating the honor of the family (4 T. R. 129).—Shortt.

[1] McBride v. Ellis, 9 Rich. Law (S. C.), 313.

[2] Young v. McCrae, 3 Best & Sur. 264; though the chief justice suggests, further on in the same case, that such an action, however, might be more in the class of actions for false representations than actions of libel (Snow v. Judson, 38 Barb. 212; Benton v. Pratt, 2 Wend. 385; White v. Merrit, 7 N. Y. 352; Gallager v. Brunel, 6 Cowen, 346; Swan v. Tappan, 5 Cush. 105; Ingram v. Lawson, 6 Bing. N. C. 212; 8 Scott, 471; Hamilton v. Walters, 4 Up. Can. Q. B. Rep. O. S. 24). In Yates' Pleadings & Forms, 436, is the form of a plea to a declaration for slander of the plaintiff's ship (Evans v. Harlow, 5 Q. B. 624; Malachy v. Roper, 3 Bing. N. C. 371; 3 Scott, 723; Kerr v. Sheddon, 4 C. & P. 528).

thereby causes an injury and special damage is averred, an action might not be maintained."

A man may very naturally be injured by slandering his wares; as if, for instance, he be a manufacturer of those wares (possibly not if he merely sold them—since he could easily keep others not open to the disparagement). But if a book be unfairly criticised it may be libelous of its author, as we shall see presently in this chapter, and as will be further illustrated in the chapter on newspapers.

The rule will be, that whenever disparaging words spoken of an article become injurious to the owner or producer of the article, the ordinary rules of libel may be invoked by the person injured. But in all such cases, undoubtedly, a special damage must be shown.

One form in which a slander of things is of frequent occurrence and well known to the law, is what is technically spoken of as "slander of title." Slandering of title consists in publishing language not of a person or of a thing, but of a person's right to a thing, whether the publication be written or spoken,[1] there being no such thing as a libel of title; and such slander, to be actionable, must be malicious, false,[2] and be productive of special damage.[3]

[1] Malachy v. Roper, 3 Bing. N. C. 371; 3 Scott, 723

[2] Like v. McKinstry, 41 Barb. 186; aff'd, 4 Keyes, 397; Kendall v. Stone, 5 N. Y. 14, rev'g S. C., 2 Sandf. 269. There must be malice which the plaintiff must prove (Smith v. Spooner, 3 Taunt. 246; Hill v. Ward, 13 Ala. 310; Stark v Chetwood, 5 Kansas, 141; McDaniel v. Baca, 2 Cal. 326; Hargrave v. Le Breton, 4 Burr. 2422; § 87, *ante;* Linden v. Graham, 1 Duer, 670; Bailey v. Dean, 5 Barb. 297; Watson v. Reynolds, 1 Mo. and Malk. 1; Paull v. Halferty, 63 Penn. 46, and note 2, p. 315, *post; re*, Madison Ave. Bapt. Church, 26 How. Pr. 72).

[3] Kendall v. Stone, 5 N. Y. 14; Paull v. Halferty, 63 Penn. 46.

As will be seen from an examination of the cases cited in the notes, a case of slander of title generally arises where one's estate in lands or real property is so impeached as to cast a cloud upon his title, or to injure or prevent a sale of the property; but it may occur also in the case of personal property. So where, at a public sale of rye, the defendant attended, and in the presence and hearing of those assembled, said, "I forbid selling the rye; it is mine," in consequence of which persons were deterred from bidding, and the rye sold, for less than it otherwise would have done, it was held an action could be maintained.[1] Or, an action would lie for alleging that plaintiff's machines were an infringement on defendant's patents.[2]

And, similarly, where the author of a work sold the copyright to the defendant, who afterwards published a new edition, purporting to be edited by the author, but which contained mistakes and errors, it was held, if this was calculated to injure A.'s reputation as an author, he might maintain an action.[3]

It has been held slanderous to say that a newspaper has a low circulation,[4] but it is not without

[1] Like v. McKinstry, 41 Barb. 186; aff'd 4 Keyes, 397; and see Carr v. Duckett, 5 Hurl. & N. 783; Hill v. Ward, 13 Ala. 310; and slander of title to a slave; Ross v. Pines, Wythe, 71; Gutsole v. Mathers, 1 M. & W. 495; 1 Tyrw. & Gr. 694; Green v. Button, 1. Gale, 349; 2 C. M. & R. 707; 1 Tyrw. & G. 118; Malachy v. Soper, 3 Bing. N. C. 371; 3 Scott, 723; Rowe v. Roach, 1 M. & S. 304.

[2] Wren v. Wield, 14 L. R. 213 Q. B.

[3] Archbold v. Sweet, 5 C. & P. 219; 1 M. & R. 162.

[4] Heriot v. Stewart, 1 Esp. Cas. 437. See also Lattimer v. West. Morning News Asso., 25 L. T. N. S. 44.

"For instance, it would be slander to say of Jones, that he is a vulgar, ignorant, and scurrilous editor; but it would not be slanderous to say that Jones' newspaper is a vulgar, ignorant, and scurrilous journal. As experience shows, this may be a benefit rather than a detriment to Jones. One may, with-

the limits of criticism to say that a picture is a "mere daub."[1]

82. A comment upon a literary production, exposing its follies and errors, and holding up its author to ridicule, will not be deemed a libel," says Broom,[2] 'provided such comment does not exceed the limits of fair and candid criticism, by attacking the character of the writer unconnected with his publication. . . . . But if a person, under the pretense of criticising a literary work, defames the private character of the author, and, instead of writing in the spirit and for the purpose of fair and candid discussion, travels into collateral matter, and introduces facts not stated in the work, accompanied with injurious comments upon them, such person may become a libeler of the author, and liable to an action.[3]

out malice, securely say that Robinson's candles are short of weight; but not that Robinson makes his candles short of weight, for that would implicate him in a wicked business. The effect of both allegations may be the same so far as the sale of the candles goes, but not the same as to Robinson's character." —Albany Law Journal, Feb. 28, 1874, art. "Defamation."

[1] Thompson v. Shackell, 1 Mo. & Malk. 187; and as to an architect, see Soane v. Knight, Id. 74. This question will be more fully discussed, *post*, in chapter on Newspapers, which see.

[2] Leg. Max. 288.

[3] The case of Reade v. Sweetzer (6 Abb. Pr. 9, note), carefully discusses the question of libel in literary criticism, and its value seems to justify its insertion here at length:

This was a trial at circuit.

The action was brought by Charles Reade, an Englishman, residing in London, as author of a novel, "Griffith Gaunt," to recover $25,000 damages, for an alleged libel published in the "Round Table," a New York weekly paper.

The complaint, after stating the plaintiff's profession as an author, and averring his authorship of the novel, alleged that when, in pursuance of arrangements therefor with the author, the book "Griffith Gaunt" was in course of publication in the "Argosy," a London magazine, and in the "Atlantic Monthly," by Ticknor & Fields, of Boston, on the 9th day of

83. If one requests, dictates, or suggests defamatory matter to another, who publishes it, even though the latter alter the form or otherwise changes the

June, 1866, "the said defendants falsely and with malice, composed, and published in said newspaper, at the city of New York, called the "Round Table," as aforesaid, of and concerning the plaintiff as an author; and of and concerning him in his said profession, business or employment, and thereby to injure him in his said business or employment, an article containing the false, libelous, and defamatory matter following." There was set forth the notice published in the "Round Table," of "Griffith Gaunt," which charged that it was "one of the worst stories that had been printed since Sterne, Fielding and Smollett defiled the literature of the already foul eighteenth century;" that the book "is not only tainted with this one foul spot, it is replete with impurity, it reeks with allusions that the most prurient scandal-monger would hesitate to make;" and the article recommended that the publishers discontinue it, as unfit for circulation in families.

For a second cause of action, the plaintiff alleged the publication, on the 28th of July, 1866, of another article of similar tenor; and for a third cause of action, alleged that the defendant published, on the 11th of August, 1866, an article, entitled "Did Charles Reade write Griffith Gaunt?" which article asserted doubts as to whether the plaintiff was the real author of the work.

The complaint concluded as follows: "And the plaintiff further shows, that by means of the aforesaid wrongful acts and doings of the said defendants, he has been and is greatly prejudiced in his credit and reputation as an author as aforesaid, and brought into public scandal, infamy and disgrace, and otherwise greatly wronged and injured, in and by the aforesaid wrongful and malicious acts and doings of the said defendants, to the damage of the said plaintiff in the sum of twenty-five thousand dollars. Wherefore," &c.

The answer admitted the plaintiff was an author, denied his authorship of the novel in question, denied that the defendants published or owned the "Round Table," but alleged ownership of it by an "association." It admitted the publication of the articles in the "Round Table," and also that the innuendoes in the complaint were true as to persons and publications. It then alleged, that the articles complained of were just and honest criticisms of the novel, and privileged as such. It then justified the publication of the articles on

same in the publication, it seems that the former will be guilty of a libel.

Thus, where the defendant told the reporter of a

the ground that they were true. In mitigation of damages, it averred that the novel was identical in plot with two other novels previously published, and that parts of it were selections from other works. It closed with a general denial.

The cause was tried at the circuit, before Mr. Justice Clerke, and a jury.

Frederick Gallatin, *Elbridge T. Gerry*, and *William D. Booth*, for plaintiff.

H. F. Dimock, *W. C. Whitney*, and *Robert Sewell*, for the defendants.

Gallatin opened the case for the plaintiff, and the articles complained of were read in evidence.

George Vandenhoff, a professor of elocution, was then called by the plaintiff's counsel, and proceeded to read at length the novel, "Griffith Gaunt." After some portion of the book had been read:

Whitney, for the defendants, objected to the further reading, on the ground that the authorship of the book was not proven.

Gerry, for the plaintiff, insisted—I. The course pursued, is sanctioned by precedent (Strauss v. Francis, 4 Fost. & Fin. N. P. 939, 1107).

II. The book was properly read in evidence as part of the plaintiff's case, to prove malice in fact. Justification was pleaded, and in no other way could the jury judge of the truth or falsity of the articles, than by having the book before them.

III. The plaintiff would be shown to have been the author before his case was rested, and it was a mere question as to the order of proof.

IV. As to authorship, the two first articles complained of, and the innuendoes admitted by the answer to be correct, proved it.

Mr. Justice Clerke overruled the objection of non-proof of authorship, but excluded the further reading of the book, on the ground that the articles complained of were libelous on their face, and the book was proper only in rebuttal of the defense of justification.

The plaintiff then proved by two witnesses who had resided with the plaintiff at the time, and had seen him prepare the work for the press, that he was the author of the novel in question; that he was paid twenty dollars a printed page for it, by

newspaper a story defamatory of the plaintiff, saying that "it would make a good case for the newspaper," and afterwards gave the reporter a more detailed ac-

Messrs. Ticknor & Fields, and a still larger sum by certain English publishers; that it had passed through three editions, of 25,000 copies each, in America; that the plaintiff had been an author twenty years, and enjoyed a reputation, as such, equaled only by Charles Dickens.

Plaintiff further proved, by the printers of the "Round Table," that the articles complained of were received by them from the defendants, and inserted pursuant to their directions; that each of the numbers in question were printed and distributed three days before its date, and that over 3,700 copies of each was so printed and published.

Plaintiff then rested.

Dimock, for the defendants, then moved for a nonsuit on the following grounds:—I. The plaintiff, a foreigner, sues for injury to him as an author. Such a character has no recognized existence in our courts, even under the copyright law.

II. There is no sufficient proof that plaintiff is author of the novel reviewed.

III. The articles being written of the book, the plaintiff cannot recover without proof of special damage (Foot v. Brown, 8 Johns. 53; Tobias v. Harland, 4 Wend. 537; Cooper v. Stone, 24 Id. 442; Swan v. Tappan, 5 Cushing, 109).

IV. The articles were privileged as criticisms (Carr v. Hood, 1 Campb. 355, per Lord Ellenborough), and express malice must be proven to sustain this action (Lewis v. Chapman, 16 N. Y., 369). This is matter of law for the court (Cook v. Wildes, 5 El. & Bl., 340; Somerville v. Hawkins, 10 Com. B., 583; Taylor v. Hawkins, 16 Q. B. 308).

Mr. Justice Clerke.—In regard to the first objection made, that because Mr. Reade sued in a representative capacity, and as a citizen of a foreign state, he could not maintain this action, the point is untenable (Pisani v. Lawson, 6 Bing., N. C. 90; Tuerlote v. Morrison, Yelv., 198; Bulst. 134; Dows v. Maloney, 8 Abb. Pr. 329). Bonaparte sued a London printer, named Peltier, for serious charges made against him as a sovereign; and it was in that case that Mr. Mackintosh first came into prominence as an advocate. But here, Mr. Reade does not sue only as an author. In his complaint, he says he was greatly prejudiced in his credit and reputation as an author, and brought into public scandal, infamy, and disgrace. The disgrace must refer to him as a man (Lewis v. Walter, 4

count, for the express purpose of inserting it in the newspaper; whereupon the reporter, from the particulars thus furnished to him, drew up an account, which,

Dow. & Ry. 813). The copyright law makes no distinction of that sort at all. That law is intended solely to protect American authors in their right to the productions. As to the articles themselves, I hold, as matter of law, that they are libelous on their face; and hence not privileged, within the rule, as to criticisms. I do not think the other points taken by counsel tenable, and therefore deny the motion.

Sewall then opened the case to the jury for the defendants. The testimony of the defendants, under stipulation, was then read to the jury in their absence, to the effect that the "Round Table" was owned and organized by a corporation, called the "Round Table Association." It was established and conducted as a literary and critical paper. The defendants were shareholders in the organization. They had never known the plaintiff personally; they had known him only through his works; they never had any communication with him. Understood from the proprietors of the "Sunday Mercury" that "Griffith Gaunt" was offered for sale to them. When the articles complained of were published in the "Round Table," they believed them to be correct. Ticknor & Fields sent copies of the "Atlantic Monthly," containing chapters of "Griffith Gaunt," to the "Round Table," with a request that the editors would pass their critical opinion upon the numbers.

Whitney, for the defense, then offered in evidence of the "Evening Post," of June 26, 1866, as showing that other similar articles had appeared in other papers.

Gerry, for the plaintiff, objected—I. This article appeared subsequent to the defendants' articles, and hence they could not have known of it when they wrote them (Bush v. Prosser 11 N. Y. [Kern.] 361).

II. At best, it is only proof that other libels were published by other parties (Hager v. Tibbits, 2 Abb. Pr. 97; Lewis v. Walter, 4 B. & Ad. 611; De Crespigney v. Wellesly, 5 Bing. 392; Ward v. Weeks, 7 Id. 211).

Mr. Justice Clerke excluded the evidence.

Whitney, for defense, then offered two novels, entitled "Queen of Hearts," and "Eighth Commandment," written by the plaintiff, to show that "Griffith Gaunt" was a plagiarism, and that the plaintiff admitted that he was a plagiarist.

Gerry objected, that there was no such defense, and that the evidence offered was not admissible, even in mitigation.

after some slight alterations, not effecting the sense, were made in it by the editor, was published in the newspaper, the court held that what the reporter pub-

Mr. Justice Clerke.—I cannot see that the evidence is relevant. Nothing is more common than for standard authors of known repute to borrow ideas from others, and dress them in their own language. Shakespeare himself copied into his plays other stories, and many of his plays are based on Cynthia's novels. But the evidence may aggravate the damages, and I will admit it.

Whitney then offered 18 Howell State Trials, 1181, to show that a speech therefrom was copied *verbatim* in "Griffith Gaunt."

Gerry objected, on the ground that part of the novel was published subsequent to the articles, and cited Bush v. Prosser (*supra*).

Mr. Justice Clerke sustained the objection.

Whitney then offered a letter of the plaintiff's, published by the defendants in the "Round Table" after the publication of the articles entitled the "Prurient Prude."

Gerry objected—I. That the publication of this letter was the act of the defendant.

II. That the whole paper should be put in evidence.

Mr. Justice Clerke admitted the whole paper.

Whitney then called Richard H. Stoddart, who testified that he had been an author and literary man for twenty years, and that it was a common custom for authors having a book to write to employ others to aid them in compiling it, and that such fact being known would not damage their reputation.

Whitney then called Richard Grant White, who testified to the same in substance, and also that he had read "Griffith Gaunt," introduced it in his own family, and that its literary merits were very high.

Gerry, on cross-examination, asked the witness what was the reputation of Mrs. Henry Wood as an authoress in the literary world.

Whitney objected.

Gerry insisted that the evidence was competent to show malice against the plaintiff, because one of the articles complained of attacked also the character of Mrs. Wood. He cited Miller v. Rutler, 6 Cush. 71; Coddy v. Barlow, 1 Moody & R. 275.

Mr. Justice Clerke allowed the question, and the witness replied he had never heard it assailed.

lished in consequence of what passed with the defendant, might be considered as published by the defendant.[1]

Gerry then asked the following question: "Suppose an article should appear in a literary weekly paper having a circulation of over 3,700 copies per week, and that article should contain a charge against an author of the position in the literary world second only to that of Mr. Charles Dickens, with having published an article which was grossly impure, a book not merely tainted with one foul spot, but replete with impurity, reeking with allusions that the most prurient scandal-monger would hesitate to make—dealing throughout with vice so familiarly, so much as a matter of course, and with such an assumption of straightforwardness, as to divest it of all the repulsiveness it should wear; should state that he is an author of position and splendid talents, and then say these splendid talents only aggravate his offense, and render the story worse than the detailed proceedings of a *crim. con.* case by just the proportion in which his writings are more graphic and fascinating than newspaper reports; and state, in addition, that the publishers of the story have no right to introduce into thousands of virtuous families, and to children and girls whose parents accept it unquestioned on their indorsement, such reading; and should assert in addition, and finally, that such a book was only fit for the avowed organ of the '*demi-monde*;'—assuming an article of this description should appear in a weekly newspaper, of high authority in the literary world, what effect would it have on the character of an author so assailed?"

Counsel cited in support of his question, People v. Lake, 12 N. Y. (2 Kern.) 358.

Whitney objected, and the court excluded the question.

Whitney then proved by a publisher, that, after the libels, he had published an edition of "Griffith Gaunt," and sold sixty thousand copies, but neither he himself or any one had paid for it; also, that hardly any novel had ever sold so well.

After proving publication, in other papers, of the "Prurient Prude" letter, defense rested.

Gerry, in rebuttal, then offered to read in evidence an editorial article in the "Round Table" of October 15, 1866, being the same number of that paper in which was published

[1] Parkes v. Prevcoll, L. Rep. 4 Ex. 169; 20 L. T. N. S. 537; 38 L. J. 105 Ex.; 17 W. R. 773.

And where the defendant asked the editor of a newspaper to "show up" the prosecutor and his brother, telling him a ludicrous story concerning them;

the letter of Mr. Charles Reade, and which article was headed, "An English Bully." He proposed to read this, as showing the *animus* of the defendants, even after the libels had been published.

Sewell objected to the admission of this article, on the ground that anything tending to an aggravation of the original libel is not admissible, and cited Root v. Loundes, 6 Hill, 518, as showing that no other matter, which would itself sustain an action for libel, can be admitted, as then the plaintiff would recover twice for the same words.

Gerry cited Rustell v. Macquister, 1 Campb. 48, n.; Tate v. Humphrey, 2 Id. 73, n.; Lee v. Hudson, Peake N. P. 167; Chubb v. Westley, 1 Carr. & P. 436; and Code, § 93, to show that the statute of limitations had run, and the case relied upon by defendants' counsel did not apply.

Justice Clerke decided that the reading of the article in question might be admitted.

Both sides then rested.

Whitney summed up for the defense, and commented on the book "Griffith Gaunt," certain portions of which he read at length.

Booth, in summing up for the plaintiff, cited and referred to People v. Crosswell, 3 Johns. Cas. 393, as showing the distinction laid down by Chancellor Kent between the liberty and license of the press.

Gallatin, for plaintiff, requested the court to charge as follows:—I. Where, under guise of reviewing a book, a criticism attacks the author's character, it ceases to be privileged as such, and is actionable as a libel (Cooper v. Stone, 24 Wend. 434; Fry v. Bennett, 3 Bosw. 210; Cooke on Defam. 58; Stuart v. Lovell, 2 Starkie, 73; Greene v. Chapman, 4 Bing. N. C. 92; S. C., 3 Scott, 340; Strouse v. Francis, *supra*). The first two articles are within this rule.

II. Language of one in his trade or profession is actionable when it imputes to him fraud, misconduct, or want of integrity, in that profession or business; and the third article charges plaintiff with defrauding Ticknor & Fields (Baboneau v. Farrell, 15 C. B. 360; Bryant v. Loxton, 11 Moore, 344; Davis v. Davis, 1 Nott. & McC. 290; Fowles v. Bowen, 30 N. Y. 20).

III. The articles complained of, in substance, charge the

and the editor told the story to a reporter for the paper, and the story appeared in the paper, with comments added; the defendant, before the publication, having

plaintiff with being author of an obscene book. This alone renders them libelous, and actionable as such (Vielé v. Gray, 18 How. Pr. 550; Brooker v. Coffin, 5 Johns. 188; Rex v. Wilkes, 4 Burr. 2527; Rex v. Curl, 2 Strange, 788).

IV. A printer of a newspaper is bound to abstain from publications, which he knows to be libelous, with more than ordinary care. It is no apology for him that he is not the author; for he who wantonly publishes a libel, is as guilty, in the eye of the law, as he who writes it. The injury is done by the publication (Dexter v. Spear, 4 Mass. 116, per Story, J.; Burdett v. Cobbett, 5 Duer, 201; Sanford v. Bennett, 24 N. Y. 20).

V. If the jury believe that the tendency of the publications complained of was injurious to the plaintiff, the law presumes that the defendants, by publishing it, intended to produce that injury which it was calculated to effect (Haine v. Wilson, 9 Barn. & Cress. 643). (1.) In their verdict, they are not limited to the actual damage he sustained, but may give further damages, suited to the aggravated character the act assumed (Taylor v. Church, 8 N. Y. [4 Seld.] 460). (2.) And the original wrong has been aggravated by their defense of justification, in which they have wholly failed (Fero v. Ruscoe, 4 N. Y. [4 Const.] 162; Hunter v. Sharp, 4 Fost. & Fin. 992, per Cockburn, Ch. J.).

Sewell, for defendants, requested the court to charge the propositions, *supra*, on motion for nonsuit, and further—

V. If the jury find from the evidence that the articles were justified by the character of the novel "Griffith Gaunt," then, whether they were privileged or not, the plaintiff cannot recover.

VI. If the jury find for the plaintiff, they are not to award damages for supposable loss resulting to the plaintiff from the sale of the edition of the novel published after the libels, and for which he received no compensation.

Mr. Justice Clerke then charged as follows:

Gentlemen of the Jury:—Among the rights of perfect obligation, which alone the law undertakes to protect, that of reputation is one of the most prominent. Many men, unfortunately for the well-being of society, are totally regardless of principle, and are therefore totally regardless of reputation. But to every member of society who, differing from the

remarked on the delay, and, after the publication, expressed approbation of it, it was held that the jury (who had found the defendant guilty) might, on this

beasts that perish, is guided by principle, reputation is necessarily very precious. He is very sensitive in relation to it, and it would be most unwise as well as most unjust, not to offer him ample and efficient means of vindicating it when it is unjustly assailed. Accordingly, the law allows an action for the recovery of damages as means of redress for injuries in cases of defamation. It allows for oral defamation an action technically called an action of slander. For written defamation, or defamation by printing or pictures, it allows an action technically called libel. Our law, like the Roman law, recognizes a very marked distinction between spoken defamation, and defamation communicated by writing, printing, pictures, or signs. Matter calculated to cast ridicule upon a man, or to degrade him in the opinion of his acquaintances, or of the community, is libelous, if written, or printed and published, although, if only spoken, it may not be actionable. For instance, to accuse a man orally of being a liar, even in the presence of hundreds, is not actionable *per se;* but to say of him, in an article published in a newspaper, that he is a liar, is actionable, and no proof of special damage is necessary. A general oral charge even of having sworn falsely, without reference to material evidence given by the plaintiff at the trial of a cause, is not actionable in itself, but it is actionable to print and publish concerning a man, "Our army swore terribly in Flanders," as said Uncle Toby; and if Toby were alive now, he might say the same thing of some modern swearers. The man is no doubt swearing to an old story. A libel, then, as applicable to individuals, may be defined to be a malicious publication, expressed either in printing or writing, or by effigy, tending either to injure the memory of one dead, or the reputation of one alive, and expose him to public hatred, contempt, or ridicule.

The plaintiff, in his allegations in the complaint, first states that he is the author of a certain work called "Griffith Gaunt," and that certain articles published by the defendants are libelous. As these have been spread before you, I will not now read them. Two of them were to the effect that this work was calculated to demoralize society, to debauch public morals, and to contaminate the purity of the youthful mind. The third article accuses—but whether it amounts to an accusation you are to determine—that he allowed an obscure per-

evidence, find that the defendant authorized the publication of the particular libel, notwithstanding the comments added, and although it appeared that the

son to assume his name, and to pass off the book here as his original production. The first two are essentially different from the third. The former accuse him of writing and disseminating works calculated to debauch and demoralize the public mind, and the latter accuses him of what the plaintiff's counsel contends is absolutely an accusation of fraud. Now, in regard to the allegation in the complaint that Mr. Charles Reade is the author of "Griffith Gaunt," you have had the evidence of two witnesses who lived in London.
for five or six months. They saw the manuscript, saw him actually engaged in the composition of the work, and saw him hand over his original manuscript to his amanuensis, and saw him receive it back again from his amenuensis, then send it to the printers, then receive the proof, correct it, and send it back to them. It is scarcely necessary for me to say that, in my opinion—though you are to judge—the proof is ample as to the authorship. With regard to the first two alleged libels, have the defendants transcended the limits of allowable criticism in these two articles?

In criticising the productions of an author, the law allows considerable latitude. The interests of literature and science require that the productions of authors shall be subject to fair criticism; that even some animadversion may be permitted, unless it appears that the critic, under the pretext of reviewing his book, takes an opportunity of attacking the character of the author, and of holding him up as an object of ridicule, hatred, or contempt. In other words, the critic may say what he pleases of the literary merits or demerits of the published production of an author; but with respect to his personal rights, relating to his reputation, the critic has no more privilege than any other person not assuming the business of criticism. For instance, he may say that the matter is crude, forced, and unnatural; that it betrays poverty of thought, and abounds with commonplaces and platitudes, being altogether flat, stale, and unprofitable; and that its style is affected, obscure, and involved. He may say, as Burke said of the style of Gibbon, that it is execrable; but he cannot say that the author himself is execrable, or that he is personally affected, or absurd, or wayward. The critic has the same liberty, under the same restrictions, in relation to all people who come before the public for praise or censure. He may

editor had heard the story before the defendant told it to him.[1]

This rule has been carried so far as to extend to a

say of the orator who uses excessive gestulation and vociferation—mistaking extravagant action and verbosity for eloquence—that he has all the contortions, without any of the inspiration, of the Sybil. He can say of the player that he mouths his speech, as many players do, or that "he saws the air too much with his hand," or that he "tears a passion to tatters, to very rags, to split the ears of the groundlings"; but he cannot abuse him as "a robustious, periwig-pated fellow," and recommend that he should be "whipt for o'er-doing Termagant." The critic can call a painting a daub and an abortion; but he cannot call the painter himself a low,

[1] Rex v. Cooper, 8 Q. B. 533; 15 L. J. 206, Q. B. "If," said Lord Denman, Ch. J., "a man requests another, generally, to write a libel, he must be answerable for any libel written in pursuance of his request: he contributes to a misdemeanor, and is therefore responsible as a principal. He takes his chance of what is to be published. Here the defendant first desires the newspaper editor to 'show up' the prosecutor, and communicates to him the particulars of the story, which afterwards appear in the newspaper. Having given this general authority, he meets the editor, and says that the article has not appeared. That which did, in fact, form the foundation of the libel, and which the editor communicated to the reporter, was what the defendant communicated to the editor; and, after the publication, it was approved of by the defendant. It is observed that there were additions; but the editor said that what the defendant communicated was substantially what was published. If we held this not to be a publication by the defendant, we must go the length of exonerating a party who gives instructions for a libel, in every case where the libel published, departs from the instructions, by a single word. It is enough that there is a substantial identity. I have no doubt that a man who employs another generally to write a libel must take his chance of what appears, though something may be added which he did not state." Wightman, J., added: "It would be very dangerous to allow a man to direct a libel to be published on a particular subject, and, after he has approved of what is published, to defend himself on the ground that something has been added to his original communications."

party presiding at a public meeting, who requests the reporters present to "take notice of" a speech, or other portion of the proceedings; and, if, following

discreditable pretender, and an abortion. The most comprehensive freedom in animadverting upon the productions and actions of public men is essential to the very existence of civil and political liberty, and to the progress of civilization; and I heartily say with Lord Ellenborough, in Tabart v. Tipper, 1 Campb. 350—"Liberty of criticism must be allowed, or we should have neither purity of taste nor of morals. Fair discussion is essentially necessary to the truth of history and the advancement of science. That publication, therefore, I shall never consider a libel, which has, for its object, not to injure the reputation of any individual, but to correct misrepresentation of fact, to refute sophistical reasoning, to expose a vicious taste in literature, or to censure what is hostile to morality." But, gentlemen, although a critic may not have directly assailed the character of an author; or ridiculed his personal appearance, his manners, his voice; or exposed any eccentricities or defects of the man—may he not, nevertheless, defame and wound him in the most vital spot by imputing to him unworthy motives, and evil designs against the well-being of society, intimating that he infers these motives and designs from the sentiments expressed, and the characters delineated, in the work which he has undertaken to review? My own opinion, gentlemen, is, that many of the works of fiction which are published in this country are very pernicious in their effects upon public morality. Not that I think that fiction, in itself, is demoralizing—very far from it. The most instructive lessons in faith and morals have been conveyed through its instrumentality. The founder of Christianity himself did not disdain frequently to employ it. Indeed, it was his favorite method of moral and spiritual instruction. But in its very fascination consists its danger; and when we see the press teeming with productions of this kind, describing scenes and portraying characters calculated to corrupt the morals, and even weaken the mental stamina, of the multitude of novel readers who seem to be absorbed in this kind of reading, it will be prudent to allow considerable latitude of criticism in in relation to these productions.

There is one virtue which women of honor have not only always observed, but have tenderly and ardently cherished, and, I may say, adored. They esteem it as a sacred jewel—its price far above rubies; and the woman who is without it is

such suggestion, the matter be reported either verbatim or summarily, if the matter be libelous, he will be held to respond therefor.[1]

deemed lost to all virtue. The want of it disfigures her whole nature; and any community in which the want of it is prevalent, depend upon it, is on the rapid road to ruin. The tendency of many of the productions, to which I have referred, is to weaken the foundations upon which this virtue is based. They are almost as mischievous as the plays which abounded in the profligate reign of Charles II., when the foulest and most hideous corruption prevailed in the court and among the higher classes. I have often wondered that society escaped the destruction which that corruption was calculated to produce. I do not say that English novels are as mischievous in this respect as similar works of fiction published in France. For there, in such works, open adultery seems to be especially admired and honored. Unholy love, like unsanctified human reason, at a memorable period of its history, seems to be deified in that land. The writer who has contributed most toward this dreadful condition of things is a profligate woman, although she has shown some token of decency by assuming the name of a man. I make these observations, gentlemen, to show that, in dealing with this kind of literature, the critic

---

[1] Parkes v. Prescott, L. Rep. 4 Ex. 169; 20 L. T. N. S. 537; 38 L. J. 105 Ex.; 17 W. R. 773. In this action, which was brought against the chairman, and one E., a member of a board of guardians, for a libel published in a newspaper report of one of the meetings of the board, it appeared that a discussion having taken place at the meeting respecting the case of the plaintiff's daughter, then an inmate of the workhouse, and reporters of the local newspapers being present in the ordinary discharge of their duty, the defendant E. said "he hoped the local press would take notice of this very scandalous case," and requested the chairman to "give an outline of it," which was done accordingly. The chairman, in the course of his statement of the case, said: "I am glad gentlemen of the press are in the room, and I hope they will take notice of it;" to which E. added, "and so do I;" the chairman further expressing a hope that publicity would be given to the matter. The libel was contained in what was proved to be a correct but condensed summary of what took place at the meeting, published in a local newspaper, and containing matter defamatory of the plaintiff. The learned judge

Nor will it be a defense to an action for libel, that the libelous matter was received from another; even though it be accompanied with the name of the real author.[1]

should not be prevented from inferring the motives and designs of the author from the inevitable effect of his writings. Of course, if he imputes motives and designs which he was not warranted in imputing by any opinion or sentiments expressed, or any character delineated in the work, or from its general tone, he is liable, and must take the consequences, and the author is entitled to redress. To charge an author with

---

(Martin, B.) who presided at the trial was of opinion that there was not sufficient evidence for the jury of the publication of the libel by the defendants, and directed a verdict to be entered for them. A bill of exceptions was tendered to this ruling; and the majority of the court of exchequer chamber (Keating, Montague Smith, and Hannen, JJ.) held

---

[1] De Crespigny v. Wellesley, 5 Bing. 392. "We do not hesitate to say," observed Best, Ch. J., delivering the judgment of the court of common pleas, in this case, "that even if we were to admit, what we beg not to be considered as admitting, that in oral slander, when a man, at the time of his speaking the words, names the person who told him what he relates, he may plead to an action brought against him that the person whom he names did tell him what he related—such a justification cannot be pleaded to an action for the republication of the libel. If the person receiving a libel may publish it at all, he may publish it in whatever manner he pleases; he may insert it in all the journals, and thus circulate the calumny through every region of the globe. The effect of this is very different from that of the repetition of the oral slander. In the latter case, what has been said is known only to a few persons, and if the statement be untrue, the imputation cast upon any one may be got rid of; the report is not heard of beyond the circle in which all the parties are known, and the veracity of the accuser and the previous character of the accused will be estimated. But if the report is to be spread over the world by means of the press, the malignant falsehood of the vilest of mankind, which would not receive the least credit where the author is known, would make an impression which it would require much time and trouble to erase, and which it might be difficult, if not impossible, ever completely to remove. . . . .

We have already alluded to the old star-chamber doctrine that a libel could be published by sending a sealed letter; although that doctrine has long since

such motives and designs is a most serious imputation, and if it is unwarranted the critic has committed a grievous wrong, which money is scarcely capable of repairing. Undoubtedly, the criticisms complained of make these imputations against the plaintiff. That can scarcely be denied. I repeat, that it is not necessary for me to read these articles. I have no doubt you understand them. The jury have the right to determine—for it is plain that the articles are *prima facie* libelous—whether "Griffith Gaunt" is obnoxious to such imputations; and if so, you have the right to infer

---

that the ruling was incorrect, Byles and Mellor, JJ., dissenting.

It was contended, on behalf of the defendants in this case, that the words used by them did not amount to a request to the reporters to publish the proceedings, but were merely the expression of a wish or hope that they would do so, nor to an authority to publish the particular reports in the words in which they in fact appeared; but the majority of the court of error were of opinion that the facts proved afforded evidence

---

Of what use is it to send the name of the author with a libel that is to pass into a country where he is entirely unknown? The name of the author of a statement will not inform those who do not know his character, whether he is a person entitled to credit for veracity or not; whether his statement was made in earnest, or by way of a joke; whether it contains a charge made by a man of sound mind, or the delusion of a lunatic. . . . . If, without any allegation that its contents were true, or that the publisher had any reason to believe them to be true, we were to hold that these pleas were a justification, we should establish a mode by which men might indulge themselves in ruining the characters of any persons they might be disposed to calumniate. There will be no difficulty in getting wretches, who would be better off within the walls of a prison than they are without, to furnish such as will pay for them with any statements they may desire respecting the character of any person whatsoever." *Vid.* also M'Gregor v. Thwaites, 3 B. & C. 24; M'Pherson v. Daniels, 10 B. &. C. 263; Watkin v. Hall, 9 B. & S. 279; L. Rep. 3 Q. B. 396; 37 L. J. 125, Q. B.; 18 L. T. N. S. 561; Shortt, p. 423.

fallen before the advance of civilization, it is by no means impossible at the present day to publish a libel by means of a letter.

the culpability of the plaintiff, and the truth of the justification. I do not mean to examine the pages of the book before you. I hope you have read the whole, or a large portion of it. The three chief characters in the work are Griffith Gaunt, Caroline Ryder, and Mrs. Gaunt—once the beautiful Catharine Peyton. Griffith Gaunt is not, to my mind, a very attractive character. He is a rough, north-country squire. He is not prepossessing in his manners, or elevated in his mind, and there is nothing whatever about him calculated to excite the admiration of the virtuous and refined; and I am very much astonished that so charming a person as Catharine Peyton should have fallen in love with him. He was guilty of bigamy. But is there anything in the work itself to set off this crime? to make it alluring? and to induce others to follow his example? That is a proper consideration. Is he so fascinating in character, or has he any other qualities—any heroic qualities, any great intellectual or moral qualities—to set off his guilt, and to recommend it to others for an example? Are the circumstances, which are represented to have caused and to have attended his conduct, calculated to entice the

---

fit at all events to be laid before the jury, of a request by the defendants to the reporters to publish an outline or summary of the proceedings, and to publish the report in such a way as to show the conduct of the plaintiff to have been disgraceful; the disclosure to the local public of what was called the plaintiff's disgraceful conduct being the avowed object of the request made by the defendants to the reporters.

"I agree with the learned counsel for the defendants," said Montague Smith, J., in whose judgment Keating and Hannen, JJ., concurred, "that loose expressions of a mere wish or hope that proceedings should be published, would not be sufficient to fix liability on the defendants in cases like the present. I think the words must be of such a kind, and used in such a manner, as to satisfy the jury that they amounted to, and were, in fact, a request to publish. If the words do amount to such a request, and the publication be made in pursuance of it by the persons to whom it was addressed, then, it seems to me, the persons making such request would be responsible for the libelous matter so published. Whether the libelous matter published is in pursuance of, and in accordance with, the

So if a man write scandalous matter in a letter, knowing or designing that that letter shall fall into the hands of certain persons, he is publishing a libel

reader into an approval, not to say imitation, of it? His guilt is not described as the result of inherent, deliberate wickedness; of depravity—gratuitous and utterly selfish. Believing that his wife was false; maddened at the thought that one whom he had loved intensely, whom he had supposed to be the paragon of purity and honor, was a hypocritical wanton—he fled from her, far away, determined never to see her again. In his new and humble home he became, immediately after his arrival, grievously and dangerously ill, and would have died but for the devoted attention of a modest and pleasing maiden; and, persuading himself that he was forever freed from his wife, he went through the form of a marriage with this girl some time after his recovery. She devoutly loved and admired him, and, of course, thought he was bound to no other woman. In his delusion about his wife's supposed guilt, in his resolution never to see her again, and in his resignation to his new attachment, which he imagined he could not avoid, he seems almost like a man in the inexorable grasp of the destinies. Not quite an Œdipus indeed, although the tumult of his mind and the horrors of his condition are described with a

---

request, or a departure from it, and so unauthorized, would be a question to be considered on the circumstanees of the particular case. It is, of course, plain, that if a man gives a copy of his speech to another to publish, he is answerable as a publisher. It cannot be contended that he would not be equally answerable, if he desired a reporter to take down his speech as he delivered it, and to publish it. Then, can it make any difference in his liability that he requests the reporter, instead of publishing the whole speech, to make and publish an outline or summary of it? Surely, in reason and principle there can be none, where the request is acted on, and a correct outline or summary made and published. It was strongly urged, for the defendants, that they could not be liable, unless they authorized the libel in the very words in which it was published. If this argument is correct, then it must follow that a man could never be liable when he desired another to make and publish an outline or summary of a speech or writing; because such an outline or summary necessitates condensation, and consequent alteration of language. But the argument cannot, as it seems to me, be correct. The man who requests

to those persons. A sealed letter addressed to a wife containing a scandal on her husband, is a libel.[1] The delivery of a writing to another that he may read it,[2]

power scarcely inferior to that with which Sophocles, in his "Œdipus the king," "Œdipus at Colonus," and in his "Antigone," describes the unexampled miseries of a doomed family of victims. Still, Griffith Gaunt greatly erred; and unlike Œdipus, he was a conscious doer of disastrous deeds. Next we have Caroline Ryder. She is the very incarnation of sensuality; and she, like the man she fell in love with, had a ruddy face, a well-developed person, a well-developed chest, and, I think the author says, had fine teeth. But is there anything in her character which can give a gloss to her crimes, or make them worthy of imitation by the reader, whether young or old? Now, gentlemen, the mere delineation of a character in a novel, the mere setting forth of a certain kind of wickedness in a character, is not necessarily demoralizing. If that were the case, every man would be obliged to send away from his library real history. If fictitious history is not allowed to do what real history does, the novel would be entirely des-

---

another to make and publish an outline or summary of a speech, writing, or proceedings, must know that the words will be, to some extent, those of him who makes such summary or outline; and he must, therefore, be taken to constitute him an agent for the purpose, and be answerable for the result, subject always to the question whether the authority has been really followed. If this be not so, a man might become a libeler with impunity. Again, if the very words of the libel, and not its substance, are in these cases to be regarded, a man who gives the manuscript of a libel to an agent to print and publish, would not be answerable if, by accident or negligence, there were variations in some of the words, although not in the substance of the libel. . . . . In the result, I come to the conclusion that, on principle, it is correct to hold that where a man makes a request to another to publish defamatory matter, of which, for the purpose, he gives him a statement, whether in full or in outline, and the agent publishes that matter, adhering to the sense and substance of it, although the language be, to some extent, his own, the man making the

---

[1] Schenck v. Schenck, 1 Spencer, 208; Wenman v. Ash, 3 Com. B. 836; Mills v. Monday, Lev. 112.

[2] Wyatt v. Gore, Holt, 289.

or that he may copy it,—since he must read it as he copies it,—is a publication of that writing as to him.[1]

And where the libelous letter is written in one

titute of interest. I repeat, that the mere delineation of a character is not necessarily demoralizing.

Look at all the histories of ancient and modern times, the history of Thucydides, the biographies of Plutarch, and modern histories and biographies; they all represent real men, who were cruel, earthly, sensual, and devilish.

In modern times, we have only to go to the last century to look at the character of Catharine, empress of Russia. She certainly was much more wicked than Caroline Ryder, for she had a lover almost every week, and when she got tired of him, she killed him. But are we not to read the history of Russia in the reign of Catharine? Still there may be something else objectionable in this work beside the delineation of character. I only wish to impress upon you that the mere delineation of a vile or vicious character, unless it is presented to the reader in some seductive shape, does not make the author criminal, or liable to the charge of demoralizing society. You are to consider, also, whether all the events which the author states in any part of his work happened to them, were calculated to

request is liable to an action as the publisher. If the law were otherwise, it would, in many cases, throw a shield over those who are the real authors of libels, and who seek to defame others under what would then be the safe shelter of intermediate agents."

Byles and Mellor, JJ., dissented from the judgment in this case. Byles, J., very much doubted "whether the expression of a hope that the press would take notice of the case, or give publicity to it, or that the chairman would give an outline of the proceedings, amounts to an authority to publish in a newspaper defamatory and unjustifiable matter spoken at a meeting." The learned judge pointed out that the libel must be proved as laid; and that though a variance is now amendable, none was in this case asked for or made, or could be made so as to cure the objection that the evidence did not show what particular facts or what particular defamatory expressions were or were not authorized by the defendant. His lordship also remarked on the great difference between the authority which will make a man liable criminally for the acts of his

[1] Keene v. Ruff, 1 Clarke (Iowa), 482.

place and opened in another, it is a publication of the libel in the place where the letter is opened.[1]

One Gibbons wrote defamatory matter of one

encourage similar conduct in others. As to the third article, gentlemen, accusing the plaintiff of allowing his name to be given to the productions of others, and that this was fraudulent, I do not intend to dwell upon that. It has been shown by several witnesses that it is a very common practice for an author to allow his name to be used, when the materials, perhaps, are furnished by others, but that he usually superintends the work, revises it, and perhaps adds to it. They say that this is a very common practice, and is not considered dishonorable. If you believe this third article amounted really to a charge of that kind, I do not know that there is anything libelous in it. It is for you to determine, however. If you believe it to be a dishonorable practice, you should find it to be libelous.

The next inquiry is as to the damages.

You have a right to consider whatever injury in mind the plaintiff has sustained by these charges, and you may go even

---

agents and that which will make him liable civilly; a principal not being civilly liable unless the agent duly pursues his authority, though liable criminally even where the agent has widely deviated from the authority. Mellor, J., said: "I think that in order to make a man responsible for a report printed and published by a third person, it ought to be shown that he had seen or heard or dictated the report himself, or approved of the libelous statements therein. . . . . I think that in order to support the allegation that the defendants caused to be printed and published the libels set out in the declaration, there ought to have been evidence of a communication, either verbal or written, of the entire substance of the libel to the reporter, as the libel to be published; or that either before or after the publication thereof, the defendants sought to be charged saw and approved of the particular libel; and that, inasmuch as in the present case the expressions used only in-

---

[1] Rex v. Johnson, 7 East, 65; Rex v. Middleton, Str. 77; Keene v. Ruff, 1 Clarke (Iowa), 482; Rex v. Watson, 1 Camp. 215; Rex v. Girdwood, East's P. C. 1116, 1120; Case of the Seven Bishops, 4 State Trials, 304; Rex v. Burdett, 4 B. & A. 717; 2 Starkie on Slander, 39–43; Commonwealth v. Blanding, 3 Pick. 304.

Trumbull, and had fifty copies printed in pamphlet form in Massachusetts. Forty-five copies he retained, and five copies he sent to his wife in New Jersey, indorsing four of them with the names of certain persons, acquaintances of the wife, but without instructing his wife to dispose of them. The wife delivered two of the copies in New Jersey to the persons whose names were indorsed thereon, and the others she delivered in New Jersey to Trumbull, who exhibited them to various persons. On Trumbull suing Gibbons in New York for libel, it was held that there was a publication by defendant within the State; that the delivery of the manuscript to be printed was a publication, although a delivery to a wife in confidence would not be a publication; the wife acted as the agent of her husband, and her delivery of the pamphlets amounted to a publication by the defendant.[1]

further; you may consider what he is entitled to as compensation for his wounded character, if it has been wounded; and you have a right to consider what injury hereafter he may suffer, for I hold that prospective damages are allowable in this action. They have been allowed in several instances, and I think it may be considered as settled that they may now be awarded, when they are incident and accessory to the action, and where no separate action can be maintained for them. The jury found a verdict for the plaintiff, and assessed the damages at six cents. And see the recent case of Johnson v. The (London) Athenæum (Athenæum, April 3, 1875), which will be examined *post*, in the chapter on Newspapers.

---

dicate a wish that gentlemen of the press present would notice the case, or call attention to it, or give publicity thereto, leaving the mode and manner to the absolute discretion of the reporters, I am of opinion that my brother Martin was justified in holding the evidence not to be sufficient to be submitted to the jury in support of the issue joined upon the pleadings" (Shortt).

---

[1] Trumbull v. Gibbons, 2 City Hall Recorder, 97

But throwing a sealed letter, addressed to the plaintiff or a third person, into the enclosure of another, who delivers it unopened to the plaintiff himself, is not a publication,[1] nor is sending to the person whom the writing concerns a sealed letter a publication; a letter always being understood to be sealed up, unless otherwise expressed.[2]

So sending letters to various persons, announcing to them that a certain person is a scoundrel or a cheat,[3] or circulating postal cards upon which scandalous or scurrilous matter is written is libelous.[4] Sending a defamatory letter sealed up is no publication of a libel.[5] But if the sender read it to a third person before sending it, such reading constitutes a publication.[6] But sending a libelous letter, unsealed, by a messenger, if the messenger do not read it, there is no publication.[7] A libel might be, undoubtedly, published by telegraph; in which case the liability of the telegraph company as publishers might be analogous to the liability of a newspaper, whose agents receive, publish and give circulation to defamatory matter written by another for reward.[8] The modern invention of the postal card is one by

[1] Fonville v. Nease, Dudley (S. C.), 303.

[2] Lyle v. Clason, 1 Cai. 581; Phillips v. Jansen, 2 Esp. 625; 1 W. Sand. 132 (note).

[3] See Note 2, *post*, p. 202.

[4] Chamberlain's Case, U. S. C. C., S. D. N. Y. 1874.

[5] Lyle v. Clason, 1 Cai. 581.

[6] Snyder v. Andrews, 6 Barb. 43; McCombs v. Tuttle, 5 Blackf. 431; Van Cleef v. Lawrence, 2 City Hall Recorder, 41.

[7] Clutterbuck v. Chaffers, 1 Stark. R. 471; Say v. Bream, 2 Moo. & R. 54. Nor where a writing is sent to the plaintiff, and he, in the presence of a third person, repeats the contents of such writing to the writer, who admits having sent it, this is not a publication of the writing to the third party (Fonville v. Nease, Dudley (S. C.), 303).

[8] No such case, however, appears to have been reported.

which a libel could be circulated with very small trouble and expense to the libeller, and to the great damage and injury of the person libeled. A postal card, carrying defamatory matter, will be regarded by the law as libel in a particularly aggravated form, and punished with great severity not only by indictment,[1] but, in a civil suit, probably, with exemplary damages.[2]

84. Libel may also be published by means of a theatrical representation, and courts will enjoin the performance of a dramatic production which is intended as a libelous caricature of a citizen, upon his bill.[3] And these observations, it seems, will apply to an actor.[4] Even a historian might possibly be construed to be a libeler.[5]

85. A libel may sometimes be conveyed by a mere carelessness and inaccuracy of detail in a published work. Thus, where the writer of a treatise on the "Law of Attorneys" referred in his book to the case of the plaintiff, as that of an attorney who had been

[1] People v. Chamberlin, U. S. Dist. Court, S. D. N. Y. *Vid. post*, vol. I., p. 510.

[2] Crane v. Walker, *post*, Id.

[3] *Post*, vol. II., chapter on Dramatic Copyright.

[4] Broom Leg. Max. 321.

[5] The son of McLauren, the distinguished mathematician, felt aggrieved by Goldsmith's statement, in his History of Animated Nature, that the senior McLauren was subject to fits of yawning, so violent as to render him incapable of proceeding in his lectures; and, although the senior McLauren and Goldsmith were both dead, yet the son bullied the publisher into canceling the offensive leaf. Dr. Johnson did not approve this course, but said, "it is of much more consequence that truth should be told than that individuals should not be made uneasy," and declared that the "uneasiness which a man feels on having his ancestor calumniated," is "too nice" (Boswell's Life of Johnson, Pickering's ed. vol. 3, p. 12).

For a more extended discussion of this species of libel, see chapter on Newspapers, *post*, vol. II.

struck off the rolls, whereas he had only been suspended for two years, as appeared from the very report of the case cited by the writer, the court, after pointing out to the jury the important distinction between the two punishments, and that the misstatement was an unintentional mistake, left it to them to say whether it was a reasonably fair statement of the report, or whether it was a mistake arising from want of reasonable diligence and care.[1]

A corporation is a person in law. It may have a reputation, which is part of its capital,[2] and therefore be the subject of a libel. Or it may entertain malice, and be itself a libeler of others. Though, as a corporation can only act by its agent, it cannot, of course, be guilty of slander, since that crime cannot be vicariously committed.[3] In the case of a libel, as both authors and publishers are always liable,[4] the corporation has no such escape.[5] They can sue or pros-

[1] Blake v. Stevens, 11 L. T. N. S. 544; 4 F. & F. 239.

[2] Abshire v. Cline, 3 Ind. 115; Long v. Brougher, 5 Watts, 437; Smith v. Wyman, 4 Shep. 13; Lewis v. Black, 27 Miss. 425; Snow v. Witcher, 9 Ired. 346; Ingham v. Lawson, 5 Bing. N. C. 60 (this latter was a case of a libel on the plaintiff's ship); Trenton Ins. Co. v. Perrine, 3 Zabris. 402.

[3] Maloney v. Bartley, 3 Camp. 210; Hecker v. De Groot, 15 How. Pr. 314. There can be no agency in a crime (Lowenstein, 54 Barb. 305; Reg. v. Bull, 7 L. T. 8).

[4] Rex v. Drake, Holt, 425; Rex v. Paine, 5 Mod. 163; Rex v. Bear, Carth. 407; Rex v. Williams, 2 Camp. 646; Dale v Lyons, 10 Johns. 461; Cochran v. Butterfield, 8 N. H. 115; Dexter v. Spear, 4 Mason, 115; Watts v. Fraser, 7 Car. & P. 369; Frescoe v. Miay, 2 F. & F. 23; Miller v. Butler, 6 Cush. 71.

[5] Phil. R. R. Co. v. Quigley, 21 How. U. S. R. 202; Aldrich v. Printing Press Co., 9 Minn. 133; Lawless v. Anglo Egyptian Cotton Co., Law Rep. IV. Q. B. 262; Maynard v. Fireman's Ins. Co., 34 Cal. 48; Latimer v. West. Morn. News Co., 25 Law Times, N. S. 44. In New York by statute (Laws 1860, ch. 90). Whitfield v. South-East. R. R. Co., 1 Ell. B. & E. 115;

ecute for a libel of themselves, upon proof of special damage, though not otherwise.[1] But a voluntary association, not chartered or organized under any general law, could not maintain an action,[2] and so no action would lie by the members of a voluntary organization known as "No. 12 Hose Company," against one who published, with other defamatory matter, that his hat had been "stolen by some of the members of No. 12 Hose Company."[3]

86. An exception arises just here in regard to what are called private publications. It is a well-known principle of the common law, that a communication made *bona fide* upon any subject-matter in which the party making it has an interest; or in reference to which he has, or honestly believes that he has, a duty, is privileged; if made to person or persons who have, or honestly believe they have, a corresponding interest or duty, is privileged accordingly; a bishop's charge to his clergy has been held privileged, although containing matter which would have been otherwise libelous;[4] and injurious reflections on the

Alexander v. N. East. R. R. Co., 34 Law Jour. Rep. N. S. 152, Q. B.; 11 Jurist, N. S. 619. Exemplary damages against a corporation (Jefferson R. R. v. Rogers, 28 Ind. 1).

[1] Townshend on Slander & Libel, 263.

[2] Giraud v. Beach, 3 E. D. Smith, 337.

[3] Id.

[4] Laughlin v. Bishop of Sodar. & Man., 4 L. R. P. C 495. 9 Moore P. C. C. N. S. 318; 42 L. J. P. C. 11; 21 W. R. 214; 28 L. T. N. S. 377, *sed vid. aliter;* Gournley v. Plimsoll, 42 L. J. C. P. 121; 8 L. R. C. P. 362; 21 W. R. 683; Dawkins v. Lord Rokeby, 8 L. R. Q. B. 255; 42 L. J. Q. B. 63; 21 W. R. 544; 28 L. T. N. S. 134; Exch. Cham. Hart v. Gumpach, 4 L. R. P. C. 439; 42 L. J. P. C. 25; 21 W. R. 365; 9 Moore P. C. C. N. S. 241; Hunt v. Goodlake, 29 L. T. N. S. 472, C. P.; Odger v. Mortimer, 28 L. T. N. S. 472, C. P.

The late celebrated charge of Judge Routhier, however, holding that a Roman Catholic priest was not responsible for words spoken in the pulpit, was reversed by ——.

character and conduct of individuals, may be rendered justifiable and necessary by the occasion, or circumstances.

Thus, it becomes absolutely necessary to the due administration of justice, that judges, jurors, witnesses, and suitors should enjoy an absolute immunity for all words spoken or written, in the course of, or necessary to any judicial proceeding, and that members of legislative bodies should not be trammeled in their deliberations by the restraints to which, as private individuals, they might be subjected.

Such publications, whether made by spoken or by written words, are known to the law as privileged publications, and are of two kinds,—those absolutely privileged, and those qualifiedly privileged,—and it will make no difference with a publication so absolutely privileged, whether or not it be influenced by malice on the part of the speaker.

Publications are absolutely privileged when made by a privileged person. Publications are qualifiedly privileged, when made not by a privileged person, but upon a privileged occasion, which will excuse everything except actual malice. Thus a judge, whether he be judge of a superior or inferior court, or a coroner, is absolutely privileged.[1] An action will not lie for defamatory matter contained in pleadings,[2] or

[1] Scott v. Stanfield, L. Rep. 3 Ex. 220; 18 L. T. N. S. 572; Floyd v. Barker, Co. Rep., part 12, p. 24; Rex v. Skinner, Lofft, 55; Miller v. Hope, 2 Shaw, Sc. App. Cas. 125; Jekyll v. Moore, 2 B. & P. N. R. 341; Revis v. Smith, 18 C. B. 126; Henderson v. Broomhead, 4 H. & N. 569; Fray v. Blackburn, 3 B. & S. 576; Thomas v. Churton, 2 Id. 475; 31 L. J. 139, Q. B.; per Kent, Ch. J., in Yates v. Lansing, 5 Joh. 282; 9 Joh. 395. But see per Cockburn, Ch. J., 2 B. & S. 479; and per Lord Denman, Ch. J., Kendillon v. Maltby, 1 Car. & Mar. 409.

[2] 1 Roll. 33; Dyer, 285; 2 Burr. 808, 817; Weston v. Dobi-

affidavits,[1] or judgments;[2] and a want of jurisdiction in

net, Cro. Jac. 432; Ram v. Lamley, Hutt. 113; Astley v. Young, 2 Burr. 809, 817.

[1] Revis v. Smith, 18 C. B. 126; Astley v. Younge, 2 Burr. 817; Henderson v. Broomhead, 4 H. & N. 569; 28 L. J. 360, Ex.; Doyle v. O'Doherty, 1 C. & Mar. 418. See Maloney v. Bartley, 3 Camp. 210; and McGregor v. Thwaites, 3 B. & C. 24. But see, however, the case of King v. Townshend, 1 King's Bench, A. D. 1822, and reported in the Appendix to Townshend on Slander & Libel, p. 641. That was an action for a libel, contained in an affidavit voluntarily made by the defendant, before a magistrate, charging plaintiff with having given information to the commissioners of customs, that one Decima Barber, a milliner, was possessed of certain uncustomed goods, which were in fact seized, whereby the plaintiff, who carried on the business of a silk mercer, sustained special damage, by reason that the said Decima Barber wholly ceased to deal with the said plaintiff in consequence of such slander. Plea, not guilty, and issue joined.

Mrs. Decima Barber, to prove the special damage, deposed that previous to the publication of this libel she had dealt almost entirely with the plaintiff, for such articles of silk as she required in her business; but that since the publication, believing that the plaintiff had been the person who caused information to be given against her to the customs, she had ceased to deal with him to so large an extent as formerly, though she had not ceased to deal with him altogether.

Abbott, Ch. J.—I am of opinion that this action is maintainable. First, I think this affidavit is not a judicial proceeding, for it is the mere voluntary affidavit of the defendant; and if such an affidavit were to be considered as a judicial proceeding, and therefore privileged, it would afford a very easy recipe for a libeler to traduce the characters of the most innocent persons. Second, I think that to designate a man as an informer, in a publication like this, if done maliciously (which is for the jury), it is libelous in a very offensive degree, and may be the subject of an action. And, Third, I have no doubt that proof of Mrs. Decima Barber having ceased to deal with the plaintiff to any extent, in consequence of the publication of this libel, will be sufficient proof of special damage to sustain this declaration; and it is for the jury to say

---

[2] Jekyll v. Moore, 2 B. & P. N. R. 341; Home v. Bentinck, 2 Brod. & Bing. 13?. See Oliver v. Bentinck, 3 Taunt. 456.

the court[1] or court martial,[2] will not abrogate the privilege. Communications made by officers and soldiers of the army, in the discharge of military or other duty, are absolutely privileged.[3]

In the case of publications qualifiedly privileged, "the occasion prevents the inference of malice, which the law draws from unauthorized communications, and affords a qualified defense, depending upon the absence of actual malice. If fairly warranted by any reasonable occasion or inquiry, and honestly made such communications are protected for the common convenience and welfare of society; and the law has not restricted the right to make them within any narrow limits."[4] "The proper meaning of a privileged communication is only this: that the occasion on which the communication was made, rebuts the infer-

what damages they will give under the circumstances of the case.

A letter complaining that the affidavit of an attorney's clerk was untrue was held privileged (Buckley v. Kiernan, 1 Ir. L. R. N. S. 75).

[1] Lake v. King, 1 Vin. Abr. 389; Hawk. Pl. Cr. 73, § 8; Hare v. Meller, 3 Lev. 169).

[2] Jekyll v. Moore, 2 B. & P. N. R. 341; Home v. Bentinck, 2 Brod. & Bing. 130; Oliver v. Bentinck, 3 Taunt. 456.

[3] Dawkins v. Paulett, 9 B. & S. 768; L. Rep. 5, Q. B. 94; 21 L. T. N. S. 584; 39 L. J. 53, Q. B; Dixon v. Earl of Wilton, 1 F. & F. 419; Keighley v. Bell, 4 Id. 763.

The Scotch law on this subject is in general the same as the English. In case of an action of libel against a judge or witness there is a *presumptio juris et de jure* in favor of the defendant, the effect of which cannot be traversed by any contrary evidence. Proof of actual malice will, however, take away the privilege from a litigant party (Borthwick's Law of Libel, ch. 5, § 1, p. 217).

[4] Per Parke, J., Toogood v. Spyring, 1 Cr. M. & R. 193. See also Somerville v. Hawkins, 10 C. B. 583; Croft v. Stevens, 7 H. & N. 570; Whiteley v. Adams, 15 C. B. N. S. 419; Cowles v. Potts, 34 L. J. 247, Q. B.

ence *prima facie* arising from a statement prejudicial to the character of the plaintiff, and puts it upon him to prove that there was malice in fact—that the defendant was actuated by motives of personal spite or ill-will, independent of the occasion on which the communication was made."[1] "The rule is, that if the occasion be such as repels the presumption of malice, the communication is privileged, and the plaintiff must then, if he can, give evidence of malice: if he gives no such evidence, it is the office of the judge to say that there is no question for the jury, and to direct a nonsuit or a verdict for the defendant."[2]

All occasions upon which a publication of defamatory or injurious matter is made by a person *bona fide* in the discharge of a public or private, legal or moral duty, or in the conduct of his own affairs in matters where his interest is concerned,[3] are privi-

[1] Per Parke, B., Wright v. Woodgate, 2 Cr. M. & R. 577.

[2] Per Campbell, J., Taylor v. Hawkins, 16 Q. B. 321.

[3] A communication made *bona fide* upon any subject-matter in which the party communicating has an interest, or in reference to which he has a duty, is privileged if made to a person having a corresponding interest or duty, although it contain criminatory matter, which, without this privilege, would be slanderous and actionable; and this, though the duty be not a legal one, but only a moral or social duty of imperfect obligation. And the court was of opinion, though it was not necessary to decide so expressly in that case, that the same privilege would be accorded to a communication made to a person who had not in fact such a corresponding interest or duty as referred to, but who might reasonably be, and is, supposed by the party making the communication to have such interest or duty (Harrison v. Bush, 5 El. & B. 344. *Vid.* also Fairman v. Ives, 5 Barn. & A. 642; King v. Bayley, cited by Bayley, J., 5 Id. 647; Scarll v. Dixon, 4 F. & F. 250).

The cases in which the law of Scotland accords this qualified privilege are those of counsel, litigants, masters giving characters of servants, literary criticisms, and communications to persons having an interest in the matters made known (Shortt, p. 429).

leged occasions, and the publication so made, is a privileged publication.[1] And so the communication of a church-member complaining of the character or conduct of the clergyman of his society, if not malicious,[2] or of an agent to his principal within the province of his agency,[3] are privileged. And as to where, in an action for slanderous words, the defendant justified, on the ground that he was the pastor of the church of which the plaintiff was a member; that by the rules and regulations of the church the ruling elders composed the session of the church, and the pastor was the moderator thereof; and that, if the words were spoken, they were used in the course of church discipline, to the session, in the progress of the investigation of certain rumors against the chastity of the plaintiff, see a very recent case.[4] A lawyer's letter to his client, or a client's to his lawyer, are privileged.[5]

So, too, are charges preferred by one member of a lodge of Odd-Fellows against another, within the rules of the order,[6] or a banker's communication to a firm who had sent him a customer's note for collection.[7]

Where the New York College of Pharmacy appointed a committee to examine certain charges as to

[1] Toogood v. Spyring, 1 Cr. M. & R. 93.

[2] O'Donohue v. McGovern, 23 Wend. 26.

[3] Wasburne v. Cooke, 3 Den. 110; Gilbert v. People, Id. 11.

[4] Kleizer v. Aymmes, 40 Ind. 562. Held, that the paragraphs of the answer were good, and that the word "crimes," in the rules, was not confined to statutory crimes, but included a violation of the moral law or of duty as a member of the church. Written charges were not necessary to authorize the investigation. Pettit, Ch. J., dissented.

[5] Warner v. Payne, 2 Sand. 195.

[6] Streety v. Wood, 15 Barb. 105. But see, however, Holmes v. Johnson, 11 Ired. 55.

[7] Lewis v. Chapman, 2 Smith, 369; reversing 19 Barb. 252.

the importation of spurious drugs, and—the committee having reported recommending that charges be forwarded to the secretary of the treasury against plaintiff, who was public inspector of drugs—the college sent such charges, it was held that such constituted a privileged communication.[1]

But a letter addressed to a superior officer having a power of removal, charging his subordinate with fraud in office,[2] or a memorial to the post-master-general in relation to the business of his department, where the plaintiff can show want of probable cause,[3] or the publication of proceedings on an *ex parte* application to a magistrate for a criminal warrant, will not be privileged. The published representations of a mercantile agent or agency, confidentially reporting the business character and standing of merchants and others, may be, however.[4]

The keeping of a mercantile agency, whose business it is to obtain information respecting the credit and responsibility of persons in business, and to furnish the same to subscribers, is a lawful business; and a communication made, in good faith, to a subscriber to such agency, is one privileged, and sanction edby the usages of commercial communities.[5] The privilege accorded to a mercantile agency, however, will not extend to the country correspondents of the agency,[6] nor is a communication by the proprietor of a mercantile agency,

[1] Van Wyck v. Aspinwall, 3 Smith, 90.

[2] Howard v. Thompson, 21 Wend. 319.

[3] Cook v. Hill, 3 Sand. 341.

[4] 4 Seld. 452; Billings v. Russel, 8 Boston Law Rep. N. S. 699; Getting v. Foss, 3 Car. & P. 160; Ormsby v. Douglass, 37 N. Y. 477; Sherwood v. Gilbert, 2 Albany Law Journal, 323; Beardsley v. Tappan, 5 Blatchf. 497; but see Taylor v. Church, 1 E. D. Smith, 279.

[5] Ormsby v. Douglass, 37 N. Y. 477.

[6] Sherwood v. Gilbert, 2 Albany Law Journal, 323.

through his clerks, to his customers and their clerks, privileged.[1]

The publication of a report of a coroner's inquest, by the coroner and a county physician, implicating the managers of the public poorhouse;[2] or, generally, matters presented to any person or tribunal not having jurisdiction in the premises,[3] are not privileged. But an abusive article in a newspaper, touching a candidate for an appointment for office, is not privileged, though such a remonstrance, addressed to the appointing power, would be.[4]

True, it has been held that when a man becomes a candidate for public honors, he makes profert of himself for public investigation. No one has the right, indeed, to impute to him infamous crimes or misdemeanors; but talents and qualifications are mere matters of opinion, of which the electors are the only judges, and it has been held that imputing weakness of understanding to a candidate for Congress (for instance), was not actionable.[5]

And to a like effect said Parsons, Ch. J.:[6] "When a man shall consent to be a candidate for a public office, conferred by the electors of the people, he must be considered as putting his character in issue, so far as may respect his fitness and qualifications for office." But the better opinion will be that, as in every other case, the existence of malice in the publication will be the criterion. "Officers and candidates for office may

[1] Beardsley v. Tappan, 5 Blatchf. 497.

[2] Greene v. Telfair, 20 Barb. 11.

[3] Hoseman v. Loveland, 19 Barb. 111.

[4] Hunt v. Bennett, 19 N. Y. 173; affirmed, 4 S. D. Smith, 647.

[5] Mayrant v. Richardson, 1 Nolt. & McC. 327.

[6] Commonwealth v. Clapp, 4 Mass. 163; but see Aldrich v. Press Print. Co., 9 Min. 133; Curtis v. Mussey, 6 Gray (Mass.), 261.

be canvassed, but not calumniated" ;[1] and some of the cases went further, and held that malice would be implied if the charge were false.[2] So in a recent case,[3] where it was claimed to be justifiable for an elector, *bona fide* to communicate to the constituency, matter respecting a candidate which the elector believed to be true and material to the election, the principle was conceded by the court to be correct, but was held inapplicable, because the communication had not been confined to the constituency of the plaintiff, but had been published in a newspaper.[4] Words which deter others from voting for him of whom they were spoken, at an election at which he is a candidate, are actionable.[5]

90. The presence or absence of actual malice is generally for the jury to determine.[6] Whether or not the occasion is privileged, and so makes the publication privileged, is, nevertheless, a question of law for the court ;[7] so also the intention of malice[8] is often a

[1] Lewis v. Few, 5 Johns. 1 ; Harwood v. Astley, 4 Bos. & Pul. 47 ; 1 N. R. 47 ; Seely v. Blair, Wright, 358, 683. See Brewer v. Weakley, 2 Overt. 99 ; Root v. King, 7 Cow. 613 ; affirmed, 4 Wend. 113, note ; 1 Stark. Slan. 301.

[2] Lewis v. Few, 5 Johns. 1.

[3] Law v. Scott, 5 Har. & J. 438.

[4] And see Cowles v. Pott, 34 L. J. 247 Q. B ; George v. Goddard, 2 F. & F. 689.

[5] Brewer v. Weakley, 2 Overt. 99.

[6] Liddle v. Hodges, 2 Bosw. 544 ; Dolloway v. Turrell, 26 Wend. 369 ; Cooke on Defamation, ch. iv.

[7] Taylor v. Hawkins, 16 Q. B. 321 ; Cooke v. Wildes, 5 El. & Bl. 335 ; Dickson v. Earl of Wilton, 1 F. & F. 426 ; Hancock v. Case, 2 Id. 711 ; Whiteley v. Adams, 15 C. B. N. S. 392 ; 33 L. J , 89 C. P.

[8] So strictly will the doctrine of malice be construed, that, it seems, though a member of congress is not responsible out of Congress for words spoken there, though libelous on individuals, yet, if he causes his speech to be published, he may be punished as for a libel, by action or indictment (1 Kent. Com.

conclusion of law.[1] But, while it is undoubtedly a question for the jury whether matter not *prima facie* libelous, is or is not so, according to the circumstances; the law will presume that one who publishes of another what is defamatory on its face, does so with that malicious intention which constitutes a libel.[2]

If one use the weapon of truth wantonly, though the occasion be a proper one, he may be guilty of libel; but where, for example, a person consents to become a candidate for a public office, conferred by a public election, he must be considered as putting his character in issue so far as regards the question of his fitness or unfitness for that particular office. For, that offices of public trust be well filled, is most certainly a matter of the greatest public interest, and the publication of truth concerning one's past character, made with the honest intention of informing the electors, will not be a libel. Where the communication is *prima facie* privileged, the burden is on the plaintiff to prove malice.[3] But a priviliged communication made with a knowledge of its falsity is actionable,[4] and if a news-

p. 236, note; Cases of Lord Abingdon and of Creevy, 3 Eq. N. P. Cases, 228; 1 M. & S. 278).

[1] Fry v. Bennett, 1 Code R., N. S. 1243; 5 Sandf. 54; Root v. Lowndes, 6 Hill, 520; Washburn v. Cook, 3 Den. 162; Howard v. Sexton, 4 N. Y. 151; Littlejohn v. Greeley, 13 Abb. Pr. 55; and see Hargrave v. De Breton, 4 Burr. 2425; Bromage v. Prosser, 4 B. & C. 247; 6 Dowl. & R. 296.

[2] Commonwealth v. Odell, 3 Pittstb. (Pa.) 449. *Vid.* Wilson v. Fitch, which discriminates as to who is or is not a public officer; also, Thorn v. Blanchard, 5 Johns. 508; King v. Root, 4 Wend. 113; Vanderzee v. McGregor, 12 Id. 545; Fawcett v. Charles, 13 Id. 473; Howard v. Thompson, 21 Wend. 319; O'Donaghue v. McGovern, 23 Id. 26; Washburne v. Cooke, 3 Den. 110.

[3] O'Donahue v. McGovern, 23 Wend. 26.

[4] King v. Root, 4 Wend. 113.

paper publish falsehood and calummy, such an excuse will not avail.[1]

88. The publisher of a newspaper in which a libel appears, is *prima facie* presumed to have published the libel, and this presumption is not rebutted by evidence that he never saw the libelous matter, and was not aware of its publication until it was pointed out to him in print, and that an apology and retraction were afterwards inserted in an issue of the same newspaper.[2] Nor that the article in question was copied from another newspaper merely as an article of news, and in the form of an extract.[3] But the publisher will be allowed the fullest opportunity to rebut all presumption of malice if he can[4]—and he may plead matters in mitigation as a partial defense.[5]

[1] Commonwealth v. Odell, 3 Pitt. & C. 449.

[2] Id.

[3] McDonald v. Woodruff, 2 Dill, 244.

[4] Wilson v. Fitch, 41 Cal. 363.

[5] Bennett v. Matthews, 67 Barb. 410.

It was held by the house of lords, on appeal from the Scotch court of session, that the publication, in a book called "The Scottish Mercantile Society's Record" (known amongst the trading community as the "Black List"), of a copy of the register of protests for non-acceptance and non-payment of bills of exchange and promissory notes, established by the Scotch acts of 1681 and 1696, and the 12 Geo. 3, c. 72, and 23 Geo. 3, c. 18, was not libelous, the contents of the register being public property, and the publication of them authorized; and the result of the various acts of parliament being to give the registration the effect of a decree or judgment of the court of session, "It is equivalent," said the lord chancellor, "to what in this country we call a judgment upon a warrant of attorney. In neither case does the court interfere, but in both, as in cases of judgment by default and decreet in absence, the party having a right to the authority of the court to confirm his claim, obtains the judgment as of course. Whether that judgment is obtained by authority of parliament, or by the consent of parties, or by the practice of the court, appears to me to be immaterial. It is for all purposes a judgment of the

89. The following have been held communications privileged by the occasion of their publication: a letter written by a person to his mother-in-law,[1] giving her advice on the subject of her proposed marriage, and containing imputations upon the person whom she was about to marry;[2] a letter written by a tenant who had been asked by his landlord to tell him if he saw

court until altered or reversed, and entitled to all the attributes of any judgment after the longest and most contested litigations. . . . . Is it, then, unlawful to state or publish the decreet or judgment of courts of justice? If their proceedings are public, so must be the result of such proceedings—namely, the judgment. For, although the steps preliminary to the judgment are not transacted in open court (the whole being incontestible in that stage), yet the whole is supposed to be the result of regular proceedings in court.

If, however, the publisher of such a "Black List" inserts in it, as a still existing liability, a judgment which has been satisfied by payment, he is, according to a decision of the Irish court of queen's bench (McNally v. Oldham, 8 L. T. N. S. 604), liable to an action of libel, and, if special damage has been caused by the publication, also to an action for a false representation.

"He would have been justified," said Lefroy, Ch. J., "if he had published the judgment as it stood in reality, as a judgment annuled and satisfied; but if, instead of that—if instead of availing himself of a legal right, which none of us mean to question, the right of publishing a judgment, a true copy of a judgment, so long as the party does not add a sting to it—if he adds the sting that it is an unsatisfied judgment, this becomes an exercise of a legal right with an addition which makes that injurious to the plaintiff, in a way that it would not have been, if he represented the truth of the transaction. . . . . The case in Scotland was very different from the present one. The party there acted under an act of parliament, and what he did, he did *bona fide* and according to the truth of the transaction. The very contrary has been the case here" (Fleming v. Newton, 1 H. L. Cas. 363).

[1] It is not libelous, however, to accuse a man of having brought suit against his mother-in-law, especially if such is the fact (Cox v. Cooper, 9 L. T. N. S. 329).

[2] Todd v. Hawkins, 2 M. & Rob. 20; 8 C. & P. 88.

or heard anything respecting game, informing the landlord that his gamekeeper sold game;[1] information given to a party asking for it, as to the respectability of a tradesman with whom that party is about to deal;[2] a letter written confidentially to persons employing a particular solicitor, containing charges as to his professional conduct in the management of certain matters intrusted to him by the writer, and in which the writer was interested;[3] a letter written *bona fide* and confidentially to the employer of a steward, informing him of certain supposed malpractices on the part of the steward;[4] a character given by a master or mistress of a servant,[5] or a retractation of a character formerly given;[6] a letter written by a subscriber to a charitable institution, to the committee, reflecting on the conduct of the secretary;[7] a communication made by one director of a company to his co-directors, respecting the conduct of one of its officers;[8] a communication addressed by a rate-payer to a parish meeting, reflecting on the parish constable;[9] a letter addressed to a bishop, informing him of a report affect-

[1] Cockayne v. Hodgkisson, 5 C. & P. 543.

[2] Storey v. Challands, 8 C. & P. 234. See Bennett v. Deacon, 2 C. B. 628; King v. Watts, 8 C. & P. 614.

[3] M'Dougall v. Claridge, 1 Camp. 267. See also Dunman v. Bigg, 3 Camp. 260.

[4] Cleaver v. Senande, referred to by Lord Ellenborough, 1 Camp. 267.

[5] Burr. 2425; Edmondson v. Stevenson, Bull. N. P. 8; Child v. Affleck, 9 B. & C. 403; Pattison v. Jones, 8 B. & C. 578; Fountain v. Boodle, 3 Q. B. 11; Dixon v. Parsons, 1 F. & F. 24.

[6] Gardner v. Slade, 13 Q. B. 796; 18 L. J. 334 Q. B.

[7] Maitland v. Bramwell, 2 F. & F. 623. See Hartwell v. Vesey, 3 L. T. N. S. 275.

[8] Harris v. Thompson, 13 C. B. 333. See Brooks v. Blanshard, 1 Cr. & M. 779; 3 Tyrw. 844.

[9] Spencer v. Amerton, 1 M. & Rob. 470. See George v. Goddard, 2 F. & F. 689.

ing the character of an incumbent in his diocese; *bona fide* applications to the proper authorities for redress for wrongs suffered;[2] letters written by the defendant in answer to a letter from a friend of the plaintiff who had been in correspondence with the defendant on the subject of certain charges against the plaintiff, with the sanction and concurrence of the latter;[3] a memorial from an elector and inhabitant of a borough, complaining of misconduct on the part of a magistrate of the county in which the borough was situated, although not addressed to the proper authority.[4] It is important to note here, however, that in cases where the occasion would render privileged a communication otherwise defamatory, the privilege may be lost by the use of language so exaggerated as to be clearly in excess of the occasion. But a letter written to the secretary of state by an inhabitant of a borough, imputing to a person holding the offices of town-clerk and clerk to the justices of the borough, corruption in the latter office;[5] or a letter written to Lloyd's, by an officer in the navy, imputing to a captain of a transport-ship misconduct and incapacity in the management of it;[6] or a letter written by an opposing creditor to a judge of the bankruptcy court, previous to the hearing of an insolvent's case;[7] or a letter written to a newspaper by members of a town council, charging contractors intrusted with the erec-

[1] James v. Boston, 2 C. & Kir. 4.

[2] Johnson v. Evans, 3 Esp. 32; Woodward v. Lander, 6 C. & P. 548.

[3] Hopwood v. Thorn, 8 C. B. 293; 19 L. J. 94 C. P.

[4] Harrison v. Bush, 5 E. & B. 344; 25 L. J. 28 Q. B.

[5] Blagg v. Sturt, 10 Q. B. 899; 16 L. J. 39 Q. B.

[6] Harwood v. Green, 3 C. & P. 141.

[7] Gould v. Hulme, 3 C. & P. 625. See chapter on Contempt of Court.

tion of a jail with misconduct in the performance of their contract;[1] or an advertisement in a newspaper, addressed to the creditors of B. & Co., who had been declared bankrupts, and containing imputations on B. of fraudulent conduct, published by the solicitor who had acted under the commission of bankruptcy;[2] or the publication in a newspaper, by a voter at an election, of statements reflecting on the character of one of the candidates: will not be considered as privileged. "However large the privilege of electors may be," said Lord Denman, Ch. J., in that case,[3] "it is extravagant to suppose that it can justify the publication, to all the world, of facts injurious to a person who happens to stand in the situation of a candidate."

A pamphlet which has *bona fide* for its object the vindication of the character of the writer against charges made by others, is undoubtedly privileged. Thus, where the plaintiff, a policy-holder in an insurance company, published a pamphlet accusing the directors of fraud, the court held privileged, if the jury should be of opinion that it was published without malice,[4] a pamphlet published in reply by the directors, declaring the charges contained in the plaintiff's pamphlet to be false and calumnious, and also asserting that in a suit he had instituted he had sworn, in support of those charges, in opposition to his own handwriting, was held of privilege, his Lordship thus directed the jury: "The law is that a publication is privileged either by the duty or the fair and honest interest of the party who has made it. And I am of opinion that the answer here was privileged,

[1] Simpson v. Downs, 16 L. T. N. S. 391. But *vid.* Harle v. Catherall, 14 L. T. N. S. 801.

[2] Brown v. Croome, 2 Stark. N. P. 297.

[3] Duncombe v. Daniels, 8 C. & P. 222.

[4] Koenig v. Ritchie, 3 F. & F. 413.

and that the publication was privileged. If you are of opinion that it was *bona fide* for the purpose of the defense of the company, and in order to prevent these charges from operating to their prejudice, and with a view to vindicate the character of the directors, and not with a view to injure or lower the character of the plaintiff—if you are of that opinion, and think that the publication did not go beyond the occasion, then you ought to find for the defendants on the general issue."[1]

Where an action of libel was brought for an advertisement, published in a newspaper, offering a reward to any person who could give notice to the defendant of the marriage of James Delany previous to a certain date, there being an innuendo that the defendant meant thereby to insinuate that J. D., the plaintiff, had been and was married before the time mentioned in the advertisement, and had another wife then living; and the defense relied upon was that the advertisement had been inserted by the authority of the plaintiff's wife, for the purpose of making a discovery which it was important for her to know, namely, whether the plaintiff had another wife then living, Lord Ellenborough, Ch. J., told the jury that, though that which is spoken or written may be injurious to the character of the party; yet, if done *bona fide*, with a view of investigating a fact in which the party making it was interested, it was not libelous, and, therefore, if the investigation had been set on foot and the advertisement published by the plaintiff's wife, either from anxiety to know whether she was legally the wife of the plaintiff or whether he had another wife living when he married her, it was justifiable, though done through the medium of imputing

[1] Ib. *Vid.* also Rex v. Veley, 4 F. & F. 1117.

bigamy to the plaintiff.[1] The soundness of this law however, was doubted by Lord Denman, Ch. J., in a subsequent case.[2] "I have great doubt," said that learned judge, "whether the interest which the wife had in the inquiry could justify the offering a reward in a newspaper."

Another class of publications which would appear to be privileged from considerations of public interest, if not of public policy, are newspaper comments on matters of daily occurrence—the news of the day, proceedings of legislative or other deliberative bodies, judicial proceedings in the courts, etc.) These will be considered further on in the chapter on newspapers.

The law of libel, it should be remarked, is in no sense in conflict with a liberty which, with us, is especially dear to the citizen, and especially guarded and secured by our constitution—the liberty of the press—"The law of libel is no more unfavorable to the press than the statute against larceny is unfriendly to the people. One perplexes thieves, the other liars, but neither is a terror to honest men, and nothing therein can militate against the principle laid down in what Judge Kent calls the 'comprehensive and accurate definition' of Alexander Hamilton: 'the liberty of the press consists in the right to publish, with impunity, truth, with good motives, and for justifiable ends, whether it respects government, magistracy, or individuals.'"

The question as to how far a newspaper may comment upon matters of public interest, which involve more or less the reputation and the rights of individuals, will be examined in the chapter on news-

[1] Delaney v. Jones, 4 Esp. 191. And see Fendin v. Westlake, 1 Mo. & Malk. 461.

[2] Lay v. Lawson, 4 A. & E. 795.

papers, except as to the question of comments upon judicial proceedings, which will be found treated of in the chapter upon contempts of court.

A defendant will not be allowed, for purposes of mitigating damages, or of justifying a libel, to inquire into a plaintiff's religious opinions, even where the libel concerns his religious creed.[1] Nor will he be allowed to read, in his address to the jury, specific books and documents, as proofs of what the doctrines of the plaintiff's co-religionists are. These are matters of fact and must be proved by witnesses.[2]

The conduct of the plaintiff in provoking the libel, is a fit subject for the jury to take into account, in estimating the amount of compensation for his injured feelings.[3]

And evidence may be given of libels on the defendant, published by the plaintiff, respecting the same subject-matter. Said Mansfield, Ch. J., "If a man is in the habit of libeling others, he complains with a very bad grace of being libeled himself; and he cannot be supposed to suffer much injury from this source."[4] But before such publications are read, it must be shown that they are connected with the libels proceeding from the defendant: for it is not a proper ground for mitigating damages that, on other occasions, the plaintiff has written libels on the defendant, on some other matter unconnected with that which is the subject of the action;[5] and it must be proved that

[1] Darbey v. Ouseley, 1 H. & N. 1. But see Turnbull v. Bird, 2 F. & F. 508.

[2] Id.

[3] Kelly v. Sherlock, 2 R. 1 Q. B. 686; 35 L. J. 209, Q. B. And see note 1, p. 222.

[4] Finnerty v. Tipper, 2 Camp. 72.

[5] May v. Brown, 3 B. & C. 113; Tarpley v. Blabey, 2 Bing. N. C. 437; Wakeley v. Johnson, 1 Ry. & Moo. 422.

they came to the defendant's knowledge before he libelled the plaintiff.[1]

[1] Watts v. Frazer, 7 Ad. & E. 223. So, too, the provocation for the libel will be considered at the trial. Thus, where the action was for imputing unchastity to the plaintiff's wife, the defendant was allowed to prove that the wife had lived alone with an unmarried man in the same house. Reynolds v. Tucker, 6 Ohio, N. S. 516; and see Bradley v. Heath, 6 Pick. 163; Shoulty v. Miller, 1 Carter (Ind.) 544; Knight v. Foster, 39 N. H. 876; Regnier v. Cobot, 2 Gilman 34; Henson v. Veatch, 1 Blackf. 369. It was remarked on page 201, that undoubtedly a libel could be published by telegraph. While these pages are going through the press, such a case (Jaffras v. McKellop. &c. Co., 4 T. & C. (N. Y.) 578) has been reported, though it does not appear that the telegraph company was pursued as a publisher.

In England, 1 of 6 and 7 Vict., c. 96, enacts that "it shall be lawful for the defendant (after notice in writing of his intention so to do, duly given to the plaintiff at the time of filing or delivering the plea in such action) to give in evidence, in mitigation of damages, that he made or offered an apology to the plaintiff for such defamation before the commencement of the action, or as soon afterwards as he had an opportunity of doing so, in case the action shall have been commenced before there was an opportunity of making or offering such apology" (Shortt L. L. 568). Upon the action, by virtue of "Fox's Libel Act" (32 Geo. 3, c. 60), the judge before whom a case of libel is tried, may give his opinion as to whether the publication is libelous (Id. 595).

CHAPTER III.

OF CONTEMPT OF COURT.

90. The original source of judicature is the people. And courts are the distributors of the justice of the people. In England, by theory of law, the king, and with us, the state, hears all disputes between man and man. "But as it would be impracticable to render complete justice to every individual by the people sitting collectively to hear each other's disputes, they have committed that power to certain select magistrates, who, with more ease and expedition can hear and determine complaints,"[1] whence it is that courts are appointed to be the tribunals wherein all disagreements shall be heard and determined.

But in order to do justice, these courts must be omnipotent. In order to protect the suppliant, they must themselves be protected.[2] If a court of justice was merely a bench, upon which a judiciary, elected or appointed, sat to arbitrate concerning the quarrels of its neighbors, to say that its doings and proceedings should be sacred against criticism, and beyond arraignment by the people, might savor of arrogance, and oligarchism, and smack of that oppression of the many by the few, which it is the boast of our constitution, cannot thrive beneath the shadow of her ægis.

But under the above definition of a court, as a

[1] Bl. Com. 267.

forum where the majesty of the state sits forever and supreme, the whole doctrine is plain and rational,[1] and consonant to the spirit of our laws. The great power—the great physical power of the state—sits in her courts. And all her engines of execution, from the constable and the *posse comitatus*, to her soldiers and her army, are at their beck to enforce obedience to their last decree. But for all this, the mightest power which centers in courts, is a moral one. A court, to be useful, must secure and maintain the confidence and respect of society, and without that, the puissance of the commonwealth is vain.

91. It is for this reason that to the author and the man of letters these courts must look for their greatest support and co-operation. The vast power of the writer, whether his vehicle of publication be through the library, the bookseller, the press, the rostrum or the stage ; can readily become the greatest and chiefest auxiliary of equity, justice, and good order ; or, with equal ease, a mighty power for their destruction. Law is the arm of justice, and is the means by which justice — the end — is to be reached. Courts are the administrators of this means, and to the learned and wise and far-seeing, the law looks with confidence, that, all the more because of their wisdom and foresight, will they be solicitous to utter nothing that shall go to undermine her sway or paralyze her arm—nay more, to those who guide and mold opinion and society with their pens, she looks not only that they refrain from lessening her authority, but for positive and substantial aid, countenance, and support. And when the author reflects that it is to this

[1] The authority to punish for contempt is granted as a necessary incident in establishing a tribunal (U. S. v. New York, 1 W. & M. 401).

law that he owes the power of following and controlling his own thoughts and clustered words, when—once uttered—they pass beyond his reach, it would seem that to him, at least, she should not look in vain.

92. There are two sorts of contempts of a court. The first arises when words are spoken derogatory of its justice, its impartiality, or its organization; the second, when its directions or decrees are disobeyed or slighted.

It is this first sort which may arise in the form of a literary composition, and with which we have to deal in this chapter. For, it is to be remarked, that the criticism of the decree of a court is not a contempt of that decree; since, once made, it is beyond the power of cavil and cannot be disarmed by clamor; the theory of literary contempts being, that they interrupt the facility of the court in arriving at, and not in enforcing, its judgments.

It is, therefore, the rule, founded in the reason of the common law, that all contempts to the personality, or organization of a court: to its judges, juries, officers, or ministers, when acting in the due discharge of their respective duties, whether such contempts be by direct obstruction, or consequentially: that is to say, whether they be by act or writing, are punishable by the court itself, and may be abated instanter as nuisances to public justice, and subject the party so offending to fine and imprisonment.[1] And it belongs exclusively to the court offended to judge of what are contempts—and of their punishment.[2]

[1] Holt L. L. 138; v. 37 N. H. 950.

[2] No other judge or court can or ought to undertake, in a collateral way, to question or review an adjudication of a contempt made by another collateral jurisdiction, though a superior court may undoubtedly review them, except perhaps in a

93. The law of contempt might at first appear to be contrary to the spirit of the common law. Personal liberty, by the law of England, was considered a strictly natural right, not to be abridged but in the exercise of the greatest possible caution, nor at the mere discretion of a magistrate.[1] This case, however, appears to be without that provision, since it seems that, in a proceeding for contempt, the party accused is not entitled to a trial by jury.[2]

Says Dr. Dwight,[3] "The power to punish for contempts is undefined, and its exercise depends on the discretion of the court or judge. It is lodged in the hands of one who may suppose himself to have been insulted, or, in other words, with the person aggrieved. It is exercised without the ordinary checks or safeguards attending criminal trials. The proceeding is inquisitorial, and the accused is compelled to answer against himself. The decision of the committing judge is without appeal. The only supervision that an appellate court can exercise, is to see that the forms of the law have been observed; as, for instance, that the person charged with contempt has had a hearing, and that the offense is stated in the order of commitment. Whether the acts were, in fact, a contempt of court, is finally decided by the court or judge before whom, in the first instance, the case is presented, and the punishment may be by fine and

matter arising on *habeas corpus. Vid.* 3 Wils. 188; 14 East. 1; 2 Bay. So. C. 182; 1 Ill. 266; J. J. Marsh. (Ky.) 575; 1 Blackf. (Ind.) 166; 2 U. P. Charlt. (Ga.) 136; 14 Ark. 538, 544; 2 Ind. 161; 6 Johns. (N. Y.) 337; 9 Id. 395; 6 Wheat. 204; 7 Id. 38.

[1] Mag. Chart. c. 29.

[2] Neel v. State, 4 Eng. 259.

[3] Paper prepared in the case of the Code Amendments, 1871.

imprisonment, or both." But the earlier and modern authorities hold the power to exist by the reason of the common law, and as vital to the very existence of courts.

94. The power to imprison for contempt of court is traced by Blackstone to Magna Charta itself.

The Magna Charta bears date June 15th, 1215, which was the seventeenth year of the reign of King John. The first enactment upon the subject of contempt was the statute of Westminster,[1] or seventy years afterward; the statute, however, having reference only to contempts in resisting the process of the King's courts, or, as Blackstone entitles them, to consequential contempts alone.[2] From this statute one writer[3] derives the present doctrine of contempts, consequential or otherwise.

95. The power of courts to imprison for contempt is declared both by our own and by English writers. It has been repeatedly asserted in the English courts (and those decisions followed in the courts of this country), as of immemorial usage and practice, since the law itself was known. It is claimed to be a vitally essential attribute and consequence of the administration of the law itself, without which it dies; since it is, thereupon, impotent to command respect or obedience to its own decrees.[4] It is held to have arisen from the very nature and necessity of things,

[1] 4 Com. 237.

[2] "If, then, the power to punish this class of consequential contempts constituted a part of 'the law of the land' so long anterior to the date of Magna Charta as to have become, at that early day, a very maxim of law, where was the necessity for legislation upon the subject?" (per Thacher v. *Ex parte* Hickey, 12 Miss. 751).

[3] Gilb. Hist. C. P. C. 3.

[4] *Ex parte* Hickey, 12 Ark. 751.

coeval with the period when the administration of the law, by means of courts and legal tribunals, was established. It is in this point of view that it is insisted by Blackstone[1] to have been confirmed by the statute of Magna Charta, when it enacted that "no freeman shall be imprisoned and condemned but by the judgment of his peers or by the law of the land."

"In this country," said Dade, J.,[2] "we know no privileges but such as exist for the public good. Many such privileges we have—from those which appertain to the legislature itself, even down to such as belong to the lowest executive officer. Those which surround the administration of justice are of the same order. Courts, their officers and process, are shielded from invasion and insult—not from any imaginary sanctity in the institutions themselves, or the persons of those who compose them, but solely for the purpose of giving them due weight and authority, and to enable those who administer them to discharge their functions with impartiality, fidelity, and effect. This is the true test of every privilege not granted by statute, and is the spirit of every one (not merely private) which is so secured. The political character of the judiciary, and the tendency of the duties which are devolved upon it, render it necessary to invest it with a considerable share of these privileges. It is confessedly the weakest branch of all governments, wielding neither wealth, force, nor patronage. Its duties consist in adjusting and settling the contested rights of individuals; in controlling their turbulence, and punishing their crimes. These duties are often of a severe and rigorous character, and as they are generally

[1] 4 Com. 237; Commonwealth v. Dandridge, Virginia Cas. 409.

[2] Commonwealth v. Dandridge, Virginia Cas. 409.

to be discharged in almost immediate contact with those on whom they act, their exercise will frequently elicit the angry passions, or excite unworthy and sinister attempts to bias or avert their operation; and where there is little real power, and no patronage, a certain degree of external dignity may have been considered necessary to supersede a too frequent resort to the actual powers of the courts."

Said Scott, J.:[1] "The doctrine of contempts, and of attachments for contempts, as it existed at common law, and has been recognized by some of the ablest American jurists, extends not only to acts which directly and openly insult or resist the power of the court or the persons of the judges, but to consequential, indirect, and constructive contempts, which obstruct the process, degrade the authority, or contaminate the purity of the court; and every case of authority seen in the books will be found to proceed upon the idea, either remote or proximate, of disrespect to the court or the judges, in reference to their official character or conduct, or of matter in derogation of the dignity of the court, or are referable to that power of self-protection, which, we have remarked, is necessarily inherent in judicial institutions.

"Although these doctrines of the common law had their origin in an idea totally unrecognized and without place in this country, and preserved, even in England, only by a fiction of law, still, in our own free government, it has always been admitted that, to a greater or less degree, they must have place, and they have rested, with us, on an idea not totally dissimilar to that original one. Anciently, in England, it is known that the king, in person, presided in his courts of justice, and sat, himself, in judgment; and the

[1] Neel v. State, 9 Eng. (Ark.) 259.

insult, resistance, or contamination, was to majesty itself, that held sway in divine right. In our day we refer it to the majesty of the law."

96. It has never been contended in this country that the common law, although it is our birthright,[1] and in force among us without express recognition by our constitution and laws, was ever actually in force in all its length and breadth, but only to an extent that was not wholly inconsistent with those great principles upon which our free institutions, purely American, have been reared and maintained. So these doctrines which we are considering, in being recognized by the courts, must be regarded as having received a corresponding abatement of those of its lineaments which are at open war with the nature and character of our constitution, and the actual state of things among us, under its legitimate operation, or it would be an exotic that could not germinate in our soil.[2]

"Contempt of court," says Blackstone, "may also, it appears, be committed by insult to a judge out of court; that contempts thus punished are either direct, which openly insult or resist the powers of the court, or the persons of the judges who preside, and elsewhere."[3] In enumerating the contempts which degrade the judicial authority, he refers to one which consists in "speaking or writing contemptuously of the courts, or judges in their official capacity."

"It is obvious," said the learned judge above

[1] The common law of England is not the common law of the United States (Van Ness v. Pacard, 2 Pet. 144). There is no common law of the United States. The constitution and laws of the Union prevail as the authority of law throughout the Union; but each independent state may have its own common law, which may not be considered so in another (Wheaton v. Peters, 8 Pet. 658; *Ex parte* Hickey, 2 Miss. 751).

[2] 4 Com. 238.

[3] Id. 285.

quoted,[1] "that, in these two clauses, the word 'judges' is not used by the writer for the mere purpose of illustrating his meaning in the use of the word 'court;' for, besides the consideration that this view is not sustained by the context, such an explanation of his meaning is so altogether futile and useless, after his luminous exposition of the courts in his third volume, as not to be attributed to a writer so able and perspicuous. On the contrary, it was evidently his purpose in the first clause, to take the distinction between a disrespect of the constitutional powers of the court and a personal disrespect of the judges therein sitting; and in the second, between a contempt of the judges while actually holding a court, and a contempt of the same persons while in discharge of judicial duties appertaining to their official character, though not performed in court. The opposite construction would produce a complete identification of the judges with the court, so as to make a contempt, of the one or the other, perfectly convertible. From which may be deduced the clear privilege of the persons of the judges in or out of court, when acting in their judicial capacity; not because of any imaginary sanctity of their persons, nor because that an indignity to their persons when so engaged obstructs the course of justice, for it might sometimes be of such a character as not to have that effect (and besides, in that aspect, it is always referable to another head of contempts; that is, for obstructing the powers of the court), but because, to use the words of Blackstone, 'it demonstrates a gross want of that respect which, when once the courts of justice are deprived of, their authority (so necessary for the good of the kingdom) is entirely lost among the people.'"

[1] Neel v. State, 9 Eng. (Ark.) 259.

Nor, to produce this effect, is it of any importance whether the contumely be used in open court, at the moment when the occasion occurs, or the moment afterward, when the sheriff has proclaimed the adjournment. The only real question in either case is, whether it is the official conduct for which the judge is challenged and insulted. Nor can a reason be offered for the protection of the person of the judge in court, that will not equally apply to a protection out of court: on the same account, in view of the remark we have already made, that whenever the indignity in open court would have the effect to interrupt its business, the attachment would be referable to the head of obstructing the powers of the court.

An ideal, imaginary being, without form, substance, or locality, needs no protection from penal sanctions. A court separate from the persons who compose it, is of this description. A sensible writer has said that the terms "nation, state, community, are words only; they do not denote anything separate from the individual members whose aggregation and association have received these names," and the like may be affirmed of a court of justice.[1]

97. In *ex parte* Hickey,[2] Mr. Justice Thatcher ably expressed himself on this branch of the subject as follows: "What is a contempt of court? Besides the various classes of contempts which were known to the common law of England and particularly described; besides those relations to officers and others connected with the courts, concerning which the law is plain and explicit, there are many which are claimed to lie exclusively within the discretion of courts. The belief in the existence of such, is alone in the breast

[1] 4 Bl. Com. 286.

[2] 12 Miss. (Sm. & Mar.) 751.

of the court. They may be construed to spring from a gesture, a word or a look."

98. "Thus, the court is constituted the judge of his own privileges, and the vindicator of his own wrongs, whether real or supposed, and his jurisdiction in this particular, is without measure. The offense is without specification and without definition; and, though, legally viewed, it is said to refer solely to the functionary, it necessarily touches and stimulates the individual who finds it hard to separate himself from the office and station. It may thus become an offense of opinion, of feeling, or of prejudice. An offense which has no other legislation than the imperfections of human nature, blinded and misled by the circumstances of the moment, notions of caprice, and the improper bias of passion, or by those powerful, but imperceptible influences from which the most upright and enlightened minds cannot be considered or trusted to be wholly exempt."

99. "The power of punishing may be extended to a degree despotic, and, as it is extended in a judicial capacity, it is irresponsible, and may therefore be used, regardless of consequences. Under such a state of things, liberty and property may become precarious, and there is no protection against expression. The rights and privileges which our constitution has retained and reserved to its citizens, may thus be despotically abridged or wholly refused, and their remedy, by due course of law, 'denied' or, at least, 'delayed,' until vindicated and restored by the slow process of the proverbially sluggish channels of jurisprudence."

"Many cases of the infringement of constitutional rights could be conceived and enlarged upon, to illustrate in strong relief this position, but the mere ad mission of the principle of entire and complete power —without responsibility—to adjudicate for the time being, upon those rights and privileges, will suggest them to all freemen who are acquainted with, and jealous of what of right belongs to them as their inheritance under our form of government. It is a legal motto, full of meaning, and not too strong in expression which declares that, '*Misera est servitus, ubi lex est vaga aut incerta.*' And certainly in no code of laws can one be pointed out more obnoxious to this reproach, than that of a supposed offense which finds its enactment, its tribunal, and its punishment in one and the same source."

100. The learned judge, however, does not hesitate to admit that the power, or rather, the potentiality of the court to exercise the discretion is the most potent engine of the authority and usefulness of courts, and, when soberly and judiciously administered, to the greatest interest of the public good; and he concludes, by denying that the fact that it is capable of abuse should constitute a reason for its abrogation, as follows:

101. "The shield which our constitution throws around the press has been held up to interpose before the power of courts to punish for contempts. The most dearly prized offspring of our national liberty is the freedom of the press. It is so because it can be made its most effectual protection at home, and because it can be employed as the apostle of those liberties, to millions abroad. The worst enemy to freedom is ignorance. Instruct men in a knowledge of their rights, and a vindication of those rights follows as surely as light follows the rising sun. Yet the freedom of the press is abused to base and unworthy purposes. Such, indeed, as sad experience teaches, is often the melancholy fate of the greatest blessings that a wise providence has bestowed upon us, or that human skill has invented. The free air we breathe is essential to our existence, but when infected with pestilential matter it becomes the most terrible weapon of death. But who would argue, because disease may float in the atmosphere, that that atmosphere should be destroyed ?[1]

It is not within the scope of the present chapter to essay a full discussion of the law of contempt; it being only where such contempt is committed by the pen that it enters into our inquiry.

Contempts by the pen arise mainly in the publication of language or statements which impair the authority of courts, or their usefulness in the course of their administration or legitimate scrutiny.

The questions of contempt of courts, and what are privileged communications by written or printed matter, are in many cases difficult of separation. It has been attempted, however, to treat the latter question according to the three classes under which all communications group themselves. Such communications, when reflecting upon individuals, we have examined in the chapter on Libel; when published in newspapers exclusively, we have treated them, as far as possible, in the chapter on Newspapers, while in the present chapter we have striven to confine ourselves strictly to its title.

102. The common law defined three classes of contempts of court, namely: Those which scandalize the court itself; those which calumniate, villify, or ridicule the parties concerned in causes before the court; and those which prejudice the public before

[1] 12 Miss. (Sm. & Mar.) 781.

the cause is heard, or the cause itself before the court. The disregard of the process of a court is also a contempt thereof. And any literary or artistic work, writing, manuscript, letter, book, magazine, or newspaper article, picture, or caricature, which, in intention or effect, would do either of the above, will bring itself under the charge of obstructing the course of justice by corrupting its sources and its channels, and incur the penalties attached to a contempt of court.

103. Contempts of court, by written matter, can arise in at least four different ways:—I. By a statement reflecting upon any officer of a court while in session, providing such reflection interfere, or have a tendency to interfere, with his duty as an officer of the court in discharge of the legitimate duty of the court. II. By a disrespect shown to the court itself. III. By such comments upon the proceedings of the court as will tend to weaken the confidence of the people in their courts; impair its usefulness or its impartiality or as will tend to produce a prejudgment of a case undergoing investigation before it; and—IV. By unauthorized reports of the proceedings of the courts. As will be seen in treating of the first of these sorts, a libel upon an individual—under any of the definitions given in the chapter on libel—will not lose its libelous character, and become contempt of court, merely because that individual is employed as an officer of a court. The latter's remedy will still be for a libel. If, however, the circumstances of the attack upon the individual cannot be separated from the circumstances of his employment, the attack will constitute contempt of court, and the remedy proceed out of the court upon its own motion.

104. "Not only contempts in the face of a court

of record," says Dr. Dwight,[1] speaking of the old common-law doctrines upon the subject, "but alleged libels published out of court, upon the administration of justice, might be regarded either as direct offenses against the king's peace, in which case they would be tried by jury, or they might be considered as attacks on the dignity of the court, when they would be regarded as contempts. In the one view, the alleged delinquent had the protection of twelve of his fellow-citizens, and of regular modes of trial, and could only be convicted upon the evidence of witnesses; in the other, the matter was examined by the court, and perhaps by a single judge, who considered himself to have been insulted. The proceeding was summary, and without the usual safeguards. The accused could be required to answer interrogatories of the most searching character. The judge could put his own interpretation on the words used, and the skill of a man of thorough training in the use of language might be employed to attach a meaning to words which was possible and plausible, though not ordinary and natural. Charges which could never be substantiated before a jury, might meet with swift condemnation and punishment at the hands of an offended magistrate. The matter of criminal contempts is left in a very undefined condition at the common law. Blackstone classifies the cases under seven general heads, the last of which is, for the present purpose, the most important. 'Contempts,' he says, 'may arise in the face of the court, as by rude and contumelious behavior; by obstinacy, perverseness, and prevarication; by breach or the peace, or any willful disturb-

[1] See a paper prepared upon the occasion of the passage of the celebrated Contempt of Court Amendments to the Code of Procedure of the State of New York, 1871.

ance whatever; . . . . by speaking or writing contemptuously of the court or judges, acting in their judicial capacity; by printing false accounts, or even true ones, without proper permission, of causes then depending in judgment; and by anything, in short, that demonstrates a gross want of that regard and respect which, when once courts of justice are deprived of their authority, is entirely lost among the people.' "

105. I. As to contempts of court by defamatory statements concerning an officer of a court in session, it is the theory of the law that officers of a court in session are ministers of the justice of the state.

The offense of contempt of court is, therefore, not an offense against the particular officer whose person or whose edict happens to be ignored or disobeyed, but against the state.

II. In speaking of contempts of court by a libel of the judge, Scott, J., said:[1] "When, therefore, the common law deemed it so necessary, for this great purpose (*i.e.*, the public good), to protect the juror, the witness, the informer, the party, the jailor, the attorney, and other persons, many of whom might never again be called into a court of justice, it was not to be expected that it would fail to cover, with its complete armor, the presiding minister of the law's majesty, who would be so often exposed to similar trials."

"Not that any higher personal privileges were arrogated to him than to the humblest of these, but because it was obvious that the principle which suggested the protection of these would be powerless if it did not also protect him, since the majesty of the law might be more degraded in the person of a higher than of a lower officer intrusted with its administration."

[1] Neel v. State, 9 Eng. (Ark.) 268.

"To the same source are to be traced the numerous cases that have settled the doctrine that a judge acting within the scope of his jurisdiction shall not be called to answer for his judgment, except by impeachment, however erroneous, malicious, or even corrupt it may have been. But while the ægis of the law is so thrown over the judge, it finds no pleasure in him when he proves recreant to the high trust reposed in him; for, in the language of one of its oracles,[1] 'If a judge will so far forget the honor and dignity of his post as to turn solicitor in a cause which he is to judge, and privately and extrajudicially tamper with witnesses, or labor jurors, he hath no reason to complain if he be dealt with according to the capacity to which he so basely degrades himself;' nor does it animadvert upon his outdoor affairs more than upon those of other citizens, unless these are forced upon him on account of his judicial functions."

When, therefore, attachments were sent out for the various kinds of contempts which are summed up by Blackstone,[2] as "demonstrating a gross want of that regard and respect, which, when once courts of justice are deprived of their authority (so necessary for the good order of the kingdom) is entirely lost among the people;" they were not issued upon the idea that the abstract ideal, invisible judicial institution known as a court, had been injured; or because the efficacy of their process, rule, order, or writ, was impaired by such contumely, but because the public good, as connected with the preservation, in its purity, of the judicial institution required them, and that the authority and dignity of the officers in whom this ideal, invisible being called a court, is realized and personified

[1] Sergeant Hawkins.

[2] 4 Bl. Com. 286.

was sunk and degraded. And that the impurity of such conduct would deprive these institutions of the aid of public opinion in carrying into effect their ordinances, and render a resort to force in all cases necessary, and thus avert a state of things in which it is not probable that any judicial system could long exist."[1]

Chief Justice Wilmot[2] in discussing the objections to a proceeding to commit for contempt for a libelous attack upon a justice, namely, that it is an invasion upon the ancient simplicity of the law; that it took its rise from the Statute of Westminster (ch. 2), that that act applies only to persons resisting process; and that—while proper to remove obstructions to the execution of process, or to any contumelious treatment of it, or to any contempt of the authority of the court—papers reflecting merely upon the qualities of judges themselves are not proper objects of an attachment; that judges have proper remedies to recover a satisfaction for such reflections by actions of *scandalum magnatum;* and that in the case of a peer, the House of Lords may be applied to for a breach of privilege; that such libelers may be brought to punishment by indictment or information; that there are but few instances of this sort of libels on courts or judges; that libels of this kind have been prosecuted by actions and indictments; and that, should attach-

[1] 9 Eng. (Ark.) 268.

[2] In an elaborate judgment, prepared, and intended to be delivered in the case of an application in 1765 by the attorney-general for attachment against J. Almon, for publishing a pamphlet entitled "A Letter concerning Libels, Warrants, Seizure of Papers, &c.," containing many libelous passages upon the court of king's bench, and the chief justice, charging the court, and particularly the chief justice, with having introduced a proceeding to deprive the subject of the benefit of the *Habeas Corpus* Act.

ments be extended to libels of this nature, judges would be determining their own wrongs, &c., and denies that attachments derived their origin from the Statute of Westminster (ch. 2). "The power which the courts in Westminster Hall have of vindicating their own authority," he says, is "coeval with their first foundation and institution; it is a necessary incident to every court of justice, whether of record or not, to fine and imprisonment for a contempt to the court acted in the face of it. And the issuing of attachments by the supreme courts of justice in Westminster Hall for contempts out of court, stands upon the same immemorial usage as supports the whole fabric of the common law: it is as much the *lex terræ*, and within the exception of Magna Charta as the issuing any other legal process whatsoever."

To the objection that there is not such necessity for summary punishment, in the case of libels upon courts or judges, as in the case of resistance of process, his Lordship said: "When the nature of the offense of libeling judges for what they do in their judicial capacity, either in court or out of court, comes to be considered, it does, in my opinion, become more proper for an attachment than any other case whatsoever. . . . . The arraignment of the justice of the judges is arraigning the king's justice; it is an impeachment of his wisdom and goodness in the choice of his judges, and excites in the minds of the people a general dissatisfaction with all judicial determinations, and indisposes their minds to obey them; and whenever men's allegiance to the law is so fundamentally shaken, it is the most fatal and most dangerous obstruction of justice, and, in my opinion, calls out for a more rapid and immediate redress than any other obstruction whatsoever; not for the sake of the judges as private individuals, but because they are the channels by which the king's justice is conveyed to the people. To be impartial, and to be universally thought so, are both absolutely necessary for the giving justice that free, open, and uninterrupted current which it has for many ages found all over this kingdom, and which so eminently distinguishes and exalts it above all nations upon the earth."

"The constitution has provided very apt and proper remedies for correcting and rectifying the involuntary mistakes of judges, and for punishing and removing them for any voluntary perversions of justice. But if their authority is to be trampled upon by pamphleteers and news-writers, and the people are to be told that the power given to the judges for their protection is prostituted to their destruction, the court may retain its power some little time, but I am sure it will instantly lose all its authority. The power of the court will not long survive the authority of it."

As to whether a judge making an order at his house or chambers is not acting in his judicial capacity as a judge of the court, and both his person and character under the same protection as if he were sitting in court: "It is conceded," he says, "that an act of violence upon his person when he was making such an order would be a contempt punishable by attachment: upon what principle? for striking a judge in walking along the streets would not be a contempt of the court. The reason, therefore, must be, that he is in the exercise of his office, and discharging the function of a judge of this court; and if his person is under this protection, why should not his character be under the same protection? It is not for the sake of the individual, but for the sake of the public, that his person is under such protection; and in respect of the public, the imputing corruption and the perversion of justice to him, in an order made by him at his chambers, is attended with much more mischievous consequences than a blow; and, therefore, the reason of proceeding in this summary manner applies with equal, if not superior, force to one case as well as the other. There is no greater obstruction to the execution of justice from the striking a judge, than from the abusing him, because his order lies open to be enforced or discharged, whether the judge is struck or abused for making it or not. It may, perhaps, merit a less punishment to libel a single judge in court or out of court, than to libel the whole court; but the question of the offense does not vary the mode of prosecuting it; it is an offense *ejusdem generis*, although *inferioris gradus;* and I cannot explore a single reason which can be urged to cover the judges in court against calumny and detraction for what they do there, which does not hold equally true, though in a less degree, when applied to what they do in their judicial capacities out of court."

106. III. Any publication pending a suit, reflecting upon the court, the jury, the parties, the officers of the court, or the counsel, with reference to the suit, or tending to influence the decision of the controversy, is a contempt of court, and punishable by attachment.[1]

A slur or innuendo cast upon a court by means of written matter, will be contemptuous.[2] Thus, where an attorney wrote on the court docket, opposite the entry of a cause in which he was engaged, the words following:

[1] Hollingsworth v. Duane, Wallace R. 77.

[2] People v. Freer, 1 Caines, 485, 518; Bayard v. Passmore,

"Having become satisfied that we cannot get the law administered, by direction of the plaintiff I hereby dismiss this action, without prejudice to the plaintiff.

"JOS. SMITH,

"March 6th, 1867." For Plaintiff.

It was held that the foreign and unnecessary matter, introduced into the order dismissing the suit, could only be regarded as a direct reflection on the integrity of the court. So in the matter of the high sheriff of Surrey,[1] where a judge of assize ordered part of the court to be cleared on account of the noise made by the persons assembled there, and the high sheriff of the county caused a placard, signed by him, to be posted up in the town opposite the court, in which he recorded his protest against "this unlawful proceeding" of the learned judge, and said, "I have given directions that the court shall be opened again to the public according to the custom and the law. All persons, so long as they conduct themselves with decorum, have a lawful right to be present in court; and I hereby prohibit my officers from aiding and abetting any attempt to bar out the public from free access to the court": it was held to be a contempt of court.

Threatening letters written to persons concerned in a trial, either as judge, parties, witnesses, solicitors, or jurymen, are alike contemptuous of the court, and there is no difference in the degree of the crime, whether it be to the officer or the person summoned.[2]

3 Yeates, 439; Morrison v. Moor, 3 Edw. Ch. 25. In Passmore's Case, the matter was written with chalk on a blackboard.

[1] 2 F. & F. 237.

[2] Smith v. Lakeman, 26 L. J. 305, ch. —; Shaw v. Shaw, 31 L. J. Prob. 35; 6 L. T. N. S. 477; 2 S. & T. 515; *re* Mulock, 33 L. J. Prob. 205; 10 Jur. N. S. 1188.

107. And so any one sitting in the place or stead of a judge, will likewise be entitled to protection. Where a barrister and member of parliament who wrote a letter in threatening and insulting terms to a master in chancery, before whom he had appeared in support of a petition presented by himself and others, the tendency of the letter being to induce the master to alter the opinion he was supposed to have formed upon the case, he was committed by the Lord Chancellor (Cottenham) to the Fleet during pleasure. His lordship saying: "the power of committal is given to courts of justice for the purpose of securing the better and more secure administration of justice. Every writing, letter, or publication which has for its object to divert the course of justice is a contempt of the court. It would be strange, indeed, if the judges of the court were the only persons not protected from libels, writings, and proceedings, the direct object of which is to pervert the cause of justice. Every insult offered to a judge in the exercise of the duties of his office is a contempt; but when the writing or publication proceeds further, and when—not by inference, but by plain and direct language—a threat is used, the object of which is to induce a judicial officer to depart from the course of his judicial duty, and to adopt a course he would not otherwise pursue, it is a contempt of the very highest order."[1]

[1] Mr. Lechmere Charlton's Case, 2 My. & Cr. 316.

Lord Abinger, C.B., and Alderson, B., seem to have taken a different view of the mode of dealing with insulting letters addressed to a judge, touching a matter under consideration. "I can only say," said Lord Abinger, "that if I received such a letter I should not consider myself at liberty to commit the writer." To which Alderson, B., added: "There would be a great many committals if such a course were pursued by the judges." "Do you mean to say," asked Lord Abinger of counsel, "that one of the judges has the power to fine a man

"The principle upon which attachments issue for libels upon courts," said Wilmot, J., "is of a more enlarged and important nature (than that upon which attachments are granted in certain other cases)—it is to keep a blaze of glory around them, and to deter people from attempting to render them contemptible in the eyes of the public." The law cannot be understood as a respecter of persons, but she will very zealously respect her own instruments.

108. As to matters disrespectful to the court: It has been very recently held to be a contempt of court for counsel in a case to hand up to the court a written paper protesting against his hearing a certain case on the ground of his personal prejudice against the prisoner. And we think that the ruling is grounded in good sense. The statutes of the various states appear to enumerate the cases in which a judge shall be disqualified from sitting; but it does not appear to be just that counsel should be at liberty to conclude, from their own opinions, or from hearsay, or from matters not upon the record, that a certain judge is unfitted to preside at a trial. Though possibly the distinction might arise just here: that it would not be contemptuous for counsel to object to the judge's sitting, in the course of their argument, if they believed it for their client's interest so to do; but only when they went so far—upon such objection being overruled or ignored—to write out a paper in the form of a protest, and hand it to the judge, personally, upon the bench.[1]

for sending him a silly letter, or an impudent letter about any matter that he has decided? I can only say I should be very much afraid of exercising it" (See Rex v. Faulkner, 2 Mont. & Ayr. 321, 322).

[1] People v. Tweed, Matter of Contempt, N. Y. S. C. 1874.

So, again, to write a letter to a judge, before whom a proceeding is depending, attempting to influence his decision therein;[1] or to the foreman of a grand jury which has before it the case of one accused of an indictable offense.[2]

Where a barrister and attorney, not in his professional capacity, but in his private capacity as a suitor, in respect of a supposed grievance and injury done him as a suitor, wrote a letter to the chief justice of Nova Scotia, reflecting on the judges and the administration of justice generally in the court, the privy council held that an order suspending the writer from practicing in the court was not an appropriate punishment for the offense, and on that ground advised her Majesty to discharge the order.[3]

"The letter," said Lord Westbury, in delivering the judgment of the privy council in that case, "was a contempt of court, which it was hardly possible for the court to omit taking cognizance of. It was an offense, however, committed by an individual in his capacity of a suitor in respect of his supposed rights as a suitor, and of an imaginary injury done to him as a suitor, and it had no connection whatever with his professional character, or anything done by him professionally either as an advocate or an attorney. It was a contempt of court committed by an individual in his personal character only. To offenses of that kind there has been attached by law and by long practice a definite kind of punishment, viz., fine and imprisonment. It must not, however, be supposed that

[1] *Ex parte* McGill, 2 Fowl. 474; Eagleton v. Duchess of Kingston, 8 Ves. 467; Gould v. Hulme, 3 C. & P. 625.

[2] Bergh's Case, Abb. Pr. N. S. See *post*, this chapter.

[3] *Re* Wallace, L. R. 1 P. C. App. 283; 14 L. T. N. S. 286; 36 L. J. 9 P. C. C.; 14 W. R. 609. See also *re* Downie, 3 Moore's P. C. C. 414.

a court of justice has not the power to remove the officers of the court, if unfit to be intrusted with a professional status and character. If an advocate, for example, were found guilty of crime, there is no doubt that the court would suspend him. If an attorney be found guilty of moral delinquency in his private character, there is no doubt that he may be struck off the roll. But in this particular case there is no *delictum* brought forward or assigned; except that which results from the fact of addressing an improper and contemptuous letter to the chief justice of the court, in respect of something supposed to have been done, unjustly to the writer, in his private capacity as a suitor. We think, therefore, there was no necessity for the judges to go further than to award to that offense the customary punishment for contempt of court."

An attorney of the king's bench, in the reign of Edward III., was committed for having written a letter to one of the king's council, reflecting on the judges, saying: "That neither Sir William Scot, chief justice, nor his fellows the king's justices, nor their clerks, any great thing would do by the commandment of our lord the king, nor of Queen Philippa, in that place more than of any other of the realm."[1]

The writer of a letter to Lord Hardwicke relative to a threatened suit, and inclosing a bank-note, was held guilty of contempt;[2] and so was the writer of a letter to Chief Baron Parker, making mention of a

[1] 3 Inst. 174.

[2] Macgill's Case, 2 Fowl. Ex. Prac. 404. And in 18—, Judge Barnard, of the New York supreme court, read from the bench a letter he had received from General Santa Anna, relating to a case in which the latter was a litigant, and which was about to be tried before him. "I will show the general," said Judge Barnard, "that this is not a Mexican court."

cause depending in the court of exchequer, and containing a scandalous offer to his lordship.

109. Where the offensive matter is directed to the judge upon the bench, the question whether it will constitute libel or contempt, will depend upon whether the charges published affect the judge's personal character or reputation as a man, or his record, character, and reputation for fairness, and general ability and reliability as a judge.

Thus, in Rex v. Almon,[1] the publisher of the letters of Junius was arraigned for contempt of court, for comments upon Lord Mansfield; but the prosecution was ultimately abandoned, and the defendant proceeded against for libel.

So, in Neel v. State,[2] where one James P. Neel, an attorney, affixed to a judge's door a writing to the effect that "Sebron G. Sneed (the judge's name) is a dam'd base and corrupt man," it was held that the words were published of the judge as a man, and not as a judge, and were not, therefore, contempt of court.

This distinction has been carried to great lengths. In the Matter of Hickey,[3] for example, a scandalous charge against a member of a court, connected with a cause pending at the time the charge was made, was held to constitute, not contempt, but libel.

In that case the circuit court was engaged in trying an indictment for murder, when an article appeared in the defendant's newspaper, charging the judge upon the bench with being a criminal abettor of the murder.

In a proceeding to commit the defendant for contempt—held, that the publication was a libel, and not

[1] 5 Burr. 2686; Bishop on Criminal Law, § 216.
[2] 4 Eng.(Ark.) 259.
[3] 12 Miss. (4 Sou. & Mar.) 751.

a contempt. But, with all deference to the learned judge's opinion, we can hardly accept this decision as satisfactory. It seems to us that this charge would come under all of the definitions of contempt that have been given. It is an attack upon an officer of the court, since it charges him with a criminal interest in the case in court before him. It is a disrespect to him. It tends to impair public confidence in the court, and its usefulness in investigating truth. And surely such a charge against the character of the presiding judge must be held to "scandalize the court itself."[1] That the charge was libelous, indeed, there

[1] It is equally indispensable to repress in the like speedy and effectual manner all attempts which may be made with relation to any trial depending at the time, or which has recently been so, to slander the proceedings of the court, or depreciate the character, or sully the honor of the judges; or to impose on their wisdom and pollute the demands of justice, to the prejudice of a fair and an impartial trial. In former times, they scrupled not summarily to inflict high corporal pains for transgressions of the first of these kinds. As in the case of Donald Campbell, who, in the course of a trial, when standing among the multitude by the courthouse, had openly accused the Earl of Athol, justice-general, of gross partiality and corruption in the case; he had sentence, therefore, to stand two hours upon the cuck-stool and make public confession of his fault, and to have his tongue bored by the common executioner. More lately, after the conviction of Nairn and Ogilvy, certain printers were rebuked (and, on account of their submission, were dismissed without further answer) for publishing an opinion of English counsel on the case, accompanied with notes highly injurious to the court and the jury. In a still later instance, an account had been published of a certain trial, equally slanderous of the proceedings of the court, and contemptuous of the persons of the judges; and here, as the offense was not followed with the like symptoms of contrition, the culprits Johnson and Drummond were sent to jail for three months, and till they should find surety for their good behavior for the future. In these several instances the court guarded their own honor. Hume, 2 Com. 139.

can be no doubt; but it seems to us that this was a contempt, as well as a libel.

In treating of the English law upon this question of libeling judges, a late writer[1] says: "There is no instance of a judge at chambers fining or imprisoning, without the authority of the court, for any insult offered to him there. We must distinguish, in this respect, between a judge of a court of record and the court of record itself." "No one of the rights, privileges, and incidents of a judge of a court of record," says Alderson, B., "necessarily carries with it the power of committing for contempt." Where the proprietor and printer of a newspaper were tried upon an information filed by the attorney-general, for a libel upon Le Blanc, J., and the jury before whom the captain of a merchant-ship had been tried for murder at the Old Bailey, Grose, J., said: "It certainly was lawful, with decency and candor, to discuss the propriety of the verdict of a jury, or the decisions of a judge; and if the defendants should be thought to have done no more in this instance, they would be entitled to an acquittal; but, on the contrary, they had transgressed the law, and ought to be convicted, if the extracts from the newspapers set out in the information contained no reasoning or discussion, but only declamation and invective, and were written not with a view to elucidate the truth, but to injure the character of individuals, and to bring into hatred and contempt the administration of justice in the country."[2]

110. IV. As to the publication of comments tending to prejudice a case in the minds of the court, the jury, or the public at large:

The publication in a newspaper, pending a cause

[1] Shortt L. L. 361.

[2] Rex v. White, 1 Camp. N. P. 359.

in chancery, of articles reflecting on the plaintiff and his witnesses, and characterizing the chancery proceedings as vexatious and unprincipled, and representing the affidavits as "containing glaring misrepresentations, which the editor believed, and heartily hoped, would lead to an indictment for perjury," is a contempt of court.[1] "If parties in the prosecution of their rights," said Lord Langdale, Master of the Rolls, "are to be exposed to this species of attack, and are to be placed in such a situation that they cannot safely proceed in the defense of their rights, and if witnesses are, in this way, deterred from coming forward in aid of legal proceedings, it will be impossible that justice can be administered. It would be better that the doors of the courts of justice were at once closed."[2] Or, if the publication comment upon affidavits filed in the case, but not yet before the court.[3] So in a recent case a motion was made on the part of the plaintiff that the publisher of the "Pall Mall Gazette" newspaper might be committed to the Queen's prison, for a contempt of the court, in having published in that paper, an article containing comments on certain affidavits which had been filed in support of the plaintiff's case, but had not yet been brought before the court. Similar applications were at the same time made to commit the publishers of certain other newspapers, for having published the same article. The vice-chancellor (Wood) said: "I have no hesitation in saying that a gross contempt of court has been committed in this case. The first observation I would make is, that, from the time of Lord Hardwicke downwards, the rule

[1] Littler v. Thompson, 2 Beav. 129.

[2] Id.

[3] *Vid.* also Felkin v. Herbert, 9 L. T. N. S. 635; 33 L. J. 294 C. H; Rex v. Clement, 4 B. & Ald. 218; Tichborne v. Mostyn, 17 L. T. N. S. 5; L. Rep. 7 Eq. 55.

which that great judge laid down in Roach v. Garvan, has been the rule which the court has adopted for its guidance, namely, the determination on the part of the court to discountenance any attempt to prejudice mankind against the merits of a case before it has been heard. I have not the slightest doubt that such an attempt has been made here, and that it has been made in the most offensive manner. An opinion has been pronounced by the author of this article (who sits down to examine these affidavits with a clear and decided bias) with all that boldness which persons under the screen of the anonymous, and having no responsibility cast upon them, think themselves entitled to indulge in. But those who have responsibility cast upon them, this court—and every tribunal which has to administer justice—is bound to protect every suitor from such an attempt to pervert the course of justice. I am not entitled to consider myself above being influenced by articles of this description, though I should hope I am. I am not entitled to think that the jury whom I may have to summon in the case are above such influences, though perhaps I ought to do so."[1]

III. And when the publication is a copy from another paper, of matter contemptuous of a court, the publisher and printer of the second paper will be, together with the publisher of the first, guilty of contempt.[2] The rule as to newspaper comments will not

[1] 2 Atk. 469.

[2] Tichbourne v. Mostyn, 17 L. T. N. S. 5; L. R. 7 Eq. 55; 2 Id. The publisher of the "Pall Mall Gazette," having made a humble submission and apology, the vice-chancellor thought it sufficient for the purposes of justice to order him to pay the costs of the motion. A similar order was made with respect to the printer of another paper which had gone beyond a mere insertion of the article from the "Pall Mall Gazette," and the

extend to comments of any description on a matter that is pending, waiting for argument, and waiting for decision; but courts will not permit comments to be made on any documents whatever, which are before the writer and not before the court, but which are afterwards to come before the court, if such comments have a clear and distinct tendency to directing and swaying the mind of the court or jury, or whoever may have to determine the cause.[1]

112. It is a contempt for the solicitor of one of the parties to a suit to write letters, for publication in a newspaper, which may tend to influence the result of the suits;[2] so, for a party to print his brief, before the cause came on, was held a contempt of court, though there was nothing in the publication reflecting upon the court in any way.[3]

motions against the other papers were abandoned. *Vid.* also Tichbourne v. Tichbourne, 22 L. T. N. S. 55.

[1] Tichbourne v. Mostyn, *ubi supra.*

[2] Dan v. Eley, L. R. 7 Eq. 49.

[3] *Vid.* per Lord Hardwicke, 2 Atk. 471; S. C., *nom.* Roach v. Garvan, 2 Dick. 794.

"It is highly important," said Lord Romilly, M. R., "that the court should not allow steps of this sort to be taken by the officers of the court, in causes in which they are engaged, which possibly may have an effect favorable to their client, or unfavorable to the other side; and I may further say that if I am to go minutely into every sentence of a letter which is written in a public newspaper, to say this is questionable, and that is doubtful, and the like, it is imposing a task and a duty upon the court which it will be impossible to perform. There is one distinct line drawn, which is this: that gentlemen who are concerned for contending clients in this court, whether solicitors or counsel, should abstain entirely from discussing the merits of those questions in public print; if they do it at all, they ought to put their names to their communications. But to let the public suppose that it is merely done by a person who takes a great interest in, and has great knowledge of, the subject, and discusses it from a public point of view, when, if the fact were known, he is the solicitor of the defendant, and

113. And, it seems, not only will the truth or falsity of the publication make no difference[1] in the

has the strongest possible interest in his suceess, is, in my opinion, highly reprehensible."

The letters published in this case were anonymous. The suit was to restrain the infringement of a patent—one of the issues raised being as to the novelty of the plaintiff's invention—and the letters written by the defendant's solicitor stated facts tending to disprove the novelty of the invention. On the appearance of the first letter, the plaintiff wrote to the editor referring to the suit, and suggesting that the writer of the published letter was an interested party. Notwithstanding this, the editor, besides refusing to insert the plaintiff's letter, as containing personal imputations, afterwards published a further anonymous letter from the defendant's solicitor, knowing that he was a solicitor, but not knowing that he was the solicitor in the pending suit. A motion was made to commit the editor, also, for a contempt of court, but the motion was refused; the editor, however, having to pay his own costs. Lord Romilly said: "The case of the editor of a newspaper is very different from that of persons who write letters to the paper for publication. His duty is simply to take no part in matters purely personal between individuals, or in matters which are the subject of a lawsuit. But it often happens that private matters are so mixed up with public matters, into which it is his duty to enter, that it is very difficult to draw the distinction between them. In this case, if the editor had inserted Mr. D.'s (the plaintiff's) letter, I should have thought that there was nothing in his conduct calling for the interference of the court; but he did not insert it, and afterwards, with notice that a suit was pending, with the knowledge that the author of the letters was Mr. C., and that Mr. C. was a solicitor—which ought to have induced him to inquire further, and ascertain the exact position which Mr. C. occupied—he allowed further letters on both sides to be published. I am inclined to think, by what the plaintiff told him, he was put upon inquiry whether 'Copper Cap' (the *nom de plume* of the letter-writer) was connected with the suit." His lordship, having taken time to consider the matter, said, on a subsequent day: "As regards the case of the editor, I think that he did not show quite the forbearance towards Mr. D. that he might have done, considering how materially interested Mr.

[1] Hollinsworth v. Duane, Wallace, 77.

offense, but even if it be neither true nor false, it may be contemptuous—as where the matter consists of an advertisement.[1]

The publication, in a newspaper, of an advertisement offering a reward for evidence tending to establish one side of a controversy pending before the court, is a contempt of court, as tending to produce false evidence;[2] and Lord Hardwicke once committed a person who published an advertisement relating to an answer in a chancery suit; saying that his reason for committing was "not only for the sake of the party injured by such advertisement, but for sake of the public proceedings in court, to hinder such advertisements which tend to prepossess people as to the proceedings in the court."[3] And it seems that even pendency of the litigation will not be deemed necessary, to give courts jurisdiction to punish where the contempt is flagrant.[4]

D. was in the matter; and that he might have made some little excuse for the warmth which Mr. D. showed upon the subject. At the same time there is nothing I can find against the editor for which I can require him either to make an apology or to pay the costs of this motion; but, for the reasons I stated on the last occasion, I cannot give him costs. That is out of the question. He has certainly shown a tendency to decide against Mr. D.; but I also feel for the difficult position in which an editor is placed in such cases. But, as I said before, with respect to him I can make no order."

[1] W. Bl. Com. 285; Respublica v. Oswald, 1 Dallas, 319; *In re* Benson & Mitchell, 12 Johns. 460.

[2] Pool v. Sacheverel, 1 P. Wms. 675.

[3] Mrs. Farley's Case, 2 Ves. Sr. 520.

[4] Shortt, 378.

"It is a reproach to the nation," said the lord chancellor (Parker), in that case, "and an insufferable thing, to make a public offer in print to produce evidence; and is tantamount to saying, that such persons as will come in and swear, or procure others to swear such a thing, shall have £100 reward, and this in a cause now depending here. If £100 is to be

In the last quoted case the court[1] granted a commitment, observing that such an advertisement tended to the subornation of witnesses, was very dangerous, and not only criminal, but "a means of preventing justice in a cause now depending."

It will be noticed that, were it not for the words above given in quotation marks, the ruling of his lordship would go to characterize the offering of the reward in the advertisement, and not the advertisement itself (a proceeding in the nature of a subornation), as the offense in this case.

114. The true liberty of the press requires the amplest and most unrestricted right of every man, not only to maintain and possess, but to publish, if he will, his own opinions. But, as we have seen (in our inquiry concerning the laws of libel), it is due to the dignity and peace of society to possess a supervisory power over the motives of such publications, to be exercised when necessary to distinguish between those opinions, expressed in the interests of good manners, of the reformation of individuals, or of institutions, and with an eye solely to the public good; and those which are intended to defame (as in the case of libel), or to delude and prejudice. To opinions of the latter description it is impossible that any good government should afford protection and impunity.

allowed, the same reason will hold as to the allowing of £500 or £1,000. And though the intention of the person so advertising may be innocent (and I, knowing the man, believe it was so, inasmuch that if a court may be said to have inclinations or impressions from thence, I must own, I should be influenced by my knowing Mr. Pool to be an honest man), yet the justice of the court nay, the justice of the nation, being concerned in so public a case, I cannot dismiss the party, though his counsel offer to pay costs to the other side, but in justice and for example's sake, he must stand committed."

[1] Parker, L. C.

"If the liberty of the press, then, is regulated by any just principle, there can be little doubt that he who attempts to raise a prejudice against his antagonist in the minds of those who must ultimately determine the dispute between them, who for that purpose represents himself as persecuted, and asserts that his judges are influenced by passion and prejudice; willfully seeks to corrupt the source and to dishonor the administration of justice."[1]

115. The publication of an article, in a newspaper printed and circulated in the place where a court is sitting, reflecting, in severe and opprobrious terms, on the character of a criminal prosecution then pending in a court, and standing in order for trial—if the publication be made at a time and in circumstances such as would naturally bring it to the notice of jurors and others who are in attendance on the court—is a contempt of that court.[2]

In the Matter of Sturoc,[3] the court said: "It must not be inferred that we question the right to criticise and censure the conduct of courts and parties when causes have been finally decided. The question, in this case, is whether publications can be permitted, which have a tendency to prejudice the decision of pending causes. The publishers of newspapers have the right, but no higher right than others, to bring to public notice the conduct of courts and parties after the decision has been made; and, provided the publications are true, and fair in spirit, there is no law—and

[1] Per McKean, Ch. J., in Respublica v. Oswald, 1 Dallas, 319.

[2] *Re* Stinoc, 48 N. H. 428; People v. Wilson, Albany Law Journal, Nov., 1872, vol. 6, p. 352; Bronson's Case, 12 Johns. 460; Yates v. Lansing, 9 Id. 417; Tenney's Case, 23 N. H. 165; State v. Matthews, 37 Id. 450.

48 N. H. 428; Bishop on Crimes, § 216.

I am sure there is no disposition—to restrain or punish the freest expression of disapprobation that any person may entertain."

116. If, during the trial of his cause, a litigant publish matter in his own defense, and reflecting upon his adversary therein, it will be deemed a contempt of court.[1]

Or if a litigant write threatening and abusive letters to parties engaged or concerned in the court or the controversy, it will likewise be construed to be contempt.[2]

A solicitor in a bankruptcy proceeding was held guilty of a gross contempt of court in publishing a pamphlet containing insulting observations on the court of review, and on certain parties engaged in litigation before it. The pamphlet spoke of the judgment of the judge as "an elaborate production, wholly beside the merits of the case, free from all allusions to the facts or statements in the affidavits, which it was but charity to suppose were never referred to by the judge; free from all denunciations against fraud; and that the only object of it seemed to have been to deter solicitors from every attempt to expose and correct abuses in bankruptcy." The court of review considered this to be a gross and scandalous contumacy of, and a gross libel upon, the learned judge, which ought to be visited as a contempt of that court; and committed the writer to custody; from which he was released, however, on humbly apologizing and paying all the costs incidental to the application.[3]

[1] Rex v. Jolliffe, 4 Term R. 285 (1791).

[2] Charlton's Case, 2 Mylne & C. 316; 2 Russ. & M. 674, n.; Macgill's Case, 2 Fowl. Sch. Prac. 474; *Re* Jones, 13 Ves. 237; Anon., 2 Ves. Sr. 520; Rex v. Fleet, 1 Barn. & A. 379; Roach v. Sarvan, 2 Atk. 464; 2 Dick. 749; Lofft, 465; *Re* Sturoc, 48 N. H. 428.

[3] Ex parte Turner, 3 Mont. D. & De G. 523, 551, 558.

117. A false and exaggerated account of a trial, published pending the trial, will be punished as a contempt.[1]

118. And it has been held that, even in cases where the publication of statements having a tendency to interfere with the administration of justice does not call for punishment, the court may, nevertheless, interfere to prohibit such publication. Thus, where one William Haire was charged with the murder of James Wilson, on the motion of the counsel for the accused, with reference to an advertisement of a forthcoming publication of the confession of William Burke, which had been amnounced in the "Edinburgh Evening Courant," the lords prohibited "the editor and publisher of the 'Edinburgh Evening Courant' from publishing or circulating any statement relative to the alleged murder of James Wilson, or anything prejudicial to the prisoner, William Haire, in the said confession, or doing anything whereby the same may be published, till the proceedings now in dependence against the said William Haire shall be brought to a conclusion; and recommended to the publishers of all newspapers to abstain in like manner from doing so."[2]

119. The publication of matter designed or tending to prejudice the public mind, in any way, in a cause depending before a court of justice, is a contempt of that court.

And even though the matter be published whilst the court is not sitting; and at a place somewhat distant, a court of record has still the power of punishing by commitment.[3] The publisher and the writer of an article in a newspaper, which reflected intemperately

[1] Shaw's Cases, No. 4; Matter of McLeod, Id. No. 6.

[2] Bell's Notes, 165; Edmond's Case, 7 December, 1829, Shaw, Id.

[3] Crawford's Case, 13 Q. B. 613.

on certain proceedings of the court of chancery of the Isle of Man, were committed to prison for the contempt, though the court was not sitting at the time of publication, and the publication took place in Douglas, ten miles distant from where the court sat.[1] "It is objected," said Patterson, J., "that the court could have no general power of commitment for a libel published out of court some time before. This point has not been expressly decided upon. In Van Sandau's Case,[2] the libel appears to have been published both in court and out of it." And, even if the publication does not, upon its face, allude to the cause depending; if it, in fact, has reference to the cause, and its tendency is to prejudice the public mind—it will be held to be in contempt.[3]

For, if the unlawful intention must appear upon the face of the writing, an artful man may escape, with impunity, even though his publication have the most pernicious effect or tendency to interrupt the course of justice.[4]

120. In the Matter of Spooner,[5] before the mayor of the city of New York, a distinction was attempted between real and constructive contempt, which, it seems to us, no other cases on the subject, either earlier or later, can be understood to warrant.

121. Comments upon the proceedings of parties who are to be litigants in a forthcoming trial, at a session of the court already begun at the time when they are published, or who are to be witnesses or par-

[1] Id.

[2] Van Sandau v. Turner, 6 Q. B. 773; 1 Phill. 445, 605.

[3] Bayard v. Passmore, 3 Yeates, 438; Anon., 2 Ves. A1. 524; *Re* Sluise, 48 N. H. 428; People v. Wilson, 6 Albany Law Journal, 532.

[4] Bayard v. Passmore, 3 Yeates, 438.

[5] 5 City Hall Recorder, p. 108.

ties, will constitute a contempt if they tend or are likely to tend to prejudice the decisions, or to throw a suspicion of bias upon a certain decision which might be made.[1]

In November, 1872, the "Chicago Evening Journal" contained an article, commenting upon a criminal trial then in progress in the city of Chicago, as follows: "The riff-raff who contributed fourteen hundred dollars to demonstrate that 'hanging is played out,' may now congratulate themselves on the success of their little game. . . . . The money is operating splendidly. The courts are now completely in the control of corrupt and mercenary shysters—the jackals of the legal profession—who feast and fatten on human blood spilled by the hands of other men."—Held, to be a gross contempt of court, and to subject the editors and proprietors of that newspaper to attachment and imprisonment.[2]

During the pendency of an election petition, the proprietor of a newspaper published in his journal a series of articles which were calculated to interfere with the due course of justice; intended to prejudice the public mind against the petitioner; to prevent witnesses affording him their evidence; to deter him from prosecuting his petition, and, if he abandoned it, to deter any other qualified person from becoming petitioner in his stead.—Held, that the publications were a contempt of the court of common pleas.[3]

122. And even in a case where judgment had

[1] People v. Wilson, Illinois Supreme Court, 6 Albany Law Journal, November, 1872, vol. 4, pp. 301, 317, 334, 348, 349, 352.

[2] People v. Wilson, Illinois Supreme Court, 6 Albany Law Journal, November, 1872, vol. 4, p. 352. *Vid.* Bishop's Criminal Law, § 216; 5 Burr. 2686.

[3] Tyrone Election Petition, *in re* Macartney v. Corry, 7 Tr. R. C. L. 242 C. P.

been finally pronounced upon a petition, but the order itself had not been drawn up, it was considered a pending proceeding for the purpose of punishing a contempt;[1] the court saying in that case:

"If the principle be the protection of the subject in all fair matter of litigation, in order that his mind may be unbiased by threat or intimidation, and that he may go on freely through that course of proceeding which the laws of his country have provided for him, I cannot but consider it the duty of the court to protect him against an impression, that, when the proceeding is concluded, he may be liable to imputations and abuse, and have no protection but by going into a court of law for damages in an action for libel. I apprehend it is the duty of the court to the suitors, to tell them that, though the matter is ended with respect to them, the court will still protect them, as if the litigation or the business of the court were still pending; and that the principle is not varied by the circumstance that the matter is altogether concluded."

Though one party to a suit in chancery publish newspaper attacks on the conduct of his opponent, the latter will not be allowed, by way of defense, to publish, pending litigation, *ex parte* garbled accounts of any of the proceedings in court, or before the examiner.[2]

[1] *Ex parte* Turner, 3 Mont. D. & De G. 544 545

[2] Coleman v. West Hartlepool, Harbow & Ry. Co., 2 L. T. N. S. 766; 8 W. R 734. In this case the court enjoined the publication of a pamphlet containing an unfair account of the evidence of a witness taken before the examiner, saying: "If the one party endeavors to prejudice the public in any way against the other litigant party, there is not the slightest justification for the other party doing the same; and this court, in the administration of justice, always takes care that neither party shall do it. . . . . I quite agree with the respondent's counsel in thinking that the present times are very different

123. The publication of proceedings in court, however, pending a suit, by a reporter, will be discriminated from a publication by a party thereto. The presumption is *prima facie* against the fairness of the report in the latter case;[1] though it is not

from those of Lord Hardwicke, and that the present feeling and the general judgment of mankind as to what is or is not proper to be published, are exceedingly different to what they were at that time. That may be at once conceded; but at the same time, even as regards the publicity of proceedings in courts of justice, and when it is a question between parties who are not litigant, but between one of the parties litigant and the publisher of a newspaper, for instance; even as between these parties the court, in these days, recognizing in the highest possible degree the importance of the public being duly and fairly informed of all that takes place, yet does take care that there shall only be such proper information published in a fair and reasonable manner. I mean that courts of justice, in giving directions to a jury as to the ultimate result in that which is or is not a fair publication, always leaves it for the consideration of such jury whether or not an independent, or supposed to be independent, person, who has published a narrative of proceedings of a court of justice, has published them in a fair and reasonable manner, being anxious to inform the public; or whether there is evidence of malice in the mode in which the report was framed. Now, this court, in dealing between litigants, takes care that the litigants shall not, by such foolish attempts as appear to me to have been made on both sides here, create public prejudice, each against his opponent, in the progress of the litigation, which ought to be conducted with all proper calmness and discretion, and for the purpose of eliciting truth.

[1] Id. "Nobody," said the vice-chancellor, "feels more sensibly than myself the advantage of having a fair publication of all that takes place in a court of justice; but I make this observation, that whenever one of the litigants is the party making the statement, that is a very strong *prima facie* presumption against its being at all fair, and that in any case in which a litigant makes a publication, it is exceedingly different from that which a newspaper reporter would publish simply in the discharge of what was his duty. Such a case is widely different. I am not aware that any case precisely like this has occurred before; but I had no hesitation in granting

infrequent that, in the course of a trial exciting great public interest, the bench will request the newspapers to abstain from comments upon the merits as the case proceeds.[1]

124. But the question is, in all cases, one purely in the discretion of the court, and cannot be demanded, as matter of right, by either party.[2]

Or, if the court, in its discretion, pending a trial promising to continue for several days, make an order prohibiting the publication of its proceedings, disobedience of such order will be a contempt.[3]

125. If one of the parties to the suit has himself supplied the newspaper with the information upon which comments are made, he cannot himself complain of the contempt.[4]

the *interim* order for the injunction in the first instance, because I was aware of what the course of all the courts at all times has been, with reference to keeping their proceedings pure from this false description of excitement, which would tend to bring witnesses into the witness-box with their imaginations colored and prejudiced by *ex parte* statements sent and circulated among them by one of the litigant parties; and, consequently, it is a case in which one ought to prevent any such undue use being made of the proceedings of the court."

[1] See request of Judge Neilson (in Tilton v. Beecher) to the newspapers of New York and Brooklyn, that they should abstain from any criticisms, or expression of opinion as to the merits of that famous controversy. It is due to the press to say that as a rule they recognized the justice of the judge's request, and readily complied.

[2] Brook v. Evans, 29 L. J. 616, ch. . So in Rex v. Gilham, 1 Mood. & Malk. 165, the exhibition in an assize town of inflammatory publications respecting a prisoner about to be tried for murder, was considered not to be a contempt which the judge of assize could interfere to stop by commitment, though they thought it "highly indecorous and improper, and one that might subject the man to punishment."

[3] Rex v. Clement, 4 B. & Ald. 218.

[4] Vernon v. Vernon, 23 L. T. N. S. 697. In this case the plaintiff procured the insertion in a local newspaper of a

126. The publication, by a newspaper, of a paragraph charging certain witnesses in a pending cause with "turning affidavit men," is a contempt.[1]

On the 19th day of March, 1875, an information was filed in the Criminal Court of Cook County, Illinois,[2]

statement of his claim, and his agent gave the newspaper proprietor a copy of the bill. A motion having been made to commit the proprietor for contempt in publishing certain articles disparaging the plaintiff's claim, Bacon, V. C., refused to make any order whatever in the matter, saying: "I am not considering the offense committed against the court by contempt, but the right which the plaintiff in the suit, who has endeavored to make use of a newspaper for his own purpose, has to come afterwards and complain of subsequent statements or comments, not malevolent and not libelous, upon the subject which he has submitted to the editor of that newspaper. What right has he to be here to complain? I cannot conceive that he has the slightest right in the world."

[1] 2 Atk. 469. Construing the words "affidavit men" to mean "persons who are ready, upon all occasions, to make affidavits without regarding whether they have any cognizance of the facts," and committed the printers to prison, observing that "nothing is more incumbent upon courts of justice than to preserve their proceedings from being misrepresented; nor is there anything of more pernicious consequence than to prejudice the minds of the public against persons concerned as parties in causes, before the cause is finally heard. . . . . There cannot be anything of greater consequence than to keep the streams of justice clear and pure, that parties may proceed with safety both to themselves and their characters."

[2] The case of the People v. Storey, excited great public interest, from the wealth and influence of the defendant, and from the fact that the articles alleged to be contemptuous as criticising the grand jury had been preceded by articles personal to the judge who delivered the opinion. "To understand the nature of the alleged offense," said the court, "we must understand who and what is assailed. The grand jury was in continuous session in the court-house, from day to day, at the time of the publication of the articles in respondent's paper. Though in a different room from the judge, it was a constituent part of the court. 1 Bishop on Crim. Prac., § 868. It was not only a part of the criminal court, but a necessary and indispensable part, without whose action no criminal could

against Wilbur F. Storey—editor and proprietor of the "Chicago Times" newspaper—alleging that the defendant had, while the grand jury was in session

even be put upon trial. It only could initiate any criminal proceeding. It was the motive power in the absence of which all the other machinery of the criminal court was motionless and useless. It was so intimately connected with the court, that witnesses brought before it are sworn in what is called open court, though not necessarily in the presence of the judge. 1 Bishop's Crim. Prac. 868. The grand jurors were for most purposes as completely under the supervision of the court as would be petit jurors in sessions in their jury-room.

"If they misconducted themselves in the grand jury-room, if guilty of drunkenness, or bribery, or personal abuse of each other while in session, they could be punished by the court. They had been summoned into court and their attendance could be enforced by fine or imprisonment. All their official action was under the solemnity of an oath that 'they will present no person through malice, hatred, or ill-will, nor leave any one unpresented through fear, favor, or reward, or for the hope or promise thereof; but in all their present threats they should present the truth, the whole truth, and nothing but the truth, according to the best of their skill and understanding.' Private citizens thus compelled, under the fear of penalties, to perform a thankless public service, under the obligations of solemn oaths, for the purpose of carrying on the business of our courts—a service often performed at great personal sacrifice by grand jurors—are entitled to some protection from the court of which the grand jury is a constituent part.

"The court that could not protect a grand jury from vindictive abuse in the discharge of its official duties, and the court which, possessing the power to protect, would, through fear of personal animadversion, fail to protect it, would alike fall into universal and deserved contempt. Failing to be protected, honorable men would resort to every artifice to escape service upon the grand jury, and would even brave fine and imprisonment, rather than subject themselves to such a fiery ordeal as the malicious and vituperative attacks of the daily press of the county in which they are impaneled. What honorable man would not rather be incarcerated for thirty days in the common jail than to sit thirty days upon a grand jury, exposed to have his character maligned by libelous publications, his family disgraced, and perhaps his business ruined? Is it

and engaged in investigating cases from day to day, "published of and concerning the grand jury in their official capacity, and of and concerning divers mem-

to be said, as it has been said upon the argument, that he has his action of libel for the injury received? Would the privilege of bringing such an action be any special consolation to the man who has been maligned?

"On the 14th instant, 'The Times' commenced the attack upon the grand jury, continuing it on the 15th, and intensifying it and publishing five different articles in its issue of the 16th. On the last mentioned day the grand jury in a body presented themselves in the court-room, moved by a common indignation, and desired to be informed by the court if it could be protected from such insults. On the morning of that day 'The Times' had heaped upon the jurors the vilest abuse for their performance of their official duties. If it could not be stopped, the paper, increasing in virulence, might be expected to charge them the following day with being thiéves and robbers. It might ruin their reputations and business standing.

"What was to be done? Was the court to say to the jurors, I have no power to protect you in the discharge of your official duties? The judge of this court did not so understand the law. Was the court to say, I have the power to protect you, but will not? Should the court say to them, in the language of the counsel who opened the argument, that 'the law for libel, the law for embracing, the law for any kind of misdemeanors, provided by the statute covering all these cases are made for your vindication.' The grand jurors did not come into court and serve therein for the privilege of bringing such suits. They came to perform a public service as a constituent part of the court. They were entitled to protection from the court which had compelled their service; and the court, upon such complaint being made by the grand jury, immediately issued a rule upon the respondent to show cause why he should not be punished for contempt. The articles show upon their face the motives which actuated the publisher. It was no regard for the interests of the public, but personal revenge against the jury for their action toward defendant. There is no proof before the court that other indictments were then pending, but there is proof that other indictments were filed in court three days later. It is more than probable that they were then under consideration. The editor of that paper had, at least, the right to suspect so much." The defend-

bers of said grand jury on account, of their action, in his paper, many slanderous and vituperative articles; calculated to impede, embarrass, or obstruct that court in the administration of justice." The articles were set forth at large in the information, and were seven in number, published in "The Chicago Times" of the 14th, 15th, and 16th insts., soon after the defendant—Storey, himself—had been indicted by the grand jury upon four different indictments, for libel, and related to the action of the grand jury in finding the same. The article published in "The Times" of Sunday, the 14th inst., was entitled, "Disreputable Vengeance," and contained, among other statements, the following:

"This action on the part of the grand jury and the state's attorney, is not in the interests of justice or decency, but wholly in the interest of the rascally elements that control the city and county. Every indictment returned by the grand jury, last week, against the editor of 'The Times,' was a mean, pitiful attempt at revenge, for his effort to invite attention to the true character of men, into whose hands has fallen the control of local affairs. 'The Times' accepts these indictments as a mean and pitiful attempt to secure revenge for the expose of official iniquity. It accepts them as such, and herewith gives notice to the state's attorney, and all others in whose interest this attempt

ant Storey had, in the course of the publication complained of, printed, as it was alleged, matter personal to the judge delivering the opinion, as appears from the following sentence in the opinion:

"I have no further defense to make of the judge of this court from the character of defendant's paper, but desire to say that the feeling of intense indignation with which he first read those charges has entirely passed away, and that he is not now conscious of the least possible animosity against the defendant."

at private vengeance is directed, that it proposes to carry the battle to the end."

In the article of Monday, March 15, the following language occurred:

"The result of the trial of this man proves what 'The Times' has asserted, to wit: That no man having money has ever been sent to Joliet from the criminal court of Cook county. Just as soon as a grand jury of honorable men can be gotten together, and can be allowed to investigate abuses under the guidance of some lawyer appointed temporarily by some judge whose integrity—of judge and lawyer—are above suspicion, then will 'The Times,' in the name of an outraged community, demand an investigation of this latest development of the peculiar practices of our criminal court."

The first article of the five contained in "The Times" of the 16th instant, contained the following language:

"Especially strong is the belief of the public in the virtue, the integrity, the purity of the men composing the grand jury which has just returned an indictment against a city newspaper for publishing 'obscene' matter. The men who have done this are themselves immaculate. Their social relations are of the highest, and their private lives are of the purest. It is only necessary to mention a few names, in order to demonstrate their standing. They are 'Fred' Erby, 'Ab' Price, B. R. Chambers, W. H. Watchtel, William Manchester, Frank Sherman, 'Jim' Brown, Walter Williams, and James Fitzgerald. Not one of these gentlemen but has a record of the most lofty character. Not one of them is a common drunkard. Not one of them is a 'sport,' or a bummer. Not one of them has a bastardy case on his hands. Not one of them keeps a one-third interest in a notorious prostitute; and not one of them is a notorious companion of abandoned women, and a regular frequenter of brothels. . . . Such being the character of the grand jury now in session, its indictments must necessarily carry weight."

The second article contained the statement:

"The state's attorney is determined to tolerate the exposure of no crime, if he has to put every male strumpet in Chicago on a grand jury to secure the punishment of the offender."

The third article, in the same paper, was as follows:

"It is a fact scarcely worthy of note, that a dozen or more members of the present grand jury, who are not bummers and notorious male strumpets, are personal friends and 'cronies' of the managing editor of 'The Tribune,' who is also wonderfully noted as not being a bummer and a male strumpet. Is this grand jury a 'Tribune' grand jury? It looks like it."

The fourth article contains these words:

"But that was before office-holding knavery found out that the grand jury could be converted from an agency for the punishment of offenders into an agency for shielding them against exposure."

The fifth is as follows:

"How to make a free press a terror to evil-doers. Get a grand jury to indict the editor that exposes them."

The court (Williams, J.) concluded its opinion delivered in the case, as follows:

"I doubt whether any city in the United States has been the scene of such events as have been transpiring in Chicago for the past few weeks. A leading public journal has been persistently employed in striving to undermine the public confidence in the officers and juries of the only criminal court existing in the city; a court whose efficiency would be destroyed in case that confidence was lost. Deprived of this confidence through the libels of the press, it would be as powerless and pitiable as Samson in the lap of Delilah."

"With the efficiency of this court destroyed, no home in this city would be safe for forty-eight hours, and robbers and murderers would hold high carnival. No one who has not sat in this court, as has the present judge and his brethren of the bench, can know how absolutely necessary it is to the safety of our citizens, especially of late, when crime seems to have taken a new lease of life. No greater offense can be committed by any man, than to stab justice in her own temple and at her own altar. What has been done by the respondent in reference to this court, is nothing, except so far as it has been an attack upon the administration of justice."

"The judge, prosecuting attorney, and jurors of this court are individually nothing to the public; but when justice ceases to be duly administered, the rights of the people are no longer secure, and their wrongs must go unredressed. The question in this case rises above every personal issue. The defendant has grossly assailed and attempted to overawe that part of this court which was the most vunerable and the least capable of self-defense—its juries. There was no way by which they could be defended, and the efficiency of this court maintained, except by the use of the only weapon of defense it possessed—the proceeding for contempt. In none of the various ways suggested by counsel upon argument, could any adequate defense be afforded. Before libel suits could be tried, the court would be without grand jurors to indict criminals or petit jurors to try them. As I have said, the act of the defendant would have been punished, without any public protest, in the case of an insignificant person. Could it be allowed to go unpunished because of the wealth and power of the defendant? It is the disgrace of our jurisprudence—a disgrace more keenly felt by those who minister at the altars of justice than by any other—that wealthy and powerful criminals go unwhipt of justice, while indigent and friendless offenders often receive an excess of punishment. Should there be no exception to this universal rule?"

"For a judge, appealed to as I have been by the grand jury in this case, to let the offender go unpunished, would be an unpardonable crime. It would be treason to the cause of justice, which, by my official oath of office, I am bound to conserve. It would be a base and cowardly desertion of the fort while the enemy was battering down the walls."

"A judge has never any right to think of the personal consequences which may ensue to himself. Duty must be his polar star. He may know that he will be assailed by the bitterest calumnies; that he will be furiously assaulted by his enemies, and deserted or feebly defended by his friends. If his is the post of honor, it is also sometimes the post of danger. I was reminded by the defendant's counsel, upon argument, that the effort to enforce the law of contempt had twice, in the state of Pennsylvania, nearly resulted in the impeachment of the judges, and that in Illinois it had driven one judge from the bench of the supreme court. I shall receive the statement of counsel, that what was said was not designed as a threat."

"But having been so recently reminded, I cannot now fail to appreciate the extent to which the malevolence of the press may be carried, and the results it may secure. I know the vindictiveness with which some of the judges of the supreme court of this state were pursued, for their conscientious discharge of duty in a case of contempt; and that one judge, who, by his integrity, purity, learning, and ability, cast a luster upon that bench, was driven therefrom. But duty cannot be learned in the school of fear. Personal popularity may be pleasant, but the serene consciousness of duty faithfully done, is infinitely better. The storm may rage, but one may patiently and calmly bide its buffetings."

"If in this case I make a blunder, though an honest one, I expect to bear the consequences. If I shall willfully do the defendant any injustice, my conduct will deserve the execration of the public. The whole facts are before it. If I am right, the sober second thought of the people, which is seldom unjust, and sometimes generous, will sustain me. If it does not, I shall still rest content."

"Such a proceeding as this, against an editor, is extremely rare. But twice before, in the history of this state, has it been resorted to, so far as I know. This is due, in part, to the press; which, while it often libels individuals, has realized that it would be a great crime, persistently to attempt to destroy the efficiency of the courts, through which alone justice can be duly administered. In case of supposed personal wrongs by the courts, editors have usually resorted to such remedies as were possessed by them in common with other citizens, and with these they have been content. But the fact is due, even more, to the extreme patience of the courts, and the great reluctance, upon the part of judges, to use the process of the court for its own protection. No action, upon the part of a judge, can be so utterly distasteful to him as the action for contempt. It is looked upon with disfavor by the public. If the process is directed against an editor, it is always attended with results which seriously prejudice the judge in the esteem of the press, and all whom it can influence."

"But if the duty should always be shunned, the independence of the courts would be soon lost. Aggressions, from whatever quarter, upon the acknowledged rights of the courts must be resisted."

"Extreme cases demand severe remedies. I believe the defendant to be the only editor in the United States who, from personal motives, by a series of articles published in his paper, day after day increasing in venom, has deliberately and persistently attempted to destroy the efficiency of a court of justice—apparently determined to ruin, if he could not rule it."

"The offense committed by the defendant has been often repeated, and in each case with greater aggravations. It was committed deliberately and willfully. Its tendency was to obstruct the due administration of justice, by the use of that almost omnipotent instrumentality—the press. It was intended to inaugurate over this court, and especially over its jurors, a reign of terror, and make the ministers of justice the subservient tools of the defendant. If the acts of the respondent had not been restrained by the proceedings in this cause, I know not to what extent of virulence and abuse the editor would not have gone. To punish such an offense merely by a fine, would be a mockery of justice. The sensational articles which would appear in 'The Times' would, in two or three days, more than reimburse the defendant for any fine which I should consider it proper to impose. Editors must understand that their rights are the same, and no greater, than other citizens, and their responsibilities no less. If they publish libels upon individuals, they may escape without loss or damage to themselves, but they cannot with impunity commit gross outrages upon jurors, tending to impede, and obstruct, and overthrow the due administration of the law. But the action of the court must be vindicatory, not vindictive. In this case the motion to vacate the rule to show cause will be denied, and the cross-motion for the issuance of the attachment will be granted. No fine will be assessed, and no costs awarded against the respondent, but for the contempt, of which he has been guilty, he will stand committed to the jail of this county for ten days."

The action of the court in this case is remarkable, in that the penalty of a fine, usual in such cases, was omitted to be imposed, either alternatively with, or as accompanying the imprisonment.[1]

[1] The defendant Storey was released upon a supersedeas from the supreme court, upon giving bonds, &c.—Chicago Times, Tuesday, March 30, 1875.

The grand jury of the city and county of New York, February 15th, 1875, made the following presentment:

NEW YORK, Feb. 15, 1875.

To His Honor, Recorder Hackett, presiding in Court of General Sessions:

DEAR SIR: The accompanying communication was received from Mr. Henry Bergh, president of the American Society for the Prevention of Cruelty to Animals, February 10, instant.

We, the members of the grand jury, consider the sending of such letter on the part of Mr. Bergh as totally uncalled for, and reflecting upon our integrity as grand jurors. It has certainly never occurred within the experience of any of us, to be called to account by a party to a criminal proceeding for what we may have done, after calm deliberation and weighing of evidence. Thinking that some action in the matter, on the part of the court, would be right and proper in order to secure to future grand juries the respect which is their due, we leave

127. It was held contempt for a newspaper to publish, before it is heard, a petition which had been

the matter in the hands of the court, to be acted upon or not, as may be deemed proper.

Respectfully submitted,

CHRISTIAN S. DELAVAN,
Foreman.

"THE AMERICAN
SOCIETY FOR THE PREVENTION OF
[SEAL.] CRUELTY TO ANIMALS,
Head Quarters, Fourth Avenue, cor. 22nd Street,
NEW YORK, Feb. 10, 1875.

To Christian S. Delavan, Esq., Foreman of the Grand Jury for the City and County, at present sitting:

SIR: On the 10th of December last were found a number of disreputable men engaged in a dog-fight in a back basement at 12 Rivington-street. Two savage bull-dogs had been fighting, a moment before the arrival of the officers; and the respective owners of the animals were at the time handling the animals, their hands at the time being covered with blood, and the dogs terribly cut up by reason of the contest. The proprietor of one of the dogs and place where they fought was present, and the lease of the vile premises is in the possession of this society. This fellow and some of his comrades have been proceeded against before; but, as in the present instance, they have escaped through means which I forbear to mention. On Monday, the 8th instant, this case came up before your jury, and, notwithstanding these facts were fully represented, as I believe, these notorious ruffians and keeper of one of the most disorderly houses in this or any other city, was relieved of all responsibility, and, in his own language, since uttered to one of our officers, 'was honorably acquitted.' I think, on reflection, you will in a measure realize the discouragement I feel at finding my earnest and unselfish labors in the public service, diverted from their legitimate ends by this decision of the grand jury, the inevitable consequence of which will be to double the already onerous duties of this society, and go far to make dog and cock-fighting, if not respectable and honorable, at least tolerable in this city. I do not mean this as a censure, for your associates acted doubtless conscientiously, but erroneously. The result, however, is the same. A scandalous stain upon our civilization has been condoned, and these execrable wretches led

presented to the court of chancery for the winding-up of a company, which contains grave charges against the directors.[1]

thereby to believe, however mistakenly, that a certain amount of sympathy exists in this community with their atrocious calling.

I have the honor to remain,

Your obedient servant,

HENRY BERGH, President."

On February 16, Mr. Henry Bergh appeared voluntarily at the bar of the court with his counsel,—

The court said—In giving my action upon this proceeding, it is proper I should submit my views in writing. I am clear that it is contempt of court at common law, for a witness or by-stander to communicate with the grand jury without its request; but to be a contempt under the statute, the commu-

---

[1] *Re* Cheltenham v. Swansea Ry. Carriage & Wagon Co., 20 L. I. N. S. 169; L. Rep. 8 Eq. 580.—It was contended, in this case, on behalf of the newspaper proprietor, that the case of a petition to wind-up was an exceptional one, because under the Act it must be advertised, and the advertisement must be accompanied by a statement that persons desiring to possess it might obtain copies from the solicitor by an ordinary application. Malins, V. C., said: "No doubt, every contributory and creditor can obtain such copies, but it is not open to any one of the public, strangers to the matter, and does not give a general license to publish the petition. It is the duty of the solicitor, before he gives copies of such a petition, which frequently contains unpleasant charges, to ascertain whether the applicants are contributories or creditors: he cannot give copies to any one who will pay for them. There is nothing in the Act or rules which sanctions the publication of a petition of this kind, any more than a bill in Chancery. It was said that there was no intention to injure in this publication; but it is a sound rule that you cannot dive into men's minds, but must draw inferences from their acts. In this case I must attribute to these proprietors, that they did not print these grave charges of fraudulent conduct against these directors unknowingly and unwittingly. They may be true or false, but that must be decided on the evidence. If you once permit such a publication as this, any person may file a petition, and any proprietor of a newspaper may print and publish it, and thus it may be made the vehicle of grievous injury to an individual character." Shortt, p. 374.

128. While the tendencies of the times are clearly to construe the offense of contempt of court with the greatest liberality, it is none the less true now than

nication must savor of the degree of contemptuous behavior committed during the sitting of the court, and directly tending to impair due respect. I think that the term behavior may cover the writing and delivery to the grand jury of a contemptuous and insulting letter. It is clear from the elementary writers, and from what the court of appeals imply in the Hackley Case, 24 N. Y. 78, that the grand-jury-room is an enlargement of the court-room, and part of the court sitting. Handing to the petit jury a letter containing remarks upon the case pending before them has been at *nisi prius* adjudged a contempt; the jury, for convenience, being outside of the court-room proper, it is true, but legally and technically, nevertheless, a part of the court sitting; and both the grand and petit jury-rooms were merely extensions of the court apartment, and are under equal jurisdiction.

The insinuation conveyed by this expression in the letter of Mr. Bergh, "as in the present instance they have escaped through means which I forbear to mention," addressed to any officer of the court during its sitting, could not be made worse for contemptuous and insolvent behavior tending to impair respect. At the commencement of the last October term of this court, I charged the then grand jury as follows:

"The minutes of some grand juries have, in the past, distinctly shown traces as well as evidences of considerations and of reconsiderations and preferences, which can only be explained upon the belief that grand juries have yielded to lobby pressure, either in finally finding or finally dismissing bills of indictment. The grand juror who suffers himself to be even impliedly approached upon subject-matters pending before the body of which he is a sworn member, not only violates his oath, but transcends the common law that forbids such approaches, either in the act of the citizen or in the consent of the juror. Should it so happen during the present term of your duty as grand jurors that any person whomsoever (except the district-attorney, who, when desired, becomes your legal adviser), shall approach either of you and seek to confer, or endeavor to influence your action for or against the prosecution of any complaint pending before you, then it will become your duty to promptly communicate the fact to this court, in order that the person so offending may be summarily dealt with. The district-attorney has done all in his power

ever before, that the usefulness of courts of justice is capable of being greatly hampered, if not wholly destroyed, by a too great license on the part of the

to destroy the opportunities for this lobby influence with the grand inquest, but if jurors allow letters to be delivered to them by accused persons, accusers, or their counsel, or visits to be made to them at their places of business, or houses, by friends of suspected persons, they cannot obviate such a scandal or frustrate the wrong intended."

It will thus be perceived that the considerations growing out of the action of Mr. Bergh are not new and were not suggested by the attitude taken by the late grand jury, and I had determined to reprehend the first instance of grand jury lobbying or outside interference which should be submitted to my consideration. But Mr. Bergh shows that he is, for the purposes of his society, both a deputy attorney-general and an assistant district-attorney by written appointments from Messrs. Pratt and Phelps. Mr. Bergh, in his affidavit swears: "Such letter was sent and intended to be sent, as an official communication in the interests of the people of this State, which deponent then honestly believed he was then representing, and not to subserve any private or personal interest, or to gratify any individual spleen or malice; and deponent firmly and conscientiously believed at the time that he was only doing his duty, and that his course was entirely justifiable under the authority derived from the attorney-general and district-attorney referred to."

In the matter of Strong, in this court, half a century since, it was held that the act of sending a scurrilous letter to the grand jury ought not to be considered a contempt, unless it clearly appeared that it was designed to interrupt the administration of justice. The supreme court has held (Weeks v. Smith, 3 Abb. Pr. 211) that if the alleged contempt be capable of a construction consistent with innocence of the party of any intentional disrespect, there is no legal contempt. It would seem that Mr. Bergh's explanation that he was acting as the agent of the prosecuting officers is consistent with innocence. The court, however, trusts it may be pardoned for observing that the representative of the attorney-general and the district-attorney owes it to those gentlemen, if not to himself, to infuse into his oral or written intercourse with grand juries, rather the *suaviter in modo* than the *forliter in re;* and to remember an old saying, "that he who impugns motives, should always rigidly examine his own."

press. It is to the good sense of the press that the doctrine of contempt of court most earnestly appeals.

129. There can be no doubt—in the case of proceedings of legislative bodies, for instance—that the newspapers should be untrammeled, by the law, in their comments thereon (and yet, as we shall presently see, wanton attacks upon such bodies, will on no hand be privileged). For in legislative proceedings the whole people are directly interested; since the result of legislative deliberations is to give to the public the laws which shall govern them; and since, to that end, they have sent thither their own representatives, armed as their mouth-pieces, with their own desires and opinions, and since it is for their unquestioned benefit that such scrutiny should accompany them.

But in the case of courts it is different; for although it is to the best interest of every citizen that a tribunal should exist in which they should have every confidence, still, when an individual case is once before that tribunal, the public interest can only extend so far as to be solicitous that justice (in whatever remedy that justice may consist) shall be done; which would be impossible if the deliberate examination of the court into the merits thereof were to be anticipated by a newspaper trial.

130. The fact that a publication, contemptuous of court, was innocent of any intention of its writer to be so, cannot be permitted to purge it of contempt. *Ignorantia juris non excusat.*[1]

It is evident, from the theory upon which punishments for contempt are based, that this must be so.

Let the rule be discharged, and Mr. Henry Bergh stands exonerated under his explanatory oath from any intentional contempt.

[1] Broom. Leg. Max. 253.

The great principle of the safety of the people (which is the supreme law), is evidently the principle upon which punishments for contempt proceed; and against the safety of the people no evidence of good or harmless intentions can be allowed to avail.

A publication, then, once being confessed; no course is left the court but to pronounce judgment. The intention can only be taken in mitigation of the punishment, not in mitigation of the offense.

During the trial of one Nixon,[1] an article appeared in the "New York Tribune," headed, "A Judicial Outrage," which was supposed to reflect upon the conduct of the judge[2] presiding. The article was supposed to have been written by Horace Greeley; and an order was issued that Mr. Greeley show cause, before that judge, why he should not be attached for contempt. Instead of showing cause, he moved for a writ of prohibition, which was denied, and the following order made:

"It is ordered, by the court, that the said Horace Greeley answer (and the answer under oath is waived) the following interrogations, and have until Monday next, being the 25th day of April inst., at 11 o'clock, A. M., to file answers thereto, and be then heard in this court in defense of the accusation that he published a grossly inaccurate report of the proceedings of this court in the 'Daily Tribune' of April 14, 1864, in the language contained in and recited in interrogatory the first.

"Interrogatory the First.—Did you write in manuscript the following matter, which appeared in page 4, in column 2 thereof, in the 'New York Daily Tribune' of Thursday, April 14, 1864?

[1] Supreme Court of New York, Oyer & Terminer, New York city, April, 1864.

[2] Geo. G. Barnard.

To wit, ("A Judicial Outrage." Here following the article, portions of which contained the alleged contempt.)

"Interrogatory Second.—If not, did you write in manuscript any part thereof?

"Interrogatory Third.—If not, did you see the same in manuscript, or in proof, before it was published?

"Interrogatory Fourth.—If not, were you or not the responsible editor of 'The Tribune' on the 14th day of April, 1864?

"Interrogatory Fifth.—If you did not write or see before publication the said matter, do you know who is the author, or writer, or composer thereof, or did you not know that it was to be published?

"Interrogatory Sixth.—If you know the said author or writer, please name him?

"A statement of the transactions in court, which were reported and commented on in 'The Tribune' followed, together with a disclaimer from the court of any complaint as to the editorial comments, but only as to what purports to be a report of the proceedings in court."

To these interrogatories Mr. Greeley filed the following statement:

"Horace Greeley, in the above-entitled proceedings referred to, protesting against the jurisdiction of this court over his person, and over the proceedings now being taken, and insisting that they are irregular and without warrant of law, and further insisting that he ought not to be asked, and cannot legally be compelled to answer questions upon a charge which is in its nature criminal, and for which he may be exposed to indictment, both as a misdemeanor for a contempt as well as for a libel; and further insisting that the said article, in the order to show cause in these proceedings referred to, is not a report of the proceedings of a court, but, on the other hand, is simply an editorial criticism, based upon a report of such proceedings contained in a newspaper called 'The Evening Express,' published two days before said editorial article was published, to wit, on the 12th day of April instant.

"For answer to the interrogatories filed and served on him, says that he is now, and ever since its foundation has been, the principal editor of the newspaper called 'The Tribune,' and is one of its proprietors, by being a stockholder of the corporation that publishes the same. That, as such editor and proprietor, he is subject to all the responsibilities that justly pertain to that relation. Believing that this avowal is a substantial answer to all the interrogatories propounded to him, he most respectfully declines to answer any questions that may expose any of his associates in the editorship and publication of said newspaper, to the discipline of this tribunal, preferring to abide the consequences, be they what they may."

The court being satisfied that no disrespect was intended, discharged Mr .Greeley.[1]

[1] And see as to this subject generally *ex parte* Jones, 13 Ves. Jr., 237; *Re* Mayer, 2 Barnard, 43; *Re* Crawford, 188 J., 225 Q. B.; *Re* Yates, 4 Johns. 317; 6 Johns. 337. As to contempts by publications reflecting on courts, &c., see *Re* Van Hook, 3 City Hall Recorder, 64; *Re* Spooner, 5 Id. 109; *Re* Strong, Id. 9; Birch v. Walsh, 10 Ir. L. R. 13; *Re* Van Saudan, 1 De Gex. 55; *Re* Crawford, 18 L. J. 225, Q. B.; *ex parte* Turner, 3 Mont. D. & G. 523; Rex v. Lee, 5 Esp. 123; Respublica v. Oswald, 1 Dallas, 319; Richmond v. Dayton, 10 Johns. 393; Folger v. Hoogland, 5 Id. 235; *Re* Bronson, 12 Id. 460; The People v. Freer, 1 Cai. 485; The People v. Few, 2 Johns. 290; Rex v. Hart, 1 Camp. 359; 1 Hawk. Pl. Cr., Ch. 73; *Re* Crawford, 13 Q. B. 613; Starkie on Slander, by Folkard, Ch. xxxvi; Moulton v. Clapham, Sir W. Jones, 431; March on Slander, 20; Hollingsworth v. Duane, J. B. Wallace, 77; Bayard v. Passmore, 3 Yeates, 438.

131. Courts cannot be permitted to be scandalized by statements and comments tending to weaken their authority, merely because those statements are published by a newspaper in giving its readers the news of the day. And if a prisoner convicted of murder and sentenced to death, while on the scaffold, and before his execution, makes a speech, reflecting upon his trial, a newspaper may not be justified in publishing a report of his speech.[1] If a highwayman shall, at the gallows, arraign the justice of the law, and of those who condemned him, he who publishes (the highwayman's language) shall not go unpunished.[2] "The defendant's excuse," said the court, "in such a case[3] is indeed entitled to be received at its fullest value; but since the wrong and injury consist, not in the intention, but in the printed word reaching the eye of the reader, the disavowal of bad intent cannot do away with the pernicious effect against which it is the aim of these proceedings to guard."

But neither, on the other hand, will the court travel behind the publication to search for a bad intent, even if the publication were intended to be contemptuous of the court, but is not so in fact, the court will not punish for the intention.[4]

Lord Erskine committed to prison the committee of a lunatic and his wife for having published a

[1] See Sandford v. Bennett, 24 N. Y. 20, and the same commented on *post*, in chapter on newspapers. In this case the language reflected on one of the prisoner's counsel, not upon the court. Townshend on Slander and Libel, p. 375. Here was a literal exemplification of Butler's lines:

> "No rogue ere felt the halter draw
> With good opinion of the law."

[2] 1 Read. Stat. Law, 151; Dig. L. L. 32.

[3] People v. Freer, 1 Caine, 485.

[4] People v. Freer, 1 Caine, 485, 518; Bayard v. Passmore, 3 Yeates, 439; Morrison v. Moat, 3 Edw. Ch. 25.

pamphlet, with a dedication to the lord chancellor, reflecting upon the conduct of certain persons acting, in the management of the affairs of a lunatic, under orders from the court of chancery. His lordship committed also the printer; holding that ignorance of the contents of the pamphlet would not excuse him.[1]

132. Even wide insinuations will sometimes be construed into a contempt at common law. In 1788 an information was granted against the members of the corporation of Yarmouth, for having entered upon their books an order, stating "that the assembly were sensible that Mr. W. [against whom an action had been brought for a malicious prosecution, and a verdict returned for £3,000 damages, which the court refused to disturb,] was actuated by motives of public justice, of preserving the rights of the corporation to their admiralty jurisdiction, and of supporting the honor and credit of the chief magistrate; and therefore they vote him the sum of £2,300." "Nothing," said Buller, J., "can be of greater importance to the welfare of the public, than to put a stop to the animadversions and censures which are so frequently made on courts of justice in this country. They can be of no service, and may be attended with the most mischievous consequences. Cases may happen in which the judge and the jury may be mistaken: where they are, the law has afforded a remedy and the party injured is entitled to pursue every method which the law allows, to correct the mistake. But when a person has recourse; either by a writing like the present, by publications in print, or by any other means, to calumniate the proceedings of a court of justice, the obvious tendency of it is to weaken the administration of justice, and in consequence to sap

1

the very foundation of the constitution itself. . . . . They say 'that W. was actuated by motives of public justice,' &c. But the judge and jury who tried the cause, confirmed as to their opinion by the court of common pleas, have said that—instead of his having been actuated by motives of public justice, or by any motives which should influence the actions of an honest man—he had acted from malice. These opinions are not reconcilable; if the one be right, the other must be wrong. It is, therefore, a direct insinuation that the court had judged wrong in all they have done in this case, and it is therefore clearly a libel on the administration of justice. . . . . The defendants have, indeed, said that they never meant to reflect on the public justice of the country; but that, alone, is no answer to this application. Where particular allegations are made, in applying for an information, some answer must be given. If the thing charged be capable of different explanations, it is fair to take the defendants' explanation in their affidavits, that they did not intend anything wrong; but if it be only capable of one interpretation, we are not to be guided by such a general answer. I am of opinion that the information should go against all."[1]

When the common council of New York city—being enjoined, by a preliminary injunction, from certain official action passed resolutions declaring the injunction illegal, proclaiming a determination to disregard it, and imputing dishonesty to the judge who granted it; the resolution was held a contempt.[2]

[1] Rex v. Watson, 2 T. R. 199.

[2] People v. Sturtevant, 9 N. Y. 263; affirming People v Compton, 1 Duer. 512. See also Morrison v. Moat, 4 Edw 25.

But a fair account of proceedings in a court of justice will be considered as privileged from proceedings by contempt.[1]

Or—even if the publication be otherwise construable as contemptuous—if it appear that no right or remedy of the parties to the suit be defeated, impaired, impeded, or prejudiced; and if the misrepresentation be not willful, the court will accept a disavowal of an intentional contempt, and withhold punishment.[2]

133. V. As to the publication of reports: courts have always claimed and exercised the right to dictate whether or not their proceedings should be published. In the time of Edward the Third, Lucius de Thacstead, a notary public, was committed to the Tower, for merely attending in court to take a note of the

[1] Hoare v. Silverlock, 9 C. B. 20; Ryalls v. Leader, 1 L. R. 298 Ex.; Pillock v. Onell, 63 Pa. St. 253; Hearne v. Stowell, 12 Adol. & El. 718; 4 Per. & D. 696; Turner v. Pullman, 6 Law Times Rep. N. S. 130; Rex v. Wright, 8 T. R. 298; Chambers v. Payne, 2 C. M. & R. 156; Cincinnati, &c. Co. v. Timberlake, 10 Ohio, N. S. 548; Flint v. Pike, 4 B. & C. 84; Saunders v. Mills, 6 Bing. 213; 3 M. & P. 520; Lewis v. Levy, 1 El. B. & E. 537; Andrews v. Chapman, 3 C. & K. 286; Smith v. Scott, 2 Id. 580; Thomas v. Croswell, 7 Johns. 264; Rish Allah Bey v. Whitehurst, 18 L. T. (N. S.) 298 Ex. No reporter, editor, or proprietor of any newspaper shall be liable to any action or prosecution, civil or criminal, for a fair and true report in such newspaper of any judicial, legislative, or other public official proceedings, of any statement, speech, argument, or debate, in the course of the same, except upon actual proof of malice in making such report, which shall in no case be implied from the fact of publication (Laws of N. Y. 1854, ch. 130, §1). Nothing in the preceding section contained shall be so construed as to protect any such reporter, editor, or proprietor, from an action or indictment for any libelous comments or remarks superadded to and interspersed or connected with such report. Id. § 2. Edsall v. Brooks, 17 Abb. Pr. 227; 26 How. Pr. 426.

[2] Morrison v. Moat, 1 Edw. ch. 25.

proceedings between Johannes de Bourne and Ricardus de Potesgrave; and a disregard of the prohibition of a court,[1] or even of a magistrate,[2] is a contempt.

Lord Eldon once remarked that, when he first came into Westminster Hall, the law was well understood that it would be a contempt to publish the proceedings of the court before they were finished;[3] and Lord Tenterden, in one case,[4] ordered that there should be no publication of the proceedings, until the several indictments against the defendant had been tried; and fined a newspaper proprietor £500 for disobedience to this order, in publishing an account of the first trial before the second had begun.

"Nothing," said Lord Hardwicke,[5] "is more incumbent upon courts of justice than to preserve their proceedings from being misrepresented; nor is there anything of more pernicious consequence than to prejudice the minds of the public against persons concerned as parties in causes, before the cause is finally heard. It has always been my opinion, as well as the opinion of those who have sat here before me, that such a proceeding ought to be discountenanced." And the jurisdiction has been exercised in very recent cases.[6]

In the state of New York, "publishing a false or

[1] See Flint v. Pike, 4 Barn. & C. 473.

[2] Cox v. Coleridge, 1 B. & C. 37; Garrett v. Ferrand, 6 Id. 611.

[3] Knight v. Knight, 1 Jacc. & Walk. 167.

[4] Rex v. Clement, 4 B. & Ald. 218. The courts upheld the action of Lord Tenterden in this proceeding, but Campbell (Lives of the Chief Justices, vol. iii. p. 208) gives it as his opinion that this transaction tarnished the fame of Lord Tenterden, and that the order forbidding the publication was "imprudently" made.

[5] In Baker v. Hart, 2 Atk. 488.

[6] So recently as 1867, a justice of the Superior Court of the city of New York prohibited the publication of proceedings

grossly inaccurate report of the proceedings of a court of record is a criminal contempt," by statute.[1]

It is very far from the purpose of the law to forbid newspaper comments upon public and well-known and accomplished facts.

If, for instance, one engaged in the trial of a cause should himself commit a contempt of court, it would not be contempt for a newspaper to chronicle the fact, or to call the attention of the public or of the court thereto.[2] So, if a newspaper remark upon the conduct of a juror, who—while engaged in the trial of a capital cause, and while apart from the public and in charge of the court officers—was furnishing articles for publication to the daily press, and call the attention of the court to the fact, in a manner irritating to the presiding judge, though not in any way impeaching his impartiality or uprightness, it is not contemptuous in the newspaper.[3]

134. In 1831, it was enacted by congress,[4] that "the power of the several courts of the United States to issue attachments, and punish for contempt of court, shall not be construed to extend to any cases except the misbehavior of any person or persons in the presence of the said courts, or so near them as to obstruct the administration of justice. The misbehavior of any of the officers of the said courts, in their official transactions, and the disobedience or resistance by any officer of the said courts, party, juror, witness,

had before him, and his course was approved by the other justices of that court. Townsend on Slander and Libel, p. 370 (note).

[1] 2 Rev. Stat. 278, §1.

[2] Stuart v. People, 3 Scam. 395.

[3] Id.

[4] Act of March 2nd, 1831. Sec. 725, Title xiii., ch. 12. Revision of 1873–74. Where the wording was slightly changed.

or any other person, or persons, to any lawful writ, process, order, rule, decree, or command of the said courts. But there may undoubtedly, and do, arise cases in which it is expedient that a court should regulate the publication of its own proceedings. As, for instance, where these proceedings might or did awaken such intense public sympathy or indignation as might prejudice or interfere with the progress and calmness of the judicial inquiry. Such a case was United States v. Holmes,[1] where the defendant was a survivor of a party who, having been shipwrecked, had found themselves forced to sacrifice the life of some of their number to save the rest, and had drawn lots for their lives. The case attracted great attention, and public sentiment was intensely agitated in the matter. In that case, Mr. Justice Baldwin said: "By act of congress, passed some years since, the court has no longer the power to punish, as for contempt, the publication of testimony pending a trial before us. We have, however, the power to regulate the admission of persons, and the character of proceedings within our own bar; and as the court perceives several persons, apparently connected with the daily press, whose object, we presume, is to report the proceedings and evidence in this case, as it advances, the court takes occasion to state that no person will be allowed to come within the bar of the court for the purpose of reporting, except on condition of suspending all publication till after the trial is concluded."[2]

135. As we have before had occasion to remark,

[1] Wallace Jr. 1.

[2] *Vid.* also Rex v. Clement, 4 B. & Ald. 218; per Lord Hardwicke, 2 Atk. 471; S. C. *nom*; Roach v. Garvan, 2 Dick. 794; Mrs. Farley's Case, 2 Ves. Sen. 520; Garnett v. Ferrand,

fair comments upon matters of public interest will be rather encouraged than otherwise, but the privilege will not be construed by courts to extend to comments on matters still pending, which have a direct tendency towards directing and swaying the mind of the court or jury by whom the cause is to be determined.[1]

136. The misrepresentation of a decision of a court, or of its views and reasons in making the decision, may be a contempt of court, or possibly the suppression of its authorized reports, made by its own reporter.[2]

6 Barn. & Cress. 616. The rule would to-day appear to be eminently the reverse, for almost as much a matter of course as the presence of the court itself, has come to be the presence of the representative of the daily press.

[1] Shortt L. L. 371; Tichborne v. Mostyn, 17 L. T. N. S. 7; L. Rep. 7 Eq. 57. In this case it was held a gross contempt of court to publish in a newspaper an article commenting on affidavits which had been filed on behalf of the plaintiff in a suit, but were not yet before the court; and the publisher, after making an ample apology, was ordered to pay the costs of a motion to commit him.

It is also a contempt to reprint in another newspaper an article of this sort. In the case last referred to, a motion to commit the publishers of two newspapers which had simply reprinted the article was refused, but the publishers had to pay their own costs. The printer of a newspaper which had gone beyond merely reprinting the article, was made to pay the costs of the motion.

Vice-Chancellor Kindersley committed to prison the publisher of a newspaper, for having published a leading article commenting on affidavits made in a suit in Chancery, which had not yet come on for hearing, and holding up to ridicule the makers of the affidavits, and characterizing their conduct as utterly disgraceful.

If a court made an order prohibiting the publication of the proceedings pending a trial likely to continue for several successive days, it is a contempt of court to disobey such order. Shortt L. L. 371.

[2] Morrison v. Moat, 1 Edw. Ch. 25.

137. As analogous to, and parcel of, the doctrine of contempt of court, is the doctrine of the contempt of legislative bodies.

The rule, as to contempts of this kind, has been stated to be that "whatever grossly reflects on the character of a member of either house, or whatever imputes to him what it would be a libel to impute to an ordinary person, is a contempt, and thereby breach of privilege; it is a direct assault upon his character, and, through the odium presumed to be excited thereby, a consequential obstruction of his political duties."[1]

The house of lords formerly inflicted fine, imprisonment, and the pillory, for offenses of this kind against its members; but in more recent times, commitment, with or without fine, has been the ordinary punishment inflicted by both houses of parliament.[2]

In the case of Arthur Hall, in 1581, himself a member of parliament, the house of commons inflicted the threefold penalty of imprisonment, fine, and expulsion, for a printed libel, "not only reproaching some particular good members of the house, but also very much slanderous and derogatory to its general authority, power, and state, and prejudicial to the validity of its proceedings in making and establishing of laws."[3]

For examples of the punishment of the pillory, see the cases of Thos. Morley, in 1623, for a libel on the lord keeper,[4] and William Carr, in 1667, for dispersing scandalous and seditious printed papers against Lord Gerard, of Brandon.[5]

[1] Rex v. Cuthell, 27 Howell's St. Tr. 642.

[2] Holt, L. L. 118.

[3] D'Ewes, 291; Hatsell, 93; 1 Com. S. 125; Hallam Const. Hist. C. 5.

[4] 39 Lords J. 314, 331.

[5] 66 Id. 704.

Commitments were made by the house of lords, in 1663, for a libel on Lord Gerard, of Brandon; in 1688, for printing a paper reflecting on Lord Grey, of Wark.[1]

In 1722, persons were attached for printing libels concerning Lord Strafford and Lord Kinnoul;[2] and in 1776, for sending an insulting letter to the Earl of Coventry, the offender in the last case being afterwards reprimanded and ordered "to be continued in custody until he find security for his good behavior;" in 1779, for a libel on the Bishop of Llandaff.[3]

One Rainer was convicted, in 1733, of having printed a scandalous libel upon the lords and commons, and sentenced by the court of king's bench to pay a fine of £50, and to be committed for two years, and until he should pay the fine, and likewise till he should find security for his good behavior for seven years.[4]

In pursuance of a resolution and address of the house of commons, John Stockdale was tried, in 1789, upon an information charging him with having published a certain false, scandalous, wicked, seditious, and malicious libel concerning the impeachment of Warren Hastings, intending to asperse, scandalize, and vilify the commons of Great Britain, in parliament assembled, and most wickedly and audaciously to represent their proceedings in parliament as corrupt and unjust, &c.[5]

[1] 14 Lords J. 144.

[2] 22 Id. 129.

[3] 42 Id. 129.

[4] 2 Barnard, 273.

[5] After a brilliant speech on behalf of Mr. Stockdale by Erskine, who took the line of defense that the intention of the author was to charge with injustice, not the house of commons as a body, but the private accusers of Mr. Hastings,

In 1796, John Reeves was tried upon an information filed against him by the attorney-general, in consequence of a resolution of the house of commons, that a pamphlet published by him entitled, "Thoughts on the English Government," was a malicious, scandalous, and seditious libel, and was also a high breach of the privileges of the house, and that an address should be presented to his majesty asking him to direct a prosecution of the publisher.[1]

In 1834, a leading article having appeared in "The Morning Post," reflecting upon the conduct of the lord chancellor (Lord Brougham) with reference to a case which had come before the house of lords on appeal, the house resolved that the paragraph was a gross breach of their privileges, and committed the editor to the custody of the usher of the black rod.

In 1686, an information having been filed against Sir William Williams, for publishing a libel called "Dangerfield's Narrative," the defendant pleaded that he was, at the time of publication, speaker of the house of commons, and, as such, had a right to publish the votes and acts of the house, and that the "Narrative" in question was printed and published as parcel of the proceedings; but the court called the plea an idle, insignificant one, and gave judgment for the king, inflicting a fine of £10,000 on the defendant; the lord chief justice (Wright) asking the defendant's counsel whether an order of the house of commons could justify a scandalous, infamous, and flagitious libel.[2]

Lord Kenyon, C. J., told the jury that he acceded to the doctrine that they must be convinced that the pamphlet "was meant as an aspersion upon the house of commons;" and the jury retured a verdict of not guilty.

[1] The jury acquitted the defendant. Rex v. Reeves, 26 St. Tr. 530.

[2] 10 St. Tr. App. 34 n.

This case of Sir William Williams happened, as observed by Lord Kenyon, C. J., in the worst of times, and the publication was a paper of a private individual published by another individual, under pretense of sanction of the house of commons. Gross, J., said of the same case, that it was declared by a great authority, to be a disgrace to the country.

In 1805, one Stuart was committed to the custody of the sergeant-at-arms for a breach of privilege in printing and publishing, in "The Daily Advertiser, Oracle and True Briton," certain libelous reflections on the character and conduct of the house. In 1810, Sir F. Burdett, a member of the house, was sent to the tower for publishing "a libelous and scandalous paper reflecting upon the just rights and privileges of the house." In 1819, the house resolved that a certain pamphlet, of which Mr. Hobhouse acknowledged himself to be the author, was "a scandalous libel containing matter calculated to inflame the people into acts of violence against the legislature, and against this house in particular," and that it was "an high contempt of the privileges and of the constitutional authority of this house;" and the writer of the pamphlet was committed to Newgate.

In 1680, two persons, named Yarrington and Groome, were committed for a libel against a member. In 1689, one Smelt was committed for spreading a false and scandalous report of a member; as was John Rye, in 1696, for having caused a libel reflecting on a member to be printed and delivered at the door. The house committed one Woodfall, in 1774, for publishing a letter reflecting on the character of the speaker; and, in 1821, the author of a paragraph in "The John Bull" newspaper containing a libel on one of the members. In 1832, two solicitors were called to the bar of the house, for a libel contained in a printed handbill, being a copy of an official letter signed by them, and addressed to a committee sitting on the "Sunderland Wet Docks Bill," reflecting on the conduct of certain members of the committee, and containing a statement of the manner in which the members had voted in the committee.

138. Burdett v. Abbott[1] was an action against the speaker of the house of commons, for breaking open and entering the house of the plaintiff (a member of parliament), arresting him, taking him to the tower of London, and imprisoning him there; acts which the defendant justified, under a resolution of the house, that a certain letter published by the plaintiff in a newspaper known as "Cobbett's Weekly Register," was a "libelous and scandalous paper, reflecting on the just rights and privileges of that house," and that the plaintiff had thereby been guilty of a breach of the privileges of the house; whereupon it was ordered that the speaker should issue his warrant to commit him to the tower. "Can the high court of parliament," said Lord Ellenborough, C. J., in his judgment, "or either of the two houses of which it consists, be deemed not to possess intrinsically that authority of punishing summarily for contempts, which is acknowledged to belong, and is daily exercised as belonging, to every superior court of law, of less dignity undoubtedly than itself? And is not the degradation and disparagement of the two houses of parliament, in the estimation of the public, by contemptuous libels, as much an impediment to their efficient acting, with regard to the public, as the actual obstruction of an individual member by bodily force, in his endeavor to resort to the place where parlia-

[1] 14 East, ‘

ment is holden? And would it consist with the dignity of such bodies—or, what is more, with the immediate and effectual exercise of their important functions—that they should wait the comparatively tardy result of a prosecution in the ordinary course of law, for the vindication of their privileges from wrong and insult? The necessity of the case would, therefore, upon principles of natural reason, seem to require that such bodies, constituted for such purposes, and exercising such functions as they do, should possess the powers which the history of the earliest times shows that they have, in fact, possessed and used."[1]

[1] The Speaker, in issuing such a warrant, does not, according to Bayley, J., act in the character of a subordinate officer, but in that of a member of the House. "When the House make an order that their Speaker shall issue his warrant, they do not direct him to do it as a subordinate minister to them, but only as being the individual member of greatest dignity in the House; by whom, on this and other occasions, the House speaks and acts; and his act in this respect is not, I think, the act of an officer, but the act of a member of the House. But if," adds the learned judge, "it were the act of an officer of the House, acting under and by virtue of its judgment on the subject-matter, I can not help thinking that, where a court has competent jurisdiction to decide upon a point, and has decided and given judgment upon it, and they direct their officer to carry that judgment into execution; the officer is protected by that judgment."

This was so decided by the Court of Exchequer Chamber (Howard v. Gossett, 10 Q. B. 359; Parke, Alderson, and Rolfe, BB., Coltman, Maule, and Creswell, JJ.), reversing the decision of the majority of the Court of Queen's Bench, who held a Speaker's warrant void, because it did not show a sufficient authority on the face of it, to justify the defendant in all he admitted to have done. Parke, B., in delivering the unanimous judgment of the Exchequer Chamber, says: "Writs issued by a superior court, not appearing to be out of the scope of their jurisdiction, are valid; and, of themselves, without any further allegation, a protection to all officers and others in their aid, acting under them; and this, although they be, on the face of them, irregular, as a *capias* against a peeress

139. "There is no power," says Kent,[1] "expressly given to either house of congress to punish for contempts, except when committed by their own mem-

(Countess of Rutland's Case, 6 Rep. 54 a); or void in form, as a *capias ad respondendum* not returnable the next term (Parsons v. Lloyd, 3 Wils. 341); for the officers ought not to examine the judicial act of the court whose servants they are, nor exercise their judgment touching the validity of the process in point of law, but are bound to execute it, and are therefore protected by it (Turner v. Filgate, 1 Lev. 95; Cotes v. Michill, 3 Id. 20). . . . . If, in these courts, the writ of attachment need not state any special grounds in order to show that the court is acting duly, formally, and regularly, what good reason can be assigned for requiring the House of Commons to do so? If the writ of attachment in the general form used, is a protection to the sheriff or the officer of the court executing it (as it undoubtedly is); and he need state nothing in his plea but the issuing of the attachment (Levinz's Entries, p. 191; Britton v. Cole, 1 Salk. 408; Com. Dig. "Pleader," 3 M. 24), why should not the warrant of the Speaker, in a general form, be equally a protection to the sergeant-at-arms, the proper officer of the House? We are clearly of opinion that at least as much respect is to be shown, and as much authority to be attributed to these mandates of the House, as to those of the highest courts in the country; and if the officers of the ordinary courts are bound to obey the process delivered to them, and are therefore protected by it, the officer of the House of Commons is as much bound and equally protected. . . . . The possibility of abuse, which is urged as an objection to the power of either House to issue its mandate in such a form, is no valid argument against its existence. If it were, it would apply equally to all the superior courts, which, without doubt, have such power; and it would apply also to the other admitted legal powers of these courts, which may be abused without adequate remedy. In case of an improper exercise of the power of attachment by a court of law or equity, or by either branch of the High Court of Parliament, there can be no appeal: the only remedy is by application to the sense of justice of each court; and it would be improper to suppose that any one of them would be more likely to abuse the power, or less likely to grant redress, than another."

The warrant of commitment is not to be construed strictly

---

[1] 1 Com. 235, 236, n. 1.

bers; but in the case of Anderson,[1] who was committed by order of the house of representatives, for a contempt of the house, and taken into custody by the sergeant-at-arms, an action of trespass was carried by writ of error to the supreme court of the United States; which court decided that the house had that power, and that it was an implied power, and of vital importance to the safety, character, and dignity of the house."[2]

It seems indisputable that such a doctrine is of vital necessity to the usefulness of a legislative assembly. But, since it contemplates only the offense against the body in session,[3] and not an offense against the laws of the land, or the dignity of the government (which offense would be sedition—a crime, as we have seen, almost unknown amongst us), the power to punish need not and does not extend beyond the

as that of an inferior court or justice of the peace, but it is to be construed as a writ of a superior court, not appearing on the face of it to be beyond the scope of its jurisdiction (Howard v. Gossett, 10 Q. B. 359); and therefore the warrant, though it does not specify the cause of arrest, furnishes a justification to the officer who executes it. Id.

[1] Anderson v. Dunn, 6 Wheat. 204.

[2] It is a power inherent in all legislative assemblies, and is essential to enable them to execute their great trusts with freedom and safety; and it has been frequently exercised, not only in Congress, but by the respective branches of the state legislatures, and may be considered as indisputably acknowledged and settled (Story's Commentaries, ii. 305, 317).

[3] In the case of Howard v. Gossett (10 Ad. & Ell. N. S. 359), the powers and privileges of parliament were very elaborately discussed; but the Court of Exchequer Chamber, in the final decision, placed itself upon the narrow ground, that the speaker's warrant must be construed as process of a superior court, not appearing to go beyond its jurisdiction.

In the case of a contempt of court, however, the case is different, for courts, being the impersonation of justice of the state, are always in session, there can be no *interregnum* to their authority.

session in which the contempt was committed, and will terminate upon the adjournment or dissolution of congress.[1]

It was held by the supreme court, in the case of Anderson v. Dunn,[2] that the house of representatives has, by necessary implication, a general power of punishing and committing for contempts, notwithstanding that the *lex scripta*, "the constitution of the United States," had expressly conferred upon it a power to punish "its members"; thereby, as it was argued, on the principle that *enumeratio unius est exclusio alterius*, prohibiting the jurisdiction in the case of persons not members of the house. "It is true," said Johnson, J., delivering the judgment of the court, "that such a power, if it exists, must be derived from implication, and the genius and spirit of our institutions are hostile to the exercise of implied powers. . . . . That a deliberate assembly, clothed with the majesty of the people, and charged with the care of all that is dear to them; composed of the most distinguished citizens, selected and drawn together from every quarter of a great nation; whose deliberations are required by public opinion to be conducted under the eye of the public, and whose decisions must

[1] 1 Kent. Com. 236. The duration of imprisonment for contempt terminates also in England upon the close of the existing session of parliament. Stockdale v. Hanford, cited in May's Treatise on the Privileges of Parliament, 62; Rex v. Crosby, 3 Wils. Rep. 138; Burdett v. Abbott, 14 East R. 1.

Even to the duration of imprisonment, "a period is imposed by the nature of things, since the existence of the power that imprisons is indispensable to its continuance; and although the legislative power continues perpetual, the legislative body ceases to exist on the motion of its adjournment or periodical dissolution. It follows, that imprisonment must terminate with that adjournment." Per Johnson, J., in Anderson v. Dunn, 6 Wheat. Rep. 231.

[2] 6 Wheat. R. 204.

be clothed with all that sanctity which unlimited confidence in their wisdom and purity can inspire—that such an assembly should not possess the power to suppress rudeness, or repel insult, is a supposition too wild to be suggested." What particular acts shall amount to a contempt of either house of congress are not defined; and are, it would seem, left to the judgment and discretion of the house, under the circumstances of each case.[1] And, we doubt not, libels which grossly interfered with the usefulness of officers or members of either house, would be held contemptuous by courts.

140. Congress has unquestionably, as we shall have occasion to consider further on, in the chapter upon newspapers, the right to control the publication of its own deliberations. But in the exercise of this right, we know of but a single instance in which that body has proceeded to its extreme powers.[2]

141. The newspapers of the Union always have enjoyed, and still enjoy, the largest liberty of criticism of Congress and of its officers and members, and show no disposition to be scrupulous of passing the line which separates criticism from vilification and abuse.

It is needless to observe that, not only legislative, but the whole law of contempt is one regarded with great disfavor with us, and it is possible that it would only be inforced by our courts with great reluctance and in rare instances.

[1] 1 Kent. Com. 236 (note).

[2] In 1873, during what has been since known as the "Crédit Mobillier Investigation." In that instance Congress, having resolved that certain of its deliberations should be secret, discovered, nevertheless, that its proceedings were being published in the daily papers, and proceeded to imprison certain reporters who refused to disclose the perpetrators or the means employed by them to obtain the prohibited news. See Congressional Globe, 1st series, 42nd Congress, part ii., 846.

142. The foregoing pages, it is believed, exhibit the American law of contempt in its extreme form. But it is well that it should be studied in that rather than in its more lenient form, in order that we may know the extreme of its operation.

The sentiment which pervades our courts, undoubtedly, is that which was well expressed by the court in Stuart v. People.[1] "Respect of courts can-

[1] 3 Scam. 397; quoted with approval by Scott, J., in People v. Wilson, 6 Albany Law Journal, 352. The question as to what is a contempt of court, its definitions and penalties, will be usually found treated by the statutes of the different states. In 1871, a successful attempt was made in the New York legislature to enact, along with others, the following amendment to the code of procedure:

"SECTION 24.—The said act is hereby amended by adding thereto an additional title, to be known as title sixteen, as follows: 'Conferring power upon courts of record, and every judge or justice of any such court, to punish for contempts.' Every court of record, and every judge or justice of any court of record, shall have the like power which courts of record, or a judge or justice thereof, possessed at common law, to punish as for a contempt of court, any person or persons for any act, matter, or thing for which courts of record or a judge or justice thereof could at common law punish any person or persons as for a contempt of court; and the proceedings for contempt shall be had and conducted in such manner as the court, or judge, or justice shall direct, and the punishment, which may include fine or imprisonment, or both, shall be in the discretion of the court, or judge or justice, before whom the proceeding is had. And all laws and parts of laws inconsistent herewith are hereby, so far as the courts of record and judges or justices thereof are concerned, repealed."

But an earnest and intelligent opposition was made by the public, and notably by the Bar Association of the city of New York; a committee of which association waited upon the Governor (Hoffman), through whose efforts the Governor was induced to veto the whole. Said Hon. Theodore W. Dwight, one of that committee:

"It can scarcely be possible that the people of the state of New York, after an experience of forty years of full liberty of speech and of the press, as far as the doctrine of constructive

not be compelled, it is the voluntary tribute of the public to truth, virtue, and intelligence, and while they

contempts is concerned, are ready to endanger, and perhaps sacrifice it, by giving deliberately such portentous powers to a single judge, having no check upon his will except the cumbrous, well-nigh obsolete and quite ineffectual method of trial by impeachment. Assuming that there is no danger at the present moment, the hour may arrive when the common-law power to commit for contempt will furnish a ready and efficient weapon in the hands of the bold and unscrupulous, to silence, not only the press, but also the utterances of advocates or counsel. Arbitrary power always frets at free speech on the part of members at the bar. So Gov. Coldon wrote to the Earl of Halifax a letter in which he refers to the dangerous influence which the profession of the law had obtained in this province more than in any other, and wishes that 'the people were freed from the domination of the lawyers.' This so-called 'domination' was nothing more than a fixed determination, on the part of the few members of the bar of that day, to insist upon a rational freedom—a determination which the governor in vain hoped to overcome. Should the struggle for free speech ever commence again, the bar will not be unfaithful to its traditions, and will strive again to 'dominate' in the same good sense. If, by the doctrine of constructive contempts, its members are cowed into silence, there will be hushed a potent voice of the tribunes of the people."

The question of contempt by written matter alone is, of course, within the province of this inquiry. What constitutes contempt, however, by other means, as by words or gestures in the presenee of a judge, can not fail to be an interesting inquiry, and we can not forbear the insertion of some additional memoranda under that head.

Calling a magistrate, in a court of justice, a fool, but not so speaking of him in his absence, and without reference to the execution of his office (Simmons v. Sweete, Cro. Eliz. 78; Reg. v. Wrightson, Salk. 698; see also 2 Roll. Rep. 78; 4 Inst. 181; *ex parte* the Mayor of Yarmouth, 1 Cox Crim. Cas. 122); giving the lie to the steward of a manor holding a court leet (Earl of Lincoln v. Fisher, Cro. Eliz. 581; Ow. 113; Mo. 470), or telling him in court that he is forsworn (2 Rol. Abridg. 78); saying to justices in session "Though I can not have justice here, I will have it elsewhere" (Rex v. Mayo, 1 Keb. 508; 1 Sid. 144); putting on one's hat in presence of the lord of a

are found on the judgment-seat, so long, and no longer, will they retain the public confidence."[1]

court leet, and saying he cared not what he could do (Bathurst v. Coxe, 1 Keb. 451, 465; Raym. 78); saying to a justice of the peace in the execution of his office that he was a rogue and liar (Rex v. Revel, 1 Str. 420); but not saying of a justice in his absence that he was a scoundrel and a liar (Rex v. Weltie, 2 Camp. 142).

And a court may be insulted by the most innocent words uttered in a peculiar manner and tone (per Lord Denman, C. J., Carus Wilson's Case, 7 Q. B. 1015). Wherever a justice may commit for such words, the offender may also be indicted for the misdemeanor (Str. 420). A justice can commit only where the contemptuous words are spoken in his presence; in other cases the remedy is by indictment of the offender (Rex v. Revel, *ubi supra*; see also Rex v. Wrightson, *ubi supra*, and 1 Vent. 169; 2 Keb. 249; Hutt. 131; 3 Mod. 139; Rex v. Selby, Mich. 4 Anne K. B.; Rex v. Penny, 1 Ld. Raym.; Rex v. Pocock, Str. 1157). A barrister may also commit a contempt of court in the conduct of a cause (*Re pater*, 33 L. J. 142 Q. B.) and so may one of the parties to the cause in the course of addressing the jury (Rex v. Davison, 4 B. & Ald. 329).

The act of congress of March 2, 1831 (*ante*, p. 291), is claimed to have been induced by the case of Judge James H. Peck, a district judge of Missouri, who, having written and published an opinion in a certain case (upon which, during the vacation of the court, one of the counsel therein, one Lawless, published a criticism), at a subsequent term, imposed an imprisonment and fine for contempt of court upon Lawless. Lawless complained to the House of Representatives, which voted articles of impeachment against Judge Peck, which were tried before the Senate in 1830, Monday, Dec. 13, and following days. Judge Peck was acquitted by one vote, but upon the ground that he had acted in good faith and in his understanding of the law (annals of congress, p. 4 *et seq*). And see Wharton's criminal law, 3439; Cole on criminal information, ch. 2; *Re* Oswald, 1 Dall.; Respublica v. Passmore, 3 Yeates, 441.

CHAPTER IV.

OF ORIGINALITY.

143. Once having satisfied itself that the work asking its protection is innocent in its nature, that is, that it does not subvert the state; or libel, deceive or injure the morals of her subjects, or undermine the sanctity and usefulness of her courts of justice; the law will, lastly, inquire whether the work be original; that is to say, whether the person asking to be protected therein, be, in any legal sense, its producer or originator, and entitled to a property by occupancy therein. For, as in the case of a title by occupancy to the solid earth, which he has not made, the author must show something in his published work of which he is the first possessor. Some idea, of which no other can claim to be in possession, must enter into its design, material, or manufacture, or employment. Something there must be new and original.

144. This question of originality is by no means one easy of solution, for many reasons. In the first place—like the fact of innocence—the originality must exist in every case, independently of any actual possession of the manuscript, either by manual custody or statutory registration. Though one be the owner, by legitimate purchase, of a written work; if it be actually the production of a foreigner, the owner cannot claim the protection of the law therefor. Nor,

again: will the fact of compliance with any formal requisites of a statute, be anything more than *prima facie* proof of his ownership so long as it remains undisputed; and equity will not fail, in either case, not only to withhold its protection from the work not original, as it did from the work not innocent, but in this case to endeavor, if possible, to restore or compensate therefor to its rightful owner.

145. In the second place, it is very clear that a legal, as contradistinguished from the popular and derivitive meaning of the word original, must be sought. For in the field of literature, any such thing as absolute originality is very rarely to be met with. As long ago as the old Librarian wrote, he declared that men were in the habit of "making new books as apothecaries make new mixtures, by pouring only out of one vessel into another;"[1] and he lived at a time when the presses of the world were not taxed with new volumes, nor the world glutted with book-writers.

That we must accept a legal definition of the words "original" and "originality," as distinguished from the strict and derivative meaning, is apparent, too, from the impossibility of following the latter at all, in these days. If we were to declare that none but he who devised from his own brain, without a knowledge of the compositions of other men, should be entitled to protection, what author could claim that protection? (And it might be added, of what value would his production be?) From the very inception of literature, language not only has been a common stock in trade of authors; but sentiments, similies, phrases, and compositions; whose recurrence might sorely tax the credulity of those who would believe them mere coin-

[1] Burton's Anatomy of Melancholy, 435.

cidences. "There is," said Dr. Johnson,[1] "a common stock of images; a settled mode of arrangement, and a beaten track of transition, which all authors suppose themselves at liberty to use, and which produce the resemblance generally observable among contemporaries. So that, in books which best deserve the name of originals, there is little new beyond the materials already provided. The same ideas and combinations of ideas have been long in the possession of other hands. And, by restoring to every man his own, as the Romans must have returned to their cots from the possession of the world, so the most inventive and fertile genius would reduce his folios to a few pages. Yet the author who imitates his predecessors, only by furnishing himself with thoughts and elegances out of the same general magazine of literature, can with little more propriety be reproached as a plagiary than the architect can be censured as a mean copier of Angelo or Wren, because he digs his marble from the same quarry, squares his stone by the same art, and unites them in columns of the same order."

". . . . As not every instance of similitude can be considered as a proof of imitation, so not every imitation ought to be stigmatized as a plagiarism. The adoption of a noble sentiment, or the insertion of a borrowed ornament, may sometimes display so much judgment as will almost compensate for invention; and an inferior genius may, without any imputation of servility, pursue the path of the ancients, provided he declines to tread in their footsteps."[2]

[1] The time came, however, when Dr. Johnson himself was the victim of a piracy. See Dodsley v. Kinnersley, Amb. 402.

[2] "Sir Fret.—I can tell you it is not always so safe to leave a play in the hands of those who write themselves.

"Sneer.—What! they may steal from you—hey! my dear Plagiary?

Virgil imitated Homer, and Horace followed Virgil.

"Hæ tibi erunt artes—
Parcere subjectis, et debellare superbos,"

said Virgil.

"Imperet, bellante prior, jacentem
Lenis in hostem,"

said Horace.

"Nisi Ilias illa extitisset, idem tumulus qui corpus ejus contexerat, nomen ejus obruisset,"

said Cicero; and this, again, we find paraphrased in Horace:

"Vixere fortes ante Agamemnona
Multi, sed omnes illacrymabiles
Urgenter, ignotique longâ
Nocte, carent quia vate sacro."

So Chaucer followed Petrarch, and Milton followed Æschylus, Virgil, and Spenser.[1] So the author of

"Sir Fret.—Steal! to be sure they may, and, egad—serve your best thoughts as gypsies do stolen children—disfigure them to make 'em pass for their own.

"Sneer.—But if your present work is a sacrifice to Melpomene—and he, you know, never——

"Sir Fret.—That's no security, a dexterous plagiarist may do anything. Why, sir, for aught I know, he might take out some of the best things in my tragedy and put them into his comedy."—The Critic, act i. scene 1.

[1] "Our sage and serious poet Spenser, &c.," says Milton, in the Arcopagitica, 19. Milton told Dryden that Spencer was his "original." (See Dryden's Fables, preface.) Without any such confession, it would have been evident from Milton's earlier works how great was the influence of Spenser over his youthful mind. To say nothing of numerous Spenserian echoes that may be detected, it is to Faerie Queene that he especially alludes in Il Penseroso, after his mention of the Squire's Tale of Chaucer:

"If aught else great bards beside
In sage and solemn tunes have sung
Of turneys and of trophies hung,
Of forests and enchantments drear
Where more is meant than meets the ear."

Shakespeare drew from almost every source known to the learned of the day; and so Byron and Tennyson have followed, as in their turn they are and will be followed, let us be certain, until the end of time. Not only the Latin, but every poet since has exclaimed at the "*sic vos non vobis*" of the craft. Literature may be aptly styled a mill, that is always grinding over and over again the same grist. An essayist is nothing more than a man who runs together, into one composition, as much as he can of what has been said by a dozen or a hundred of his predecessors, upon the theme which he has chosen. As every opinion of a judge upon the bench is drawn from the volumes in his library, so the work of every author has grown from his reading and his lore, as well as from his genius and his fancy. A lexicographer is not the originator of language; nor a commentator, of the law; and all these difficulties and complexities must be contemplated and construed, in considering the question of originality before the law.

146. A legal definition of "originality" might, perhaps, well be, that which is, in some ascertainable feature, original. It would evidently be incorrect to substitute the words "part," or "portion," for the word "feature,"—for a work partly original, and partly copied from another, has been repeatedly held to be original, in the eye of the law, only as to the portion not copied; and no amount of original matter added, can justify use of borrowed matter *in solido*, or vest its ownership in the transcriber.

If ten chapters of my novel or cantos of my poem are entirely original, and the eleventh taken from

He quotes at length from the fifth book of the Shepherd's Calendar in his Animadversions upon the Remonstrant's Defense.

another book, the eleventh is none the less another's; neither does it lose its identity by being printed along with my ten. But, even though not a single line of my work be new or original, if the feature of the plan and arrangement of those lines be so, it is my book. If I should print one play of Shakespeare along with ten plays of my own, or one novel of Charles Dickens, or of George Eliot, along with ten novels of my own, I would not become by the process the owner of Shakespeare's play, or of Dickens's, or of George Eliot's novel. But if I took every word of Shakespeare's plays, and arranged them into a concordance, the concordance would be mine; or, if I arranged his sentiments alphabetically, the Shakesperian dictionary would be mine. And so I might arrange a cyclopædia of Charles Dickens's or George Eliot's Thoughts; and even though I wrote no single original line, yet the words to which I contributed the feature of plan and arrangement, the idea of which was mine by occupancy, would be my own. In one case I have contributed originality without obtaining ownership, while in the other I have contributed only ingenuity and industry, and have rightfully acquired ownership.

The distinction becomes still more subtle, when we reflect that there might be a dozen (and doubtless, in fact, there are more than that number) different dictionaries of Shakespeare, or of elegant extracts therefrom, upon the plan of alphabetical arrangement, and yet each of them original in the legal sense; for although in general a plan may be original, yet an alphabetical plan cannot be monopolized by any one; and concordances, like commentaries, are likewise capable of being produced indefinitely, without infringement upon each other.

It is very apparent that equity cannot stop to pull over the libraries of the world every time an injunction is asked, or a piracy is alleged. If we were to insist upon rare and absolute originality in a work, our courts must be furnished not only with complete legal but complete literary libraries—must be turned into academies, and our judges into critics and librarians, which we cannot evidently do.

147. A learned French commentator,[1] with the facility of his language, has thrown much light upon this question, by dividing all literary composition into works *de genie*—of genius, and *de l'esprit*—of ingenuity or intelligence. And the legal meaning of "originality" may be said to include both of these. Thus, it was a genius who wrote Shakespeare. It was an intelligence that could compile from his plays a history of his native land, or a concordance of his speech. We have but to remember that the title to literary property is a title by occupancy, and assume that, in the case of literary property, the occupancy may be in any feature of the things occupied, and the whole way will become plain. If the work contain an idea, even though it be only an idea as to the plan, arrangement, or adaptability of old and well-worn matter: so that idea is first occupied and possessed by the arranger and adapter, the law will give him his proprietorship therein, equally as if the matter itself were produced entirely by himself. But—as we shall see, when we presently come to discuss the decisions upon this subject—some such idea the writer must possess; and he is not entitled to seize upon anything that can be traced to the ownership of another, any more than he will be allowed to possess himself of a

[1] M. Merlin, Repertoire de Jurisprudence, title contrefacon, § xi.

horse that wanders near his own preserve, or of a house whose door stands open before him.

148. The word 'author,' which is, as we shall presently see, the one used both by the English and American statutes of copyright law, is not, in itself, one readily capable of exact definition. Some light may be thrown upon its precise significance by the expression used in the French copyright statute or decree of July 19th, 1793, to which we have already referred. Instead of the word authors, the expression "les auteurs d'ecrits eu tout genre" was there substituted,—in the construction of which expression M. Merlin says: "Mais il ne faut pas necessaire, dans cet article, les mots ecrits 'en tout genre,' de l'expression 'auteurs;' et la propriété dont cet article déclare que les ecrits en tout genre sont susceptibles, ne peut evidemment etré reclamée que par ceux qui en sont auteurs, dans la véritable acception de ce terme."

Or, "le mot 'auteurs' quel sens a-t-il en general? Quel sens a-t-il relativement aux écrits? Quel sens a-t-il dans la loi du 19 Juillet, 1793?"

"En general, le mot auteur designe Quivant la definition qu'en donnes le dictionnaire de l'acadamie Francaise celui que est la premiere cause de la quelque chose: et il est aussi, suivant la même définition, synonyme d'inventeur.

"Applequé aux écrits, le mot auteur se del (toujours suivant le même dictionnaire) de celui qui a composé un livre, qui a fait quelques ouvrages d'esprit, en vers ou en prose, et il est bien clair qu'en ce sens, le mot auteur est opposé a copiste.

"Enfin la loi du 19 Juillet, 1793, ne permit pas de douter qu'elle n'exclue également les copistes de la denomination d'auteurs. Les littérature ou de gravure, dit-elle, art. 7, ou de toute autre production de l'esprit ou du génie, qui appartient aux beaux-arts, en auront la propriété exclusive pendant dix années Ces termes, " ou de toute autre production de l'esprit ou du génie, qui appartient aux beaux-arts," ne sont ni obscurs ni équivoques. Ils signifient clairement que les productions de l'esprit ou du génie sont de deux sortes ; que les unes consistent en ouvrages de littérature ; que les autres appartienment aux beaux-arts ; mais que nul ne peut être réputé auteur soit d'un ouvrage de littérature, soit d'un ouvrage d'arts, si ce n'est pas à son esprit ou à son génie qu'en est due la production.

" Donc, les expressions " d'écrits en tout genre," ne sont employées dans l'art. 1er de la même loi, que pour désigner tous les genres de compositions littéraires.

" Donc, elles n'y désignent pas les écrits qui ne seraient pas des compositions, mais de simples copies.

" Donc, celui qui ne fait que copier une composition littéraire, ne peut jamais être réputé auteur de la copie de cette composition, ni par conséquent en avoir la propriété, dans le sens attaché à ce mot par la loi du 19 juillet 1793 et par le Code penal 1810."[1]

149. The essential attribute of one who would establish himself to be "an author" of anything, is, that he must be the first producer of the thing composed. As for instance, let us state that Shakespeare was the author of the plays which bear his name: Schlegl was the author of a translation of those plays into German: Halliwell was the author of an edition of those plays: Furness was the author of a variorum collection, from various sources, of notes to certain of those plays, Price was the author of an alphabetical

[1] Merlin, Répertoire de Jurisprudence, titre Contrefacon,

arrangement of sayings and proverbs taken from those plays. Now here Shakespeare, Schelgl, Collier, Furness, and Price were all authors, " de l'esprit," though only the first was, primarily, an original writer, " de génie." And so there may be, besides, an author of original matter, an author of secondary matter, such as a translation, an edition, a collection, or an arrangement. And yet the authors of all of these are authors, in the legal sense of the word, and will be protected by law in the product of their labors.

Or, again, take the case of legal reports. A reporter collects, in book form, a certain number of opinions of judges, accompanied by statements of the cases in which they were uttered. A compiler of digests takes a certain number of these reports; and, by drafting resumés of the point involved in each case found in them, forms a digest. After a certain number of digests have been published, still another compiler forms from them a table of the names of cases contained in the digests, with the volumes and pages where they occur. And still another writer may, from the reports or the digests, or both, compose an abridgment, or an index, or a compendium of practice, or innumerable volumes of use to the practicing lawyer. Now, every one of these volumes are of value to the profession. No case involving a legal question can be tried without their aid—no opinion given, or pleading drawn—and yet, if we were to insist upon the derivative meaning of "originality" and "author," neither the compiler of the reports, of the digest, nor of the index, abridgment or compendium, could be protected in the profits of his toil, in what the profession know to be its most laborious and important branches. For, in the latter case, not one of the persons mentioned have exercised the slightest invention. Even the judges arrived at their opinions from the perusal of the opinions of other judges, and carefully guarded themselves from the exercise of any such faculty as invention—they merely pronouncing over again what had been enunciated thousands of times before.

150. In the mercantile law there is such a thing as admixtion, and rules are laid down, following the ownership of the things mixed, to the very limits of possibility, and providing for the rights and remedies of all concerned. But in the law of literature no such provision is possible.

The utmost that the law can do is to require and insist that the secondary author shall have exercised original labor in devising the plan, selection, arrangement, and presentation of the materials which he has found to be *in medio*, and open to all. It will not be sufficient, on the one hand, that he has bestowed upon his work the manual labor of copying or clipping the material; nor will it be necessary, on the other, that he have used such judgment in discovering the wants of the public, and such skill in catering to them, as to have produced a really valuable book. But the product of actual mental labor, whether valuable [1] or worthless, will be protected by law.

[1] "The mere utility of a book, or its adaptation to the end which it professes to answer—its value in a critical point of view—can not determine its legal originality. The law takes upon itself none of the functions of the critic, in this sense. It looks only for some substantial product of individual thought or labor, and leaves to public taste or judgment to determine its value, and to bestow its due reward. So that whether a book be more or less useful, more or less successful, or brilliant, or important, if in a just sense the claimant is the author of that in which he claims an exclusive property, he is entitled to his copyright *valere quantum, valere potest.* It is true, there may be cases, in which the question will arise, whether a subsequent author has made any im-

So, as we shall presently see, the science of mathematics is a subject *in medio;* and the law will protect a man in the ownership of a set of mathematical problems or tables, calculated by himself, even though everybody knows that the problems cannot be varied because their principles are immutable; and although a calculation by any other person must, *ex necessitate*, produce identically the same tables, the same problems, and the same results.[1] "Sans doute," says the learned commentator, before quoted, "Sans doute, il est des compilations d'ouvrages littéraires qui, par l'immensité des recherches qu'elles supposent, par le discernement et le goût qu'elles exigent, peuvent et doivent passer pour de véritables productions de l'esprit, et qu'il n'est pas plus permis de contrefaire que si elles étaient réellement des compositions originales.

"Par exemple, les Pandectes de Pothier ne sont, à peu de chose près, qu'une compilation des Institutes, du Digeste du Code et des Novelles de Justinien; c'est-à-dire, de recueils qui, depuis plusieurs siècles, sont incontestablement dans le domaine du public.

"Cependant, si Pothier vivait encore, et qu'un imprimeur s'avisât de publier une édition de ses Pandectes, sans sa permission, qui est-ce qui oserait con-

provements upon his predecessors; and, in such cases, it may become necessary to apply collaterally, as a test of originality, an inquiry into the practical and relative value of his publication. But this will be done, in order to determine whether he has borrowed any, and how great a part of his matter from sources common to all writers—whether he has actually produced anything of his own, and not whether his production is better or worse than the productions of others. If it appears that he has produced anything of his own, not borrowed or adopted from a previous writer, its effect in advancing or retarding the progress of knowledge, or its value in a critical point of view, can have no influence upon his title to a copyright." Curtis on Copyright, 172.

[1] Bailey v. Taylor, 3 Law Journal, 66; and see *post*.

tester à Pothier le droit de la poursuivre comme contrefacteur? Qui est-ce qui oserait dire que Pothier, en compilant à sa manière les Institutes, le Digeste, le Code et les Novelles de Justinien, n'a pas fait un ouvrage qu'il n'appartenait qu'à un jurisconsulte du premier ordre d'entreprendre et d'achever? Qui est-ce qui oserait dire qu'un simple copiste eût pu, comme lui, tirer tous les textes du droit romain de l'espèce de chaos dans lequel ils sont dispersés; les ranger dans un vaste cadre où, enchaînés les uns aux autres, ils s'expliquent mutuellement; rapprocher de chaque règle générale toutes les exceptions qui la limitent; placer à côté de la loi ancienne, la loi moderne qui la modifie; et la loi plus moderne encore qui l'abroge; en un mot, substituer l'ordre à la confusion, la lumiere, a l'obscurité, la facilité d'etudier et d'apprendre aux dégouts et aux épines qui arretent, des leurs premiers pas, tous les aspirants à l'exacte connaisance des lois romaines?

"Compiler de cette manière ce n'est pas copier c'est créer; c'est faire ce que ferait un architecte qui, apres avoir demoli un edifice gothique—en emploierait tous les materiaux pour élever un superbe palais, un temple majestueux."

"Mais il est aussi des compilations qui se font comme—on le dit vulgairement—avec des ciseaux, qui n'exigent, qu'un travail de manœuvre et qui, pour cette raison, ne peuvent pas mériter a leurs artisans le titre d'auteurs."[1]

151. In the legal sense, then, of the word, the originality of a literary production will be found to exist:

First. In its author (if an original work).

Second. In its compiler or arranger—(if a com-

[1] Merlin, Repertoire de Jurisprudence, titre Contrefacon, § xi.

pilation, such as a dictionary, glossary, gazetteer, encyclopedia, abridgment, guide-book, text-book, manual of an art, of a science, or, generally; any other book of reference),—or,

Third. Its translator—(in case of a translation). And the ownership of the work will follow the individual or individuals in whom its originality exists, until he or they part with the same by his or their own act.

152. An author is well described, by Dryden, as one who "has the choice of his own thoughts and words." And, following him, we may define an author as, one who by his own intellectual labor produces a new work, composed in his own thoughts and words.[1]

A compiler is one who by his own intellectual labor, makes, arranges, or frames a composition or collection of literary or scientific matter, not originally produced by him; but which he has himself first brought together in an arrangement new with himself.[2]

It is important, at the outset, to remark that the words compiler, editor, arranger, codifier, abridger, &c., though technically distinguished, will be regarded by the law as one and the same; that is, in so far as their legal rights and liabilities are concerned.

If it were otherwise, the law of copyright might be-

[1] Author.—(Latin, auctor; Italian, autore; Spanish, autor; French, autour or auteur).—He to whom anything owes its origin; originator; maker; first cause; one who composes a work of science or literature; the first writer of a thing; distinct from a translator or compiler; a composer; a writer. —Worcester.

[2] Compiler.—(Greek, πιλόω, to press close; Latin, pilo; Italian, compilare; Spanish, compilare; French, compiler).—One who frames a composition from various sources; a collector of literary fragments.—Worcester.

come a complicated and intricate mass of subtleties instead of the simple and logical thing it is.

153. The law can recognize but two classes of intellectual labor, viz., original labor and secondary labor. An original work alone has, properly speaking, an author. The producer of a secondary work, that is, a work consisting of parts, passages, or matters collected, condensed, or amplified from various sources, is a compiler,[1] editor, arranger, or abridger, as the case may be.

An editor is also one who superintends, revises, or prepares a work for publication, or—in popular language—one who conducts a newspaper, but none the less his labors are secondary, and not original.

154. There is, however, a third sort of literary laborers, in the classification of whom, and of the results of whose labors, an apparent, though—as we think will presently appear—no real difficulty arises. This class of intellectual laborers are translators.

A translator is one who renders or interprets literary matter from one language into another, retaining the idea and the sense, which are not his, and clothing them in words which are his own.

Now, a translation, under the division above indicated, is clearly a secondary work. A translator, however, is not a secondary laborer; and it is not erroneous, but perfectly correct and proper, to speak of the author of a translation.[2]

[1] In the time of Alfred the local customs of the several provinces of the kingdom were grown so various that he found it expedient to compile the Dome Book. 4 Blackstone Com. ——. Atwill v. Ferrett, 2 Blatchf. 45; DeWitt v. Brooks, MS. N. Y. 1861; Nelson, J., cited in Law's Digest of Patent and Copyright Cases, 174.

[2] All translations, I suppose, may be reduced to these three heads: first, that of metaphrase, or turning an author, word for word and line by line, from one language into another.

155. The apparent paradox, therefore, arises, that while the labor is original, the result is secondary; and hence the difficulty to which allusion has been made.

The work of a translator is clearly original, since it not only presupposes and requires knowlege, care, foresight, and a wide appreciation of the difference between the real and popular significance of idioms, expressions, phrases, and words in the language into which, as well as in the language out of which, he translates; but a positive primary labor—as contradistinguished from the secondary labor of selecting transcribing, and compiling, which the mere collector or editor performs.

Again, the labor of a conscientious and faithful translator is much more original and primary, for instance, than the labor of a mere paraphraser; since a creditable paraphrase may be produced without the slightest knowledge of, or familiarity with, or reference to, the language of the original work, by mere reference to a previous translation, and a book of synonyms. The paraphraser's labor might be secondary, but the work of a translator is at least original, in the contemplation of the common law and statutes of copyright,

This manner was: Horace—"His Art of Poetry," translated by Bengonson. The second way is that of paraphrase, or translation with latitude, where the author is kept in view by the translator so as never to be lost; but his words are not so strictly followed as his sense, and that, too, is admitted to be amplified, but not altered. Such is Mr. Waller's translation of Virgil's fourth Æneid. The third way is that of imitation, where the translator (if now he has not lost that name) assumes the liberty, not only to vary from the words and sense, but to forsake them both, as he sees occasion, and taking only some general limits from the original to run divisions on the groundwork as he pleases. Such is Mr. Cowley's practice in turning two odes of Pindar's and one of Horace's into English. Dryden's Works, Scott's Ed. xxii.

and of the definition given by them of the word "author."

In the earliest days of our literature, the translator's work was regarded as one of much greater merit and genius than the author's. The mere faculty of invention was formerly little prized; while the learning required to translate, was of the highest value, and exacted the highest respect.

Chaucer, the father of English literature, never attempted invention; neither did the author of Shakespeare, whose stories are, without exception, taken from the classics, or the Italian, and from other and foreign sources.

The reason undoubtedly was, and is, that education does not develop (possibly by affording ruts and grooves for the intellect, it rather retards) the faculty of literary invention; and in the days when education was a thing very rarely met with, the mere faculty of story-telling was of no estimation whatever.[1]

It is an interesting reflection that stories, legends, and tales—what in fact is now learnedly known as "folk-lore," sprung entirely from the lowest classes intellectually—from the utterly uneducated, in whom superstition and imagination go hand in hand—the imagination of one generation becoming, in the course of time, the superstition of the succeeding, and the fancy of each lending new exaggerations and amplifications to the superstition of the age before it.

It is essential, of course, that the translated work should be in a language foreign to the one into which it is translated. One who should take a work by an author of his own country, and carefully change each word into a synonym, thus destroying the identity

[1] For curious confirmation of this fact, see Prof. John Fisk's "Folk Lore." Boston, 1872.

of the language, but in reality leaving the ideas and thoughts the same, would not be held, by this exercise of disingenuous ingenuity, to be entitled to the rights of a translator.[1] It is of the utmost importance that these classes of secondary works should be carefully approached and examined; for it is in regard to their construction that the questions of originality arise, which we are about to consider.

156. In the copyright law of the United States, these three classes of writers we have alluded to are undoubtedly included under the word "author," or at least under the three words "author," "designer," or "proprietor," in the first sentences, which are as follows:

"Any citizen of the United States, or resident therein, who shall be the author, inventor, designer, or proprietor of any book, map, chart, dramatic or musical composition, engraving, cut, print, or photograph, or negative thereof, or of a painting, drawing, chromo, statue, statuary, and of models or designs intended to be perfected as works of the fine arts, and the executors, administrators, or assigns of any such person shall, upon complying with the provisions of this chapter, have the sole liberty of printing, reprinting, publishing, completing, copying, executing, finishing, and vending the same; and, in the case of a dramatic composition, of publicly performing or representing it, or causing it to be performed or represented by others. And authors may reserve the right to dramatize or to translate their own works."[2] But,

[1] The rights of a paraphraser do not appear to have ever been recognized as such in the law.

[2] Revision of 1873-4, § 4952; 3 Feb. 1831, ch. 16, § 1, v 4, 436; 18 Aug. 1856, ch. 169, § 1, v. 11, 138, 139; 3 Mar. 1865, ch. 126, § 1, v. 13,540; 8 Pet. 662; 14 How. 530; Hopk. ch. 351; 1 Blatchf. 625; 1 Story, 17; 3 Story, 778; 4 McLean, 316, 317; 5 Id., 37; 2 Wood & Min. 46; 2 Bla. 46, 170, 336 · 2 Paine. 383.

in the interpretation of this law, the distinctions above alluded to arise, and make it of the utmost importance to carefully examine and determine them.

157. Whenever an author can identify his own labor in the book or production of another, he can claim damages for its use, or protection by injunction against its further illegitimate employment. It is a maxim of the law that wherever there exists a wrong, there also exists somewhere a remedy. But if it should appear that the portion used was so insignificant or so trifling as to be unworthy the consideration of the dignity of the bench, the above rule might not apply; —for *de minimi non curat lex.* Mere quotation (i. e., fair quotation) is always optional; the only test, as we have seen, is whether the author has been injured by the use of his language.[1]

If the unwritten law which prohibits larceny and theft were capable of being applied to a man's thoughts, as well as to his watch or his purse, no statutes of copyright would be necessary. Their existence is only important because of the impracticability of carrying the law's recognition of *meum* and *tuum* so far. Their principle and spirit is precisely the same; and the law of copyright is only the eighth commandment applied to intellectual and immaterial labor. Upon this point it is unnecessary to dwell further.[2]

The simple rule is, that a man is entitled to the product of his own literary labor. And the simple question that the law will ask, without reference to the form or the pretension of the work is, Is it inclusive of any genuine product of his own labor? is it an original conception, an original composition, an original compilation, an original translation, codification, ex-

[1] Curtis on Copyright 247, 249, 250, 252.

[2] See *post*, chapter on piracy.

emplification, arrangement, analyzation, or annotation?

"In truth, in literature, in science, and in art," says Judge Story,[1] "there are and can be few, if any, things which, in an abstract sense, are strictly new and original throughout. Every book in literature, science, and art, borrows, and must necessarily borrow and use, much which was well known and used before. No man creates a new language for himself—at least if he be a wise man—in writing a book. He contents himself with the use of language already known, and used and understood by others. The thoughts of every man are more or less a combination of what other men have thought and expressed, although they may be modified, exalted, or improved by his own genius or reflection. If no book could be the subject of copyright which was not new and original in the elements of which it is composed, there could be no ground for any copyright in modern times; and we should be obliged to ascend very high even in antiquity to find a work entitled to such eminence."

158. "The law does not require that the subject of a book should be new, but that the method of treating it should have some degree of originality about it," not merely colorable.[2]

Thus, for instance, the composing receipts, or arranging them in a book, will give a copyright to the compiler; but the mere collecting them and handing them over to a compiler will not.[3] Or, one may have

[1] Emerson v. Davies, 3 St. 779; *Vid.* also Gray v. Russel, 1 St. 16.

[2] Copinger on Copyright, 21; Sayre v. Moore, 1 East, 361; King v. Reed, 8 Ves.; Jarrould v. Houlston, B. K. & J. 708; Reed v. Carusi, 98 Law Rep. O. S. 411; Wilkins v. Atkins, 17 Ves. 422.

[3] Rundell v. Murray, Jac. 314; Newton v. Cowrie, 4 Bing. 234.

copyright in mathematical tables, actually calculated by himself, although, on a similar calculation, precisely the same tables would be produced from the same sources, upon an application of the same principles by anybody else, and although they may have been published previously, and before his appeared.[1] Upon this principle, mere indices of title,[2] and school-books, no matter how elementary their character—as we have remarked elsewhere in this chapter—will be protected.[3]

"Anything like absolute originality in the composition of a work nowadays," says a late and learned writer, "seems to be almost an impossibility. The range of human ideas on any subject is limited; and the productions of the busy brains and pens of preceding thinkers are so numerous, that, if books are to be written, the writers must be, to some extent at least, beholden for their materials to those who have written before. If no copyright exist in a work, of course subsequent writers may make of it what use they like, and reproduce it to any extent they please. But if a copyright does exist in it, then the important and somewhat difficult question arises: In what manner, and to what extent, may subsequent authors make use of the materials contained in it without an infringement of the copyright? In other words, how far may

[1] Bailey v. Taylor, 3 L. J. 66; "I admit," said Lord Eldon (in Matthewson v. Stockalde, 12 Ves. 275), "that no man can monopolize such subjects as the English Channel, the Island of St. Domingo, or the events of the world; and every man may take what is useful from the original work, improve, add, and give the public the whole, comprising the original work, with the additions and improvements."

[2] Banker v. Caldwell, 3 Minn. 94.

[3] Emerson v. Davies, 3 Story, 768; Lennie v. Pillans, 5 Sess. Cas. 2 Law, 416; Constable v. Brewster, 3 S. 215 (N. E. 152).

one writer avail himself of the product of another's labor in which copyright exists, without subjecting himself to the charge of piracy?"[1]

He who claims the originality must show something which the law can recognize as the result of his own, and not of another's industry and skill. "Something he must show to have been produced by himself; whether it be a purely original thought or principle, unpublished before, or a new combination of old thoughts and ideas and sentiments, or a new application or use of known and common materials, or a collection, the result of his industry and skill. In whatever way he claims the exclusive privilege accorded by these laws, he must show something which the law can fix upon, as the product of his own, and not another's labors. But, in order that the law should do this ample justice to the great variety of claimants, it is necessary that its rules should be capable of adaptation to the objects of their labor. They must include in their range everything that can be justly claimed as the peculiar product of individual efforts; otherwise, they would exclude from the benefits of literary property, objects which are as clearly the products of individual labor as the most original thoughts ever written, namely, new and important combinations and arrangements, or collections of materials known and common to all mankind."[2]

159. No matter how original in his conception the author may be, or at what date he writes, or how soon after the discovery, or invention, or introduction of his theme, he clearly cannot copyright his subject-matter. He may even own it, but still it is free to the

[1] Shortt, 171.
[2] Curtis on Copyright, 171, 172.

world, to be described and commented upon by whomsoever will.[1]

One who has written a treatise, for example, on the moon, cannot copyright the moon as a subject, and give out that thereafter he intends to monopolize it. Nor can he copyright the name of a cardinal virtue, and prevent the use of that title forever afterwards.[2] Nor, if one happened to be the owner of land upon which an aereolite had fallen, or upon which a curious boulder happens to rest, which attracts the attention of scientific men, could he copyright the subject of that aereolite, or that boulder, and prevent its description by others. He would have power, indeed, to prevent an incursion upon his premises for the purpose of their examination, but his power over his property would not extend to words. He could not enjoin their discussion.

Neither, on the other hand, will the fact that the subject-matter is common, deprive the author of the product of his original labor, *bona fide* performed, in creating that subject-matter.

160. "I do not see why," said Lord Eldon, "if a person collects an account of natural curiosities, and such articles, and employs the labor of his mind by giving a description of them, that is as much a literary work as many others that are protected by injunction

[1] See, however, the case of Prince Albert v. Strange, 2 De G. & Sm. 674.

[2] Isaacs v. Daly, N. Y. Times, March 3d, 5th, and 6th, 1874. In that case the defendant, who was proprietor of the Fifth Avenue Theater, in the city of New York, had advertised and announced his intention of producing at that theater, on a certain night, a play called "Charity;" the plaintiff, who claimed to have written and copyrighted a play by that name, some time before, moved for an injunction, not pretending that the play was the same as the one he had written, but merely claiming the title "Charity." Curtis, J., refused the injunction. See this case reported *post*, chapter on Dramatic Copyright.

and by action. It is equally competent to any other person, perceiving the success of such a work, to set about a similar work, *bona fide* his own; but it must be in substance a new and original work, and must be handed out to the world as such.[1]

The fact that the subject of the work is common, does not deprive an author of copyright in the product of the labor which he has *bona fide* spent on it, or render it less necessary for any subsequent author to have recourse to the original sources. So in Longmans v. Winchester,[2] the plaintiffs were held entitled to copyright in the "Court Calendar," a work consisting of lists of members of the houses of peers and commons, &c., and an injunction was granted restraining the defendants from copying and publishing the plaintiffs' work. "The question before me," said Lord Eldon, "is whether it is not perfectly clear that, in a vast proportion of the work of these defendants, no other labor has been applied than copying the plaintiffs' work. From the identity of the inaccuracies, it is impossible to deny that the one was copied from the other *verbatim et literatim.* To the extent, therefore, in which the defendant's publication has been supplied from the other work, the injunction must go; but I have said nothing that has a tendency to prevent any person from giving to the public a work of this kind if it is the fair fruit of original labor, the subject being open to all the world; but if it is a mere copy of an original work, this court will interpose against that invasion of copyright."[3]

A work entitled "The Guide to Science," which

[1] Hogg v. Kirby, 8 Ves. 221.

[2] 16 Ves. 269; *Vid.* also Kelly v. Morris, L. Rep. 1 Eq. 702; 14 L. J. N. S. 222; 35 L. J. 423; ch. 14, W. R. 496.

[3] Longmans v. Winchester, *ubi supra.*

laid no claim to any originality with reference to the scientific doctrines treated in it, but contained, in the form of questions and answers, a scientific exposition of some of the ordinary phenomena of human life, in parts digested from different works; was held to constitute an original work, in which the author was entitled to copyright. Wood, V. C., said, "That an author has a copyright in a work of this description is beyond all doubt. If any one, by pains and labor, collects and reduces, into the form of a systematic course of instruction, those questions which he may find ordinary persons asking in reference to the common phenomena of life, with answers to those questions and explanations of those phenomena; whether such explanations and answers are furnished by his own recollection of his former general reading, or out of works consulted by him for the express purpose, the reduction of questions so collected, with such answers under certain heads and in a scientific form, is amply sufficient to constitute an original work, of which the copyright will be protected.[1]

In Cary v. Faden[2] the question is fully illustrated. In 1797, the plaintiff Cary was employed to make a survey of certain roads and highways in Great Britain. Upon the completion thereof, he published a book called "Cary's New Itinerary," which followed the plan and contained much of the materials of an older work called "Patterson's Road Book," but contained also many corrections of and additions to it. Faden having published a book bearing the same relation to Cary's that Cary's did to Patterson's, Cary filed a bill in chancery to restrain Faden from publishing his work, on the ground that it was not original, but,

[1] Jarrold v. Houlston, 3 K. & J. 708.

[2] 5 Ves. 23.

either in whole or part, a copy of Cary's. The lord chancellor (Loughborough) refused an injunction. He said, "What right had the plaintiff to the original work? If I were to do strict justice I should order the defendants to take out of their book all that they have taken from the plaintiff, and reciprocally the plaintiff to take out of his all he has taken from Patterson. I think the plaintiff may be contented that a bill is not filed against him."[1] An action was brought in 1801 by the same plaintiff against Messrs. Longman & Rees for publishing a pirated edition of the same or a similar work, the book published by the defendants being professedly a twelfth edition of the original work by Patterson, but containing nine-tenths of Cary's alterations and improvements. The plaintiff was held entitled to recover. Lord Kenyon, Ch. J., said, "Certainly the plaintiff had no title on which he could found an action to that part of his book which he had taken from Mr. Patterson's; but it is as clear that he had a right to his own additions and alterations, many of which were very material and valuable: and the defendants are answerable at least for copying those parts in their book. . . . . The courts of justice have been long laboring under an error, if an author have no copyright in any part of a work unless he have an exclusive right to the whole work."[2]

161. "The identity of a literary work," says Blackstone,[3] "consists entirely in the sentiment and the language. The same conceptions, clothed in the same words, must necessarily be the same composition; and whatever method may be taken of exhibiting that composition to the ear or the eye of another, by recital,

[1] 1 East, 358.
[2] Cary v. Kearsley, 4 Esp. 169.
[3] Com. 406.

by writing, or by printing, in any number of copies, or at any period of time, it is always the identical work of the author which is so exhibited."

162. If the author of a work be unknown, and impossible to be ascertained, the copyright will be held to belong to the publisher.[1]

Where one procures from another the subject-matter or data of a work, and, upon procuring them, frames them into a work—the authorship of the work exists in the person composing it, and not in the one furnishing the material.[2]

Accordingly, in the case of De Witt v. Brooks,[3] it was held that where the incidents of a person's life were furnished by him to one who prepared them for publication, and the copyright was taken out in the name of the person furnishing the facts, it was held that he was not the author, and that a person claiming as his assignee, could not maintain an action for an infringement.

But a judicious, careful, and useful new arrangement of old and well-known material, may be produced by original labor; and if so, will be entitled to protection.[4]

And so, under the copyright law of 1831, it was held that, to constitute a person an author, he must, by his own intellectual labor, applied to the materials of his composition, produce an arrangement or compilation new in itself;[5] but he cannot obtain an owner-

[1] McLean v. Moody, Scotch Sess. Cas. 2nd series, vol. 20, 1163.

[2] DeWitt v. Brooks, MS. cited Law's Digest of Patent and Copyright Cases, 174.

[3] MS. cited Law's Digest of Patent and Copyright Cases, 174.

[4] Per Lord Jeffrey in Alexander v. McKenzie, 9 Scotch Sess. Cas. 2 ser. 758.

[5] Atwill v. Ferrett, 2 Blatchf. 39.

ship in those materials in the same state in which he finds them, or in which they are furnished to him.[1]

In the case of Alexander v. Mackenzie,[2] the pursuer had copyrighted a manual of practical forms and styles of the writs and instruments introduced by the heritable securities and infeftment acts, those acts giving only general descriptions of the forms to be used.

The court, in rendering its judgment (per Lord Fullerton) remarked: "It is said, that owing to the particular nature of the styles they cannot be the subject of copyright, because they are drawn up precisely after the form prescribed in the statute, and because any styles relating to the same subjects as those given by the complainer must, if the directions of the statutes and phraseology of conveyancers were used, be expressed in the same manner exactly as those proposed by the complainer. Now, it may be quite true that, if the statute had supplied certain forms by which the operations intended to be thereby regulated were to be done, if the statute had contained, as such statutes sometimes do, an appendix exhibiting certain schedules of forms which it was only necessary for anyone to copy in order to avail himself of the provisions of the act, then I hold that the reprinting of such forms in a separate publication would not give him a copyright in those forms. But the case here is different, for the statute only gives very general directions and descriptions of the styles that are to be used. The schedules are very general in their terms, and it is no doubt of great practical importance to suit these general directions to each case falling under the statute as it may arise. The preparing and adjusting of such writings require much care and exertion of mind. As

[1] Id.

[2] 9 Scotch Sess. Cas. 2nd ser. 758.

to invention, that is a different thing; it does not require the exercise of original or creative genius, but it requires industry and knowledge." And he was, therefore, held to have in them such a property as courts of equity would protect.

163. A work, to be entitled to recognition as sufficiently original for the purposes of protection, must, therefore, contain internal evidence of labor, thought, and skill, on the part of the one claiming the originality of the secondary labor.

164. A not unusual case arises where a person compiles a list of names of public men for reference. In such cases, the first compiler undoubtedly has a copyright in his compilation, though the material is in no sense original, and is equally accessible to any person seeking it. But how far a second compilation of the same will be an infringement upon the first, does not appear to be fully settled.

In the case of Longman v. Winchester, where this question arose, it was evident, from the identical reappearance in the second compilation of certain inaccuracies in the first, that the defendant had performed scarcely any other labor than merely to copy, *verbatim et literatim*, from the plaintiff. "To the extent," said Lord Eldon, "in which the defendant's publication has been supplied from the other work, the injunction must go;" and he adds, by way of *obiter*, "but I have said nothing that has a tendency to prevent any person from giving to the public a work of this kind (a 'court calendar,' or lists of members of the houses of lords and of commons, &c.), if it is the fair fruit of original labor, the subject being open to all the world.[1] . . . . Take the case of a map describing a particular country, and a map of the same country afterwards

[1] 16 Ves. 271.

published by another person: if the description is accurate in both, they must be pretty much the same; but it is clear the latter publisher cannot, on that account, be justified in sparing himself the labor and expense of actual survey, and copying the map previously published by another."

The circumstances here supposed by Lord Eldon, appear actually to have arisen in the case of Kelly v. Morris.[1]

And the court, in its judgment, stated the rule with great clearness, as follows:

"The compiler of a directory or guide-book containing information derived from sources common to all, which must of necessity be identical in all cases, if correctly given; is not entitled to spare himself the labor and expense of original inquiry, by adapting and republishing the information contained in previous works on the same subject. He must obtain and work out the information independently for himself; and the only legitimate use which he can make of previous works is for the purpose of verifying the correctness of his results,[2] as Lord Eldon said in Longman v. Winchester."[3]

Lord Eldon had previously said, with reference to a "Road Book," "It is certainly competent to any other man to publish a book of roads; and if the same skill, intelligence, and diligence are applied in the second instance, the public would receive nearly the same information from both works; but there is no doubt that this court would interpose to prevent a

[1] L. Rep. 1 Eq. 702; 14 L. J. N. S. 222; 35 L. J. 423, ch. 14; W. R. 496.

[2] *Vid.* also Lewis v. Fullerton, 2 Beav. 14; Murray v. Bogue, 1 Drew, 353.

[3] 16 Ves. 271.

mere republication of a work which the labor and skill of another person had supplied to the world."

165. This fact, perhaps, can only be established by the testimony of individuals employed on the second work. In Kelly v. Morris, canvassers and employees of the defendant were examined; and one of them admitted that he had "done his work carelessly, and had not taken the trouble to make the necessary inquiries; and such testimony, where internal evidence (as in the case of Longman v. Winchester, where the inaccuracies of the first work had been copied along with the rest[1]) is wanting, will be the safest test.

166. As to in how far portions of one original work may be quoted, contained, or incorporated in another, without interfering with the originality of the second—it would be difficult to state any one principle of universal application. The decisions will be found mainly to be governed by the circumstances of the particular cases. A quotation is, of course, a reprinting of the portion quoted. Without doubt, the author has a right to every line of his work; and the only question can be—at least the only question for the court—is the author injured, or in danger of being injured, by the publication of quotations from his book?

The gist—the valuable part of a work—might readily be copied, and credit therefor duly given, and yet the quoting be illegal. The value of the matter taken, rather than the quantity thereof, must be regarded. If the tendency of the quotation be to supersede the sale of the work quoted from,[2] then it will

[1] It is curious to observe that the first conclusive proof of the forgeries of Chatterton was of this description. Skeat's Chatterton, vol. 1, p. 16.

[2] Emerson v. Davies, 3 Story, R. 768, 797.

be illegal. "When it comes to a question of quantity," said Lord Cottenham, "it must be very vague. One author might take all the vital part of another's book, though it might be a small proportion of the book in quantity. It is not only quantity, but value that is always looked to."[1]

There are several cases where courts of equity have refused interference, on account of the minuteness of the injury occasioned by short extracts or quotations. Where the value of the extract or the amount of injury is minute and trifling, courts will discourage the practice of occupying their time by applications in which it would be harassing and difficult to ascertain, by account, the precise value of the injury alleged to have been committed.[2] But the court, however, would not refuse to allow an attempt to assess the damages by a jury. "There is no doubt," said Lord Eldon, "that a man cannot, under pretense of quotation, publish the whole or a part of another's book, though he may use —what, in all cases, it is very difficult to define—fair quotation.[3] And in determining the question of fair quotation, the intention of the person quoting will make no difference.[4] The question must be, has the quotation the effect of injuring the sale of the book quoted from? The work might be quoted from with a view, even, of advertising or complimenting it; and Lord Ellenborough instanced—[what has become of such habitual custom in these days]—the practice of reviewers and literary critics, who include large extracts

[1] Bramhall v. Halcombe, 3 Mylne & C. 737, 738.

[2] Whittingham v. Wooler, 2 Swanst. 428; Tonson v. Walker, 3 Id. 672; Bell v. Whitehead, 17 L. J. 142; Wilkins v. Aikin, 17 Ves. 422, 424.

[3] Wilkins v. Aikin, *supra*.

[4] Curtis on Copyright, 245 (note).

of works criticised by them.[1] But the case viewed by his lordship was that of an encyclopædia, which had taken from the plaintiff's book and reprinted seventy-five of the one hundred and eighteen pages of which it consisted. Said he: 'The question is, whether the defendant's publication would serve as a substitute for the plaintiff's? A review will not, in general, serve as a substitute for the book reviewed; and even there, if so much is extracted that it communicates the same knowledge with the original work, it is an actionable violation of literary property.' The intention to pirate is not necessary in an action of this sort; it is enough that the publication complained of is, in substance, a copy whereby a work vested in another is prejudiced."

Upon the appearance of Dr. Johnson's "Rasselas," it was seized upon by "The Gentleman's Magazine," which printed the story, leaving out the "moral reflections." Now this was claimed to be an abridgment only; and the court held, with a reasoning that later decisions can hardly be said to sustain, that an abridgment was an advantage to the author, as being not only, perhaps, a testimonial to the value of his work, but as serving the end of an advertisement.[2] This reasoning of the Master of the Rolls was very much the same as saying, If your goods are stolen, it is testimony that they are worth stealing; and the gratification of the compliment should compensate you for your loss. And perhaps it might, if writers wrote for "glory," as we have seen, unhappily for this line of argument, is not the case. "This latitudinarian right," said Chancellor Kent, in commenting upon this case, "is liable to abuse, and to trench upon the copyright of the author. The question as to a *bona fide* abridg-

[1] Roworth v. Wilkes, 1 Camp. 94.
[2] Dodsley v. Kinnersley, Aub. 403.

ment may turn—not so much upon the quantity, as the value of the selected materials."[1]

Somewhat later, in the case of Charles Dickens's "Christmas Carol," where the defendant had taken the story, and without altering incident, character, scene, or name, had set out the narrative in somewhat fewer words; the court would not permit the defense, of abridgment to be set up, saying that it "was not aware that one man had the right to abridge the works of another; that—although it would not pronounce that such a thing as a lawful abridgment was impossible—to say that one man had the right to abridge, and publish in an abridged form, the work of another, without more: was going much beyond his notion of what the law of this country was.[2]

And so an injunction was granted against the sale of a work entitled "An Abridgment of Cases," &c., which appeared to be a *verbatim* copy of a preceding work of the same name, except that the former work left out certain portions of the cases, such as the arguments of counsel. The injunction was granted.[3]

Where the publication of the quotation is a substitute for the quoted work, or for so much of it as may be, the quotation is an infringement. As to the "giving of credit," that goes merely to the question of the intention of the quoter, and is mainly immaterial; for, as an injury may be inflicted without in-

[1] 2 Com. 382 (note), and see Gyles v. Wilcox, 2 Alk. 141. 2 Story Eq. Jur. § 939; Campbell's Lives of the Chancellors, v. 56.

[2] Dickens v. Lee, 8 Jur. 183.

[3] Brellerworth v. Robinson, 5 Ves. 709; and see Bell v. Walker, 1 Bro. C. C. 451, and see also Sweet v. Shaw, 1 Jur. 212; Whittingham v. Wooler, 2 Swanst. 428; Mecklin v. Richardson, Amb. 694.

tention, so no injury may result from an intention to injure. The law will look at the effect, as we have said before, whether intentional or unintentional.[1] This question, and the questions arising in the cases of abridgments, are often so inseparable as to be practically identical.

167. To constitute a true and proper abridgment of a work, the whole must be preserved in its sense. The act of abridgment thus becomes an act of the understanding, employed in carrying a large work into a smaller compass, and, by rendering it less expensive, and more convenient both to the time and use of the reader, making the abridgment a new and meritorious work. In the case of an abridged edition of an extensive work, which might be read in a fourth part of the time, and all the substance preserved and conveyed in language as good or better than in the original, and in a more agreeable and useful manner, Lord Apsley said that he and Mr. Justice Blackstone were agreed, "that an abridgment, when the understanding is employed in retrenching unnecessary and uninteresting circumstances, which rather deaden the narration, is not an act of plagiarism upon the original work, nor against any property of the author in it, but an allowable and meritorious work."[2]

But though a *bona fide* abridgment of another work is no infringement of the copyright in that work, a merely colorable abridgment may be. "Where books are colorably shortened only," said Lord Hardwicke, "they are undoubtedly within the meaning of the act of parliament, and are a mere evasion of the statute, and cannot be called an abridgment;"[3] and

[1] Curtis on Copyright, 247.
[2] Lofft's Rep. 775.
[3] Gyles v. Wilcox, 2 Atk. 142.

his lordship considered a book published by the defendant entitled "Modern Crown Law," not to be a *bona fide*, but a mere colorable abridgment of Sir Matthew Hale's "Pleas of the Crown," with the omission of some repealed statutes, and a translation of the Latin and French quotations.

A mere selection or different arrangement of parts of the original work, bringing it into a smaller compass, will not be regarded by the law as an abridgment. "There must be," said Mr. Justice Story,[1] "real, substantial condensation of the materials, and intellectual labor and judgment bestowed thereon; and not merely the facile use of the scissors; or extracts of the essential parts constituting the chief value of the original work." Many mixed ingredients enter into the discussion of such questions. In some cases, a considerable portion of the materials of the original work may be fused—if I may use such an expression—into another work, so as to be undistinguishable in the mass of the latter, which has other professed and obvious objects, and cannot fairly be treated as a piracy; or they may be inserted as a sort of distinct and mosaic work, into the general texture of the second work, and constitute the peculiar excellence thereof, and then it may be a clear piracy.

In the case from which the above remarks are taken, the question was as to whether a "Life of Washington," in two volumes of 866 pages, was an invasion of the copyright in "Sparks's Life and Writings of Washington," a work in twelve volumes; 353 pages of the former work being copied from the latter, 64 pages being official letters, and 255 being

[1] Folsom v. Marsh, 2 St. Rep. 107, and see Lewis v. Fullerton, 2 Beavan, 6, 8.

private letters of Washington, first published by Sparks under a contract with the owners of the original papers of Washington. It was held by Story, J., to be such an invasion, and the injunction was granted.[1]

The question of quotation will constantly arise. In volumes of "Elegant Extracts," where the defendant published a book of specimens of modern English poetry, with criticisms and biographical notices, and inserted therein entire poems and extracts from the poems of Campbell, which were under the protection of copyright, an injunction was granted against the publication, and the *animus furandi* held to be implied by law, from the taking.[2] And said Story, J.,[3] "If a person should, under color of publishing 'Elegant Extracts' of poetry, include all the best pieces at large, of a favorite poet, whose volume was secured by copyright, it would be difficult to say why it was not an invasion of that right, since it might constitute the entire value of the volume."

The addition of words, prelude, and accompaniment to an old air was held to give the adapter a copyright in the whole composition; and where a a person adapted words to an old air and procured a friend to compose an accompaniment, his assignee was held entitled to describe himself, in an action for piracy, as proprietor of the copyright in the entire composition.[4] And it was said in Bogue v. Houls-

[1] Folsom v. Marsh, 2 Story, 100.

[2] Campbell v. Scott, 11 Simons, 31.

[3] In Folsom v. Marsh, 2 Story R. 100, 115, and see also Mawman v. Feof, 2 Russ. 383, *post* chapters on legal reports and piracy.

[4] Leader v. Purdy, 7 C. B. 4. As to how far an arrangement for the pianoforte of the score of an opera is an orginal work, see Wood v. Boosey, 7 B. & S. 869; 9 B. & S 175;

ton,[1] that where there are designs forming portion of a book in which a person has copyright under the act, such copyright extends to the illustrations and designs of the book, as well as to the letter-press. Where the plaintiff had published a book, containing letter-press illustrated by wood-engravings, the engravings being printed on the same paper as the letter-press itself, and defendants published a work with a different title and different letter-press, but containing pirated copies of the wood engravings—which are especially excluded from the English statutes[2] (the plaintiff having complied with the requisitions of 5 & 6 Vict. c. 45, but not with those of the act for the protection of engravings, by printing the date of publication and the name of the proprietor on each copy), the vice-chancellor granted an injunction, the plaintiff undertaking to bring an action to try the right at law. "It appears to me," said Sir James Parker, "that a book must include every part of the book, it must include every print, design, or engraving which forms part of the book, as well as the letter-press therein, which is another part of it. Prints published separately do not appear to have been within that act by that express definition. But the case now before the court is not the case of separately published prints, but the case of designs forming part of a book. There is no decision of any court of law, or of this court, either way upon this point."

168. If one, not claiming any originality whatever, reduces to question and answer a certain science or subject-matter, courts, as we have seen, will not

L. Rep. 2 Q. B. 340; L. Rep. 3 Q. B. 223; 18 L. T. N. S. 105.

[1] 5 DeG. & S. 275.

[2] 5 & 6 Vict. C. 45.

travel behind it to ascertain whether the questions and answers were framed from the writer's own surmises, opinions, or recollections on the particular subject, or from works consulted by him for the purpose; but will hold his work to be original, for the purposes of copyright and protection.[1]

169. We have seen that, where the sources from which the material or subject-matter are common, and of general availability and recourse—that is, *in medio*—any novel arrangement of them can be the subject of ownership.[2]

But though any person may thus acquire a copyright in his own arrangement of common materials; the materials themselves remain, as always, open to the next comer who chooses to have recourse to them, and different copyrights may be acquired in different arrangements of the same common materials. Different arrangements of common materials must, however, be independent. A later arrangement must not be a servile imitation or reproduction of an earlier one.

In Kelly v. Morris,[3] application was made for an injunction to restrain the publication of "The Imperial

[1] Jarrold v. Houlston, 3 K. & J. 108 *ante*, 40. See this principle applied in the case of a book of chronology (Trusler v. Murray; cited in note to Cary v. Longman, 1 East, 363); and to the case of an annotated catalogue of books published by a certain publishing house (Hatten v. Arthur, 11 W. R. 934); to a work on architecture (Wilkins v. Aikin, 17 Ves. 422); maps (Kelly v. Morris, 1 L. Rep. Equity, 697; *Vid.* also Carnan v. Bowles, 2 Bro. C. C. 80); and as to the protection accorded (2 Story Eq. Jur. § 941; Eden Inj. ch. 13, 286; *Vid.* also Gray v. Russel, 1 Story, 11; Emerson v. Davies, 3 Id., 768.

[2] Alexander v. Mackenzie, 9 Scotch Sess. Cass. 2nd ser 758; *Vid.* also Emerson v. Davies, 3 Story, 781; Blunt v. Patten, 2 Paine, 395.

[3] L. Rep. 1 Eq. 697; 35 L. J. 423 ch.; 14 L. T. N. S. 222.

Directory of London, 1866," on the ground that it was a mere piracy of a work belonging to the plaintiff, entitled "Post-Office London Directory." The defendant set up, as defense, that from 1862 to 1864, he had published a work called "The Business Directory," in which appeared the names of about 100,000 persons, in trade or business, which had been obtained by a large number of canvassers whom he had employed for the purpose; that, wishing to extend his operations, and bring out "The Imperial Directory," which should comprise street, conveyance, postal and other sections, he acted on a similar principle to that which had guided him in taking the names of persons in business whom his canvassers were unable to see, and procured his information from any source "where the persons had made it public at their own expense, for their own benefit"; that he considered that the name of a private resident belonged to the public when that resident had "gratuitously given it to the public through some recognized medium of publicity," and that the publisher merely "held it in trust for a purpose, receiving for his trouble any benefit he could make of the information, but that the right of using that information belonged to the public, as soon as the information was made public"; that any person might go round with a list of names already published, and ask permission to render the work of publication more complete by reproducing it, and if any error had been made in the first publication, it rested with the original owners of the names to point out the error when submitted to them for permission to reproduce which opportunity was afforded the residents by means of circulars sent round to them through the defendant's canvassers, asking the residents to fill up a form with their name and address for publication in "The

Imperial Directory." It was admitted that one of defendant's canvassers, afterwards discharged by him, had not taken the trouble to make the necessary inquiries, from house to house, so that most of the errors in the defendant's directory, identical with those in the plaintiff's, would be thus accounted for. On the other hand, several instances were adduced of corrections and large supplementary additions to the plaintiff's work contained in the defendant's, and the manuscript of the latter work was produced.

In granting an injunction the lord chancellor said: "The defendant has been most completely mistaken in what he assumes to be his right to deal with the labor and property of others. In the case of a dictionary, map, guide-book, or directory, where there are certain common objects of information, which must, if described correctly, be described in the same words, a subsequent compiler is bound to set about doing for himself that which the first compiler has done. In the case of a road-book he must count the milestones for himself. In the case put of a newly-discovered island, he must go through the whole process of triangulation, just as if he had never seen any former map; and generally, he is not entitled to take one word of the information previously published, without independently working out the matter for himself, so as to arrive at the same result, from the same common sources of information; and the only use that he can legitimately make of a previous publication, is to verify his own calculations and results, when obtained. So, in the present case, the defendant could not take a single line of the plaintiff's directory for the purpose of saving himself labor and trouble in getting his information. The defendant, from the description of the way in which he had in the first instance compiled his 'Business

Directory,' seems to have known exactly what he might do. . . . . The defendant goes on in his affidavit to propound a most extraordinary doctrine as to the right of publicity in the names of private residents, who had, as he expressed it, 'given their names for public use.' What he has done has been just to copy the plaintiff's book, and then to send out canvassers to see if the information so copied was correct. If the canvassers did not find the occupier of the house at home, or could get no answer from him, then the information copied from the plaintiff's book was reprinted bodily, as if it was a question for the occupier of the house merely, and not for the compiler of the previous directory. Further than this, the defendant tells us that he had a number of new agents, and that one of them had performed his part of the work carelessly, thus at once showing how easy it would be, on the system adopted by the defendant, for any negligent agent to send back his list all ticked as if correct, without having taken the trouble to make a single inquiry. . . . . The work of the defendant has clearly not been compiled by the legitimate application of independent personal labor, and there must be an injunction to restrain the publication of any copy of the defendant's work containing the portions called the 'Street' and 'Court' Directories, with liberty for the defendant to apply, when he shall have expunged from such portions all matter copied from the plaintiff's work."[1]

A compiler may not cut out slips from the former work and go and see whether they are accurate, and if accurate, copy them bodily into his own work, as

[1] *Vid.* also Matthewson v. Stockdale, 12 Ves. 275; Cornish v. Upton, 4 L. T. N. S. 862; Morris v. Ashbee, L. Rep. 7 Eq. 34; 19 L. T. N. S. 550.

was done in both the cases referred to; but he is quite justified in referring to the former book "in order to guide himself to the persons on whom it would be worth his while to call."[1] He is not entitled to take a single line of the plaintiff's directory for the purpose of saving himself trouble in getting his information.[2] Not that he may not look into the book for the purpose of ascertaining whether it was worth his while to call upon that person or not; but he may not cut out a slip or portion of the first work, and then take that particular slip, and show it to the person, and get his authority as to putting that particular slip in.[3] He must not take the passage of the directory and go and see whether it happens to be accurate, and if it is accurate, bodily copy the passage into his directory.

Nor will the fact that the publisher of the directory receives payment from some of the persons whose names are contained in it, for printing their names in large letters, or with lines of additional description, make those names, when so inserted, common property, so as to justify the compiler of a rival directory in reprinting them from slips cut from the former.[4] Nor the fact that the persons, whose names were so printed, had been applied to by the compiler of the second directory to verify the information contained in the first, and had authorized the second insertion of

[1] Morris v. Wright, L. Rep. 5 ch. app. 279; 22 L. T. N. S. 78.

[2] Kelly v. Morris, L. Rep. 1 Eq. 697; 35 L. J. 423 ch.; 14 L. T. N. S. 222.

[3] Pike v. Nicholas, 20 L. T. N. S. 909; 38 L. J. 529 ch. The decision of the vice-chancellor in this case was reversed on appeal, but only as to the question of degree in which the defendant had in fact made use of the plaintiff's work. L. Rep. 5 ch. app. 251; *vid.* also Stowe v. Thomas, 2 Amer. Law Reg. 229.

[4] Morris v. Ashbee, L. Rep. 7 Eq. 34; 19 L. T. N. S. 550.

their names in capital letters and added lines,[1] make the work an original one.

The rule, as applied to dictionaries, is illustrated in a late English case,[2] holding, that labor having been employed upon any subjects, however humble, gave a copyright which no one had a right to interfere with; and that, "as to dictionaries, while there might be a certain degree of skill exhibited as to order and arrangement, and a certain amount of ingenuity exhibited in the selection of phrases and illustrations which were the best exponents of the sense in which the word was to be used; there might also be great labor in the logical deduction and arrangement of the word in its different senses, when the sense of the word departed from its primary signification; on the other hand, there was always this to be said, that as a large mass of the words admitted of only one acceptation, and could be translated in one way only (and the large mass of dictionaries were composed of words of this description): numerous dictionaries had necessarily been published from time to time, and the new dictionary maker must, of necessity, use much of the information and of the results of his predecessors. . . . . Of course there could be no copyright in much of the information contained in the numerous dictionaries published, each necessarily having a large number of words identically similar." In the case before it the court applied the test "whether there was a legitimate use of the plaintiff's publication in the fair exercise of a mental operation deserving the character of an original work," and the result, after an elaborate comparison of the two dictionaries, was an opinion that though the defendant had taken a good

[1] Morris v. Ashbee, L. Rep. 7 Eq. 34; 19 L. T. N. S. 550.

[2] Speers v. Brown. 6 W. R. 352.

deal from the plaintiff's work, yet a good deal of labor had been bestowed upon what had been taken, and, on the whole, it could not be said that the defendant had gone beyond what the court would allow; having produced that which, in the result, was, in fact, a different work from the plaintiff's.[1]

170. Abridgments—possibly from the fact that their spirit and tendency is by cheapening and making less laborious the perusal of learned works, to diffuse more widely education and culture—have generally been regarded with favor by the law, and liberally protected.

"An abridgment," said Lord Hardwicke,[2] "may, with great propriety, be called a new book, because not only the paper and print, but the invention, learning, and judgment of the author is shown in them, and in many cases are extremely useful, though in some instances prejudicial, by mistaking and curtailing the sense of an author." The abridgment must not only contain the arrangement of the book abridged; the idea must be taken from the pages: it must be in good faith an abridgment, not a treatise interlarded with citations: to copy certain passages from a book, omitting others, is in no just sense an abridgment: the judgment is not exercised in condensing the views of the author; the language is copied, not condensed.[3]

"Between a compilation and an abridgment," said Mr. Justice Leavitt,[4] "there is a clear distinction; and yet it does not seem to have been drawn in any opinion cited. A compilation consists of selected extracts from different authors; an abridgment is a condensa-

[1] The bill praying for an injunction was dismissed; but, on account of the doubtfulness of the case, without costs.

[2] Gyles v. Wilcox, 2 Atk. 143; *vid.* also Tonson v. Walker 3 Swanat, 681; Bell v. Walker, 1 Bro. C. C. 451.

[3] Story's Executors v. Holcombe, 4 McLean, 311.

[4] Id.

tion of the views of the author. The former cannot be extended so as to convey the same knowledge as the original work; the latter contains an epitome of the work abridged, and consequently conveys substantially the same knowledge. The former cannot adopt the arrangement of the works cited; the latter must adopt the arrangement of the work abridged. The former infringes the copyright, if matter transcribed, when published, shall impair the value of the original book; a fair abridgment, though it may injure the original, is lawful."

And modern jurists have not been as unanimous as their predecessors in favorable regard for abridgments; and, perhaps, the greater cheapness and ease with which original works are now produced, render it right that it should be so. In Tinsley v. Lacy,[1] Lord Chancellor ——— said: "I do not agree in the reasons for upholding such a work, given by some learned judges, viz., that an abridger is a benefactor. I should myself regard him rather as a sort of jackall to the public, to point out the beauties of authors"; and in the case of Story's Executors v. Holcombe,[2] Mr. Justice Leavitt expressed himself to the same effect, and observing that the same rule of decision should be applied to a copyright as to a patent for a machine. "The construction," he says, "of any other machine which acts upon the same principle, however its structure may be varied, is an infringement on the patent. The second machine may be recommended by its simplicity and cheapness; still, if it act upon the same principle of the one first patented, the patent

[1] 11 W. R. 876; 1 H & M. 747; 32 L. J. ch. 535. See *post*, chapter on Piracy.

[2] 4 McLean 311. And see, to the same effect, Curtis on Copyright, pp. 272, 273.

is violated. Now an abridgment, if fairly made, contains the principle of the original work, and this constitutes its value. Why, then, in reason and justice, should not the same principle be applied in a case of copyright, as in that of a patented machine? With the assent of the patentee, a machine acting upon the same principle, but of less expensive structure than the one patented, may be built; and so a book may be abridged by the author, or with his consent, should a cheaper work be wanted by the public. This, in my judgment, is the ground on which the rights of the author should be considered. But a contrary doctrine has been long established in England, under the statute of Anne, which, in this respect, is similar to our own statute; and in this country the same doctrine has prevailed. I am, therefore, bound by precedent; and I yield to it, in this instance, more as a principle of law than a rule of reason or justice."[1]

The case of Story's Executors v. Holcombe, from which the above remarks are taken, was one in which the plaintiffs complained of an infringement of the copyright in Judge Story's "Commentaries on Equity Jurisprudence," the defense being that the work complained of (an "Introduction to Equity") was a *bona fide* abridgment of the Commentaries. It appeared that the chapters and the subjects were the same in both books; the former book contained 1856 octavo pages, including notes, the latter 348 octavo pages, including notes; a page in the latter contained a little more than one in the former: reduced to the same sized page, the ratio in the amount of matter in the latter book to that in the former, was about two to nine. In the entire work of Story there were 226 pages, constituting nearly an eighth part, on which

[1] *Vid.* also Curtis on Copyright, pp. 272, 273.

there was some matter which had been extracted in the same language, or very nearly so, into the defendant's book, this matter comprising 879 lines, or about 24 pages of his book, and 30 pages of Story, which made one-fifteenth part of the defendant's book and one-sixtieth of Story; this matter being found in scattered paragraphs in the first third of the defendant's book: all the other portions of Judge Story's book were abridged without any transcription of his common language, the part so abridged comprising two-thirds of the defendant's book. The court, in granting an injunction as to the first 100 pages of the defendant's work, said:

"What is the character of the work complained of? Upon its title-page it does not purport to be an abridgment, but 'An Introduction to Equity Jurisprudence, on the Basis of Story's Commentaries'; and in the preface the author says, 'It is not intended to supply the place of the Commentaries with any class of readers, but to serve simply as an introduction, a companion, and a supplement to their study. The text is substantially an abridgment of that work, &c.'; . . . . but he also says that 'he has felt at liberty to make very considerable alterations and additions.' Alterations of the original work, and additions to the text, are not appropriate to an abridgment. In saying, therefore, that 'the text is substantially an abridgment,' Mr. Holcombe could have meant nothing more than that, in writing his book, he followed the arrangement of the Commentaries, extracting certain parts, condensing others, with 'very considerable alterations and additions' of his own. A supplement to the Commentaries, which, Mr. Holcombe says, in some sense, is the character of his work, may supply defects in the original, but it can in no sense be considered an abridgment. This remark seems to have been made in reference to the notes added by the author. It may not be essential to exclude extracts entirely from an abridgment, but in making extracts merely there is no condensation of the language of the author, and, consequently, there is no abridgment of it. Much looseness is found in the decisions upon this subject. Some of the judges would seem to consider that where a book is greatly reduced in the size, though made up principally of extracts, it is an abridgment. In a book of reports, such as 'Bacon's Abridgments,' the language of the court is necessarily adopted often to show the principle of the decision. But the same necessity does not exist, and the same license can not be exercised in abridging an elementary work. . . . . Nearly one-half of the text, in the first hundred pages of Mr. Holcombe's book, appears to have been extracted from Story. . . . . To class these extracts under the head of 'abridgments,' would seem to be a perversion of terms. Whatever else this part of Mr. Holcombe's book may be called, it is not an abridgment. With greater propriety it may be called a compilation, as the extracts contained in it are taken from various authors. As a compilation, this part of the book must be considered an infringement of the right of the plaintiffs, by the copious extracts made from the Commentaries, and the classification of the subjects copied from them. . . . . Looking at the smallness of Mr. Holcombe's book, in comparison of that from which it was principally taken, one might suppose that the former was a short abridgment of the latter. But this comparison of size or number of pages affords no guide to a proper decision. The character of the work must depend upon its matter; and it would seem from the considerations stated, that the first third part of Mr. Holcombe's book, including one hundred pages, cannot be justly and legally called an abridgment, as it does not possess the essential ingredients of such a work; and that, viewing it as a compilation, it is an infringement of the plaintiff's right, on the ground that the plan of the Commentaries is copied; and also for the reason that the extracts extend beyond the proper limit of such a work. The remaining two-thirds of the book may be comprehended under a liberal construction of an abridgment. The matter is greatly condensed by Mr. Holcombe, in his own language, and in a manner highly creditable to him."

The case of Dickens v. Lee,[1] is interesting as illustrating the extent to which publishers have ventured to take advantage of the privileges of abridgers and abridgments. In that case the defendant published in a number of "Parley's Illuminated Library" (a weekly publication) a portion of a story entitled "A Christmas Ghost Story, re-originated from the original by Charles Dickens, Esq., and analytically condensed expressly for this work," which, with the exception of a few colorable alterations, was in all respects similar to the "Christmas Carol" of Charles Dickens, this was held to be a clear invasion of Mr. Dickens's copyright in that work.

It was contended that the work was neither a colorable imitation nor a piracy of the other, but a fair abridgment, the result of the defendant's mental labor, and falling within the principle of Dodsley v. Kinnersley;[2] and it was urged that—so far from any attempt being made to induce the public to believe they were buying, for one penny, what the eminent author of the

[1] 8 Jur. 183, *ante*, p. 339.
[2] 4 Esp. 169.

"Christmas Carol" had written and published for five shillings—the defendant, in his work, had a dedication of his labors to Mr. Dickens himself. "The plaintiff," said the court, "appears to be the author, and to own the copyright of a work of fiction—a novel—the copyright of which has not been contended to be not entitled to protection. The defendant has printed and published a novel, of which, fable, persons, names and characters of persons, the age, time, country, and scene, are exactly the same; the style of language in which the story is told is in many instances identical, in all similar, except when certain alterations, by way of extension or substitution have been made; as to which, whether they improve or do not improve upon the original composition, it is not necessary for me to express my opinion. Now this has been said to be an abridgment, and as an abridgment to be protected. I am not aware that one man has the right to abridge the works of another. On the other hand, I do not mean to say that there may not be an abridgment which may be lawful, which may be protected; but to say that one man has the right to abridge and so publish in an abridged form the work of another, without more, is going much beyond my notion of what the law of this country is. The expressions of Lord Eldon, applied to a subject of copyright very different from the present, but still applied to the subject of copyright, are these: 'The question upon the whole is, whether this is a legitimate use of the plaintiff's publication in the fair exercise of a mental operation deserving the character of an original work.'[1] And I agree that there may be such an use of another man's publication as, involving the exercise of a new mental operation, may fairly and legitimately involve it. It does not appear

[1] 17 Ves. 426.

to me that there is anything in the present case which brings that which the defendant had done within a legitimate use of the plaintiff's publication, within the terms 'fair exercise of a mental operation,' or within the expression of 'deserving the character of an original work.' I think it, therefore, entirely excluded from Lord Eldon's definition, if as a definition Lord Eldon meant it. It appears to me to be a mere borrowing, with alterations and departures merely colorable; and when it is said that the difference of price and other circumstances of difference belonging to it, are such as to render the invasion of no practicable mischief to the plaintiff, the person whose property has been taken, is entitled to judge for himself how far he will consider that abstraction of his property to be prejudicial or not prejudicial. It is a valuable property, and he is entitled to be protected from the unauthorized use of it by another. I do not, however, as at present advised, at all accede to the argument that, whatever may be the relative merit of the two publications, whatever their relative prices, the publication and circulation of the cheaper may not in a pecuniary point of view, at least, if not otherwise, materially prejudice the plaintiff. There are various points of view into which it is unnecessary for me to enter, in which such a case may be put, in which material damage may arise from the subject, considered merely and solely as a question of property, which is the only point of view in which it is my duty or business to consider it."

171. The case of Bradbury v. Hotten[1] applies the principle of unlawful abridgment to pictures and engravings. Between the years 1849 and 1867, there appeared, in the London "Punch," nine cartoons, with

[1] 8 L. R. Exch. 1; 42 L. J. Exch. 28.

descriptive writing underneath, referring to the emperor Napoleon III. In 1871, the defendant published a work called "The Man of his Time," consisting, first, of the "Story of the Life of Napoleon III., by James M. Haswell," and, secondly, of "The Same Story as Told by Popular Caricaturists of the Last Thirty Years." Among the caricatures in Part II. were copies in a reduced form, sometimes with, and sometimes without, the descriptive writings of the nine cartoons above mentioned. No consent from the proprietors of "Punch" to this reproduction had been obtained. In an action by them for infringement of their copyright in the several books or sheets of letter-press containing the cartoons, they were held entitled to recover therefor.

A collection of indices of abstracts of titles to the real estate in certain precincts, is an original work, and entitled to protection as such.[1]

172. An important aspect of this question presents itself in regard to school and college text-books,[2] which in the United States are multiplied almost by hundreds yearly, and form, perhaps, the most profitable of publishers' ventures.

The originality of these productions consists entirely and exclusively in the method of treatment or arrangement of primary, cardinal, and fundamental rules and principles, and they therefore present this branch of our inquiry in its purest phases. As was well said by Mr. Justice Story, in a leading case,[3]

[1] Banker v. Caldwell, 3 Minn. 94. See further discussion of this case in the chapter on Piracy.

[2] As to school books, see also Lennie v. Pillans, 5 Sess. Cas. 2 Ser. 416. Constable v. Brewster, B. S. 215 (N. E. 152). Greene v. Bishop, 1 Cliff R. 186.

[3] Emerson v. Davies, 3 Story, 786. *Vid.* also Gray v. Russel 1 Story, 17. As to how far a re-arrangement of scientific-

"The preparing and adjusting of such writings require much care and exertion of mind. . . . . It does not require the exercise of original or creative genius, but it requires industry and knowledge."

The case of Emerson v. Davies[1] is a leading one in the United States. In the year 1829, Frederic Emerson published a text-book entitled "The North American Arithmetic, containing Elementary Lessons, by Frederic Emerson." This book was extensively adopted; continued to be popularly used in schools; and was several times revised, re-copyrighted and re-published in various editions previous to the year 1843. In that year Professor Charles Davies published a work entitled "First Lessons in Arithmetic, Designed for Beginners, by Charles Davies."

Mr. Emerson thereupon brought his bill against Professor Davies for alleged piracy of his first-mentioned work, claiming that its distinctive features had been boldly pirated by Davies, in his work, and that the "First Lessons in Arithmetic, by Charles Davies," was really and substantially "The North American Arithmetic, by Frederic Emerson."

The complainant claimed among other, that the progressive steps by which he (Emerson) had proposed to teach children the elements of arithmetic, was his own original invention. "That, in the execution of his plan he arranged a certain set of tables in the form of lessons, with a gradation of examples to precede each table, in such manner as to form, with the table, a peculiar and symmetrical appearance of each page;" and had further illustrated his lessons by

artistic matter (as, for example, the arrangement of the score of an opera for the pianoforte), is an original work. See Wood v. Boosey, 7 B. & S. 869; 9 Id. 175; L. Rep. 22 B. 340; Id. 32 B. 223; 18 L. T. N. S. 145.

[1] 3 Story, 786.

attaching to each example unit-marks, representing the numbers embraced in the example, which features were his own original contrivance and invention. He further alleged, that these peculiar features, *i. e.*, the tables, the examples, and the unit-marks, were imitated, copied, and employed in the work by Davies. The defendant denied all the allegations, and claimed that, whatever resemblance there was between the two text-books, was owing to the identity of the subjects treated.

The ability and fullness of the arguments on both sides of this case, and the exhaustive opinion therein by Mr. Justice Story, entitle it to be considered as one leading in questions of this kind.

In his opinion in that case, Judge Story said: "It is a great mistake to suppose, because all the materials of a work, or some parts of its plan and arrangements and modes of illustration may be found separately, or in a different form, or in a different arrangement in other distinct works; that therefore, if the plan, or arrangement, or combination of these materials, in another work, is new, or for the first time made, the author, or compiler, or framer of it (call him what you please), is not entitled to a copyright. The reverse is the truth in law, and, I think, in common-sense also. It is not, for example, in the present case, of any importance that the illustrating of lessons in arithmetic, by attaching unit-marks representing the numbers embraced in the example, may be formed by dots, in 'Wallis's Opera Mathematica,' or—in 'Colburn's Arithmetic,' in the form of upright linear marks, in a pamphlet detached from the main work. That is not what the plaintiff claims to found his copyright upon. He does not claim the first use or invention of unit-marks for the purpose above mentioned. The use of these is a part of, and included in, his plan; but it is not the whole of his plan. What he does claim, is—1. The plan of the lessons in his book. 2. The execution of that plan, in a certain arrangement of a set of tables, in the form of lessons to illustrate those lessons. 3. The graduation of examples to precede each table in such manner as to form with the table a peculiar and symmetrical appearance of each page. 4. The illustration of his lessons, by attaching, to each example, unit-marks representing the numbers embraced in the example. It is, therefore, this method of illustration in the aggregate, that he claims as his invention, each page constituting, of itself, a complete lesson; and he alleges that the defendants have adopted the same plan, arrangement, tables, gradation of examples, and illustrations, by unit-marks in the same page, in imitation of the plaintiff's book, and in infringement of his copyright; and, in confirmation of this statement, he refers to divers pages of the book of the defendants. Now, I say that it is wholly immaterial whether each of these particulars—the arrangement of the tables and forms of the lessons, the gradation of the examples to precede the tables, the illustration of the examples by unit-marks—had each existed in a separate form, in different and separate works, before the plaintiff's work; if they had never been before united in one combination, or in one work, or on one page, in the manner in which the plaintiff has united and connected them. No person has a right to borrow the same plan and arrangement and illustrations, and servilely to copy them into any other work. The same materials were certainly open to be used by any other author; and he would be at liberty to use unit-marks, and gradations of examples, and tables, and illustrations of the lessons, and to place them in the same page. But he could not be at liberty to transcribe the very lessons and pages, and examples and illustrations, of the plaintiff, and thus to rob him of the fruits of his industry, his skill, and his expenditures of time and money."[1]

And in the case of Gray v. Russell,[2] which was a suit brought to protect the well-known "Adam's Latin Grammar" against a so-called "improvement" thereon, the same eminent judge, with equal clearness, enunciated the principles from which our courts would very reluctantly depart. Said Story, J., in answer to the argument that there was nothing really new or novel in Mr. Gould's notes to Adam's Latin Grammar, and that all his notes were taken from works that had been subsequently printed: "That is not the true question before the court. The question is, whether these notes are to be found collected and embodied in any former single work. It is admitted, that they are not so to be found. The most that is contended for, is, that Mr. Gould has selected his notes from very various authors, who have written at different periods, and that any other person might, by a diligent examination of the same works, have made a similar selection. It is not pretended, that Mr. Cleveland undertook or accomplished such a task by such a selection from the original authors. Indeed, it is too plain for doubt, that he has borrowed the whole of his notes directly from Mr. Gould's work; and so literal has been his transcription, that he has incorporated the very errors thereof."

"Now, certainly, the preparation and collection of these notes from these various sources, must have been a work of no small labor and intellectual exertion

[1] 3 Story, R. 782.
[2] 1 Story, 11.

The plan, the arrangement, and the combination of these notes—in the form in which they are collectively exhibited in Gould's Grammar—belong exclusively to this gentleman. He is, then, justly to be deemed the author of them, in their actual form and combination, and entitled to a copyright accordingly. If no work could be considered by our law as entitled to the privilege of copyright—which is composed of materials drawn from many different sources, but for the first time brought together in the same plan and arrangement and combination—simply because those materials might be found scattered up and down in a great variety of volumes, perhaps in hundreds, or even thousands of volumes, and might, therefore, have been brought together in the same way and by the same researches of another mind, equally skillful and equally diligent, —then, indeed, it would be difficult to say, that there could be any copyright in most of the scientific and professional treatises of the present day. What would become of the elaborate commentaries of modern scholars upon the classics, which, for the most part, consist of selections from the works and criticisms of various former authors, arranged in a new form, and combined together by new illustrations, intermixed with them? What would become of the modern treatises upon astronomy, mathematics, natural philosophy, and chemistry? What would become of the treatises in our own profession, the materials of which—if the works be of any real value—must essentially depend upon faithful abstracts from the reports, and from juridical treatises, with illustrations of their bearing? Blackstone's Commentaries is but a compilation of the laws of England, drawn from authentic sources, open to the whole profession: and yet it was never dreamed that it was not a work in the highest sense original: since never before were the same materials so admirably combined and exquisitely wrought out, with a judgment, skill, and taste absolutely unrivalled."

173. The principle already examined, which obtains in questions of this kind is, that the fact of the imitation or infringement may depend upon the value rather than the quantity of the selected and conveyed materials, as where, for example, in a review or an abridgment only the unimportant parts are omitted, and the substance of the original work retained.

It is upon this principle that the decision in Low v. Ward,[1] assigning copyright in part only, of a work which was only valuable as a whole, would seem to depend. And so the addition of words, prelude, and accompaniment to an old musical air, would give the adapter a copyright in the whole composition;[2] and the rule will be the same if the adapter procured another to compose the accompaniment instead of doing it himself.[3]

In the case of Boucicault v. Wood,[4] it was held that a person who writes a play, and borrows certain incidents from a published novel, will still be held to be its author. "The mere copyist," said the judge in that case (Shipman), "or the slavish imitator, who produces old materials substantially in their old form, without new combination, is entitled to no protection under the statute. But the law rests upon no code of comparative criticism. It protects alike the humblest efforts at instruction or amusement; the dull productions of plodding mediocrity and the most original and imposing displays of intellectual power. The

[1] L. R. 6 Eq. 418, *post*, chapter on Copyright.

[2] Lover v. Davidson, 1 C. B. N. S. 182.

[3] Leader v. Purday, 7 C. B. 4.

[4] 5 Blatchf. 87.

law should be liberally construed in favor of authors, and, leaving their comparative merits to be settled by critics, at the tribunal of public opinion, it should protect and encourage their labors. The fruits of their literary toils should be secured to them by the highest title, for they keep open the springs of thought which feed the intellectual life of the nation."

174. A question of some nicety, however, arises as to translations. While a translation of a foreign work, not under the protection of copyright in the country where the translation is made, is, of course, an infringement of no one's rights, it is a matter of some legitimate doubt whether or not, if the untranslated version is protected by copyright, the translation would violate it. Translations are, it would seem, from the considerations already submitted, original works, although not productions de génie, but rather productions de l'esprit (to use the French distinction of M. Merlin). They are laborious and diligent works, involving the individual mental labor of the translator; and as a no unimportant means of spreading and diffusing knowledge, they are regarded with favor by the law, and will be encouraged by the law as far as possible, consistently with vested rights.[1]

The law of England unquestionably treats translations as original works, and this is probably the rule in the United States. The particular question as to where a work in a language classical, or "caviar to the general," seems not to have met with any authoritative decision in either country. A case exactly in point, however, was that of Burnett v. Chetwood,[2] where a bill was brought to restrain the publication of a trans-

[1] Curtis on Copyright, p. 187.

[2] 2 Meriv. 441 (note).

lation of "Burnett's Archæologica Sacra,"—a book in which the complainant had a vested right under the statute 8 Anne, c. 19. The opportunity for an enunciation upon this mooted point was all that could be desired; but the lord chancellor (Parker) ignored the question altogether, and granted an injunction to restrain its publication, upon entirely different grounds, namely, that the work was one not innocent in its character as tending to disturb religious beliefs; grounds which, to say the least, were gratuitously suggested by his lordship, which, at the present day, appear to be sufficiently absurd.[1]

The opinion seems to be, that in cases where a copyright of the original exists within the jurisdiction when the translation is made, that the unauthorized translation would be considered as an interference with the rights of the proprietor.

Still, much is to be said in favor of an opposite view. The translation would not only have given the work a new dress, have increased its circulation and influence, but it would be a new labor expended upon old materials, which, as we have seen, cannot be forbidden. If the work was scientific in its character, however, the original writer in the foreign tongue might

[1] The lord chancellor said that, though a translation might not be the same with the reprinting of the original on account that the translator had bestowed his care and pains upon it, and so not within the prohibition of the act, yet—this being a book which, to his knowledge (having read it in his study) contained strange notions intended by the author to be concealed from the vulgar in the Latin language, in which language it could not do much hurt, the learned being better able to judge of it—he thought proper to grant an injunction to the printing and publishing it in English; that he looked upon it that this court had a superintendence over all books, and might, in a summary way, restrain the printing or publishing any that contained reflections on religion or morality.

claim protection in the peculiar system, arrangement, and design of his treatise, under the well-known rule of Judge Story,[1] who draws an analogy from the law of patents. Said he, "A man who constructs a new machine, is entitled to a patent therefor, if the combination and arrangements thereof are new and his own invention, although he uses old materials and old mechanical apparatus and powers, in constructing such machine. He may use wheels, or levers, or screws, or toggle-joints, or cranks, or any other known modes of accomplishing given mechanical ends, if he combines them in a new manner, and thus produces a beneficial result. The steam-engine, the steamboat, the cut-nail machine, the card machine, are all but new combinations of old materials, old processes, and old mechanical powers and apparatus. And so," he argues, "although the last compiler or arranger, does not, by his new arrangement, acquire the right to appropriate to himself the materials which were common to all persons before, so as to exclude those persons from a future use of such materials, still he is entitled to use such materials, with his improvements superadded, whether they consist in plan, arrangement, or illustration, or combinations; for these are strictly his own." And so, also, a patent will be granted for an improvement, just as no inconsiderable number of the more useful and laborious works in all the range of literature, are annotations of preceding texts, and, of course, copyrightable.

175. There may be cases, however, in which the ownership of literary property centers in one, not its actual author, and not its proprietor by contract of assignment or purchase, though, undoubtedly, the

[1] In Emerson v. Davies, 3 Story, R. 968; and see Gray v. Russell, 1 Id. 11.

principle upon which they depend, is one of implied contract.

Such cases are those in which the real author, at the time he produced the composition, was in the employment of another. This principle is sometimes called the law of literary accession, and is as follows: where, in the course of the production or composition of a literary scientific production, an author employs another or others to assist him, the product of their individual labor will belong to him who is the author or proprietor of the whole.[1]

The difference between the doctrine of literary accession and the preceding cases, where the labor of others was merged, consists in the fact of the employment. In the cases of the musical adaptation of an old air, and of the plot of a novel in a play, the point hinged upon, was, that ownership of the particular features of these compositions became merged in the ownership of the composition as a whole (and which was only valuable as a whole), and it made no difference that the feature happened to be the theme of the whole production, if, separated and isolated from the production, that theme was of no market value.

Still another variety of this general principle is to be found in what we have treated, further on in this chapter, under the head of proprietary copyright.

176. The doctrine of literary accession, however, will only be applied in favor of innocent parties, and those who have not willfully used or appropriated the property of others.

A wrong doer will not be permitted to derive benefit from the otherwise accessorial character of that

[1] Pothier, proprieté, 170, 175. Hatton v. Keene, 7 Com. B. N. S. 268, 29 L. J. 20 C. P.; 1 L. T. N. S. 10. 9 Am. Law Reg. 33. *Vid.* Code Nap. 566, 567.

which he converts to his own use.[1] And, as against such, the accessorial part will be held to be the principal and vital part. Accordingly, the publication of a book will be restrained or suppressed for piracy, where the matter pirated is accessorial only to former compositions in which there could be no copyright, and forms only a small portion of the whole contents.[2]

The law of literary accessions is well illustrated in the case of a calico printer,[3] who had discharged his head color-man. The color-man brought suit against him in trover for a book of entries of processes of mixing the colors used in his employ, which he had kept while in the defendant's employ. It was held that, even though many of the processes therein set forth were of the plaintiff's own invention, he could not recover, because they were the result of his employment; and that the master had a right to something beside the mere manual labor of the servant in the mixing of the colors; and though the plaintiff invented them, yet they were to be used for his master's benefit.

So where the plaintiff, an artist, accompanied an expedition to Japan, fitted out by the United States government, as a master's mate, and signed the shipping articles, and drew and received his pay as such, with the understanding that all sketches and drawings that he might make were to belong to, and become

[1] Sweet v. Bunning, 2 T. J. ch. 90; 2 S. & S. 1; 16 Com. B. 459; 3 Jur. 217; 5 Carr. & P. 58. Merlin: Questions de Droit, "Contrefacon," § II. vol. 2, p. 659; "Proprietée Litterraire," § II. vol. 6, p. 498, 4th ed.; Keene v. Wheatley, 9 Am. Law. Reg. 33; Keene v. Clarke, 5 Rob. 38.

[2] 3 Swanst, 680, 681; 5 Ves., 709; 3 Mylone & Co., 736, 737, 738; Sweet v. Benning, 16 Com. B. 459; Hatton v. Keene, 29 L. J. N. S. C. P. 20; 7 Com. B. N. S. 268; Keene v. Wheatley, 9 Am. Law. Reg. 33.

[3] Makepeace v. Jackson, 4 Taunt. 770.

the property of, the government,—and he did make certain sketches and drawings, which were afterwards incorporated in a report of the expedition to the navy department, and ordered printed by congress,—it was held, that he was not the "author or proprietor" of the prints and engravings, in such a sense as to be capable of taking out a copyright, after the publication by government.[1]

In another case, where an inventor, in the course of his experimental essays, had employed an assistant, who suggested and adapted a subordinate improvement, it was held an incident or part of the employer's main invention.[2] Where an actor in the employ of a manager of a theater, who was also the proprietor of a manuscript play, took the leading part in the representation of the play on the stage, and in so doing introduced many new and original "gags" and interpolations, consisting of words, phrases, and sentences, some of which were written in pencil on the margin of the manuscript copy of the play, and some of which were retained only in the memory of the actor,—it was held that these "gags" and interpolations were the property of the proprietor of the play, and not of the actor in her employ.[3] And, upon a like principle, in the case of a musical composition, it was held that a person who adapted words to an old air, and procured a friend to arrange an accompaniment, would acquire a copyright in the whole.[4]

This principle, however, will be exercised with great care, and should be considered in connection with

[1] Heine v. Appleton, 4 Blatchf. 125.

[2] And see Lover v. Davidson, 1 Com. B. (N. S.) 82; Maclean v. Moody, 20 Scotch Sess. Cas. 2d series, 1164.

[3] Keene v. Wheatley, 9 Am. Law. Reg. 33.

[4] Cocks v. Purday, 2 Car. & Kirw. 269.

the rules before noticed, namely, that to constitute one an author he must, by his own intellectual labor, applied to the materials of his composition, produce an arrangement, combination, or performance new in himself.[1] He cannot become entitled to its proprietorship by merely procuring another to do the work.[2]

177. A question has arisen whether a greater degree of originality is necessary to sustain a claim to a copyright than would be sufficient to support a title to a patent. In the case of patent inventions, suggestions of servants employed in perfecting a discovery, tending to facilitate its practical application, may be adopted by the employer and incorporated into his design without detracting from his claim to originality. In Barfield v. Nicholson,[3] Sir John Leach suggested the application of a similar principle to copyright. Chief Justice Jervis, however, leaned to a different opinion in the case of Shepherd v. Conquest,[4] remarking that the enactments upon which literary property and patents for inventions are respectively founded, differ widely in their origin and details; and that in order to show that the position and rights of an author within the copyright acts are not to be measured by those of an inventor within the patent laws, it is only necessary to bear in mind that, whilst on the one hand a person who imports from abroad the invention of another previously unknown here, without any further originality or merit in himself, is an inventor entitled to a patent; on the other hand, a person who merely reprints for the first time in this country a valuable foreign work, without bestowing

[1] Atwill v. Ferrett, 2 Blatchford, 46. *Ante pp.* 360, 362. Per Story, J.

[2] Id. Pierpoint v. Fowle, 2 Wood & Minn. 46.

[3] 2 Sim. & St. 1; 2 L. J. 90, 102 ch.

[4] 17 C. B. 444.

upon it any intellectual labor of his own, as by translation, which to some extent must impress a new character, cannot thereby acquire the title of an author within the statutes relating to copyright. The chief justice proceeded: "We do not think it necessary, in the present case to express any opinion whether, under any circumstances, the copyright in a literary work, or the right of representation can become vested *ab initio* in an employer, other than the person who has actually composed or adapted a literary work. It is enough to say in the present case, that no such effect can be produced where the employer merely suggests the subject, and has no share in the design or execution of the work, the whole of which, so far as any character of originality belongs to it, flowed from the mind of the person employed. It appears to us an abuse of terms, to say that in such a case the employer is the author of a work to which his mind has not contributed an idea; and it is upon the author in the first instance that the right is conferred by the statute which creates it."[1]

Or again: as in the case of succeeding essays or treatises upon identical subjects, or of new and improved editions of standard works, the same question, founded on a supposed analogy between patents and copyright, occurs.

It has seemed to us, however, that such an analogy, from the very nature of the things treated, cannot and does not exist.

The thing patented is actual, palpable, and material. The thing copyrighted is an invisible, impalpable idea—a thought clothed in words. The idea is the common property of him to whom it shall occur; the language is the common heritage of the race. Does

[1] Shortt, L. L. p. 85.

it not follow, therefore, that there must be a difference in their treatment, and that, because the subjects of patent and copyright will generally be found treated of together—bound together in the same treatise; or because both are alike a property created by the state; or even because authors and inventors have common and analogous rights, and seek the identical remedies or protection—there is any analogy (except, possibly, an analogy of treatment) between them?

The theory of copyright recognizes the possibility of a new work, arising from a re-arrangement or republication of old matter, without an interference with, or infringement upon, the former, which is a case unknown to the theory of patents.

For instance: the patentee of a sewing-machine, in 1874, which employs the needle of a sewing-machine patented in 1862, must pay to the owner of the patent on the needle a royalty for every one of his needles used. But the writer of a legal work in 1874, who treats a branch of the subject-matter in identically the same method; making, perhaps, identically the same remarks, in the same order and even in almost the precise words as a treatise-writer on that same subject, who published ten years before him—since, as we have seen, he could not copyright the subject-matter—so long as his work is not a mere conveyance of the preceding one, is not bound to pay a royalty for the method.

The explanation is, that a work is copyrighted simply because it cannot be patented. If the law of patents was capable of protecting every possible product of intellectual labor, there would be no necessity for a law of copyrights; and, so far from their being similar, it is only because they are dissimilar that they exist separately, or that copyright exists at all.

178. The question of proprietory copyright (which, perhaps, is only a variation of the doctrine of literary accession, and reduceable to that head), arises principally in considering as to how far the proprietor of a periodical containing translations made from foreign works, by persons employed and paid by him, or from works imported by him at considerable expense, seems to be settled in favor of the proprietor.[1] So, any assistant, employed to compile matter for catalogues or other works of reference, will be held to have no claim to authorship in the labor thus performed at their principal's instance. As, for example, persons employed by publishers of a shipping list to compile from books of a custom-house, to which the publishers had the sole right of access, for purposes of publication, will not be held to be authors.[2]

But, on the other hand, a person employed as a performer and stage manager of a theatre, who agrees to write a play to be performed in the employer's theatre, so long as it continues to draw good audiences, and who thereupon does write such play, will not be held by the agreement as to its performance to have parted with his ownership therein.[3]

One who merely procures a drawing or design to be made,[4] or who procures alterations to be made in

[1] Wyatt v. Barnard, 3 Ves. & B. 77.

[2] McLean v. Moody, 20 Scotch Sess. Cas. 2nd ser. 1164.

[3] Roberts v. Myers, 13 Month. L. Rep. 400; *post*, chapter on Dramatic Copyright.

[4] The plaintiff has not made a case for relief within the statute (8 Geo. 2 C. 13) which was made for the encouragement of genius. . . . . If he is any author, then any person who employs an engraver or printer, is an author. Lord Hardwicke in Jeffreys v. Baldwin, Amb. 164; *vid.* also Pierpont v. Fowle, 2 Wood & Min. 46, and Binns v. Woodruff, 4 Wash. 53.

a musical composition not original with himself,[1] will not be, in either case, an author. And the employment of an author to write a play, even where the employer suggests the subject, does not constitute the employer the author of the play.[2]

To constitute a joint authorship the work must have been the result of a preconcerted joint design between two co-workers, and the mere introduction of alterations, additions, or improvements by another person, whether with or without the real author's sanction, will not entitle the other person to be considered a "joint anthor" of the work in question.[3]

179. The important inquiry as to what will constitute a new edition of a work, is one of constant importance. This question was ably discussed in the late Scotch case of Black v. Murray,[4] which held that a person may, by publishing a reprint of a work of which the copyright has expired, with notes and illustrations from other works, create a new copyright, which will be protected from piracy; and that it is a piratical use of such copyright work to borrow from it any considerable number of those illustrations.

It was contended on behalf of the defenders in this case (which was an action for infringing the pursuers' copyright in the works of Sir Walter Scott, by publishing what purported to be a reprint of the original edition of the "Minstrelsy of the Scottish Border"), that the copyright claimed by the pursuers was a copyright of an edition of a work, not of the original text, the copyright in which had admittedly

[1] Lover v. Davidson, 1 C. B. N. S. 182; Leader v. Purday, 7 C. B. 4.

[2] Levi v. Rutley, L. R. 6 C. P. 523.

[3] Id.

[4] 9 Scotch Sess. Cas. 341, 3d series.

long since expired; that the pursuers' claim to copyright was chiefly based on notes contributed to their alleged copyright edition; that to make notes the subject of copyright, they must, in a reasonable sense, form a "book," and must constitute the value of the new edition; that that was not the case with the pursuers' edition, the notes added by their edition being 200 in all, many of them unimportant, and not extending to 25 small pages; that only 40 were taken by the defenders, 10 of them being found in editions not copyright; and, finally, that it was open to the defenders to quote, even from copyright books, for the purpose of illustration; but the court of session affirming the interlocutor of the lord ordinary, held the defenders liable for piracy.

"Questions of great nicety and difficulty," said the Lord President, "may arise as to how far a new edition of a work is a proper subject of copyright at all; but that must always depend upon circumstances. A new edition of a book may be a mere reprint of an old edition, and, plainly, that would not entitle the author to a new term of copyright running from the date of the new edition. On the other hand, a new edition of a book may be so enlarged and improved as to constitute in reality a new work, and that, just as clearly, will entitle the author to a copyright running from the date of the new edition. Take for example, in illustration of this, a new edition of a scientific work which is published twenty or thirty years after the date of the first edition. The progress of science in the interval necessarily leads to the new edition being a very different book from the old. That old edition will, probably, in the course of these twenty or thirty years, have become comparatively worthless, while the new edition, particularly if it is the production of the original author himself, will be as valuable, at the later period, as the original edition of the book was at the time when it was published. But there are many cases between these two extremes; and the difficulty will be to lay down any general rule as to what amount of addition, or alteration, or new matter will entitle a second or a new edition of a book to the privilege of copyright, or whether the copyright extends to the book as amended or improved, or is confined only to the additions or improvements themselves, as distinguished from the rest of the book. I think, in the present case, that we shall not find that we are in reality much troubled with such difficulties."

"It is not necessary," observed Lord Ardmillan, "that a work shall be entirely a new work in order to be the subject of copyright. A new edition is not necessarily a subject of copyright, but it may be so. There must be some originality in it; it may be in new thought, or in new illustration, or in new explanatory and illustrative annotation, or even, in some peculiar instances, in simply new arrangement. If, in any of these respects, there is independent mental effort, then in the result of that mental effort, there may be copyright."

Lord Kinloch said: "I think it clear that it will not create copyright in a new edition of a work, of which the copyright has expired, merely to make a few emendations of the text, or to add a few unimportant notes. To create a copyright, by alterations of the text, these must be extensive and substantial, practically making a new book. With regard to notes, in like manner, they must exhibit an addition to the work which is not superficial or colorable, but imparts to the book a true and real value, over and above that belonging to the text. This value may, perhaps, be rightly expressed by saying that the book will procure purchasers in the market on special account of these notes. When notes to this extent and of this value are added, I can not doubt that they attach to the edition the privilege of copyright. The principle of the law of copyright directly applies. There is involved in such annotation, and often in a very eminent degree, an exercise of intellect and an application of learning, which place the annotator in the position and character of author, in the most proper sense of the word. The skill and labor of such an annotator have often been procured at a price which cries shame on the miserable dole which formed to the author of the text his only remuneration. In every view, the addition of such notes as I have figured, puts the stamp of copyright on the edition to which they are attached. It will still, of course, remain open to publish the text, which, *ex hypothesi*, is the same as in the original edition; but to take and publish the notes will be a clear infringement of copyright."

It is not necessary that the notes should be original. If skill and labor are bestowed in their selection and application, the annotator is entitled to copyright in them.

"Of the 200 notes," said the lord president, in the case just referred to, "the defendants' counsel tells us further that fifteen only consist of original matter, and are the composition of Mr. Lockhart himself, while the remaining 185 are quotations from other books and authors. Now this seems to be considered, also, to be a sort of disparagement of the value of the notes, in which I cannot at all agree. It seems to me that notes of this kind are almost chiefly valuable in bringing together, and in combination, the thoughts of the same author in different places, or the thoughts of other authors, or of critics, bearing upon the point that is under consideration; and nothing could better illustrate it than a number of the notes which we see in these very volumes, and which are exceedingly interesting and valuable as matter of literary and critical taste and judgment. The quotations are, in many places, most apposite, and highly illustrative of the text, and exceedingly interesting to the reader; and, certainly, the selection and application of such quotations from other books may exercise as high literary faculties as the composition of original matter. They may be the result both of skill and of labor and of great literary taste; and, therefore, I think the circumstance that the notes consist, to a great extent, of quotations, is anything but a disparagement of their value." So Lord Kinloch: "It was, perhaps, thought that to repeat quotations from well-known authors was not piracy. If so, I think a great mistake was committed. In the adaptation of the quotation to the ballad which it illustrates—the literary research which discovered it—the critical skill which applied it—there was, I think, an act of authorship performed, of which no one else was entitled to take the benefit for his own publication, and thereby to save the labor, the learning, and the expenditure, necessary even for this part of the annotation."

This question would arise more properly under the consideration of the subject of piracy, to which chapter we refer the reader for a further discussion of the question of originality.

180. An examination of the subject of originality in literary matter, drawn from the decided cases on the subject, is more or less an examination of the subject of piracy; for piracy is the name which the law gives to the wrongful appropriation of intellectual property, in which the ownership has been asserted in accordance with its own rules, just as larceny is the wrongful appropriation of personal and tangible property: the solitary difference being that, while the latter is a criminal, the former is only a civil offense.[1]

Though, indeed, why this should be, there is no logical reason. And, as the recognition by the law in any form, of this species of property is still comparatively new and recent, the day may not be far distant when even this last distinction will be rejected.

Resulting from the fact that literary and intellectual matter is property in the eyes of the law, and can, therefore, be transferred from man to man, it follows that the ownership may exist in others than its author; were it not for this, the subject of originality and of piracy might well be treated concurrently. The cases not examined, therefore, in this chapter will be found treated of further on, in the chapter on Piracy.

[1] This is, however, not the case in all countries. In France, Holland, and other kingdoms, piracy is a misdemeanor. See synopsis of copyright in different nations in chapter on Copyright, *post*.

BOOK II.

OF PROPERTY IN LITERARY COMPOSITION BEFORE PUBLICATION.

CHAPTER I.

OF MANUSCRIPTS.

181. We have stated that, as soon as the author's property in ideas is put into any tangible, visible form, and the "airy nothings" have taken to themselves a "local habitation:" the law, from that instant, asserts its recognition and protection, and will, if appealed to, take measures to enforce it.

The first form which literary composition must take outside the composer's brain, is evidently the form assumed upon its being written upon a surface, and this occupied surface is called a manuscript, which, as the name implies, means something written with the hand,[1] as contradistinguished from a printed or published "book."

Lord Ellenborough seemed to think[2] that the word "book," as used in the statute of Anne, implied a plurality of sheets, and would not cover words printed upon a single sheet. But in Beck v. Long-

[1] Latin:—*Manuscriptum* from *manus*, the hand, and *scribere*, to write.

[2] Hime v. Dale, 2 Camp. 27 (note); Clementi v. Golding, Id. 25.

man,[1] it was decided that musical compositions, printed upon a single sheet, might come under the definition of that word. If a different construction were put upon the act, many productions of the greatest genius, both in prose and verse, would be excluded from its benefits. The papers of the "Spectator," or "Gray's Elegy," might have been pirated as soon as published, because they were first given to the world on single sheets. The voluminous extent of a production cannot, in an enlightened country, be the sole title to the guardianship the author receives from the law. Everybody knows that mathematical and astronomical calculations, which will confine the student during a long life, in his cabinet, are frequently reduced to the compass of a few lines. And is all profundity of mental abstraction—on which the security and happiness of the species in every part of the globe depend—to be excluded from the protection of jurisprudence? There is nothing in the word "book" to require that it shall consist of several sheets, bound in leather or stitched in a marble cover. "Book" is evidently from the Saxon "bot;" and the latter term is from the beach-tree, the rind of which supplied the place of paper to our German ancestors. The Latin word "*liber*" is of a similar etymology, meaning originally only the bark of a tree. "Book" may, therefore, be applied to any writing, and it has often been so used in the English language. Sometimes the most humble and familiar illustration is the most fortunate. The horn-book, so formidable to infant years, consisted of one small page protected by an animal preparation; and in this state it has universally received the appellation of a "book." So in legal proceedings, the copy of the pleadings, after issue

[1] Cowp. 623.

joined, whether it be long or short, is called the paper "book," or the demurrer "book." In the court of exchequer, a roll was anciently denominated a "book," and so continues, in some instances, to this day. An oath as old as the time of Edward I. runs in this form: "And you shall deliver into the court of exchequer a book fairly written," &c. But the book delivered into court, in fullfillment of this oath, has always been a roll of manuscript.[1] The present familiar form of a book, or folio of two pages, was invented by Julius Cæsar, who adopted that form for his letters to the senate, instead of the ordinary roll in use among the Romans. But before the law the import of the term "manuscript" will doubtless be less derivatively exact, and the distinction disregarded, and by "manuscripts" the law will imply any unpublished work.

182. A literary composition may be a book entitled to copyright without being printed. Mr. Justice Yates, one of the jurists who rendered an opinion in the greatest case of literary property that English jurisprudence has ever seen,[2] in a peculiarly felicitous illustration compared the ideas of an author to birds in a cage, "which none but he can have a right to let fly. For, till he thinks proper to emancipate them, they are under his own dominion. It is certain every man has a right to keep his own sentiments as he pleases. He has certainly a right to judge whether he will make them public, or commit them only to the sight of his friends. In that state, a manuscript is, in every sense, his own peculiar property;[3] and no man can take it from him, or make any use of it which he has not authorized, without being guilty of a violation

[1] Erskine for plaintiff in Hime v. Dale, 3 Camp. 27 (note).
[2] Millar v. Taylor, 4 Burr, 2378.
[3] Roberts v. Myers, 13 Month. Law. Rep. (N. S.) 396.

of this property."[1] The cage is the manuscript, and the slightest public use, is an invasion. Its contents are sacred from notice, in whole or in part,[2] or even from the publication of a resumé, synopsis, abridgment, description, or even a catalogue of its contents.[3] This incorporeal right to publish will be most zealously guarded, nor can it be construed as belonging even to a creditor who has seized an author's manuscripts,[4] or as passing to assignee in bankruptcy.[5] He has a right to them as chattels, but he cannot publish their contents.[6] Neither can an author be forced to publish his works for the benefit of his creditors. Even under such circumstances, the author's right of withholding the publication will continue till the very moment his book is actually given out to the public. Even the printer of the book will not be entitled to sell it for his payment, although there is not the smallest doubt that he has a complete lien over it till delivery, to prevent the author or his creditors from taking advantage of the publication till he shall be paid. When a book is published, the property of it forms a subject which creditors are entitled to attach and sell; and the price unpaid by the bookseller is as completely open to the diligence of creditors, as the price of any other commodity or piece of merchandise. And so,

[1] Per Yates, J. 4 Burr, 2378.

[2] Wheaton v. Peters, 8 Pet. 657. Hoyt v. Mackenzie, 3 Bart. ch. 323. Bartlett v. Chittenden, 4 McLean, 301. Prince Albert v. Strange, 13 Jur. 112, 1 M. & G. 42. Maughan on Literary Property, 74, 137. Webb v. Rose, 4 Burr, 2330. Pope v. Curl, 2 Atk. 342. Manly v. Owens, Burr, 2320. Southey v. Sherwood, 2 Meriv. 342. 2 Story on Eq. § 943.

[3] Prince Albert v. Strange, 13 Jur. 112, 1 Mac. & T. 42.

[4] 1 Bell's Com. 268. Curtis on Copyright, 85.

[5] 1 Bell's Com. 68. 4 Burr, 2396, 2397. Curtis on Copyright, 218. Dodson on Patents and Copyright, 2nd ed. 430.

[6] 1 Bell's Com. 68.

where one had compiled an abstract of public records of title, with great labor and care, it was held, in a very recent case, that although a sheriff might seize them upon execution, he would have no right to publish them to satisfy the judgment.[1]

And a sculptor may distribute plaster casts of his model, among his friends, without losing a right to first publish it.[2] The public exhibition of a picture, for the purpose of obtaining subscriptions to engravings of it,[3] and even the publication of a representation of a picture, accompanied by a description in a periodical, has been held to abridge no author's rights therein.[4]

The author may even limit the circulation of his manuscript to his own particular friends, guests, or pupils,[5] and such private circulation will not be construed to license the appearance of either a catalogue description or a copy of it, for the benefit of any one else.[6]

For the purposes of their regulation, the law will make no discrimination between the forms of unpublished works; so, whether in manuscript or in print (*i.e.* privately printed), both will be controlled by the law relating to manuscripts. In either case, a mere possession will not imply a right to publish.

The principles of the common law are mainly invoked in dealing with manuscripts. In this country, however, they are protected also by statute.

The act of Congress of July, 1870,[7] which was passed to revise, consolidate, and supersede all existing statutes of copyright, provides that any person who

[1] Banker v. Caldwell, 3 Min. 94. See this case discussed *post*, in chapter on Contracts, &c.

[2] Turner v. Robinson, 10 W. ch. Rep.

[3] Id.

[4] Id.

[5] Bartlett v. Chittenden, 5 McLean, 32.

[6] Prince Albest v. Strange, 13 Jur. 112; 1 Mac. & T. 42.

[7] U. S. Stat. at large.

shall print or publish any manuscrips whatever, without the consent[1] of the author or proprietor first obtained (if such author or proprietor be a citizen of the United States, or resident therein), shall be liable to said author or proprietor, for all damages occasioned by such injury, to be recovered by action in any court of competent jurisdiction.—And this protection was held (in the similar enactment in the statute of 1831, to extend to any part of, as well as to the whole of a manuscript),[2] but that it did not operate to take away the right of property which the auther possesses in his unpublished works by common law.[3] This right of an author to his manuscripts is often alluded to as "copyright before publication," and is often so spoken of by writers upon literary property. This copyright before publication is the more ancient of the two. It is the exclusive privilege of first publishing any original material product of intellectual labor. Its basis is property, and it depends entirely on the common law.[4]

The first question settled in the leading case of Donaldson v. Beckett[5] was, that the author has the prior right to the publication of the contents of his own manuscript under all circumstances. Eleven judges, including Lords Mansfield and DeGray, and Messrs. Justices Blackstone and Yates, were unequivocal as to this point.

[1] The act of 1831 (now repealed) required this consent to be in writing, signed in the presence of two or more credible witnesses; but the provision is retained in section 4964 of the revision of 1873–74.

[2] Wheaton v. Peters, 8 Pet. 657; Woolsey v. Judd, 4 Duer, 385; Bartlett v. Chittenden, 5 McLean, 301; Jones v. Thorne, 1 N. Y. Leg. Obs. 409; Hoyt v. Mackenzie, 3 Barb. ch. 320.

[3] Id.

[4] Phillips on Copyright, 2.

[5] Maughan on Literary Property, p. 37.

183. The whole gist and substance of the law of literary property, as relating to unpublished works, consists solely in the right to first publish. And in this the law has a regard to the nature of the property itself. It assumes that the only value of an unpublished work is the power to publish,—either by oral delivery, exhibition, expression by gesture, pantomime, or by the multiplication of its contents by mechanical processes, such as transcribing, printing, engraving, and the like. There are exceptional cases, indeed, where the value of the unpublished work in the author's hands, seems to be insisted on, as apart from a right to publish. As, for instance, where men of culture and wealth have accumulated collections of their own sketches or descriptions, which they exhibit only to personal friends.[1] But it is submitted that the principle is not affected by these exceptions. The right claimed here is in reality the same as in all other cases, differing in degree rather than in kind. It is still the right to a first publication; that is to say, if the matter is to be published at all, the author claims the right to publish it himself; the exhibition to personal friends being nothing more or less than a publication where the public or audience is chosen by the exhibitor. Of course, a manuscript, like any other chattel, may have a historical or sentimental value. It may be an antique or a curiosity, like a palimpsest or a parchment; it may be an heirloom, a souvenir, or an ornament. In such cases it will not be considered under the head of literary property, but rather of property personal, like any other.

184. The earliest case in which a court was called upon to adjudicate concerning the common-law rights of an author to his manuscript, was prob bly

[1] As in the case of Prince Albert v. Strange, 13 Jur. 112.

the case of the famous Dr. Priestley, already examined.[1] On the trial of an action brought by him against a hundred, to recover damages sustained by him in consequence of the riotous proceedings of a mob at Birmingham, amongst other property alleged to have been destroyed, and for the loss of which he claimed compensation, were certain unpublished manuscripts. It was alleged, by way of defense, on behalf of the hundred, that the plaintiff was in the habit of publishing works injurious to the government of the state, but no evidence was produced in support of that allegation. Lord Chief Justice Eyre is stated to have observed, however, that if such evidence had been produced, he should have held it was fit to be received as against the claim made by the plaintiff.

But we have taken the liberty [2] to question if such a rule would be followed to-day. A man's manuscript is a chattel, and we doubt if a possible and prospective damage that its publication might do, would destroy its owner's property therein. If this case decided anything, it decided that there can be property in a manuscript.

Another early enunciation upon the subject was in Webb v. Rose,[3] in 1732, where equity granted an injunction to restrain the clerk of a deceased conveyancer from printing certain conveyancing drafts, which had been used by the latter. In 1741 an injunction was granted against the printing of plaintiff's notes surreptitiously abstracted from him;[4] and in 1755, certain printers who had purchased, from the lord mayor of London, the copy of the sessions paper

[1] Cited 2 Meriv. 437. *Ante*, pp. 25, 27.

[2] *Ante*, p. 25.

[3] Cited 4 Burr, 2330.

[4] Forrester & Walter, Id.

of trials, were granted an injunction restraining other parties from printing the same.[1]

In 1820, Lord Eldon enjoined the performance of a comedy called "The Young Quaker," of the manuscript of which the plaintiffs were possessed.[2] This decision is remarkable as foreshadowing the tendency of the law which resulted in the first English dramatic copyright act,[3] coming many years later, which gave to authors of plays the sole right of representing them, and therefore could only have rested on the common-law ground of proprietorship in the manuscript, including the matter written thereupon.

The common law or statute right of an author in his manuscript being conceded, the whole question, then, in treating of this branch of the subject, will be: has the author relinquished his right to say when, how, and where his compositions shall be published; or, in legal language, has he dedicated it to the public; and what damage has he suffered by the publication against his will?

185. I. Such a dedication to the public as will overcome an author's right to first publish his own manuscript, must be positive and actual. It must be the sole and voluntary act of the author himself. An act which amounts to a publication, if it be entirely or partially the act of another than the author; or, if the author begin and the other complete the act which is construably a publication, it will not be the author's own act, nor amount to a dedication.

For instance: it will not matter how the unpub-

[1] Manley v. Owen, cited 4 Burr, 2329.

[2] Morris v. Kelly, 1 Jac. & W. 481; *vid.* also Macklin v. Richardson, Amb. 694.

[3] 3 & 4 Will. 4, C. 15

lished work of any one who does not intend to publish, may have come into the hands of another person; that other person cannot publish it without the author's consent. "If any person takes it to the press without his consent, he is certainly a trespasser, though he came by it by legal means, as by a loan or by devolution; for he transgresses the bounds of his trust, and therefore is a trespasser."[1] And the law is the same whether the case be mechanical or literary; whether it be an epic poem or an orrery. The inventor of the one as well as the author of the other has a right to determine "whether the world shall see it or not."[2]

The leading case of Southey v. Sherwood[3] might at first appear to overrule this principle. In that case a motion was made on the part of the poet Southey to restrain the defendants from printing or publishing a poem called "Wat Tyler," which had been composed by the plaintiff about twenty-three years previously; and had lain unpublished during the whole of that period in the hands of the bookseller, to whom Southey had first sent it for his perusal and consideration as to the advisability of publishing it. But the decision of Lord Eldon, in refusing the injunction, was expressly on the ground that the poem in question, from its libelous tendency, was of such a nature that there could be no copyright in it. Lord Eldon, in refusing the injunction, remarked, "that, in some cases, the refusal of the court to interfere by restraining such may operate so as to multiply copies of mischievous publications; but to this my answer is, that, sitting here as a judge, upon a mere question of property, I have nothing to do with the nature of the

[1] Millar v. Taylor, 4 Burr, 2379.
[2] Id. 2386
[3] 2 Meriv. 438.

property, nor with the conduct of the parties, except as relates to their civil interests; and if the publication be mischievous, either on the part of the author or of the bookseller, it is not my business to interfere with it."[1]

This decision of Lord Eldon's, however, has not commanded universal assent, and appears to have been somewhat hasty and ill-considered. A single glance at the case of Southey v. Sherwood, and its supposed precedent in Dr. Priestley's case, must be sufficient to disclose the difference.

In the latter case (the reports of which are principally traditionary, after all), we have said that the most that the court in that case actually ruled, was that, if Dr. Priestley's manuscripts were not innocent in their character, he could have had no property in their contents, had those contents been published, which the law would have recognized, and that it certainly could not be expected to award damages for presumptive profits, which, if they had accrued at all, would have accrued from a positive injury done to the morals of the community. Surely, this ruling does not justify the publication of the contents of a doubtful or non-innocent manuscript, against its author's and owner's will and protest. Mr. Curtis[2] criticises this decision or dictum of Lord Eldon's with much reason, saying:

"There is, or ought to be, some difference between the publication of an author's manuscript, against his will and protest, and the case of Dr. Priestley's MSS., which was destroyed by the act of a mob. There are two kinds or degrees of property in a literary work,

[1] 2 Meriv. 343. Lord Eldon expressly states that he followed the case of Dr. Priestley in this ruling. See Wolcot v. Walker, 7 Ves. 1.

[2] On Copyright, p. 157.

one consisting in the right to take the profits of a book when published, the other in the right to the exclusive possession and control of a manuscript, or the right to publish or withhold from publication altogether. In no case has it been considered that the author's right depends on his intention to publish and to make a profit; but the cases proceed upon the ground of a right of property, by which seems to be intended, a right to the possession and control of the manuscript, and to publish or to withhold it from publication; and this holds equally in the case of a non-innocent and an innocent work. When, therefore, an author has not published, or does not intend to publish, a work existing in manuscript, but, on the contrary, desires and intends to withhold it from publication, the question as to its innocence does not arise, because that question affects only so much of his right of property as consists in the right to take the profits of the publication."[1]

The mere parting with the possession of a manuscript, or intrusting its possession to another; or even a permission to another to take and hold a copy of the manuscript, will not amount to an authority to that other person to publish. All such acts will be construed strictly in favor of the author, and against the recipient, by the intention of the supposed licensor, and the circumstances of the act; and unless it is the express intention and effect of the gift, to pass—with itself—permission to use the contents of the manuscript for purposes of publication, profit, or gain, at the pleasure of the recipient, no such permission will be inferred by construction of law.

"To make a gift," said the court, in a leading case,[2]

[1] Curtis on Copyright, cited Shortt, 1 L. L. 7 (note).

[2] Bartlett v. Crittenden, 4 McLean, 5 McLean, 301.

"of a copy of the manuscript, is no more a transfer of the right, or abandonment of it, than it would be a transfer or an abandonment of an exclusive right to republish, to give the copy of a printed work."[1]

186. An author may loan, or even, perhaps, present his manuscript to another, or may print its contents for private circulation, without waiving his right therein, or dedicating it for the purpose of publication.[2]

Neither can the rights of an author be lost by the publication of anything else than the thing itself. And the author will not be deemed to lose his rights in the literary property itself, even if he publish an abridgment of it before the thing itself.[3]

The author of a manuscript may deliver the contents of his manuscript in the form of lectures, to his pupils, or others; or may loan it to them, to copy in portions or entirely, without being held to have published it.[4]

187. The question as to this right of an oral lecturer to restrain the publication for profit of lectures delivered by him,[5] first came before the courts in 1824, when Abernethy, the distinguished surgeon, delivered a series of lectures on the principles and practice of surgery to the medical students of St. Bartholomew's Hospital. "The Lancet" newspaper proceeded to publish these lectures; and, besides publishing some, it contained an announcement that the re-

[1] *Vid.* also Story Eq. Jur. 943.

[2] Jeffreys v. Boosey, per Erle, J. 4 H. S. 867. Bartlett v. Crittenden, 5 McLean, 37. But see Duke of Queensbury v. Shebbeare, 2 Eden, 329.

[3] Prince Albert v. Strange, 2 De G. & S. 652; 1 Mac. & C. 25; 13 Jur. 45, 109, 507.

[4] 5 McLean, 33.

[5] T. L., 19.

maining lectures would also be published as they were delivered. A bill was filed by Abernethy against the proprietor of "The Lancet," to restrain the publication.[1] It was contended, on behalf of the defendants, that no man could have any right of property in ideas and language not reduced into writing; and it was acknowledged by Mr. Abernethy, that although a good deal of the materials for his lectures had been reduced by him to writing, yet, at the time of delivering the lectures he did not read or refer to any writing before him, but that he delivered them orally. As the written notes were not produced, the lord chancellor,[2] when the case first came before him, treating the lecture as orally delivered, refused to grant an injunction, on the ground of a right of property in sentiments and language not deposited on paper, because no case had determined that there was such copyright in unpublished productions not reduced to writing; although the injunction was granted on another ground, namely, the existence of an implied contract, between the lecturer and his hearers, that the latter would make use of the lectures only for their own information; and not publish, for profit, that which they had not the right of selling.[3] The lord chancellor is reported to have stated his reasons to be, that, where the lecture was orally delivered, it was difficult to say that an injunction could be granted upon the same principle upon which literary composition was protected; because the court must be satisfied that the publication complained of was an invasion of the written work, and this could only be done by com-

[1] Abernethey v. Hutchinson, 1 H. & T. 39; 3 L. J. 209 ch., and see Morrison v. Moat, 9 Hare, 257.

[2] Lord Eldon.

[3] And see Webb v. Rose, cited 4 Burr, 2330; 2 Bro. P. C., 1338; where the reports "cases temp. Talbot," were pirated.

paring the composition with the piracy. But it did not follow that, because the information communicated by the lecturer was not committed to writing, but orally delivered, it was, therefore, within the power of the person who heard it to publish it. On the contrary, he was of opinion that, whatever else might be done with it, the lecture could not be published for profit. He had no doubt whatever that an action would lie against a pupil who published these lectures; and whether an action would or would not lie against a third person obtaining the lectures from a pupil, an injunction undoubtedly might be granted; because, if there had been a breach of contract on the part of the pupil who heard the lectures, and if the pupil could not publish for profit, to do so would be regarded by the court as a fraud in a third party.[1]

[1] But now a distinct property in lectures is given to the lecturer by Stat. 5 & 6, Will. 4, c. 65. After stating that printers, publishers, and other persons have frequently taken the liberty of printing and publishing lectures delivered upon divers subjects without the consent of the authors of such lectures, sect. 1 enacts, "that from and after the first day of September, one thousand eight hundred and thirty-five, the author of any lecture or lectures, or the person to whom he hath sold or otherwise conveyed the copy thereof, in order to deliver the same in any school, seminary, institution, or other place, or for any other purpose, shall have the sole right and liberty of printing and publishing such lecture or lectures, and that if any person shall, by taking down the same in shorthand or otherwise in writing, or in any other way, obtain or make a copy of such lecture or lectures, and shall print or lithograph or otherwise copy and publish the same, or cause the same to be printed, lithographed, or otherwise copied and published, without leave of the author thereof, or of the person to whom the author thereof hath sold or otherwise conveyed the same, and every person who, knowing the same to have been printed or copied and published without such consent, shall sell, publish, or expose to sale, or cause to be sold, published, or exposed to sale, any such lecture or lectures, shall forfeit such printed or otherwise copied lecture or lectures, or parts there-

Closely following this case is Bartlett v. Chittenden,[1] decided in the United States circuit court for the seventh circuit. There the complainant was a teacher of the art of book-keeping, who had reduced

of, together with one penny for every sheet thereof which shall be found in his custody, either printed, lithographed, or copied, or printing, lithographing, or copying, published or exposed to sale, contrary to the true intent and meaning of this Act, the one moiety thereof to His Majesty, his heirs or successors, and the other moiety thereof to any person who shall sue for the same, to be recovered in any of His Majesty's Courts of Record in Westminster, by action of debt."

Sect. 2 enacts, "that any printer or publisher of any newspaper who shall, without such leave as aforesaid, print and publish in such newspaper any lecture or lectures, shall be deemed and taken to be a person printing and publishing without leave within the provisions of this Act, and liable to the aforesaid forfeitures and penalties in respect of such printing and publishing."

And sect. 3 provides, "that no person allowed for certain fee and reward, or otherwise to attend and be present at any lecture delivered in any place, shall be deemed and taken to be licensed or have leave to print, copy, and publish such lectures only because of having leave to attend such lecture or lectures."

Sect. 4 makes an exception in the case of lectures published with leave of the authors or their assignees, and of which the statutory term of copyright had expired, and also in the case of lectures published before the passing of the Act (9th September, 1835).

Sect. 5 makes a further exception. It enacts "that nothing in this Act shall extend to any lecture or lectures, or the printing, copying, or publishing any lecture or lectures, or parts thereof, of the delivering of which notice in writing shall not have been given to the justices living within five miles from the place where such lecture or lectures shall be delivered two days at least before delivering the same, or to any lecture or lectures delivered in any university or public school or college, or on any public foundation, or by any individual in virtue of or according to any gift, endowment, or foundation, and that the law relating thereto shall remain the same as if this Act had not been passed."—Shortt, L. L., p. 21.

[1] 4 McLean, 300.

to writing, upon separate cards, the system of instruction he was in the habit of pursuing, for his own convenience and the convenience of his pupils. He had at various times permitted his pupils to copy these cards, with a view to their own instruction, and to enable them to instruct others. One Jones, having been qualified in the complainant's instruction, and, having copied these manuscripts or cards, engaged, in connection with him, to open a similar school in another city; and the defendant, having entered this latter school, and having been permitted to copy these manuscript cards, composed from them, with certain alterations, the first ninety-two pages of a work denominated "An Inductive and Practical System of Double Entry Book-keeping, on an Entirely new Plan," which was thereupon published. This book the complainant sought to restrain. The defendant contended that the complainant, by suffering copies of his manuscript to be taken, had abandoned them to the public. That the principle was the same in regard to copyrights as in regard to patents; and that permission or consent of the author to use the manuscript, is as fatal to his exclusive right, as the consent of an inventor to use the thing invented.[1] The court, however, said, "There was no consent of the complainant that his manuscripts should be printed. That they

[1] To sustain this view the defendants cited Rundell v. Murray, Jac. 314; Barfield v. Nicholson, 2 Sim. & S. 1; Whittmore v. Carter, 1 Gall. 478; Miller v. Sillsbee, 4 Mason, 108; Wyeth v. Stone, 1 Story R. 282; Act of March 3rd, 1839, which declares that a purchaser from the inventor of the thing invented before a patent is obtained, shall continue to enjoy the same right after the obtainment of the patent as before it; and that such sale shall not invalidate the patent, unless there has been an abandonment, or the purchase has been made more than two years before the application for the patent.

were not prepared for the press is admitted. They were without index or preface, although, as alleged, they may have contained the substantial parts of the complainant's system—which, in due time, he intended to print. Copies of the manuscripts were taken for the benefit of his pupils, and to enable them to teach others. This, from the facts and circumstances of the case, seems to have been the extent of the complainant's consent.

"It is contended that this is an abandonment to the public, and is as much a publication as printing the manuscripts; that printing is only one mode of publication, which may be done as well by multiplying manuscript copies. This is not denied; but the inquiry is: does such a publication constitute an abandonment? The complainant is, no doubt, bound by this consent; and no court can afford him any aid in modifying or withdrawing it. The students who made these copies have a right to them, and to their use as originally intended. But they have no right to a use which was not in the contemplation of the complainant and of themselves when the consent was first given. Nor can they, by suffering others to copy the manuscripts, give a greater license than was vested in themselves. Popular lectures may be taken down *verbatim*, and the person taking them down has a right to their use. He may not print them. The lecturer designed to instruct his hearers, and not the public at large. Any use, therefore, of the lectures, which should operate injuriously to the lecturer, would be a fraud upon him for which the law would give him redress. He cannot claim a vested right in the ideas he communicates, but the words and sentences, in which they are clothed, belong to him."

Analogous to this was a case where a parliamentary

agent has noted down at different times in the course of business, various observations as to the methods of passing bills through parliament, and his clerk, who had access to his papers, purloined them and published them with some trifling alterations, under the title, "Practical Instructions for Passing Private Bills Through Parliament. By a Parliamentary Agent." It was held, that, although the substance of the plaintiff's manuscripts might not have been original, he was entitled to an injunction against the publication of an edition of the above-entitled work by a third party.[1]

188. The protection afforded by the common law to unpublished compositions cannot be evaded by translation, abridgment, summary, or even review.[2]

How complete the right of the author is to prevent even the slightest infringement of the property in his unpublished production is forcibly shown by the case which may now be considered the leading one on the subject. In Prince Albert v. Strange,[3] it appeared that the queen and the prince her husband had occasionally, for their amusement, made drawings and etchings,[4] principally of subjects of private and domestic interest to themselves, and procured lithographic impressions thereof to be struck off by means of a private press kept for that purpose, for their own use,

[1] Stevens v. Sherwood, cited Maugham on Literary Property, 139.

[2] 5 & 6 Vict. c. 45, sec. 20.

[3] Per Knight Bruce, V. C., in Prince Albert v. Strange, 2 DeG. & Sm. 693.

[4] 2 DeG. & S. 652; 1 Mac. & G. 25; 13 Jur. 45, 109, 507. There was also an information filed by the Attorney-General v. Strange, for the purpose of protecting the interests of Her Majesty in those portions of the etchings which were the property of Her Majesty, and praying relief as to them similar to that prayed in the bill of Prince Albert.

and not for publication. Some few impressions had indeed been given to private friends, but no further publication was intended or desired. Some further copies being required, the plates for the purpose of printing them were sent to a printer at Windsor, and, while in his possession, one of his workmen surreptitiously took some impressions of them. These surreptitiously-procured impressions were subsequently obtained by one Judge, and from his possession they passed into that of the defendant, Strange, a London publisher. Strange printed a catalogue of the etchings, in which was expressed an intention of publicly exhibiting the impressions of them, which had come into his possession through Judge. The catalogue was entitled "A Descriptive Catalogue of the Royal Victoria and Albert Gallery of Etchings," and contained, after a long introduction stating the general nature of the subjects, a detailed list of sixty-three etchings, with observations upon them. The bill prayed that the defendant might be ordered to deliver up to the plaintiff all impressions and copies of the said several etchings made by the plaintiff; and that they, their servants, &c., might be restrained by injunction from exhibiting the said gallery or collection of etchings, and from selling or in any manner publishing, and from printing the said descriptive catalogue, or any work being or purporting to be a catalogue of the said etchings, and that all the copies of the said catalogue in the possession or power of the said defendants might be given up to be destroyed. An interim injunction having been granted, extending to Judge as well as Strange, the defendant Strange answered, stating, amongst other, his original belief that the impressions had come honestly into Judge's hands: that Judge wrote the descriptive catalogue, which he (Strange) then printed, striking off only fifty-one copies, after which the type was broken up: that the catalogue had never been published or sold, or exposed for sale, and that on receiving the first information that the contemplated exhibition was disapproved of by her majesty and the prince, he had abandoned the whole scheme; and expressly denied any intention to make such exhibition, or to make any copies or engravings of the etchings. Upon motion made to dissolve the injunction granted against Strange, so far as it sought to restrain him from selling, or in any manner publishing or printing the descriptive catalogue of the etchings—leaving unquestioned the remaining portion of the injunction against exhibiting, publishing, or parting with the etchings described in the catalogue—it was contended, that although the owner of a print might prevent another from publishing a copy of it, it was impossible to prevent the other from describing it, and printing and publishing such description; that the law of England could not prevent a party obtaining knowledge through the medium of perceiving these etchings, from using that knowledge, and from conveying that information to others; nor could a court of equity, in the absence of contract, interfere with the use of that knowledge; that no one's rights could be interfered with by the making of a catalogue describing the articles and making remarks upon them in the shape of friendly, if not flattering criticism (for such appeared to be the general character of the observations); that if a spectator had a right to contemplate any of the productions of so exalted a personage (which he might do without any invasion of domestic privacy), he had a right to communicate full information connected with those productions; and this, substantially, was all that had been done by the descriptive catalogue; that privacy was not essential to the right of property, for though the cwner of anything may use every means in his power to prevent that thing been seen by another, yet, if that other person sees it, the owner can have no right of property in the notion or idea created in the mind of the person who has seen it; that there is no property in the ideas created by seeing the etchings—the property is confined to the etchings; and no regard could be paid to a mere injury to private feelings, and that in substance the complaint is of an offense not against law but against manners.

Notwithstanding, however, the distinction between the publication of copies of the (unpublished) etchings themselves and that of a mere descriptive catalogue of them sought to be established, it was held that the plaintiff was entitled to restrain the publication of the one as well as the other. Though the fraudulent manner in which the impressions of the etchings had been originally acquired formed one of the grounds on which the decision rested, the right of the plaintiff to restrain the publication of the catalogue on the sole ground of his property in the things described, was unmistakably asserted by the judges. "Property in mechanical works or works of art," said the court, "executed by a man for his own amusement, instruction, or use, is allowed to subsist certainly, and may, before publication by him, be invaded, not merely by copying, but by description or by catalogue, as it appears to me. A catalogue of such works may in itself be valuable. It may also as effectually show the bent and turn of the mind, feelings, and taste of the artist, especially if not professional, as a list of his papers. The portfolio or the studio may declare as much as the writing-table. A man may employ himself in private, in a manner very harmless, but which, disclosed to society, may destroy the comfort of his life, or even his success in it. Every one, however, has a right, I apprehend, to say that the produce of his private hours is no more liable to publication without his consent, because the publication must be creditable or advantageous to him, than it would be in opposite circumstances. Addressing the attention specifically to the particular instance before the court, we cannot but see that the etchings executed by the plaintiff and his consort for their private use; the produce of their labor, and belonging to themselves, they were entitled to retain in a state of privacy—to withhold from publication. That right, I think it equally clear, was not lost by the limited communication which they appear to have made; nor confined to prohibiting the taking of impressions, without or beyond their consent, from the plates, their undoubted property. It extended also, I conceive, to the prevention of persons unduly obtaining a knowledge of the subjects of the plates, from publishing (at least by printing or writing, though not by copy or resemblance) a description of them, whether more or less limited or summary, whether in the form of a catalogue or otherwise." And said Lord Cottenham, upon the appeal: "It being admitted that the defendant could not publish a copy—that is, an impression—of the etchings, how in principle does a catalogue, list, or description, differ? A copy or impression of the etching would only be a means of communicating knowledge and information of the original, and does not a list and description do the same? The means are different, but the object and effect are similar; for in both, the object and effect is to make known to the public more or less of the unpublished work and composition of the author, which he is entitled to keep wholly for his private use and pleasure, and to withhold altogether, or so far as he may please, from the knowledge of others. . . . . Upon the first question, therefore—that of property—I am clearly of opinion that—the exclusive right and interest of the plaintiff in the composition or work in question being established, and there being no right or interest whatever in the defendant—the plaintiff is entitled to the injunction of this court to protect him against the invasion of such right and interest by the defendant, which the publication of any catalogue would undoubtedly be."

"The elaborate judgments in this important case," says Shortt,[1] in his valuable work, "have established the following points:—That the right of property of the author or composer of any works of literature, art, or science, in such works, so long as they remain unpublished, is so complete and absolute that no one else, without his permission, may publish even a list or descriptive catalogue of them; that the circulation amongst a few private friends of impressions of etchings not otherwise published, is not such a publication of them as disentitles the owner to the protection of the aforesaid right, and that this right is but part of the general common-law right of property."

189. A manuscript being, as we have seen, the personal property of its author, that peculiar value, differing from the value of other personal property, which is in the future, and which it is to derive from publication of some sort, is also the property of its author. He can part with it by barter or sale; in which case the right to publish most probably would

[1] L. Lit. 54.

go with the manuscript, unless reserved by contract. The question does not appear even to-day to be fully settled. As nearly, perhaps, as the rule may be stated, it will doubtless be, that the license to publish must be express and unmistakable. The present copyright law of the United States, however, has stepped in to settle the question, enacting, "That any person who shall print or publish any manuscript whatever, without the consent of the author or proprietor first obtained (if such author or proprietor be a citizen of the United States, or resident therein), shall be liable to said author or proprietor for all damages occasioned by such injury, to be recovered by action on the case in any court of competent jurisdiction."[1]

Under a like provision in the English statute, Lord Macclesfield, C., is said to have held that the author might grant the right of the copy to a subsequent publisher, after it had been once published by the person to whom he had originally delivered the manuscript, the bare delivery amounting only to a license to print the first edition.[2] In a more modern case, Lord Ellenborough said, that "the statute having required that the consent of the proprietor, in order to authorize the printing or reprinting of a book by any other person, shall be in writing, the conclusion from it seemed irresistible that the assignment must also be in writing; for if the license, which is the lesser thing, must be in writing, *à fortiori* the assignment, which is the greater thing, must also be."

[1] Rev. Stat. U. S. (Rev. 1873–74) § 4967. And this consent must be in writing, signed by two witnesses. And see the English act, 8 Anne. c. 19, § 1; 54 Geo. III. c. 156, makes the consent of the proprietor first had and obtained in writing, signed in the presence of two or more credible witnesses, a requisite of the lawful publication of a manuscript.

[2] Vin. Abr. 278.

But if he part with it by gift merely, or loan it, or allow it to be copied, without express license to publish, it will not be implied to be dedicated. Even in the case of a manuscript work that is too extensive and elaborate for mere personal perusal in that form (such as a history, for example), the gift of, or license to, copy the manuscript will not imply a right to publish.

Where the son of the Earl of Clarendon gave permission to a Mr. Gwynne to take a copy of the manuscript of his deceased father's "History of the Reign of Charles II.," and Mr. Gwynne's son and administrator sold it to a Dr. Shebbeare, the court of chancery, at the suit of the Duke of Queensberry (the personal representative of the Earl of Clarendon and his son), restrained Dr. Shebbeare from printing and publishing the copy of the manuscript. Lord Keeper Henley said, "It was not to be presumed that Lord Clarendon, the younger, when he gave a copy of his work to Mr. Gwynne, intended that he should have the profit of multiplying it in print; that Mr. Gwynne might make every use of it except that."[1]

We have seen, however, that where the author of a poem had sent it to a bookseller, and had allowed it to remain in his hands unpublished for twenty-three years, Lord Eldon was of opinion that the writer had abandoned his right, as an author, and refused to grant an injunction to prevent the publication of the poem by the bookseller.[2]

190. A prior publication by the author himself, in a foreign country, or in the country itself, if without a copyright, is a dedication of the second publication to the public in the country in which it is made.

[1] Duke of Queensberry v. Shebbeare, 2 Eden, 329.

[2] Southey v. Sherwood, 2 Meriv. 434; and see Rundell v. Murray, Jacobs, R. 311.

This question will be found to mainly arise in the case of dramatic manuscripts.

In the case of manuscripts other than dramatic, a publication of their contents by their author, or any one entitled to publish them, through the press, without a formal compliance with the statutes of copyright, would be a waiver of the author's rights therein.[1] But in the case of dramatic copyright, the question as to what amounts to a waiver is more complicated.

Publication may be either a publication to the ear or to the eye. To the latter, through the medium of printing, or of some other art; or to the former, from the rostrum, the stage, or the pulpit.

The value of a literary work, such as a novel, a history, an essay, or a poem, intended for the perusal of the public, is measured by, and depends upon, the ability of the publisher to multiply and circulate copies of it over as extensive a territory as possible. The value of a dramatic work, on the contrary, consists entirely in the ability of its author to prevent the multiplication of copies thereof; to prevent its publication, through the printing-press, absolutely; and to limit its publication, by word of mouth, to one or more particular places and occasions, and to the knowledge and audience of the comparatively few who shall have obtained, for value, the license to witness it.

Hence, to prevent any other publicity to his work, it is manifestly to the interest of the dramatic author to confine literal copies of his production to a manuscript form; or if he print it, to do so privately, and for his own use alone.[2]

[1] See *post*, chapters on Copyright and Piracy.

[2] The value of dramatic productions, in these days, has largely increased, and the dramatic author is now more or less protected by statute, as well as by common law, in the enjoy-

So, although the public exhibition of a picture at a picture-gallery is, in one sense, a publication of it, yet it is a publication which may be restricted by the rules of the place of exhibition, by which the managers may preclude any use being made of their rooms for the purpose of copying; and an exhibition, under such circumstances, would not disentitle the proprietor to an injunction to restrain the piracy of the picture;[1] and musical compositions in manuscript, engravings, etchings, maps, and charts, also, while unpublished, stand on a like footing with literary matter unpublished, and so do in England, both by common law and by express statute.

A strong ruling in their favor occurs in White v. Geroch,[2] where it was held that, even though the author of a musical composition had sold several thousand copies of it in manuscript, a year before it was printed, he had not, thereby, lost the copyright. Abbot, Ch. J., in that case, was of opinion that it was not the intention of the legislature, in conferring a copyright upon authors, to impose on them, as a condition precedent, that they should not sell their compositions in manuscript before they were printed.

191. It seems to have been settled long since that the representation upon a stage of a dramatic production, will not dedicate the contents of its manuscript to

ment of his franchises. The subject of dramatic productions, both in manuscript and copyright, has been thought of sufficient importance to merit a chapter by itself, further on in this treatise. It is necessary, however, to glance, under the general subject of manuscripts, at the treatment which they will receive by common law; referring for more extended treatment of the subject to that chapter.

[1] Turner v. Robinson, 10 Tr. Ch. Rep. 121, 516.

[2] 2 B. & Ald. 298.

the public, unless that first representation takes place abroad.[1]

In Macklin v. Richardson[2] as early as 1770, it was decided that the public performance of a play, by the author's permission, is not such a publication of it by him as disentitles him to restrain the unauthorized printing or publishing of it by any other person, and is not a dedication to the public. The plaintiff in that case was the author of the farce called "Love à la Mode," which was performed, by his special permission, at the different theatres several times in 1760, and the following years, but never printed or published by him; and it appeared that, when the play was over, the plaintiff used to take the copy away from the prompter. The defendants employed a shorthand writer to go to the playhouse and take down the words of the farce from the mouths of the actors. These notes having been corrected, by one of the defendants, from his own memory, the first act of the farce was published by them in a magazine called the "Court Miscellany," of which they were the proprietors, and notice was given that the second act would be published in the next month's "Miscellany." The plaintiff filed a bill to restrain this publication; and

[1] Boucicault v. Delafield, 1 H. & M. 597; 9 L. T. N. S. 709; 39 L. J. 38 ch. This point is further enunciated in England by statute. Sect. 19 of 7 Vict. c. 12, now enacts that "neither the author of any book, nor the author or composer of any dramatic piece or musical composition, nor the inventor, designer, or engraver of any print, nor the maker of any article of sculpture, or of such other work of art as aforesaid, which shall, after the passing of this Act, be first published out of her majesty's dominions, shall have any copyright therein respectively, or any exclusive right to the public representation or performance thereof, otherwise than such, if any, as he may become entitled to under this act."

[2] Amb. 694.

the Lord Commissioner (Smythe) granted an injunction. He said, "It has been argued to be a publication by being acted, and therefore the printing is no injury to the plaintiff; but that is a mistake, for besides the advantage from the performance, the author has another means of profit from the printing and publishing; and there is as much reason that he should be protected in that right as any other author."

And in the equally leading case of Coleman v. Wathen,[1] decided in 1793, it was ruled that the acting of a pièce is in no case a publication thereof.

In the cases of Keene v. Kimball[2] and Keene v. Wheatley,[3] it was said that "The sole proprietorship of an author's manuscript and of its incorporeal contents, wherever copies exist, is, independently of legislation, in himself and his assigns, until he publish it. Where a copyright under statute exists, the publication can not affect this right, but where a copyright does not exist, an unqualified publication and one unrestricted by any condition, such as the making or sanctioning its literary or dramatic representation, is a dedication to the public, and its proprietor can not thereafter maintain an objection to such representations or representation as others are enabled, either directly or secondarily, to make from its having been retained in the memory of any of the audience. In other words, the public acquire a right to the extent of the dedication, whether complete or partial, which the proprietor has made of it to the public."

"It is to be carefully observed, however, that the distinction between a general and a limited publication, is not affected by this ruling," said Judge Hoar.[4]

[1] 5 T. R. 245.
[2] 16 Gray (Mass.), 543.
[3] 9 Amer. Law Reg. 33; *vid.* also Keene v. Clarke, 5 Rob. 38
[4] Keene v. Kimball, *ubi supra.*

"There may be a limited publication by communication of the contents of the work, by reading, representation, or restricted private circulation, which will not abridge the rights of the author to the control of his work, any further than necessarily results from the nature and extent of this limited use which he has made or allowed to be made of it.

"These principles," continued the judge, "sustain the demurrer in the plaintiff's bill. She has publicly represented the play, 'Our American Cousin,' before audiences consisting of all persons who chose to pay the price charged for admission to her theater. She has employed actors to commit the various parts to memory, and, unless they are restrained by some contract, express or implied, we can perceive no legal reason why they might not repeat what they have learned, before different audiences and in various places. If persons, by frequent attendance at her theater, have committed to memory any part or the whole of the play, they have a right to repeat what they have heard to others. We know of no right of property in gestures, tones, or scenery, which would forbid such reproduction of them, by the spectators, as their powers of imitation might enable them to accomplish."[1]

192. The publication of a work in a foreign country disentitles the author to a copyright in it in England. This, before the legislature interfered in the matter, had been judicially determined in several cases. In Clementi v. Walker,[2] it was decided that if an author first published abroad, and then, instead of

[1] We doubt the value of this ruling, however, at least under later authorities; see a fuller examination of the three cases, Keene v. Wheatley, 9 Am. Law Reg. 33; Keene v. Clarke, 5 Rob. 38; Keene v. Kimball, 6 Gray, 545; see chapter on Dramatic Composition, *post*, vol. ii.

[2] 2 Barn. & C. 861.

using due diligence to publish here, forebore to publish until some other person had honestly published here, the author could not insist upon his privilege, and at a distance of time stop a publication which, in the interim, had taken place here, or treat the continuance of that publication as a piracy. "Whether the act of printing and publishing abroad," said the learned judge who delivered the judgment of the court in that case, "makes the work at once *publici juris*, it is not necessary now to decide; but we have no doubt that it becomes *publici juris*, if the author does not take prompt measures to publish it here."[1] And in Guichard v. Mori,[2] an injunction was refused on the ground that there had been a publication abroad before there was any publication in this country.

But where there was a contemporaneous publication abroad and in England, it was held that the copyright of the author here was not infringed by the foreign publication.[3] And Clementi v. Walker is in favor of the author's title to copyright, provided he print and publish here "promptly," and with due "diligence," after the publication abroad.[4]

In Keene v. Wheatley,[5] it was expressly held that the ninth section of the act of Congress (Act of 1831, c. 16) which gave redress for the unauthorized printing or publishing of manuscripts, operated in favor of a resident of the United States who had acquired the proprietorship of an unprinted literary composition

[1] *Vid.* also Page v. Townsend, 5 Sim. 395, as to publication abroad of prints and engravings.

[2] 9 L. J. (1831), 227 Ch. See also Hedderwick v. Griffin, 3 Sess. Cas. 2nd ser. 383.

[3] Erle, J., Cocks v. Purday, 2 Car. & K. 269, N. P.

[4] 2 Barn. & C. 870.

[5] 9 Am. Law Reg. 33. *Vid.* chapter on Dramatic Copyright

from a non-resident alien author.[1] The publication in order to be such as will amount (in the absence of the copyright) to a dedication, must be a publication of the thing itself, and not the publication of something else that resembles it; so that the author of a literary work does not lose his common-law right of property in it before its publication, by previously publishing an abridgment of it.[2]

The distribution, by a sculptor amongst his friends, of copies of a plaster cast taken from the bust of a statue is not a publication of the statue itself.[3] The exhibition of the picture itself, for the purpose of obtaining subscribers to an engraving of it, is not a publication of the picture.[4] The private circulation among friends, of lithographic impressions or drawings, is not a publication of the drawings themselves.[5] Nor is the publication of an engraving of a picture in a magazine, with an article describing the picture, a publication of the picture itself.[6]

The case of Boucicault v. Delafield,[7] where the plaintiff prayed for an injunction to restrain the defendant from producing a drama ("The Colleen Bawn") written by the plaintiff, and, as it appeared on the hearing of the case, represented by the plaintiff at

[1] The property which an author has in his unpublished ideas embodied in a tangible shape being independent of statute, it should seem that an alien friend might prevent the unauthorized publication here of any of his unpublished works (Shortt, L. L. 36).

[2] Prince Albert v. Strange, 5 De G. & S. 652; 1 Mac. & G. 25; 13 Jur. 45, 109, 507.

[3] Turner v. Robinson, 10 Jr. Ch. Rep. 134.

[4] Id.

[5] Prince Albert v. Strange, *ubi supra.*

[6] Turner v. Robinson, 10 Jr. Ch. Rep. 121, 516.

[7] 1 H. & M. 597; 9 L. T. N. S. 709; 33 L. J.; 38 Ch. This was, however, under and by virtue of the statute.

New York prior to its being represented in England, where the vice-chancellor refused to grant the injunction and dismissed the bill with costs, was decided upon statutory grounds, and will be considered hereafter.[1]

The principle of literary accessions treated in the chapter on Originality[2] is also applicable to manuscripts. So, where one contracts for hire and reward to write certain portions of a book to be published by another, equity will not aid him by injunction to prevent his portion of the work being printed and published in an altered or mutilated form.[3] Wood, V. C. intimated an opinion, though the point did not arise in the case before him, that, unless there be a special contract, either express or implied, reserving to the

[1] The vice-chancellor being of opinion that the words of the 19th section of 7 & 8 Vict. c. 12, took away whatever rights the plaintiff might otherwise have had. If he had first represented his drama here, he would have been entitled to the provisions of the dramatic copyright act. Then 7 & 8 Vict. c. 12, was passed, enabling her majesty to make arrangements conferring on other nations the privileges accorded to all people who first publish their works here. If the plaintiff had this sort of double right, it was the very thing which the 7 & 8 Vict. c. 12, was intended to extinguish. The statute says in effect (sect. 19) that "if any person, British subject or not, chooses to deprive this country of the advantage of the first representation of his work, then he may get the benefit of copyright, if he can, under the arrangement which may have been come to pursuant to 7 & 8 Vict. c. 12, between this country and the country which he so favors with his representation; but if he chooses to publish his performance in a country which has not entered into any treaty or made any such arrangement with regard to copyright, then this country has nothing more to say to him; he must be taken to have elected under which of the two statutes with respect to copyright he wishes to come, by performing his work in one country instead of the other; and he is thereby excluded from all advantage of publishing in the other" (Shortt, L. L. 35).

[2] *Ante* ——.

[3] Cox v. Cox, 11 Hare, 118.

author a qualified copyright, the purchaser of a manuscript is at liberty to alter and deal with it as he thinks proper. The court is not moved in such a case by the possible effects of the alterations as affecting the writer's reputation.[1]

But it seems that if a publisher puts forth an inaccurate edition of an author's work, purporting to be executed by him, the author may maintain an action against the publisher for injury to his reputation, even where the publisher is the owner of the copyright.[2]

193. I. As to the injury sustained by the author from the trespass upon his manuscripts or unpublished works, until the case of Prince Albert v. Strange, it seemed to be settled that such injury would consist in the loss of his right or the frustration of his intention[3] to first publish himself, and of his prospective profits thereof, to arise from such publication, and that no measure of damages could be considered looking to his own personal feelings of sensitiveness, or difference, or reputation.[4] But that case appears to hold exactly the reverse, and as going further than its predecessors, may be looked upon as leading upon the subject.

A manuscript going through the press is as we shall see[5] at the owner's risk, and unless the printers

[1] Archbold v. Sweet, 1 M. & Rob. 162; S. C. & P. 219.

[2] Id.

[3] Bartlett v. Chittenden, 4 McLean, 301.

[4] In Cox v. Cox, 2 Hare. 110. "The possible effect on reputation," said Wood, V. C., "unless connected with property, is not a ground for coming to this court, though it may be an ingredient for the court to consider, when the question of a right of property also arises." But see Archbold v. Sweet, 1 M. & Rob. 162; *post* Southey v. Sherwood, 2 Meriv. 437.

[5] Mawman v. Gillett, 2 Taunt. 325, and see *post* chapter on Contracts concerning Literary Property.

expressly insure it, they would not be liable in damages for its loss, to the author. It might be a damage to an author, also to have his art or method of trade disclosed as we have seen,[1] but the publication of his private opinions, sentiments or doings, even though by such disclosures he were rendered unpopular in certain quarters, or were defeated in an election or choice to a position of emolument or influence, would probably be no ground for an action of damages.

The question as to damage by such publication will be found to arise mainly in the case of letters of persons living, or of deceased persons, in the hands of their executors, and others.

As to the manuscripts of deceased persons in other hands than those of the executors, it has been held in England that a right on their (the executors,) part to restrain a publication of such manuscripts can only depend upon whether the estate will suffer damage by such publication.[2] The right to prevent such publication is no part of the assets in the executor's hands.[3] This question, therefore, will be treated as incidental to our examination of the general rules of law applicable to letters and correspondence.

194. The most difficult question with regard to the property and proprietorship of literary composition embodied in manuscripts, arises in the case of those manuscripts which, from their nature, pass from one ownership and possession to another, and may be said, at times, to have more than one owner: *i.e.*, letters.

[1] Bartlett v. Chittenden, 4 McLean, 300.

[2] Stevens v. Sherwood, cited Maugham L. Prop. 139.

[3] Id. 140.

Gerard Vassius,[1] remarking on the surprising discovery of the art of letter-writing,[2] a phenomenon which

[1] De Quatuor Artibus Popularibus, iii. 1.

[2] Next to the invention of printing, the invention of paper has done most toward educating and enlightening the world. The earliest races of men probably used to plant groves and set up pillars or heaps of stones, or to institute games or festivals to recall or perpetuate the memory of events. The composition and singing of historical songs was a still more popular way of accomplishing the purpose (Tac. Mor. Germ. 2). Small cords, sometimes variously colored and regularly knotted, were used by the Chinese in ancient times before the reign of Fo-hi, and by the Peruvians (Quipos) at a later period; notched or marked sticks were also employed. Probably the next step in the communication of thought, was the use of pictorial representation. When Cortez had his first interview with the Aztec chiefs he found that news of his arrival on the coast had already been conveyed to them by means of pictures of ships, strangers, horses, and artillery. Nor could they have more rapidly comprehended the power, mission, and intentions of the Spaniards, by means of language itself. The probability is that, next to pictures came hieroglyphical characters, which, without doubt, originally were abbreviations of pictures, each character meaning a word, or perhaps more than one. The Hebrew alphabet, for instance, betrays marks of this origin. The first letter, aleph, signifies an ox, and the picture of the head and horns of that animal very probably suggested its form. A zigzag line is a natural symbol for water as expressing undulation—and the Hebrew letter M, pronounced mem, is the word for water. The waving line is also the symbol of aquarius in the zodiac. So the Arabic numerals were originally the simple form of marks; a single stroke or mark meaning the digit one; two marks, forming a right angle, the digit two; a second downward stroke, attached to the right angle, the digit three, and so on And so, too, the Chinese characters disclose in their formation their natural derivation from the like simple sources. The more these symbols were employed, of course, the greater the tendency to abbreviate them; and when, from these initiative methods, the art emerged, from the historical and representative system, to the employment of mere marks and dots to express ideas or letters, a great step had been taken, and the time had come for a material to present itself. At first these materials were of so rude a description as to render the appli-

has lost its hold upon our admiration only by its frequency and familiarity, relates a pleasant story to show at what an elevation it stands above the vulgar apprehen-

cation of the character very laborious and wearisome, and while we wonder at the slow progress of improvement in an art of such urgency in the commonest affairs of life, we are forced, at the same time, to admire the refinement and perfection to which some of the languages of primitive antiquity were matured and polished in spite of all these discouragements and difficulties. The language of Homer is as graceful as it is vigorous and comprehensive, and yet, in the public and private transactions with which his poems have to do, very little occurs which indicates that the art of writing was known and practiced. The story of Prœtus, Jobates, and Bellerophontes, in the sixth book of the Iliad, is the only instance in which such allusion is made; and even there the word used to denote what was carried was *σηματα*, which may mean "signs," as well as written characters. Judicial decisions, civil compacts, stipulations, pledges, obligations of kindred, rights of inheritance, conditions of combats, suspensions of hostility, treaties of peace—all appear to have been verbal. Witnesses, symbols, sacrifices, and libations were in most cases relied upon as memorials and ratifications of the most solemn and weighty transactions. When lots were cast to see who should answer the challenge of Hector, the marks and not the names of the heroes were cast into the helmet of Agamemnon (Iliad, vii. 175). It was on hard materials that the art of inscription was first practiced. According to Pliny, the Babylonians wrote their astronomical observations on bricks. Tables of stone are among the most ancient monuments of Chinese literature, though it would seem that the Chinese in very early times manufactured a sort of silk paper. There are traces of Abyssinian writings which were inscribed on clay, this clay being afterwards baked into bricks. The Decalogue, and Joshua's copy of the Law, were on stone, and metal was often substituted. In Job allusion is made to writing on lead with a style of iron; and plates of copper were also used in early days (Plin. xxxiv. § 21; Ovid, Metam. I. v. 91, 92). Themistocles writes a letter on stone, to be conveyed to the Ionians (Herod, Uram. 22), while Xerxes wrote to the Lacedemonians by means of the tablet of wood covered with wax, such as the Roman authors used to compose upon at a much later day—only for greater secrecy Xerxes wrote upon the wood itself, and covered his writing with the wax

sion of an uncultivated mind. In the country of the Brazils, he says, a slave was sent by his master to a nobleman, his friend, with a basket of figs as a present, accom-

(Herod, Polym. 239). The skins of animals, the leaves of plants, or the bark of trees came next in order. The Cumean Sybil wrote her prophesies upon leaves. Under the words *Εκφυλλοφορησαι* and *Εκφυλλοφορειν* in Suidas, we are told by him that the votes expelling a senator from his rank and office were taken on leaves. "Senatores nomina eorum in foliis oleæ scripta in echinos demittebant, argumentis et rationibus latæ sententiæ simul adscriptis." *Αντι της ψηφου φυλλοις επισημαινε την αυτου γνωμην εκαστος, και ελεγετο τουτο εκφυλλοφορησαι.* The Hindoos also used leaves for purposes of transcribing. In the time of Cyrus the interior barks or membranes of trees, especially of the linden-tree, were used; and that monarch, to prevent ennui (*ἱνα μη αλυν*) always carried a tablet of that material with him on his journeys (Ælian, Var. Hist. xiv. 12). It would seem, from many passages in the Greek and Latin classics, that these tablets were sometimes waxed, and sometimes polished, to enable the scratching of letters readily upon its surface; and for this purpose the box-wood seems to have been employed. *Παλαι γαρ ποτε πιναξιν, ητοι σανισι, και ταυταις εκ πυξου μαλιστα, τα γραμματα ενεκολαπτον· και το γραφειν δε παλαιας ενεργειας ονομα· ξυσμοις γαρ τισιν ετυπουντο στοιχεια, το δε ξυειν γραφειν ελεγετο.* "Tabellæ autem istæ etiam scalpendo et radendo poliebantur, quod itidem voce *ξεειν* et *ξυειν* dentabatur." These writing tablets were compactly folded, whence they were called by the Romans pugillares, since they could be carried within the grasp of the fist. The manufacture of the Egyptian papyrus was a great step forward into the world of letters, and its discovery was almost immediately followed by the beginning of the great libraries of Alexandria and Pergamus. The manufacture of papyrus is said by Varro to have been begun soon after the building of the city of Alexandria by Alexander; but others say that papyrus was manufactured at Memphis three hundred years before the reign of Alexander. The reed papyrus grew plentifully on the banks of the Nile, the Tigris, and the Euphrates, but appears only to have been manufactured in Egypt. The Egyptians themselves, however, often used linen cloth for writing; much of which is found in their mummies. As the demands of literature increased, the supply became inadequate, and we are told that, in the age of Tiberius, there was such a

panied with a letter. Tempted by the excellence of the fruit, the bearer of the present devoured it. The plunder, however, was detected, of course, by means

scarcity of paper in Rome that its use, even in contracts, was dispensed with by a decree of the senate.

Pliny the elder, who says he saw in the house of Pomponius Secundus the books of the Gracchi, written with their own hands on papyrus, and that the works of Virgil and Cicero were written in the same manner, treats expressly of the Egyptian papyrus in three chapters of his thirteenth book, upon which Guilandrinus has based his copious and curious commentary; which, however, is criticised severely by Scaliger. The Roman paper was often very finely wrought and polished, the charta dentata being paper made smooth by polishing with the tooth of a boar, or other animal. There was a famous factory for dressing Egyptian paper in Rome, conducted by one Fannius (Plin. xiii.). This paper was prepared by dividing the pellicles or fillaments of the plant, laying them in sheets transversely, and pressing them together by a machine, or with blows of mallets. Nondum flumineas Memphis contexere biblos noverat (Lucan). Besides this, papyrus had other properties, and was sometimes eaten for food. The Egyptians were often called παπυροφαγοι, or papyrus-eaters. It has an insipid taste, and was eaten by the Cossacks and the inhabitants of Oxai and Tscherchaskoy, according to Dr. Clark, in modern times. Vospiscus says that Firmus, who owned vast regions of papyrus-growing country, boasted that he could support an army with its revenues; but Salmasius says the emperor meant that he could feed them on the papyrus itself. (For an elaborate account of the manufacture of papyrus into paper for writing, see Roberts, 21–22, *et seq.*).

In the rolls or volumes of papyrus, the sheets or leaves were glued to each other at the edges and carried out in successive lengths, the first sheet or scheda, on which was usually nothing but the manufacturer's mark, or the title of the book, being first fastened or glued, and called on that account the πρωτοκολλον, whence comes the word protocol, in such frequent diplomatic use. The same term also denotes the prima scheda of the books composed of membraneous leaves, whether skin or bark. The papyrus being cut at the middle, the first pellicle or strip was the finest, and was known in Rome as Augusta (from the time of Augustus to that of Claudius); the second strip, which was the next finest, was called Livia, from Augustus' wife, and so on to the out

of the letter, and the slave found it of no avail to deny the fact, against the evidence of the letter, though utterly unable to comprehend the way in which the

side of the plant, which was so coarse as only to be used for the commonest purposes. The paper called Augusta was too fine for ordinary purposes, however, often being penetrated by the reed or Roman pen (calamus) and showing the writing on the other side; and the Emperor Claudius caused a mixed paper to be made to remedy this defect. There are accounts also of a paper made in Madagascar from the papyrus growing in that country, which is manufactured by putting the leaves into a mortar, beating them to a paste, washing this paste with clear water on a frame of bamboos, expanding them into sheets, and glazing the surface with a decoction of rice water.

Large numbers of manuscripts of papyrus were found in Herculanean, and out of 1,756 found in one room, some 210 were successfully unrolled; a process, from the fact of the vegetable juices of the material having been thoroughly baked by the heat, of no little difficulty; once opened they are quite legible and, but for the utter want of punctuation, which appears to be a mod rn invention, could be easily read. The manuscripts discovered at Pompeii crumbled upon exposure to the air, or upon being touched. The Herculanean manuscripts were unrolled by the use of goldbeater's skin being applied to the b ıck.

As we have said before, the Chinese appear to have been familiar with the process of making silk paper at a very early day. In the time of Confucius they wrote on the finely-pared bark of bamboos with a style, and at about A. D. 95 appear to have invented paper. About the middle of the seventh century, they introduced it to Samarcana; when the Saracens took that city they found the art, which they transported to Mecca, where cotton was afterwards substituted for silk, and paper made therefrom in that city, early in the eighth century. From this source the manufacture found its way into Spain, and in the twelfth century a flourishing manufactory of paper was established at Valentia, where flax, which grew abundantly in that region, was substituted for cotton.

Monfancon considered that cotton paper was familiar in E iro, e for six or seven hundred years before his time, and it is known to have been in common use in the tenth century. It had the name of charta bombycina. Some very ancient manuscripts in Arabic and other oriental languages are writ-

communication had been made. Some time after, he was again dispatched with some figs and a letter to the same person. Being again overcome by the

ten upon a paper apparently made of silk, linen, or cotton intermixed (Prideaux, Conn. 1, B. 7). The patronage of literature by the kings of Pergamus, which began about the middle of the third century before the Christian Era, in the reign of Eumenes, excited the envy of one of the Ptolemies, who interdicted the exportation of papyrus. Invention thus being stimulated among the subjects of Eumenes, the present mode of preparing the skins of animals was discovered and pergamenum or parchment became the surface upon which books were written. Papyrus, however, continued to be the favorite, whenever procurable; but after the Saracens overran Egypt, in the eighth century, it ceased to be procurable, and it was about this time that the art of manufacturing paper from linen rags made its appearance. This great invention has been claimed by almost every civilized nation in turn, though the testimony procurable seems to assign the honor to the Chinese. Not only did the invention of paper open the way to the civilization, culture, and learning of modern times to an extent which it is perfectly impossible to calculate, but it has preserved to us a vast storehouse of the learning of the ancients; since for many centuries before its appearance, the practice of erasing from parchment books the classical remains of antiquity, in order to write upon the surface thus obtained, the legends and chronicles of monkish invention, was in general vogue, and the palimpsests of the middle ages are among the most curious of its vestiges.

The style used by the ancients was an instrument made of wood, metal, or other material, pointed at one end and blunt at the other. With the sharp end they wrote upon their tablets, covered with a sort of wax, using the obtuse end to obliterate the writing, or any part of it, when necessary. But when they wrote upon parchment or papyrus, they made use of a reed dipped in some staining or coloring liquor. Baruch is said, in the thirty-sixth chapter of Jeremiah, to have written his prophesies with ink, which is probably the earliest mention of this method of writing to which we can refer, though there is reason for supposing that the use of the reed (Du Halt. Descr. Chin. vol. I. p. 363; Phil. Trans. No. ccxxvii. p. 155) dipped in some marking liquor existed in very ancient times in China, and other parts of the East (called by the Romans stylus, or graphium). It is the instrument at this

temptation, and conscious of the tattling propensities of the letter, he was determined that it should have, this time, no knowledge of his roguery; so, putting it

day used in writing by the Turks, Persians, and Arabians. The Indian, or more properly, the Chinese ink, needs only to be slightly rubbed in water to afford a substance rather solid than fluid, well adapted to the purpose of writing. In the work on "The Empire of China and its Inhabitants, by John Francis Davis, Esq., late his Majesty's Chief Superintendent in China," 1836, will be found the following information on this subject: "The date of the invention of paper seems to prove that some of the most important arts connected with the progress of civilization are not extremely ancient in China. In the time of Confucius they wrote on finely-pared bark of the bamboo with a style. They next used silk and linen. It was not until A. D. 95 that paper was invented. The materials which they use in the manufacture are various. A coarse yellowish paper, used for wrapping parcels, is made from rice-straw. The better kinds are composed of the liber or inner bark of a species of the morus, as well as of cotton, but principally of the bamboo." And we may extract the description of the last from the Chinese Repository, vol. iii. p. 265: "The stalks are cut near the ground, and then sorted into parcels according to age, and tied up in small bundles. The younger the bamboo the better is the quality of the paper which is made from it. The bundles are thrown into a reservoir of mud and water, and buried in the ooze for about a fortnight to soften them. They are then taken out, and cut into pieces of a proper length, and put into mortars with a little water, to be pounded to a pulp with large wooden pestles. This semi-fluid mass, after being cleansed of the coarsest parts, is transferred to a great tub of water, and additions of the substance are made until the whole becomes of a sufficient consistence to form a paper. Then a workman takes up a sheet with a mold or frame of proper dimensions, which is constructed of bamboo in small strips, made smooth and round like wire. The pulp is continually agitated by other hands, while one is taking up the sheets, which are then laid upon smooth tables to dry. This paper is unfit for writing on with liquid ink, and is of a yellowish color. The Chinese size it by dipping the sheets into a solution of fish-glue and alum, either during or after the first process of making it. The sheets are usually three feet and a half in length, and two in breadth. The fine paper used for letters is polished after sizing, by rubbing it with smooth stones."

underneath a large stone, he sat upon it and regaled himself with the figs, when he proceeded on his errand and delivered the letter. He was again accused, and,

"What is commonly known in this country under the name of Indian ink, is nothing more than what the Chinese manufacture for their own writing. The writing apparatus consists of a square of their ink; a little black slab of schostus, or slate, found in the mountains called Leu-Shän, on the west side of the Poyang lake (where the last embassy saw quantities of these slabs manufactured for sale), polished smooth, with a depression at one end and hold water; a small brush or pencil of rabbit's hair, inserted into a reed handle, and a bundle of paper." The Chinese, or, as it is miscalled, Indian ink, has been erroneously supposed to consist of the secretion of a species of sepia or cuttle-fish. It is manufactured from lampblack and gluten, with the addition of a little musk to give it a more agreeable odor. A black dye is also obtained from the cup of the acorn, which abounds in gallic acid. Pere Contanein gave the following as a process for making the ink: "A number of lighted wicks are put into a vessel full of oil; over this is hung a dome or funnel-shaped cover of iron, at such a distance as to receive the smoke. Being well coated with lampblack, this is brushed off and collected upon paper. It is then well mixed in a mortar with a solution of gum or gluten, where it receives those shapes and impressions with which it comes into this country. It is occasionally manufactured into a great variety of forms and sizes, and stamped with ornamental devices, either plain or in gold and various colors. They consider that the best ink is produced from the burning of particular oils, but the commoner and cheaper kinds are obtained, it is said, from fir wood. The best ink is produced at Hoey-chow-foo, not far from Nanking; and a certain quantity annually made for the use of the emperor and the court, is called Koong-me, "tribute ink." The best ink is that which is the most intensely black, and most free from grittiness. In the Himalayan provinces there is a plant found in the greatest abundance, called Sitabhoua, from which a coarse paper is made by first detaching the bark of the stem and branches, and then submitting the same to the process of boiling, pounding it into a paste, straining it through a cloth to get rid of the coarser fibres, drying it in the sun, and finally spreading it upon a cotton cloth stretched upon a frame; and this has probably been practiced for centuries. The fabric is coarse, but

with greater confidence than before, denied the charge, "until," says the narrator, "a smart castigation con-

capable of great improvement. See the description of the plant Daphne Cannavina, by Dr. Wallich, Asiatic Researcher, vol. i. 13; and of the mode of making paper from it, in Journ. of the Asiatic Society, vol. i. 8. Paper is said to be manufactured in Kashimire, in considerable quantities, from old cloth of the Janhemp and from cotton rags. See Travels of Moorcroft and Trebeck from 1819 to 1825."—Murray.

Ink-stands, with pens (reeds) lying by them, are represented in pictures found in Herculaneum. Those reeds were dipped in some liquid substance, various in its composition and color, but for the most part black, and expressed by the word *atramentum*, in Latin. It sometimes had the name *cæpia* among the Latins, which signified the black or dark liquor emitted by the cuttle-fish. In Greek it had the general name of *γραφικον μελαν*. St. John, in his Third Epistle, says he did not intend to write with pen (reed) and ink. Allusions also to this mode of writing occur in most of the authors of the Augustan history, and their literary successors. Sometimes, in order to make the writing more visible, where the person addressed labored under an infirmity of eyesight, the letter was written with black ink (atramento) upon ivory; and these epistles were called pugillares eborei (*Armido*, fistula, and canna, split at the point). Thus the Roman epigramatist:

> Languida ne tristes obscurent lumina ceræ,
> Nigra tibi niveum littera pingat ebur.
> Mart. lib. XIV. Ep. 5.

The Romans found it generally convenient, in compos,ing to write their thoughts first upon waxen tables, for the facility of making alterations or corrections, and perhaps also for expedition, as they had no occasion to leave off for dipping the pen; and when the draft was thus made correct, it was transcribed upon paper or parchment. They had also a blotting-paper of a coarse contexture, which they called charta deletitia, and which had also the Greek name of *παλιμψεστος* from *παλιν*, rursus, and *ψαω*, rado, from which what was written upon it might be easily rubbed out or erased (Cic. Farrs, lib. VII. Cicero to Trebatius). The better sort usually carried about them their *pugillares*, or small writing-tables, on which they set down anything which occurred. Thus Pliny, in his agreeable letter to his friend Tacitus, tells him that he took care to have about him, even when hunting, his stylus et pugillares, "ut si manais vacuas, plenas tamen ceras reportarem"

vinced him that he had not escaped the scrutiny of the letter."

(Plin. lib. I. Ep. 6). As the Romans wore neither sword nor dagger when in the city, they sometimes had recourse to the inon style, which they carried about their persons as a weapon of defense, Accordingly, we read in Suetonius, that Julius Cæsar, when assaulted by the conspirators, upon receiving his first wound pierced the arm of the assassin with his stylus, or graphium. Quintus Antyllius, one of the lictors of the consul Opimius, who offended the followers of Caius Gracchus, in the forum of Rome, by his pushing them aside with contempt, as they were supporting their friend, was fallen upon by them, in the fury of their resentment, and slain with their styles, or writing instruments (Florus, l. iii. c. 15). We are told that the friends of Caius Gracchus and Fulvius were greatly exasperated by his rejection, on his standing for the tribuneship the third time. His disappointment was followed by the elevation of his great enemy, L. Opimius, to the consulship, who exerted the whole power of his office to procure the repeal of Caius's popular laws. Caius, it is said at the instigation of Fulvius, the triumvir, collected his friends, to defeat the consul's measures. On the day for proposing the abrogation of the laws in question, both parties repaired early in the morning to the capitol. While the consul was performing the customary sacrifices, Q. Antyllius one of the lictors, while carrying away the entrails of the victims, said to the friends of Caius and Fulvius, "Make way, ye worthless citizens, for honest men." And it is addcd, that he accompanied these words with a contemptuous motion of his hand. Whereupon, they fell upon him and killed him with their styles, or pens of their tables. Seneca, in his tract on Clemency, makes mention of a Roman knight, who, having whipped his son to death, was himself put to death by the people in the forum, who stabbed him with their styles. "Populos in foro graphiis confodit (Seneca, de Clement, lib. i. cap. 14). From which occasional use of this instrument it is probable that the word "stiletto," in the modern language of Rome, had its origin.

The case for holding the implements of writing was called by the Romans scrinium, or capsa (Horat. Sat. lib. i. 4 lin. 22), and by the Greeks *κιβωτος* or *κιβωτιον*, a very essential part of the furniture or equipment of a person or any rank or importance in the more polished nations of antiquity. The use of black lead pencils, both for writing and drawing, is

Letters are said to have been invented by Atossa, the daughter of Cyrus, wife of Cambyses and Darius Hystaspes, and mother of Xerxes.[1] Pliny considered

of old standing, though hardly, if at all, traceable to the times of Greek and Roman antiquity. There is, indeed, a hint of it in the works of Pliny, where we have the words argento, ære, plumbo, lineæ, ducuntur (Plin. lib. xxxiii. 136). But the passage seems to signify nothing more than the use of these substances in making lines by the help of the rule. This application of these materials, and especially of lead, as being soft and easily rubbed out, appears to have been in practice many centuries ago. We know that above a thousand years ago transcribers made their writings even and regular by means of parallel lines, to be erased after having answered their purpose. In very old MSS. the traces of those lines are very visible; but, according to Beckman, this practice became rare after the fifteenth century, about which period the MSS. exhibit a want of the parallelism which is characteristic of the more ancient specimens.

The use of the lead pencil in writing has an early date in modern history. Gerner, in his book on Fossils, printed at Zurich, 1565, says, that pencils for writing were used in his day, with wooden handles and pieces of lead, or, as he rather believed, an artificial composition, called by some stimmi angliamum (De Rerum Fossilium Figuris, 104). Towards the end of the same century, Imperati mentions the graffio plombino, and says it was more convenient for drawing than pen and ink. The mineral, he says, was smooth, greasy to the touch, had leaden color, and a sort of metallic brightness. One kind was mixed with a clay, which they called rubrica (Del. Historia Naturale di Ferrante Imperato, el Napoli, 1599, 122).

---

[1] Aul. Gell. xv. 23; Strom. i. 132. *Πρωτην επιστολας συνταξαι Ατοσσαν την Περσων βασιλευσσαν φησιν Ἑλλανικος.* Tatian, in his oration against the Greeks, says that none of those institutions of which the Greeks were so boastful, were of their own invention, but came invariably from the Barbarians. *Ὁτι ουδεν των επιτηδευματων οίς Ελληνες καλλωπιζονται Ελληνικον· αλλα εκ Βαρβαρων την ευρεσιν εσχηκος.* Quod nihil eorum quibus Græci gloriantur studiorum apud ipsos natum, sed omnia a Barbaris inventa sunt.—Bentley fixes Alossa as having lived 70 years after Phalaris, tyrant of Agrigentum, who died, according to him, Olymp. lvii. 3.

as epistles only those letters which were inscribed on paper, as distinguished from the ancient codicilli[1]—the term he gives to the writings that Bellerophontes

But the pencils principally in use in Italy, at the period of the revival of letters, were composed of lead and tin, the proportion being two parts of the former to one of the latter; which pencil was called a style. It seems that the oldest certain account of the use of the quills in writing, which has reached us, occurs in a passage in Isidorus Hispalensis, who died in 636. He mentions reeds and feathers as instruments employed in writing. There is besides, a small Latin poem on a writing pen, to be seen in the works of Anthelmus; the first Saxon, says Beckman, who wrote Latin, and who made the art of Latin poetry known to his countrymen. He is said also to have inspired them with some taste for compositions of this kind. He died in 709. The poem De Penna Scriptoria, begins thus:

"Me pridem genuit candens onocrotalus albam," which, if not descriptive of a goose-quill, at least supposes an implement furnished by a feathered animal. Writing pens are mentioned by Aleuin, who lived in the eighth century, somewhat later than Anthelmus, and composed poetical inscriptions for every part of a monastery, and, among others, for the writing study; of which, he says, that no one ought talk in it, as it was very important that the pen of the transcriber should go correctly on without mistake.

Tramite quo recto penna volantis eat.

Mabillon saw a MS. of the Gospels written in the ninth century, in which the Evangelists were represented with quills in their hands. In the curious little work of Hericus Ackerus, called "Historia Pennarum," in which he treats of the pens of the famous Academicians, published at Altenburgh, in 1726, we read of the one pen of Leo Allatins, with which he wrote his Greek for forty years, and on losing which, he is said to have with difficulty refrained from tears. "Et eo tandem amisso tantum non lacrymasse." P. Holland, the translator of Pliny, performed his work with a single pen, and he has handed down the fact in the following verse:

---

[1] The epistola were always sent to the absent. Codicilli were given to those present as well, as sent to the absent, as were also the libelli, as for example Cæsar's letters to the Senate, in the form of our present book, which form was adhered to by the other emperors.

carried from Prœtus to Jobates,[1] enjoining the death of the bearer. Licinius Mucianus, a writer of the time of Vespasian, mentions having seen, when governor

With one sole pen I wrote this book,
Made of a gray goose-quill;
A pen it was when I it took,
A pen I leave it still.

Cicero, in a letter to his brother Quintus, makes some pleasant allusions to his bad pen, in which he tells him that he is apt to snatch up whatever pen (calamus) comes first to hand: "Calamo et atramento temperato, charta etiam dentata res agetur. Scribis enim te meas litteras superiores vix legere potuisse: in quo nihil eorum mi frater, fuit, quæ putas. Neque enim occupatus eram, neque perturbatus, nec iratus alicui: sed hoc facio semper, ut, quincumque calamus in manus meas venerit, eo sic utar tamquam bono" (Ad Quint. Frat. lib. ii. ep. xv.)

Haerlem, Mentz, and Strasburg seem to have the best pretensions to the original invention of the art of printing. Venice has a better claim to the improvement than to the first rudiments. For Nicolas Jenson, who is generally supposed to have first taught it to the Venetians, did not begin printing there till the year 1470; and if John de Spiras's claim should be allowed, who says "that he was the first who had ever printed in that city," yet his pretensions go only a year or two further backward. And even admitting that another book was printed at Venice before John de Spiras's "Cicero's Epistles ad Familiares," in 1469; (namely, "Fr. Maturantii de Componendis Versebus Hexametro et Pentametro," by Ranolt, Venet. 1468"), yet that would carry it back but one year more in support of the Venetian claim; whereas the first rudiments of

[1] ———Πορεν δ' ὁγε σηματα λυγρα,
Γραψας εν πινακι πτυκτω θυμοφθορα πολλα.
Hom. Iliad, ζ'. 168.

Thucidides relates a similar story of Pausanias, and similarly David sent a letter by Uriah to Joab, and Hamlet wrote letters for Rosencrantz and Guildenstern. And the like is told of Giangiacomo. But Homer's πιναξ πτυκτος would seem rather to correspond to the Latin "tabellæ," or "pugillares," rather than litteræ or epistolæ. Pliny, while distinguishing pugillares and codicilli from epistolæ, assumed on the authority of the above passage: Pugillarium usum fuisse etiam ante Trojana tempora.

of Lycia, in a temple, an epistle from Sarpedon, written on paper. But Pliny distrusted the account; "since," says he, "even in Homer's time, and therefore long

the art, the first rough specimens, the first essay with separate wooden types, if not elsewhere, yet at least at Haerlem, was about thirty years anterior to those dates.

At Haerlem, the use of separate type blocks appears to have been first thought of, by Laurentius, about 1430, and practiced. It was afterwards practiced at Mentz with metal types, first cut and then cast, invented by one of the two brothers of the name of Geinsfleich—probably by elder John Geinsfleich, about the year 1442, when he published his first essays on wooden types, which did not answer his expectations. However, both the brothers have been called protocharagmatici. This invention of printing with metal types was called "Ars characterizandi." The cut metal types were further improved by John Faust, of Mentz, who, in 1462, completed the art by the help of his servant, Peter Shoeffer, whom he adopted for his son, and to whom he gave his daughter in marriage, pro dignâ laborum multarumque ad inventionum remuneratione. So that the original foundation of the art of printing, in general, seems to have been laid at Haerlem, and the improvements made at Mentz. As to Strasburg, it can have no pretensions nearly equal to either Haerlem or Mentz. Gutenberg endeavored to attain the art whilst he resided in that city, and his first attempts were made, in 1436, with wooden types. But he and his partners were never able to bring the art to perfection. He quitted Strasburg in 1444 or 1445, greatly involved in debt, and obliged to sell all that he had.

The true inventor of printing seems to have been Laurentius, of Haerlem, son of John, who was son of another Laurence. This Laurence, the grandson, was born at Haerlem, about 1370, and died in 1440. He was Æditiuus or Custos of the cathedral of Haerlem; and was called Custer from his office, not from his family name. His descent is said to have been from an illegitimate branch of the Gens Brederodia. He was a man of large property, and his office was both respectable and lucrative. Hadrian Junius gives a full narrative of the accident which led Laurentius into the happy train of this useful invention (see his Batavia, Ed. Ludg. Bat. 1588, 253). This Laurentius being a man of ingenuity and judgment, he proceeded step by step, inventing a more glutinous ink, and then forming whole pages of wood with letters cut upon them; pasting the backsides of the pages together, thus

after Sarpedon, the part of Egypt which produces paper was nothing but sea, being afterwards thrown up by the Nile."

making a single sheet printed on both sides. He changed his original beechen letters for leaden ones, and those again for a mixture of tin and lead, as a less flexible and more solid and durable substance. In one of his first works, the "Speculum Salutis," he introduced pictures on wooden blocks, printed on separate movable wooden types, fastened together by threads.

He did not live to see the art brought to perfection, as he died in 1440, aged 70; and was succeeded, either by his son-in-law, Thomas Peter, who married his only daughter, Lucia, or by his immediate descendants, Peter, Andrew, and Thomas, who seem to have acquired the art of printing, neatly with separate wooden types. Their last known work was printed at Haerlem, in 1472; soon after which they disposed of all their materials, and probably quitted their employment. Laurentius' types were stolen soon after his death. The thief was one of his workmen, named John, a native of Mentz; to which place he conveyed them, and settled there; it is not so certain what was his surname. John Fust or Faust has been suspected; but it seems to be an unjust charge upon him. So also, upon John Gutenberg, whose residence was at Strasburgh, from 1436 to 1444, endeavoring with fruitless labor and expense to attain the art. Neither does it seem just to suspect John Meidenbachius, an assistant to the first Mentz printers; nor John Petersheimius, some time a servant to Fust and Schoeffer, who set up a printing house at Frankfort, in 1459.

It is most probable that the culprit was John Geinsfleich, senior, elder brother of Gutenberg, who was born at Mentz, but had resided in other places. He took the shortest route, through Amsterdam and Cologne, to Mentz, where he fixed his residence, in the year 1441, and in 1442 published two small works. Ulric Zell, in his Chronicon Coloniæ, 1499, attributes the invention, or at least the completion of the art, to Gutenberg, at Mentz, though he admitted that some books had been published in Holland earlier than in that city; and from Mentz, he says, it was first communicated to Cologne; next to Strasburg; then to Venice. There is no certain proof of any book having been printed at Strasburg till after 1462, after which period printing made rapid progress in Europe. In 1490, it reached Constantinople. In the middle of the next century it advanced into Africa and America, and about 1560 was in-

The age of Homer, synchronizing with the time of Solomon, may be regarded as preceding the Christian Era by about one thousand years.[1] But the Scrip-

troduced into Russia. After this it was even carried into Iceland, the farthest north (as Mr. Bryant observes) of any place where arts and sciences have ever resided. We find mention of a book, written in Latin, by Arngrim Jonas, a native of Iceland, and printed ("Typris Hollensibus in Islandia Boreali, Anno, 1612, entitled Anatome Blefkiniana"). It was formerly the general opinion and belief, and seemed to be agreed by all our historians, that the art of printing was introduced and first practiced in England by Mr. William Caxton, a citizen of London, who had been bred a mercer, having served an apprenticeship to one Robert Large, who died in 1441, after having been sheriff and lord mayor of London, leaving a legacy to Caxton, in testimony of his good character and integrity. From the time of his master's death Mr. Caxton spent the following thirty years (from 1441 to 1471) beyond sea, in the business of merchandise. In 1464, he was employed by King Edward the Fourth in a public and honorable negotiation, to transact and conclude a treaty of commerce between that king and his brother-in-law, the Duke of Burgundy. By his long residence in Holland, Flanders, and Germany, he had opportunity of being informed of the whole method and process of this art; and returning to England, and meeting with encouragement from great persons, and particularly from the then abbot of Westminster, be first set up a press in that abbey (in the almonry or ambry), and began to print books soon after the year 1471, and is said to have pursued his business there till the year 1494, or, as some affirm, until the year 1491. He was probably upwards of four-score years of age when he died. The "Recuyel of the Historyes of Troye," is supposed to have been the first book that he had printed in England. All English writers before the Restoration, who mention the introduction of the art of printing, give Caxton the credit of it, without any contradiction or variation. For

---

[1] According to Theopompus, Homer lived 500 years after the siege of Troy (684 B. C.)—Clem. Alex. Strom. 1. i. s. 21, p. 389. According to Plutarch, some affirmed that Homer lived at the time of the Trojan war, 1184 B. C. Plut. in V. Hom. 44. So that if, as Mr. Roberts suggests, we take a mean between these extremes, the age of Homer must stand at about 100 years after the age of Solomon.

tures mention a letter from David to Joab, sent by the hand of Uriah;[1] and, about forty years after, one from Jezebel, written in Ahab's name.[2] The king of Syria

example, Stowe, Trussell, Sir Richard Baker, Leland, and Howell, and the more modern authorities of Mr. Henry Wharton and M. Du Pin—are all in favor of this opinion. In opposition, however, to all these great and seemingly invincible testimonies and authorities on behalf of Caxton—a book which had been scarcely observed before the Restoration, was soon after that time taken notice of, and looked upon as a strong argument, if not a full and clear proof, "that the art of printing had been exercised "in the university of Oxford before Caxton exercised 'it at Westminster, in 1471.'" This book bears for its title, "Expositio Sancti Jeronimi in Simbolum Apostolorum ad Papam Lamentium;" and at the end, "Explicit," Expositio, &c. Impressia Oxonie, & finita Anno Domini M.CCCC.LXVIII., xvii. die Decembris."

A record which had long lain obscure and unknown at Lambeth Palace, in the register of the See of Canterbury, which record is mentioned by the reporter in a note to Miller v. Taylor, 4 Burr. 2345, as apparently drawn up at the very time, stating "that Thomas Bouchier, Archbishop of Canterbury, moved King Henry the Sixth to use all possible means for procuring a printing mold to be brought into this kingdom. The king readily hearkened to the motion, and, taking private advice how to effect his design, concluded that it could not be brought about without great secresy and a considerable sum of money given to such person or persons as would draw off some of the workmen of Haerlem, in Holland, where John Gutenberg had newly invented it, and was himself personally at work. It is resolved, that less than one thousand marks would produce the desired effect, towards which sum the said archbishop presented the king three hundred marks. The management of the design was committed to Mr. Robert Turnour, of the robes to the king, and much in favor with him. Mr. Turnour took to his assistance Mr. Caxton, a citizen of good abilities, who, trading much into Holland, might be a credible pretense, as well for his going, as staying in the low countries. Mr. Turnour was in disguise (his beard and hair shaven quite off), but Mr. Caxton appeared known and public. They went first to Amsterdam, then to Leyden, not

[1] 2 Sam. XI. 14, 15.

[2] 1 Kings, xxi. 8, 9.

wrote to the king of Israel, by Naaman, the leper,[1] nine hundred years before the Christian Era; and about twenty years later, Jehu wrote letters and sent

daring to enter Haerlem itself; for the town was very jealous, and had apprehended and imprisoned divers persons who had come from other parts for the same purpose. They stayed till they had spent the whole thousand marks in gifts and expenses; so as the king was fain to sent five hundred marks more. Mr. Turnour had written to the king, that he had almost done all his work; a bargain being struck betwixt him and two Hollanders, for bringing off one of the under workmen, whose name was Frederick Corsells (or rather Corsellis); who, late one night, stole from his fellows in disguise, in a vessel prepared for that purpose, and got safe to London. It was not thought prudent to set him on work in London, but by the archbishop's means (who had been first vice-chancellor, and afterwards chancellor of the university of Oxford), whose guard constantly watched this Corsellis, to prevent him from any possible escape till he had made good his promise in teaching them how to print."

"So at Oxford printing was first set up in England, which was before there was any printing-press or printer in France, Spain, Italy, or Germany, except the city of Mentz, which claims seniority as to printing even of Haerlem itself, calling her city Urbem Moguntinum, artis typographicæ inventricem primam, though it is known to be otherwise, that city gaining that art by the brother of one of the workmen of Haerlem, who had learned it at home, of his brother, and after set up for himself, at Mentz. The press at Oxford was afterwards found inconvenient to be the sole printing place of England, as being too far from London and the sea; wherefore, the king set up a press at St. Alban's, and another in the city of Westminster, where they printed several books of divinity and physic. For the king (for reasons best known to himself and council) permitted then no law-books to be printed; nor did any printer exercise that art, but only such as by the king's sworn servants, the king himself having the price emolument for printing books." Upon the authority of this record, all our latter writers have declared Corsellis to have been the first printer in England. This is admitted by Dr. Middleton; and he specifies Antony Wood, Mattaire, Palmer, and Bagford, by name, as persons who were clear in that opinion.

[1] 2 Kings, v. 5–7; ch. x. 1–2, 6–7.

them to Samaria. Then there were the threatening letter from the king of Assyria to Hezekiah,[1] and the complimentary letter from Berodact-Baladan to the

But he says, "it is strange that a piece so fabulous, and carrying such evident marks of forgery, could impose upon men so knowing and inquisitive." He asserts, that as it was never heard of before the "publication of Atkyns's books, so it has never since been seen or produced by any man." He cites Palmer himself as owning "that it is not to be found there now; and he thinks it clear that Archbishop Parker must have very carefully examined the registers of Canterbury, and that it was not there in his time. In fine, he declares in express terms, "that we may pronounce this record to be a forgery." But though he seems to exult in having cleared his hands of this record, yet he admits "that the book itself stands firm as a monument of the exercise of printing in Oxford six years older than any book of Caxton with date." He acknowledges the fact to be strong, and "what in ordinary cases passes for certain evidence of the age of books;" but he says, "that in this there are such contrary facts to balance it, and such circumstances to turn the scale, that he takes the date in question to have been falsified originally by the printer, either by design or mistake, and an X to have been dropped or omitted in the age of its impression;" and he argues, with sagacity and acuteness, to show not only the possibility of his conjecture, but the probability of it, and (as he says) "to make it even certain." Mr. Bowyer, whose general learning and particular knowledge in his profession seem to qualify him for being at least as good a judge of this dispute as any man that ever lived, does by no means agree with Dr. Middleton in this point of Caxton's priority to the Oxford book, or in the arguments adduced by the doctor in support of his opiuion, any more than he does in the former point, of the place where the art was first invented and practiced abroad. He is of opinion that the Oxford press was prior to Caxton's, and thinks those who have called Mr. Caxton the "first printer in England," and Leland in particular, meant that he was the first who "practiced the art with fusile types, and consequently first brought it to perfection;" which is not inconsistent with Corsellis's having printed, earlier at Oxford, with separate cut types in wood, which was the only method he had learned at Haerlem. The speaking of Mr. Caxton as the first printer in England, in this sense of the

[1] 2 Kings, xix. 14.

same king, after his sickness;[1] and Hezekiah himself wrote letters to the tribes of Ephraim and Manasseh, summoning them to Jerusalem.[2] Cyrus, after decreeing to the Jews liberty to return to their own country and rebuild the house of the Lord at Jerusalem, wrote letters recommendatory to the governors of several provinces to assist them in their undertaking, one of which Josephus[3] has recorded as being directed to the governors of Syria, and commencing with the usual epistolary salutation: "Cyrus, the king, to Sysina and Sarabasan, sendeth greeting." And during the rebuilding (about 520 B. C.), there was a frequent correspondence between the enemies of the Jews and Artaxerxes, king of Persia, on the subject.[4]

"The Greek epistles of heathen writers which have come down to us, which are entitled to be considered as genuine, are, for the most part, studied and elaborate compositions, the vehicles of argument or disquisition on matters of general interest or contemplative inquiry,[5] and as different as possible from our modern ideas of a letter. Thirteen of these letters are ascribed to Plato,[6] though two of the number are sometimes assigned to Dion. The letters which have been ascribed to Themistocles were first printed at Rome, in the year 1626, from a manuscript in the

expression, is not irreconcilable with the story of Corsellis."—Note to Millar v. Taylor, 4 Burr., p. 2418.

[1] 2 Kings, ch. xx. 12.

[2] 2 Chron. xxx. 1, 6.

[3] Jew. Antiq. lib. xi. c. 1.

[4] Ezra, iv. 8, 11, 18; Nehemiah, ii. 8, 9, vi. 17, 19; Esther, iii. 13, viii. 5, ix. 25; Isaiah, xxxvii. 14, xxxix. 1; Jeremiah, xxix. 1, 25, 29. And Mordecai wrote and sent letters to the Jews. Esther, ch. ix. 20.

[5] Roberts, p. 91.

[6] *Επιστολαι ηθικαι*, xiii., according to Fabricius, 1 Dionis, 2.

Vatican, and although doubted as spurious by most authorities,[1] are received by some as genuine. They all bear date posterior to his banishment, and from places to which the general is supposed to have retired during his exile, such as Argos, Corcyra, Epirus, Ephesus, and Magnesia. The epistles of Socrates and his scholars, Xenophon, Aristippus, and others, were collected and published in the year 1637, also from a Vatican manuscript, by the celebrated Leo Allatius. But, from internal evidence, these have been rejected as spurious.[2] Besides these, there were also

[1] Plato to Dionysis; 4 to Dion; 5 to Perdiccas; 6 to Hermias, Erastus, and Corsicus; 7 and 8 to the friends of Dion; 9 to Archytas of Tarentum; 10 to Aristodorus (or according to Laërtius, Aristodemus); 11 to Leodamus; 12 to Archytas; 13 to Dionysius. Siudas acknowledges thirteen under *Ευπραττειν*, which was the salutation used by Plato; the others using *χαιρειν*, *γαθειν*, *ευδιαγειν*, or *ευλογειν*. Laërtius mentions 10 and 12 as above. The third is said by Bentley to be genuine; but Meinursius declares that, and all the others as well, to be spurious, "in judico de quibusdam Socraticorum reliquiis."—See Comment. Socrat. regiæ Gottingensis, Ann. 1783, Classis. Histor. et Philog. But Guil. Gottlieb Tenneman contra Meinursium disputans, maintains their genuineness (p. 17, *et seq.*), except as to a part of Ep. 13, all of which Wesseling contends is genuine. Roberts, p. 84.

[2] The correspondence of Socrates with the King of Macedon has the air of puerile romance.—In one of these letters Xenophon invites some friends to come and see him at his plantation, near Olympia, informing them that Aristippus and Phædro have been visiting him there, to whom he had been reciting his memoirs of Socrates, which both had approved of: Now, this Aristippus was always on the worst terms with Xenophon, and could hardly have given his approbation to a book which, says Bentley, was a satire against himself.—The letters abound in manifest anachronisms and errors, assigning two wives to Socrates, and but one, indiscriminately.

A curious letter from Xenophon to Xantippe, after her husband Socrates' death, runs as follows:

"I have committed to the hands of Euphron, the Megarite, six small measures of wheaten cakes, and eight drachms, also a new cloak for winter wear. Accept these trifles, and be

five epistles alleged to have been written by Euripides, which, however, were said by Apollonides, who wrote a treatise on false history, to have been forged by Sabirius Pollo, "the same who counterfeited the letters of Aratus."[1] Every one of these letters, as has been

assured that Euclid and Terpsion are very good and worthy persons, full of kind-feeling toward you, and of respect to the memory of Socrates. When the children show an inclination to come to us, do not oppose their wishes, as it is but a little way for them to come to Megara. My good lady, let the abundance of the tears you have shed, suffice. To mourn longer, will do no good, but rather harm. Remember what Socrates said, and endeavor to follow his precepts and counsels. By incessant grief you will greatly injure yourself and the children. These are young Socrateses, and it not only becomes us to support them while they live, but to endeavor to continue in life for their sakes. Since, if you or I, or any other who feels a tender concern for the children of the deceased Socrates, should die, they will suffer loss by being deprived of a protector and a contributor to their support and subsistence. Therefore try to live for these children, which can only be done by attending to the means of preserving your life. But grief is among the things opposed to life, as those can testify, who experience its hurtful effects. The gentle Apolliodorus, for so he is called, and Dion, give you praise for not receiving assistance from anybody standing in no particular relation to you. You say you abound, and you are much to be commended for so speaking of yourself as far as I and your other intimate friends are able to assist you, you shall feel no want. Take courage then, Xantippe, and let none of the good instructions of Socrates be lost, for you know in what honor that great man was held by us; and consider well the example he has left us by his death. For my own part, I really think his death was a great benefit to us all, if it be regarded in the light in which it ought to be."—Now Xenophon did not return from his Asiatic expedition, until some time after Socrates' death, and so could hardly have been at Megara, as recently after the event as this letter appears to have been written. Nor does it seem probable that he was at Megara at all after his return, since he did not leave Agesilaus, until he went to settle at Scyllum (See Diog. Laërt. ii. 52).—Roberts.

[1] The Letters of Aratus are not extant.

pointed out,[1] contains unquestionable evidence of its spurious nature.[2]

"The letters attributed to Phalaris are also doubted, as are the letters attributed to Pythagoras, his wife Theano, and certain of his immediate scholars.[3]

"In the works of Herodotus, Thucydides, and other Greek historians, however, letters of statesmen, sages, princes, governors, and military commanders, are not infrequent.[4]

"Little or nothing in the shape of letters or letter-writing has survived to us, from among the Romans, until the time of Cicero. Their military ardor and warlike customs, their absorbing ambition, restless political agitations, and their addiction to brutal shows, left the Romans small leisure or taste for the refinements of epistolary intercourse. 'Those Republicans,' says Roberts, 'were characterized by a dryness

[1] Roberts, 87, citing Bentley and others.

[2] As, for instance, one of them appears to have been written from the court of Archelaus, King of Macedonia; in this, in answer to some reproaches which had been cast upon him for leaving Athens, the writer expresses himself as paying no regard to what might be said of him at Athens, by Agatho or Mesatus. Now, this Agatho, unfortunately, was all the time himself at the court of Archelaus with Euripides. Again, the injury done to Euripides by Cephisophon, seems to have been overlooked by the fabricator, since Euripides is made to address one of his letters to that personage.

[3] Roberts, 67.

[4] There are very few examples of such among the Romans. Plutarch, in his life of Pyrrhus, gives a letter from Fabricius to that monarch, communicating to him the proposal of Nicias, his physician, to poison him; also mentioned by Livy. The letter is as follows: "You seem to be unhappy in your choice both of your friends and your enemies. When you have read the letter sent us by one of your own people, you will perceive that you are making war with good and honest men, while you are trusting to the dishonest and wicked. We

of genius, and certain coarse and homespun habits of thinking, which ill-qualified them for the graceful play of thought and expression which properly belongs to good letter-writing. Nor do letters of business and grave affairs appear, but very rarely, among the transactions recorded by the historians of the Roman Republic. The mind of the nation took a sudden spring under the influence of Cicero's genius, who at once gave and completed the pattern. With the pen of Cicero, letter-writing began to take its rank in polite literature as a specific head or department of composition." [1]

make you acquainted with these things, not out of regard to you, but lest your destruction should bring a slander upon us, and we should appear to have accomplished this war by treachery, for want of ability to conclude it by valor." Upon receipt of this letter, Pyrrhus is said to have exclaimed, "This is a man whom it is harder to turn aside from the ways of justice than to divert the sun from its course." P. 114, 118.

[1] The Romans sealed their letters usually with some device or symbol, to notify the writer and identify the person written to. Plautus makes the bearer of a letter thus accost the person to whom he brings it:

> Nosce imaginem; tute ejus nomen memorato mihi,
> Ut sciam te Ballionem esse ipsum (Plaut. Pseud. 1).

The wax, with the impression, kept the letter closed, hence the phrase, Solvere Epistolam: and as the impression or signum was generally defaced or broken in opening the letters, the messenger or bearer usually required the person to whom it was to be delivered to acknowledge the signum, and name the writer, that it might with the more certainty appear that he was the person to whom the letter belonged. Thus Cicero, in his third oration against Catiline: "Ostendi tabellas Lentulo, et quæsivi cognosceretne signum."

Alexander Severus, according to Lampridius, after midday, always gave his attention to the reading and dispatch of letters, when he was regularly attended by the three principal officers "ab epistolis, et libellis, et a memoria," who generally continued standing in his presence, unless laboring under any indisposition, when they were permitted to be seated.

Augustus Cæsar at first adopted a sphinx for the device of

The earliest English correspondence extant, is that of the Paston family, written between 1422 and 1485. Letters of familiar correspondence are

his seal, both in his public acts and in his epistles; afterwards the figure of Alexander the Great; and ultimately his own likeness, engraved by Dioscordes; which impression his successors continued to use; and we are imformed by his accurate biographer, that he was so precise in dating his letters, that he added the hour of the day or night in which they were written (Suet. Aug.).

It was not unusual with the great men among the Romans to use one of the alphabetical characters in the place of the other, where it was their design to convey certain intelligence or orders to be understood only by the person written to; the transposition having been previously concerted. Upon these occasions Julius Cæsar, instead of the proper letter, made use of the letter that came fourthly after it in the alphabetical order; as D for A, and so on. And Augustus used the letter immediately following the letter which should properly have been used (Suet. Jul. Aug. Aul. Gell. xvii. 9).

The Romans always put their own names first in the prae logium, and afterwards the person to whom the letter was to be sent, as "L. Catilini, Q. Catullo, S., Claudius Lycius, unto the most excellent governor Felix, send the greeting" (Acts, xxiii. 26). Paulino Ausonius; metrum sic suasit ut esses tu prior, et nomen progrederere meum (Aus. ep. xx). Seu leviter noto, seu caro misso sodali; omnes ista solet charta vocare suos (Mart. Epig. xiv. 11).

Sometimes, in flattery to the emperors, the writer added "*Suus*," as an expression of peculiar homage and devotion, to his name. Similar, as Casaubon observes, to the Greek ὁ αυτου ιδιος.—Epithets expressive of any peculiar dignity in the receiver, or of esteem, or affection, such as "optimo dulcissimo," and the like, were not unfrequently added. The Roman letter began with *Salutem*, like the Greek χαιρειν, following the writer's names, and ended with *Vale*, like the Greek εῤῥωσο. Often the Roman letter closed with "Cura ut valeas," take care of your health; "fac ut diligentissime te ipsum custodias;" or "Deos obsecro ut te conservarint," Heaven preserve you. In the East letters often began with "Thus says," ὡδε λεγει. In this manner begins the letter of Amasis, the Egyptian king, to Polycrates, and of Orœtes to the same tyrant of Samos, as given us in the Third Book of Herodotus; Αμασις Πολυκρατει, ὡδε λεγει, Ὀροιτης Πολυκρατει, ὡδε λε-

rarely met with in Scotch records before the sixteenth century.

γει; and to the letter in Thucydides, i. 129, ὧδε λεγει βασιλευς Ξερξης Πανσανια. The letter of the king of Assyria to the king of Jerusalem is commenced with similar introductory words: "Thus saith the king of Assyria," 2 Kings, xviii. 31. Wesseling, in his note on the passage in Herodotus, above cited, says of this epistolary form of commencement, "Nihil simplicius et per Orientem olim probatius hac in Epistolis et Regum edictis formula."

Ælian, in his Book of Various Histories, l. xii. c. 51, has a pleasant story, of which we are here reminded. "Menecrates a physician of Syracuse, was so elated with the extraordinary cures performed by him, that he assumed the title of Jove, as being the dispenser of life to man; and accordingly, in a letter to Philip, king of Macedon, he adopted the following address: *Φιλιππω Μενεκρατης ὁ Ζευς ευ πραττειν*: 'To Philip Menecrates Jupiter sends felicity;' to which the monarch replied, heading his letter thus: '*Φιλιππος Μενεκρατει ὑγιαινειν*; 'Philip to Menecrates sends sanity.'" The anecdote which follows is amusing. Philip having ordered a sumptuous banquet, invited the celestial physician. The invitation was condescendingly accepted by Menecrates, who being introduced, was respectfully seated by himself at a separate table, with a censer placed before him; in which situation he was left to regale himself with the fumes of the incense. At first he was much pleased with the homage shown him; but after a while growing hungry, and finding nothing more substantial proposed to him, he left the place with much dissatisfaction.

The first use of the salutation *χαιρειν* is ascribed by many of the Greek grammarians to the demagogue, Cleon, who, they say, prefixed it, instead of *ευ πραττειν*, to his letter informing the Athenians of his victory at Pylum. But Xenophon, who would not have borrowed from Cleon, prefixed it to the pleasing letter which he makes Cyrus write to Cyaxares; *Κυρου Παιδ*. lib. iv. Artemidorus, who wrote about a century before Christ, says, that the words *χαιρειν* and *ερρωσο*, were the familiar beginning and ending of every epistle, *ιδιον πασης επιστολης*. And Horace alludes to the custom in lib. i. ep. 8:

> "Celso gaudere et bene rem gerere Albinovano
> Musa rogata refer."

According to Lucian, Plato censured the practice as *μοχ-*

A letter is an object of property.[1] There is nothing a man may so emphatically call his own, or more incapable of being mistaken, than his ideas thrown upon paper.[2] By the Roman law, a messenger detaining a letter was prosecuted as for forgery. *Nuntius non restituens litteras ei, cum mandatum restituere susceperit, incidit in crimen falsi.*[3]

The laws of France recognize a letter as a chattel which may be the object of larceny. An action lies; and even a criminal proceeding may be instituted against a person who, having undertaken to carry a letter, detains it. "Il y a action en justice, et même on peut prendre la voie extraordinaire contri celui qui s'etant chargé de porter une lettre, se n'est point acquitté de son message et la retient."[4]

"It is said to have been the opinion of Lord Hardwicke," says Waddeston,[5] "that the receiver of letters has no legal right[6]—I speak not of the delicacy or propriety of such a measure—to publish them; be-

θηρον (poor and vulgar), though he himself uses it in his third epistle to Dionysius. He prefers the word *σωφρονει*, or the words *γνωθι σεαυτον*, as a better salutation. But he did not banish the word *χαιρειν*. It is prefixed to the letter sent by the apostles and elders to the brethren at Antioch, to which *ἐῤῥωσο* is subjoined; and so also the letter from Claudius Lysias to Felix, Acts xxiii., which letter has a claim, from the situation in which we find it, to be regarded as genuine; the words *περιεχουσαν τον τυπον τουτον*, being properly translated in our Bible, "after this manner," and not "in this form," or "tenor." Diogenes Laërtius notices the different salutations prefixed to the letters of the Greek philosophers. —Diog. Laërt. lib. iii. s. 61.

[1] Denis v. Leclerc, 1 Miller (La.) 294.

[2] Millar v. Taylor, 4 Burr. 2345.

[3] Bartolus in lege Titio, 36 n. 3.

[4] 3 Collection de Jurisprudence, 312.

[5] 2 Atk. 345.

[6] Lectures, vol. 3, p. 715, § 56.

cause, at most, he has but a special property in them, jointly with the writer. The same doctrine[1] has been since confirmed and established. But the reason, attributed to Lord Hardwicke, that a special property is left in the writer, seems, at least, so equivocally expressed as to need explanation, for surely every receiver of letters may destroy them. It is, however, a different thing to publish them to the world, without the writer's consent, from which mischievous consequences might ensue."

As to the question whether the sender and receiver of a letter have each a joint property therein, and as to Lord Hardwicke's[2] opinion that such a joint property existed, a late writer[3] says: "If his lordship used this language, it serves to show that he had not considered the subject so as to have formed a definite opinion. A special property, and a joint property, are two very different things. It may not be amiss to note that the case came up on motion, and may, therefore, have had less consideration than it would have had on a regular hearing."[4]

"Again, if the receiver and the sender have a 'joint property' in the letter, they would enter joint tenants or tenancy in common."

"If such were the case, how could one burn a letter received by him. If he were only a tenant in common he would be accountable in law and in equity, from the moment he received the letter, for its cus-

[1] Amb. 737.

[2] Pope v. Curl, 2 Atk. 341.

[3] Am. Law Reg. vol. 1, p. 437.

[4] *Vid.* Gyles v. Wilcox, 2 Atk. 143, where Lord Hardwicke said, in relation to Reade v. Hodges, cited before him, "that case was upon a motion only, and at that time I gave my thoughts without much consideration, and therefore I shall not lay any great weight upon it."

tody and its use, and who would be a correspondent on those terms? There is certainly no suggestion of any such right anywhere that we know of. The Roman law asserted that the owner of the manuscript was the owner of the thing written upon it, except that it directed that the manual labor of writing should be recompensed for to the scribe,[1] but no intimation was made of any "joint property."

"Neither," says the same writer above quoted, "it seems to us, is there a general or a special property remaining in the writer of matter not literary, which he has sent to its destination. If he has a special property, who has the general, and if he has the general, who has the special? Letters in regard to matters of business or friendship—aside from the question whether they had a literary value, although they pass to the executor or administrator, are not assets in their hands, and cannot be made the subject of sale or assignment by them, but belong to the widow or next of kin. If the writer has the special property and the receiver the general, then the writer is the bailee of the receiver, which is absurd; and if the writer has the general and the receiver the special property, then the receiver of a letter is, from the moment of its reception, the bailee of its writer, and liable to respond to him in law and in equity, which, it appears to us, is equally absurd."

Clearly the only right to be enforced by the sender of a letter against the holder, is a right to prevent publication of literary matter in which he has a property. The receiver may read it aloud, recite its contents to others; he may perhaps copy it (if he do not

[1] Inst. 2, 1, 33; 3 Inst. 109; and the same law provides for the case of one man's painting on another's canvas (Inst. 2, 1, 34). See *ante*, p. 14.

print it), and distribute copies; he may sell it, if he efface the contents, but it seems he should not do so otherwise.[1]

In Eyre v. Higbee,[2] where the plaintiffs were the executors of Colonel Tobias Ford, private and military secretary to General Washington (and whose letters to Colonel Lee are the subject-matter of the controversy), it was also held that (says Story, J.) "the mere sending of letters to third persons is not to be deemed, in cases of literary composition, a total abandonment of the right of property therein by the sender; *à fortiori* the act of sending them cannot be presumed to be an abandonment thereof in cases where the very nature of the letters imports, as matter of business or friendship, or advice, or family or personal confidence, the implied or necessary intention and duty of privacy and secrecy."[3]

And the same learned jurist, sitting in the case of Folsom v. Marsh,[4] summed up on the whole law in the words following:

"The author of any letter or letters, and his representatives, whether they are literary compositions or familiar letters, or letters of business, possesses the sole and exclusive copyright[5] therein; and no

[1] Am. Law Reg. vol. 1, p. 437.

[2] 22 How. Pr. 198. *Vid.* also Gee v. Pritchard, 2 Swans. 402; 2 Story Eq. § 945; Eden on Inj. 2 Am. ed. 324, 325; Drannard v. Dunkey, 1 Rol. & Beat. 209.

[3] 1 Eq. Jur. 947.

[4] 2 Story's Rep. 111.

[5] *I.e.*, the right to copyright. We think in this case Judge Story unquestionably uses the word in this sense, as identical with the word "copy," in the common law. "I use the word 'copy,'" said Lord Mansfield,in Millar v. Taylor, 4 Burr. 2396, "in the technical sense in which that name or term has been used for ages, to signify an incorporeal right to the sole printing and publishing of somewhat intellectual, communicated by

persons—neither those to whom they are addressed, nor other persons—have any right or authority to publish the same upon their own account, or for their own benefit. But, consistently with this right, the persons to whom they are addressed may have—nay, must, by implication possess—the right to publish any letter or letters addressed to them, upon such occasions as require or justify the publication or public use of them; but this right is strictly limited to such occasions. Thus, a person may justifiably use and publish in a suit at law or in equity such letter or letters as are necessary and proper to establish his right to maintain the suit, or defend the same. So, if he be aspersed or misrepresented by the writer, or accused of improper conduct in a public manner, he may publish such parts of such letter or letters (but no more) as may be necessary to vindicate his character and reputation, or free him from unjust obloquy and reproach. If he attempt to publish such letter or letters, on other occasions not justifiable, a court of equity will prevent the publication by an injunction, as a breach of private confidence or contract, or of the rights of the author, and *à fortiori* if he attempt to publish them for profit; for then it is not a mere breach of confidence or contract, but it is a violation of the exclusive copyright of the writer. In short, the person to whom letters are addressed has but a limited right or special property (if I may so call it) in such letters, as a trustee or bailee for particular purposes, either of information or protection, or of support of his own rights and character.

letters." "The 'copy' of a book," said Aston, J., in the same case, Id. 2346, "seems to have been not familiarly only, but legally used as a technical expression of the author's sole right of printing and publishing that work." See also per Willes, J., Id. 2311.

The general property, and the general rights incident to property, belong to the writer, whether the letters are literary compositions, or familiar letters, or details of facts, or letters of business. The general property in the manuscripts remains in the writer and his representatives, as well as the general copyright. *A fortiori*, third persons standing in no privity with either party are not entitled to publish them, to subserve their own private purposes of interest, or curiosity, or passion."[1]

195. We have seen that the mere parting with the possession of a manuscript, or intrusting its possession to another person, or a permission to that person to take and hold a copy of the manuscript, will not amount to an authorization of its publication by that other person. Such acts must be deemed strictly limited, in point of effect, to the very occasions expressed or implied, and ought not to be construed as a general gift or authority for any purposes of profit or publication to which the receiver may choose to devote them.[2]

And yet, nobody has ever called in question the right of the recipient of a letter to burn, or otherwise destroy it, to sell it for waste-paper, or to part with it to a collector of autographs or chirographical specimens; and yet, if the writer of that letter have still a property in the composition, which, if not valuable in his lifetime, might become so after his death, what is there, logically, to prevent the recipient's being called

[1] *Vid.* also Wetmore v. Scoville, 3 Edw. Ch. 543; Woolsey v. Judd, 4 Duer, 379.

[2] St. Eq. Jur. 943. See Bartlett v. Crittenden, 4 McClean, 303; 5 Id. 41, where the court says, "To make a gift of a copy of the manuscript is no more a transfer of the right or abandonment of it than it would be a transfer or an abandonment of an exclusive right to republish, to give the copy of a printed work."

upon to answer for the property which was in his possession without being his, and of which he was, if anything, only a trustee, or at least an involuntary bailee, liable only for gross negligence in the custody of property deposited with him?

Such a principle as this—the accompaniment of all other property—it is very evident cannot exist in the case of the special property of the receiver in letters sent to him in the course of correspondence. Such a rule would convert the most ordinary of all human procedure into a nice and complicated transaction, reviewable by the strict rules of equity, and render every individual, who received a letter from his friend, liable at any time to account, in a court of chancery, for the disposition made by him of an inchoate and impalpable property, undefinable and immeasurable, which existed by theory of a careful law, and with which he never sought any connection.

To escape this logical deduction and result, we must either assume that the property of the author in his sentiments and expressions, has never left his possession, or that it is a property *sui generis*, to which the ordinary rules and principles governing property will not be applied.

Both of these hypotheses are in some measure correct. In one sense, the ideas of the author never leave his possession, being still his, and capable of being used by him alone. And as we have seen in its every phase, literary property is a property unlike all other sorts and kinds, and capable of being construed by comparison with no other.

So, therefore, if the receiver of a letter destroys it, even though he may have thereby destroyed its contents as well as its material, he has done no wrong and no action can lie.

If, after its destruction, his memory still retains its contents, he cannot be summoned to repeat such contents to the writer.[1] And, if, on the other hand, the writer recollect the contents of the letter, or have retained a copy, the letter in his possession does not differ in any respect from any other manuscript, and he has the same rights that he would have in any manuscript, not in the least altered or abridged, or affected by the fact that the composition was originally written and despatched in the form of a letter.

There is nothing, in the law, to prevent one person's possessing the original, and the other a copy of a thing, and both having a property in that which they possess, the one in what his original contains, and the other, in what his copy contains. If the manuscript of a work should be retained by the author, after its contents had been published in book form, the manuscript would be none the less his own, because a thousand others possessed copies of his book. Nor does the original of a famous picture possess a lessened value, because a copy has been made and sold, nor are the visitors to the Rospigliosi Gallery and the "Aurora" of Guido any less numerous, because the author's countrymen, from his day to ours, have assiduously copied his masterpiece.

196. The rights, therefore, of the sender and receiver of letters are entirely distinct and independent, each of the others.[2] What rights the sender has, he retains,

[1] If, however, the receiver remember the contents, and publish them from memory, can equity prevent or interfere? If the ruling of Buller, J., in Coleman v. Wathen, 5 T. R. 245, that the transportation of anything in one's memory is not a piracy thereof, he evidently could, but this ruling has been doubted. See De Witt v. Palmer, 7 Amer. 480, 47 N. Y. 532, M.; *post*, vol. ii. Dramatic Copyright.

[2] But if it were even held that there could be but one prop

subject to no special right of the receiver; and what rights the receiver obtains in the reception, he enjoys and will continue to enjoy, subject to no rights of the sender.

The rights of the sender of a letter are, then, to recapitulate: First. The receiver has a title by gift to everything that passed into his possession when he received the letter. The paper, the characters, the autograph, the ink, the envelope, the superscription—the postage stamp, the postal mark. Whatever value these may have—actual, or historical, or otherwise—is his, and his only.

Second. The writer of the letter has his title by occupation (according to Blackstone) to the literary composition, the sentiment and the thought of the letter, as separated from all its above enumerated or other material adjuncts, and whatever value these may have—actual, personal, literary, or historical—is his and his only, and vests in him and his executors or assigns, until he shall have parted with that title by the various methods of abandonment (*i.e.*, by alienation, publication, or dedication) to which we have alluded.

197. While the material upon which the transmitted letter is inscribed is undoubtedly in the nature

erty in the ideas or contents, as a literary composition, and that the entire property did not pass to the receiver, then that whole property must remain in the writer as an entire thing; for it seems very clear that if in such case he has not transferred the entire property, in what is sent, to the receiver, he has not given him any special property to which his own general property is subject, making his right in the nature of a reversionary or servient interest. There may be general right of property, and there may be one or more special rights or properties in the same thing, yet all these will but constitute the whole property, and the general will be subject to the special right (1 Am. Law Reg. p. 460).

of a gift to the recipient, from the impracticability of its ownership still centering in the sender after its leaving his possession; the law, at a very early day, recognized the injustice of allowing the writer's private matters, if forming the theme of his letter, from becoming the property of another. Of the offense against common decency committed in the publishing of private letters, Cicero spoke with much earnestness in his oration against Philip: "Quis enim unquam, qui paulum modo bonorum consuetudinem nosset, literas, ad se ab amico missas, offensione aliquâ interposita, in medium protulit, palamque recitavit? Quid est aliud, tollere e vitâ vitæ societatem quam tollere amicorum colloquia absentium? Quam multa joca solent esse in epistolis, quæ prolati si sint, inepta videantur! Quam multa seria, neque tamen ullo modo divulganda!"[1]

But, unfortunately for the species, it was found that it would not answer to trust this valuable right, upon which, not private feelings alone, but the peace of families or of the state itself might depend, to any general sense of decency, or taste, or manners. It was enunciated, at a very early day, that the gift of the manuscript of a letter carried with it no license to publish. But for a long time courts based this ruling upon a right of "literary" property in the writer; and hesitated to do more than protect letters which, as they expressed it, were "literary in their character," from unlicensed publication.[2] Equity declined to interfere in the case of merely friendly or commercial letters; holding, as one judge expressed it, that "though the form of familiar letters might not pre-

[1] Cic. Orat. Philip, ii. c. 4. See Sir S. Romily; 2 Swans. 419.

[2] Percival v. Phipps, 2 V. & B. 19; and see *ante*, p. 447.

vent their approaching the character of literary works, every private letter, upon any subject, to any person, is not to be described as a literary work to be protected upon the principle of copyright. The ordinary use of correspondence by letters," he continued, "is to carry on the intercourse of life between persons at a distance from each other in the prosecution of commercial or other business, which it would be very extraordinary to describe as a literary work in which the writers have a copyright."

198. The old rule that letters, to be protected, must be literary in their character, was laid down by Plumer, V. C., in the year 1813, in Percival v. Phipps.[1] In that case, the defendant was proprietor of a newspaper, called "The News," in which were published, from time to time, articles and paragraphs on a subject which then engrossed the public attention—which articles and paragraphs were supplied to Phipps by a Mr. Mitford, but were written, as Mitford informed Phipps, by Lady Percival, and in her handwriting. A piece of intelligence in one of these published articles being found to be false, Phipps applied to Lady Percival on the subject, who denied that the intelligence had ever been sent, and stated that the papers containing it were forgeries. Mitford positively asserted the contrary; and to enable Phipps to justify himself to the public, delivered to him several letters written by Lady Percival to Mitford, upon similar subjects, materially tending to show that the false intelligence, published in "The News," had come from Lady Percival through Mitford. Phipps published in "The News" one of the letters given to him by Mitford, and announced an intention of publishing the others. A bill was filed, on the part of

[1] 2 V. & B. 19.

Lady Percival, to restrain the publication of those letters written by her to Mitford, as being of a private nature, and having been sent to him in confidence that he would not part with them or communicate their contents to any other person. The answer denied that the letters had been sent in any such confidence. It was urged, on behalf of Phipps, that a gross imputation had been cast upon him; and that, though he might derive a profit from publishing the letters in his own paper, his object was not profit, but the vindication of his character from the imputation thrown upon it, and to effect that object he was entitled to use the letters. The vice-chancellor held that he was entitled to make this use of the letters. "Whatever degree of confidence," he said, "or reservation of property may be implied, from the transmission of a private letter, it would be too much to hold that the individual who receives it can in no case use it for the purpose of protecting himself from an unfounded imputation—stating that to be the sole and *bona fide* object of the publication; and, upon the answer, in this case, it must be taken that the defendant has no purpose of gain, or to deprive another of the benefit derived from a literary composition; but that his only object is, by proving agency, to answer the imputation cast upon him."

"An injunction," continued the vice-chancellor, "restraining the publication of private letters must stand upon this foundation: that letters, whether of a private nature or upon general subjects, may be considered as the subject of literary property; and it is difficult to conceive in the abstract that they may not be so. . . . . We find Lord Eldon, however, five years later, criticising this case severely, when cited before him,[1] on the ground of the 'difficult and

[1] Gee v. Pritchard, 2 Swanst. 422.

endless questions of literary character which it would be forced upon courts to decide.'"

And the distinction has long since been abandoned as impracticable and absurd. The right which every man has to the control of the product of his own hands, can hardly be discriminated against on account of the character or merit of the production. "Why should a writing of inferior composition be precluded from being a subject of property. To establish a rule that the quality of a composition must be weighed previous to investing it with the title of property, would be forming a very dangerous precedent. What reason can be assigned why the illiterate and badly-spelt letters of an uneducated person, should not be as much the subject of property as the elegant and learned epistle of an author. The essence of the existence of the property is, the labor used in the concoction of the composition, and the reduction of ideas into a tangible and substantial form; and can it be contended that the labor is less in the former than in the latter case? Every letter is, in a general acceptance, a literary composition, however defective it may be in style, grammar, or orthography, or however trivial or elaborate in design or composition. The result of literary labor may differ widely in merit and value, but the basis upon which it rests in regard to the law of property, all kinds and sorts are alike.

The property of the author is the labor he has expended on his manuscript; which, in the case of the illiterate, might be even greater in amount than that expended by the fluent and facile and cultivated. No matter how labored or crude or inartificial the attempt to set down thoughts in words, the law will protect the author's right to it, however valuable or valueless. To a volume of burlesques—like the collection of sketches, by "Artemus Ward"—nobody would deny a copyright, yet they were burlesques of the letters of an illiterate person—and why should we protect a burlesque more than the thing burlesqued?

Again, mere printing and publishing cannot make a composition literary. If it be not literary in manuscript, it will not become so between covers. If the rule as to "literary character" would apply to letters, it would apply equally to more extensive works. We have already seen that the question of the value or merit of a literary production, will not be considered in granting it the privilege of copyright."[1]

No matter how trivial or how finished, we incline to think that the writer of a letter is the owner of its substance—and so long as he continues to be—can control the multiplication of copies of the same.

Again, were a destinction between literary and non-literary property allowed to exist, what would be the test, and who would apply it? Is it a question of law or of fact? Would the court decide the question itself, or would it cite experts to appear, and leave their testimony to a jury?

Clearly it could do neither; for the decision of the judge or the testimony of the expert, could only be the assertion of his own taste or appreciation; and the one or the other would be compelled, under oath, to decide upon a question *de gustibus*, which—it is a proverb—is *non disputandum.*

Must the test be whether the letters had been, or could, or might be published, or whether any one wanted to publish them? Clearly not, since the appeal is to equity to prevent their being published at all.

If an author's title to the copyright of his own work were to rest upon its intrinsic merit, our judges

[1] *Ante*, p. 316.

must labor to prepare themselves to be critics as well; our courts must be stocked with miscellaneous as well as legal libraries, and become lyceums and debating societies, instead of the solemn tribunals of impartial justice.

The jurisdiction of a court of equity must evidently rest upon the right of the author in whatever original ideas he has written down for preservation upon his manuscript, and it is quite immaterial, even could everybody agree upon that point, whether they are worthy of such preservation or not.

199. Again, a man's reputation and honor are as much his own as his manuscripts, or anything else that is his, and that courts of equity have a right to restrain his reputation from injury and his private feelings from outrage,[1] as in the case of Cadell v. Stewart,[2] where letters written by Robert Burns, the poet, to a lady whom he designated as Clarinda, had been given by her to a bookseller, who published them, and where the poet's family were held—as interested in his literary reputation—entitled to enjoin their appearance.

Equity also might interfere to stay the publication of letters, on the ground that such publication would be a breach of contract or of confidence, and, *à fortiori*, when they are intended to be made a source of profit, in addition to all that would be a violation of the author's actual or presumptive copyright.[3]

So, upon the principle of breach of contract, an

[1] Copinger on Copyright, 30; Dodsley v. McFarquhar (Feb. 27, 1775), which was the case of Lord Chesterfield's letters (Mor. Dict. of Dec. Lit. Prop. App. 1, 5; Br. Sup. 509).

[2] June 1, 1804, Mor. Dict. of Dec. Lit. Prop. App. 4.

[3] Copinger on Copyright, 30.

injunction was granted to restrain publication of letters written by an old lady to a young man to whom she had been foolishly attached, there being an agreement not to publish them, but to surrender them for a valuable consideration.[1]

"Were the court of chancery," says Copinger, "to interfere on any other principle than that already stated, individuals would be deprived of their defense in proving agency; orders for goods; the truth of an assertion, or some other fact, merely because the testimony establishing the true and genuine circumstances was contained in letters in which a pretended copyright was claimed."[2]

"Independent of property," said Vice-Chancellor McCoun,[3] "and disconnected therefrom, there is no ground or principle on which the jurisdiction to restrain the publication of private letters can properly rest. . . . . The publication of letters having relation exclusively to matters of private concern, written in the confidence of friendship, and being of a private and confidential nature, not intended for the public eye, carries with it the evidence of a wicked, depraved, and sinister purpose, and its own dishonor; for I know of no other law, than that which may be found in a just sense of propriety and honor, to forbid the publication of private letters or papers, not having the character of property about them. . . . . It is a gross breach of honor and trust. . . . . After all that can be done by the judicial tribunals of the country, much must be left to the dictates of conscience, to the usages

[1] Anon. v. Eaton, cited 2 V. & B. 247. *Vid.* also Story Eq. Jur. 2 Esp. 944, 950; Denis v. Leclerc, 1 Martin (La.), 297; Eyre v. Higbie, 35 Barb. 502.

[2] On Copyright, 30; Godson on C. 330.

[3] Wetmore v. Scoville, 3 Edw. Ch. 515.

of society, and to the corrective influence of public sentiment and opinion."[1] And Chancellor Walworth cites these words approvingly in a later case in the same state; and, while characterizing the violation of good morals and good manners,—which, however, a court of chancery cannot undertake to enforce—says further: "It is evident however, in relation to all these letters, that the complainant could never have considered them as of any value whatever as literary productions; for a letter cannot be considered as of value to the author, for the purpose of publication, which he would never have consented to have published,[2] either with or without the privilege of copyright. But we have already seen that the doctrine upon which the vice-chancellor proceeded must now be abandoned as impracticable, and that the sender's literary property in a letter cannot be restricted by the pupular meaning of the word "literary."

The case of Earl of Granard v. Dunkin,[3] seems very distinctly to sustain and to protect the doctrine of property in the receiver of a letter. In that case, it was sought to restrain the defendant from publishing letters from Lady Moira and Lady Granard to Lady Tyrawley during her lifetime. Lady Granard claimed these letters, not as their writer, but because she was the executrix of Lady Tyrawley; and it was

[1] These rights are, however, reciprocal; for if a letter contain private and confidential matter, which it would be scandalous or injurious to publish, it cannot make any difference, if it be published at all, whether it be published by writer or sender; and if the writer could enjoin the receiver from publishing such matter, the receiver could equally have his remedy to restrain its publication by the writer.

[2] This was before the doctrine laid down in Prince Albert v. Strange, however, which would seem to hold emphatically the reverse (2 De G. & Sm. 694, &c.).

[3] 1 Ball. & Beat. 207.

decreed that her own, as well as Lady Moira's letters, being Lady Tyrawley's, vested in her executrix.

200. Neither will equity leave the firm ground and province of contracts and borrow jurisdiction from its sister courts, for the purpose of punishing a crime,[1] nor can it enforce, apart from the right of property of which alone it will take cognizance, the performance of purely moral duties.[2] She will only restrain the publication of letters, written and sent in the course of epistolary correspondence, when there is a right of property in the writer, upon which its jurisdiction can rest.

So, in the case of an application[3] for an injunction to restrain publication of a pamphlet, entitled "The Life, Exploits, Comical Adventures, and Amorous Intrigues, of Benjamin Brandling, M.D., V.P.L.V.S., a distinguished pill-vendor, written by himself, &c.," the court held, that, as it did not appear to be an invasion of any right of either literary or medical property, although unquestionably a gross libel upon the complainant, equity could not interfere to grant one.

"It is very evident," said Chancellor Walworth in that case, "that this court cannot assume jurisdiction of the case presented by the complainant's bill, or of any other case of like nature, without infringing upon the liberty of the press, and attempting to exercise a power of preventive justice which, as the legislature has decided, cannot be safely intrusted to any tribunal." "The court of star chamber in England," said the chancellor, "once exercised the power of cutting off the ears, branding the foreheads, and slitting

[1] *Ante*, p. 29.

[2] Hoyt v. Mackenzie, 3 Barb. Ch. 320; 2 Story Eq. 948, a.

[3] Brandreth v. Lance, 8 Paige, 24.

the noses of the libelers of important personages. And, as an incident to such a jurisdiction, that court was undoubtedly in the habit of restraining the publication of such libels by injunction. Since that court was abolished, however, I believe there is but one case upon record in which any court either in this country or in England has attempted, by an injunction or order of the court, to prohibit or restrain the publication of a libel, as such, in anticipation. In the case to which I allude, the notorious Scroggs, chief justice of the court of king's bench, and his associates, decided that they might safely be intrusted with the power of prohibiting and suppressing such publications as they might deem to be libelous. They accordingly made an order of the court prohibiting any person from printing or publishing a periodical entitled 'The Weekly Packet of Advice from Rome, or a History of Popery.' The house of commons, however, considered this extraordinary exercise of power on the part of Scroggs, as a proper subject of impeachment, and I believe no judge or chancellor, from that time to the present, has attempted to follow that precedent."[1]

In case, however, of an explicit agreement by its receiver to refrain from publishing a letter, courts might interfere to prevent its publication upon other grounds, namely, to enforce and uphold a trust, or to decree a specific performance of the agreement.[2] That is, where the agreement was made before the receipt of the letter.[3]

201. The leading case upon the subject of letters

[1] Hudson's Star Chamber, 2 Collect. Jurid. 224; 8 Howell's State Trials, 198.

[2] Gee v. Pritchard, 2 Swans. 402.

[3] 1 Am. Law Reg. 456.

still continues to be Pope v. Curl,[1] decided in 1741, in which Lord Hardwicke continued an injunction, obtained by the poet Pope, to restrain the defendant from publishing a collection of his letters.

"The first question," said Lord Hardwicke, "is whether letters are within the grounds and intention of the statute.[2] I think it would be extremely mischievous to make a distinction between a book of letters, which comes out into the world either by permission of the writer or the receiver of them, and any other learned work. . . . Another objection has been made by the defendant's counsel, that, where a man writes a letter, it is in the nature of a gift to the receiver. But I am of opinion that it is only a special property in the receiver. Possibly the property of the paper may belong to him, but this does not give a license to any person whatsoever to publish them to the world, for at most the receiver has only a joint property with the writer." And to the objection insisted on by the defendant's counsel, that this was a sort of work which did not come within the meaning of the act of parliament, because it contained only letters on familiar subjects, and inquiries after the health of friends, and therefore could not properly be called a learned work, his lordship replied: "It is certain that no works have done more service to mankind than those which have appeared in this shape, upon familiar subjects, and which, perhaps, were never intended to be published, and it is this makes them so valuable; for I must confess, for my own part, that letters which are very elaborately written, and originally intended for the press, are generally the most insignificant, and very little worth any person's read-

[1] 2 Atk. 342. See remarks of Lord Mansfield in Millar v Taylor, 14 Burr, p. 2397.

[2] 8 Anne, c. 19.

ing." The injunction was continued, by the lord chancellor, only as to those letters in the book which were written by Pope, and not as to those which were written to him.

This ruling, however, militates against Lord Ellenborough's declaration in Du Bost v. Beresford,[1] that, upon an application, he would have granted an injunction to restrain the exhibition of a libelous painting. A note to Horne's Case,[2] says that this declaration "excited great astonishment in the minds of all the practitioners in the courts of equity."

Subsequent to Pope v. Curl, the next leading case in this branch of the law is that of Thompson v. Stanhope,[3] wherein the executors of Lord Chesterfield, in 1774, brought suit against Stanhope,—his natural son, —to restrain the publication, by him, of his lordship's famous "letters."

These letters were written, as is well known, to Lord Chesterfield's natural son, Philip Stanhope, who lived abroad, and was "a public character." On the latter's death, his widow came to England, where she was affectionately received by Lord Chesterfield, to whom she delivered certain of the letters in which his lordship had drawn the characters of different living persons (first keeping copies of the same), but retaining the others which treated of politics, education, and manners. After his lordship's death, the widow agreed with one Dodsley, a publisher, to deliver to him the letters treating of education, manners, &c., for publication; and accordingly these were, from time to time announced. Lord Chesterfield's executors, upon seeing the announcements, brought suit to restrain the publi-

[1] 2 Camp. R. 511.
[2] 20 Howell's State Trials, 779.
[3] Amb. 737.

cation of the letters. The widow Stanhope, in her answer, stated that, being frequently in conversation with his lordship, she had one day mentioned to him that she thought the letters he had written her late husband would form a fine system of education if published, to which he had answered: "Why, that is true, but there is too much Latin in them;" but did not express any disapprobation of the plan, only stating that he wished to destroy the letters in which he had sketched the characters of persons then living; that these letters had thereupon been restored to him, but that he had given her permission to keep the others. But the court seemed to hold that permission to keep the letters did not imply permission to publish them—and granted the injunction sought.

202. There are, however, it is to be noticed, circumstances under which the law will not allow a writer of private letters to insist on his special property in them, and to hinder their publication by others. He may, by his own acts, disentitle himself to prevent the publication of his letters to another person, and justify that other person in giving them to the world. A false accusation, brought by the writer against the recipient of the letters, which may be disproved by their publication, for example, will justify such publication; and courts of equity have refused to aid, by injunction, the writer of the letters in such a case. Sir Thomas Plumer, V. C.,[1] refused an injunction to prevent the publication of the letters, under such circumstances, where the receiver was forced to the publication, in his own justification, against charges of dishonesty and a circulation of false news.

[1] Lord & Lady Perceval v. Phipps, 2 V. & B., 19. *Vid.* also Gee v. Pritchard, 3 Swanst. 416, 419, and Folsom v. Marsh, 2 Story, 100–111.

"The distinction in that case," says Shortt,[1] "between the publication of private letters without the writer's consent, for the purpose of profit or gain, and publication for a different purpose, is treated by Lord Eldon, in Gee v. Pritchard,[2] as of no moment. His lordship considered the previous cases to have decided that, *ultra* the purposes for which the letter was sent, the property was in the sender. 'If that is the principle,' he observes, 'it is immaterial whether the publication is for the purpose of profit or not. If for profit, the party is then selling; if not for profit, he is giving that, a portion of which belongs to the writer.' The defendant in this case was the illegitimate son of the plaintiff's deceased husband, and had received many letters from the plaintiff during her husband's life-time. After her husband's death, the plaintiff ceased to be on terms of friendship with the defendant, and denied the truth of statements made by him as to the expectations which he had been led to entertain from the plaintiff and her husband. The defendant returned to the plaintiff the original letters which she had written to him, but took copies of the letters before returning them, without the plaintiff's knowledge, and advertised his intention to publish the letters, but, as he stated in his answer, for private circulation only. This he did, as he alleged, in order to clear his character from the charge of want of veracity which the plaintiff had brought against it. In this case the defendant, by returning the originals, had abandoned whatever property he had—for if he had any right of property it was in the originals—and Lord Eldon restrained the threatened publication. In giving judgment he observed, 'I do not say there may not be a

[1] L. Lit. 16.

[2] 2 Swanst. 415.

case, such as the vice-chancellor (Sir T. Plumer) thought the case before him, where the acts of the parties supply reasons for not interfering; but that differs most materially from this case. In April last, the defendant having so much of property in these letters as belongs to the receiver, and of interest in them as possessor, thinks proper to return them to the person who has in them, as Lord Hardwicke says, a joint property, keeping copies of them without apprising her, and assigning such a reason as he assigns for the return [his "being unworthy of the sentiments and expressions of kindness contained in them"]. Now I say, that if, in the case before the vice-chancellor, Lady Percival had given to Phipps a right to publish her letters, this case is the converse of that; and that the defendant, if he previously had it, has renounced the right of publication.'

"Lord Eldon was careful to rest his decision in this case on the ground of the plaintiff's property in the letters (as determined by previous cases), and not on any considerations as to wounded feelings. When reference was made to such considerations by the defendant's counsel, his lordship interposed: 'I will relieve you from that argument. The question will be, whether the bill has stated facts of which the court can take notice, as a case of civil property, which it is bound to protect. The injunction cannot be maintained on any principle of this sort, that if a letter has been written in the way of friendship, either the continuance or the discontinuance of that friendship affords a reason for the interference of the court.'"[1]

203. We have seen that—by what has been

[1] 5 T. R. 245. *Vid.* also Wetmore v. Scoville, 3 Ed. Ch. 527; Woolsey v Judd, 4 Duer, 382.

called the law of literary accession—if the literary composition is the result of labor performed by one in the employ of another, the literary property therein belongs to the employer.

So, if the writer of a letter be employed by a principal, and write a letter in the course of the employment, and concerning its subject-matter: that peculiar property in letters which we have ascertained to remain in the writer, would, by the same rule, inhere in the principal. And if the principal be also the recipient of the letter, the principal would own not only the paper and material part of the letter, but also the property of the writer thereof. So, if the agent or servant of a company write a letter, apparently on behalf of the company, to a shareholder, it is the property of the company, and the agent or servant cannot prevent the company from publishing the letter.[1] Where the solicitor of an insurance company established in London, wrote a letter not marked "private" or "confidential," to one of the shareholders in the country, in reference to certain shares allotted to the country shareholder, he was held not entitled to restrain the publication of this letter in a pamphlet, published after the winding up of the company by its late manager, to whom a copy of it had been sent by the shareholder. "If the solicitor of an insurance company established in London," said the master of the rolls, in this case, "by the direction of the directors, wrote a letter to one of the shareholders in the country, it is clear that such letter is not the property of the solicitor, and that he cannot say that the company have not a right to publish it. Take it a step further, and assume that the solicitor wrote a letter, but not by the direction or on behalf of the directors, though

[1] Howard v. Gunn, 32 Beav. 465.

it had all the appearance of being written on their behalf, and by their direction. Thus, if it were written to a person who proposed to take shares in the company, and it related to the affairs of the company, and contained authoritative information on behalf of the company, in answer to an application for shares, and the person who receives it treats it as such, and sends back to the company, objecting to its contents, shall the solicitor be allowed to complain of its publication, and to insist that it is a private letter, though it appears to be written on behalf of the directors? The answer is, if that be so, it ought not to have been written. It has all the appearance of having been written by the plaintiff, on their behalf, and the shareholder to whom it is addressed so treats it, for he writes to the manager in answer to it. Can the plaintiff be allowed to say that the company have no right to publish it? and if they have, is not the defendant entitled, as regards the plaintiff, to bring it forward? It is obvious that this was not a private letter, and was not intended to be a private letter."

But all manuscript letters and communications sent expressly or impliedly for publication to any periodical,—such as a newspaper, review, or magazine,—and received by its editors or proprietors, become the property of the person or periodical to whom they are addressed or directed, and cannot be published by any other person obtaining possession of them.[1] Book manuscripts are ranked as third-class matter by the United States post-office department; can be sent by mail, to the publisher, at the same rates as transient printed matter, proof-sheets, and corrected proof-sheets, &c., at the prepaid rate of one cent for each ounce or fraction of an ounce. All matter of this description

[1] Copinger on Copyright, 32; Hogg v. Kirby, 8 Ves. 215.

which is inclosed in an envelope, which conceals it so as to prevent the post-office authorities examining it, without breaking the envelope, will be charged letter postage.[1] It has been held that publishers are liable for the loss of manuscripts sent them—even when they have not requested them from their authors, or are not in the habit of paying for those accepted—where the author's address accompanied the manuscript, and no notification was sent him that it would be returned to him on receipt of the postage which it was necessary to prepay.

A dramatic manuscript can be copyrighted at any time, even though its contents have been previously represented on the stage; and such representation will in no case be a dedication of its contents to the public.[2]

204. A manuscript written in another country, if brought to this, will not lose its character of personal property which it possessed in that.[3] But if such manuscript, or a copy thereof, be brought against the will of its proprietor, the literary property in its contents will not vest in the possessor of the manuscript.

And the manuscript may be a personal chattel on this side of the water, although its contents have been copyrighted on the other.[4]

205. If an author sell and dispose of his manuscript, in specie, to a publisher, with the express agreement and understanding that he parts with its possession, he

[1] U. S. Official Postal Guide.

[2] Roberts v. Myers, 13 Month. Law Rep. N. S. 396.

[3] Story Conf. L. § 376, *et seq.*; Keene v. Wheatley, 9 Am. Law Reg. 33; Keene v. Clarke, 5 Rob. 38; Keene v. Kimball, 6 Gray (Mass.) 542; Palmer v. De Witt, 47 N. Y. 532; Crowe v. Aiken, 2 Biss. 208.

[4] Id.

cannot afterwards copyright the work in his own name, but the copyright belongs to the publisher.[1]

206. The right to take out copyright of a work, as a rule, belongs to the owner of the manuscript.[2] Copyrights of manuscripts may be entered, at any time, by depositing a printed title thereof; and the time of completion of the manuscript work does not affect the title. In the case of unprinted dramatic compositions, the notice of copyright, required by the act, does not apply; neither does the requirement of two copies of the publication. But if the title, once deposited, is changed, or in any way altered, a distinct entry must be made; and there must continue to be a distinct entry for every such change in the title. This rule also applies to photographs, prints, and engravings, of every description. The librarian of congress is not at liberty to record or issue certificates of copyright upon written titles. The law explicitly requires a printed copy of the title of the article, for which the copyright is desired, to be sent to the office of the librarian, before the author or proprietor can be entitled to receive his copyright. The particular form or style of type is immaterial; and only the precise words of the title need be printed. It does not appear to be necessary that the whole title-page shall be filed.[3]

207. It may not be out of place, in connection with the subject of property in letters, to allude to postal facilities, regulations, and laws. The conveyance of dispatches, and royal letters and messages, by regular couriers, was a feature that appears, at a very early date, to have entered into the policy of every ancient state. In the book of Job, which is conceived, by some, to be a fragment of the earliest literature, the

[1] Paige v. Banks, 7 Blatchf. 152. [2] Id.

[3] *Post*, chapter on Copyright, Vol. II.

transitoriness of life is compared to the fleetness of a post[1]—the Hebrew word there employed signifying a runner or courier. And again, in Jeremiah,[2] we read: "One post shall run to meet another, and one messenger to meet another, to show the king of Babylon that his city is taken." So, in the third chapter of the book of Esther,[3] we read that "letters were sent by the posts into all the king's provinces." In Persia, more especially, the institution of regular posts appears to have been an object of attention, as early, at least, as the reign of Cyrus. A passage in the Cyropædia of Xenophon is very clear and particular on this head: "We have been informed, also, of another invention of Cyrus for promoting the prosperity of his empire, by providing a method of communication whereby intelligence might be brought of what happened in places the most remote. Having considered what journey a horse was capable of performing, in the course of a day, he ordered stables, accordingly, to be prepared at the proper distances from each other, and stationed horses in each of them, with persons to take care of them, and have them in readiness. He placed also a person at each of these stations, who might receive the letters brought to them and hand them over to the others, taking due care of the tired men and horses, and providing others fresh and prepared for going forward. In this manner the conveyance was to be carried on successfully by night as well as by day,—an arrangement so complete, that Xenophon continued: "Some say the progress was more rapid than the flight of cranes. If this be an over-statement, it is, however

[1] Job, ix. 25.
[2] Jeremiah, li. 31.
[3] Verse 13.

certain, that no journey by a human being, made on land, was ever so expeditious."[1] The same institution of posts in the Persian empire, as it existed in the time of Xerxes, is thus noticed in Herodotus. A man and horse were posted at the regular intervals of a day's journey, to deliver the letters to each of the succession, till they reached the place of their destination. From one relay to the other, the journey was to be performed in the time prescribed, whatever might be the state of the weather or the obstacles of the way; and the historian remarks, "that nothing mortal was ever known to proceed with greater celerity."[2] This institution is expressed by the word *αγγαρειον*; in the Ionic idiom of Herodotus *αγγαρηϊον*, a term borrowed from the language of Persia, where it appears, if not to have had its origin, at least to have attained to great perfection. The messengers employed had the name of *αγγελοι*, angari; and the noun, from its primary use in designating the institution and conduct of the posts, came at length to indicate any compulsory service, but especially a journey by constraint. The verb *αγγαρευειν*, has also its derivative sense, and is used by St. Matthew:[3] "Whosoever shall compel thee to go (*αγγαρευσει*) a mile, go with him twain." The force of which word in the original is not properly understood but by adverting to the authority of the *αγγαροι*, to press others into their service by way of expediting the post.[4] The principal couriers, or postmasters of Persia, appear to have been persons of some importance in the dominions of the Persian monarchs, and, if we may credit Plutarch,

[1] Xenoph. *Κυρου Παιδειας, βιβλ. Η.* 642; Ed. Hutch. 1727.
[2] Herod. Uran. 98.
[3] Matt. v. 41.
[4] Roberts, p. 40.

Darius Codomannus, was originally one of that order; a circumstance, among many others, affording some confirmation to the testimony which history bears to the pains bestowed in this quarter of the globe, at an early period, on the means of conveying intelligence and instruction between places at great distances from each other. Throughout the eastern states a similar attention to the establishment of posts, or the provisions for the rapid conveyance of important despatches, appears to have been paid, and continued to modern times. In the dominion of the Mogul emperors, as well as in provinces subjugated by the Turks and Tartars, the speed of couriers on foot, or on the backs of horses or dromedaries, has been always an object of great importance. A modern traveler, who in 1840 published accounts of travels in British India and Bochara, alludes to the post as follows: "We continued our march to Tugduluk, and passed the Soorkh road, or Red river, by a bridge, with a variety of other small streams, which pour the melted snow of the Sufued Kob into that rivulet. On our way we could distinguish that a road had once been made, and also the remains of the post-houses which had been constructed every five or six miles by the Mogul emperors to keep up a communication between Delhi and Cabool. They may even be traced across the mountains of Balkh; for both Humaioon and Aurungzebe, in their youth, were governors of that country. "What an opinion," adds the traveler, "does this inspire of the grandeur of the Mogul empire; it had a system of communcation between the most distant provinces as perfect as the posts of the Cæsars."

Up to this time, however, and, indeed, for a long period thereafter, we find no traces of any provision for the employment of the post by private parties or by the public, even had there been (as there probably was not) a disposition on their part to take advantage of it. These conveyances were contrived only for the service of the state, or rather of the court, and for the transmission of instruction and dispatches; and if they were occasionally made use of by private persons, or for personal communication, the risk of disclosure must have made it an unfit and unsafe vehicle. Servants, hired messengers, or traveling friends, furnished the only means of carrying on a free correspondence; and it is easy to imagine how greatly the uncivilized, unsettled, and tumultuous state of those ancient communities multiplied the chances of miscarriage, not to mention the negligence or treachery of the private, irresponsible hands to which the charge was necessarily committed. The old historians record numerous instances of subtle expedients and contrivances to transmit intelligence so as to avoid the danger of treachery or discovery. Mention of a table, covered with wax after the letters had been engraved on the wood, and sent by Demaratus to the Lacedemonians, is made by Herodotus,[1] who abounds in similar anecdotes.

The transmission of information by letters was always attended with risk or uncertainty in the disorderly state of ancient manners—the establishment of posts remaining for a long period the organ of courts and governments rather than a medium of general communication.

Private hands and special messengers were perpetually betraying their employers, as we may learn from the history, as well as the drama, of the ancients. Herodotus records a striking instance of treachery in

[1] Herod. Polym. 239.

the conduct of the internuncius of Histiæus, who, instead of carrying the epistles of that general to his friends, in Ionia, who were plotting with him against the Persian government, delivered them to Artaphernes, the great Persian satrap and commander in that province.[1] The stratagem of Harpagus, who dispatched a letter in the body of a hare to the young Cyrus, to persuade him to take up arms against his grandfather, Astyages, is one among several curious methods of eluding discovery, in the conveyance of secret intelligence, which we meet with in the same historian.[2] The story of Artabazus is as follows: That general having laid siege to Potidæa, was informed that Timoxenus was disposed to deliver up the city by treachery; and it being a matter of the greatest difficulty and danger to interchange intelligence with him, the following expedient was adopted: A letter was written on a scroll, and wound round an arrow, which was shot from a bow so as to reach a certain place agreed upon, and an answer was sent back by the same method. On one occasion, however, Artabazus missed the mark; and the arrow, instead of falling where it was intended, struck the shoulder of one of the citizens. The people, gathering round him and taking up the arrow, on which they found the letter, carried it to the proper authorities, and thus the plot was discovered.[3]

Another more subtle method[4] is related of Histiæus. Being detained at Susa, by the Persian king, and wishing to convey to Aristagoras, at Miletus, in Ionia, information of his intended defection, he shaved the head of one of his servants on whose fidelity he

[1] Herod. Lib. vi. s. 4.
[2] Id. Lib. i. s. 123-4.
[3] Id. Lib. viii. s. 128
[4] Id. Lib. v. s. 95.

could rely, and wrote, or rather engraved, upon his skull, a letter containing the secret. After this was done, the hair was suffered to grow again; and as soon as the head was covered, the man was sent to Miletus, where he safely arrived, and delivered his message to Aristagoras, who was to cause his head to

[1] Humboldt, in his "Vues Pittoresques des Cordillères," relates, that in order to maintain postal communication between the shores of the South Pacific and the province of Jaen de Brancamoros, Indians are employed, who, during two days, descend the river Guancabamba, or Chamaya, and afterwards the Amazon river, as far as Tomependa. The courier, before he commits himself to the water, wraps the few letters, with which he is charged monthly, sometimes in a handkerchief, and at other times in a species of drawers called guayuco, and this he disposes in the form of a turban round his head. In this turban he also places the large knife or cutlass with which he is always provided, less as means of defense than to assist him in making his way though the underwood, for the Guancabamba is not navigable throughout, by reason of the great number of falls and rapids; these the postman passes by land, taking again to the water as soon as all danger from them is over. To assist him in swimming, the Indian provides himself with a log of very light wood, generally the trunk of the bombax. These men, who are known in the country as the swimming couriers—el coreo que nada—have no occasion to encumber themselves with provisions, their wants being abundantly supplied by the hospitable inhabitants of the cottages which they pass on the banks of the rivers. A similar mode of securing the letters entrusted to their care, is adopted by the couriers of Hindostan. When compelled, as they frequently are, to cross a river by swimming, they deposit their letters in the turban, and thus convey them safely to the opposite shore. One of these men having failed to make his appearance at the appointed time, messengers were dispatched to search for him. On the banks of a river which flowed across the route lay the dead body of an alligator, with its jaws distended as if it had suffered a violent death. They proceeded to examine it more closely, and discovered the head of the unfortunate courier completely choking up the passage of the throat, so that the animal had died from strangulation; the letter was found uninjured in the turban.

be again shorn, and to read what was inscribed upon it.[1]

The scytale of the Spartans was a contrivance made of two small cylinders of wood, smoothed and polished, and of the same length and size. One of these was taken by a general on his departure for service, and its fellow retained by the magistrates at home. Round one of these pieces of wood a leather strap was wound, the edges touching each other in every part with a perfect adjustment, and ending exactly with the wood at each extremity. When a secret despatch was to be sent, it was written along the cylinder and over the places where the edges of the strap were in contact. When the strap was removed, the letters and words were detached so as to fall into illegible disorder and confusion; and in this state it was sent to the general, who alone could make out the sense, by winding the strap round his own cylinder, which brought again all the letters into their proper places, making them coincide as they had done when they were written upon the cylinder in the hands of the council at Sparta; and thus secrecy was maintained between the parties.[1]

It was customary with the Roman generals, when writing to the senate the news of a victory gained by their valor and conduct, to fold their letters in laurel leaves. A report had reached Rome of a defeat supposed to have been sustained by Posthumius, in a battle with the Æqui, which spread great consternation through the city. But the tide of success was turned; and the Romans achieved so complete a victory as nearly to annihilate the army of the Æqui.

[1] Aul. Gell. Noct. Att. lib. xvii. c. 9.

Litteræ laureatæ announced the event, and proclaimed that the enemy's army was routed.[1]

The Romans were far behind the eastern nations in adopting the convenience of the post. It does not appear, even in the time of Cicero, that any public provision had been made for the conveyance of letters of any description. The carriage was committed to some private hand, or special messenger, usually a slave, who was called tabellarius. Men of high condition often employed slaves, for freedmen, to write their letters, called amanuenses; which domestics were held in great consideration, as persons of a very confidential character. Sometimes, indeed, the proper and expedient time for the delivery of the letter was left to the discretion of the tabellarius.[2]

It appears, from Suetonius, that Augustus Cæsar felt the inconvenience arising from the want of a public provision for the transmission of important despatches; and that, in order to establish a speedy intercourse with the provinces of the empire, he first stationed young men at moderate intervals along the high roads, and afterwards chariots, to facilitate the transport of letters, and oral intelligence.[3] And this

[1] "Æquorum exercitum deletum" (Tit. Lib. I. v. c. 28).—Roberts.

[2] Cicero writes to Brutus (Cic. ad Fam. lib. xi. ep. xvi.; and see Harat. lib. i. ep. xiii.): "Permagni interest, quo tibi hæc tempore epistola reddita sit: utrum cum sollicitudinis aliquid haberes, ad cum ab omni molestia vacuus esses. Itaque ei præcepi, quem ad te misi, ut tempus observaret epistolæ tibi reddendæ. Nam quemadmodum coram qui ad nos intempestive adeunt, molesti sæpe sunt; sic epistolæ offendunt non loco redditæ. Si autem ut spero, nihil te perturbat, nihil impedit: et ille, cui mandavi, satis scite, et commode tempus ad te cepit adeundi: confido me, quod velim, facile a te impetraturum."

[3] Sueton, August.

continued to be the practice of his successors. The word post is Roman, if we suppose it, as is probable, to be derived from positus, the carriers being placed, or posted, at certain settled distances from each other. It does not seem, however, that regular relays of horses were part of the institution. The messengers seized any horses they could find, till Trajan appointed regular horse-stations for the conveyance of despatches and intelligence, of which a particular mention is made in the Theodosian Code, "de Cursu Publico." It was not, however, till in quite modern times, that this most useful provision came under a regular and general management, so as to be a system of popular economy and common convenience. Lewis Hornigk, who has furnished, in the German language, a full and accurate treatise on posts, tells us that they were first settled on this large scale, by the Count de Taxis, at his own expense; in acknowledgment of which the Emperor Matthias, in 1616, gave him in fief the charge of postmaster under him and his successors.

It is said that Charlemagne established stations for couriers, who rode upon horseback, delivering messages and parcels; but that the custom lapsed at his death, and was revived in France by Louis XI., who made his stations four French miles apart. But Rollin relates that France was indebted, for the great conveniency of the post, to the university of Paris. That university being at the time of its institution the only one in the kingdom, and having great numbers of scholars resorting to it from all parts of the country, took into its employment messengers, whose business it was, not only to bring clothes, silver, and gold for the students, but also to carry bags of law proceedings, informations, and inquests; and, in process of time, to conduct all sorts of persons, indifferently, to and from Paris, finding horses and diet; as also to convey letters, parcels, and packets for the public, as well as the university. In the university registers of the faculty of arts these messengers are often styled *nuncii volantes.* Until, in 1576, by a royal edict, Henry III. granted certain privileges to royal messengers, similar to those which his predecessors had granted to the messengers maintained at the charge of the university, the students were the only post-riders, and the university the only postal department of France. It was in recognition of its services that Louis XV., by his decree of the council of state, of the 14th of April, 1719, and by his letters patent, registered in parliament, and in the chamber of accounts, ordered that, in all the colleges of the university, the students should be taught gratis; and to that end, for the time to come, appropriated to the university one-twenty-eighth part of the revenue arising from the general lease or farm of the posts and messengers of France, which twenty-eighth amounted in that year to 184,000 livres, or about $37,000. In England we find but little trace of anything like a post establishment till about the twenty-third year of Elizabeth. In the early stages of society, private persons departed but seldom from their homes or families, and the business of commerce was transacted with very little complication. The king's letters and writs to summon his barons, command his sheriffs, and collect his revenues, were carried, by special messenger, through the medium of a general establishment, charges for the conduct and expenses of which, make frequent items in the records of the royal household; and this practice was imitated by the more powerful nobles, who had their *nuncii* among their retainers.

For these *nuncii*, by degrees, fixed posts and stations were established, for the maintenance of regular relays; and in the time of Edward IV., during the war with Scotland, certain posts, twenty miles apart, are said to have been fixed for a succession of carriers, who were so well equipped and furnished with means, as to expedite the conveyance at the rate of one hundred miles per diem. By statute 2 and 3 Edw. VI., ch. 3, "the rate for the hire of post-horses, for the conveyance of letters, was fixed at one penny per mile."

In 1581, Thomas Randolph was appointed chief postmaster-general of England, and seems to have occupied himself more with the establishment and supervision of post-houses, than with the introduction of any great improvements in the transmission of the mails.[1] There was no complete organization of mail service, in England, until during the reign of James I., who constituted the office of postmaster of England for foreign parts, and appointed Matthew Le Quester the first postmaster, with reversion to his son. Le Quester appointed William Frizell and Thomas Witherings his deputies. The latter became postmaster-general in 1635, and was directed to establish running-posts between London and Edinburgh, to go night and day, and come back in six days. In 1644, Edmund Prideaux, a member of the house of commons, was appointed master of the posts, and first established a weekly conveyance of letters into all parts of the nation. In 1656 an act was passed to

[1] When the Spaniards invaded Peru, fifty-four years before Randolph's appointment, they had found an admirable system of postal communication in operation from Quito to Cuzco, the couriers winding around their waists the quipu, a species of sign-writing by means of knotted cords. News of the invaders was thus transported to the capital, as it had been by pictures, when the Spaniards landed in Mexico.

settle the postage of England, Scotland, and Ireland, fixing the rates of letter postage and the prices for post-horses.[1] Rowland Hill proposed, in a pamphlet, the sweeping changes which have connected his name illustriously with the postal service in 1837.

Parliament adopted the changes in 1839, and they went into operation in 1840, under Hill's supervision. Inland postage was reduced to the uniform rate of one penny for a single half ounce; the franking privilege was abolished, and to the dispatch of the mails at more frequent periods, and increased speed in the delivery of letters, was added prepayment, by stamps. In 1848 the transmission of books by post was granted, at first, at 6*d.* per lb. This was subsequently modified so as to give increased facilities for forwarding proofs, pictures, &c., at low prices.[2] The money-order system

[1] "The rates of postage, previous to the act of 1645, were, for a single piece of paper: Under 80 miles, 2*d.*; between 80 and 140 miles, 4*d.*; above 140, 6*d.*; and on the borders and in Scotland, 8*d.* That act raised the rates to 14*d.* for a distance of more than 300 miles, from which sum they were diminished according to the distance, down to 2*d.* for 7 miles and under. Between this period and 1838, although a multitude of acts relative to postal affairs were passed, the rates were not materially changed. All manner of devices for avoiding the payment of postage were adopted. The franking privilege was at an early period granted to members of parliament and officers of the government, and was much abused; and franks were sold openly."—American Encyclopædia.

[2] In 1849, the French mail tariff was fixed as follows: For letters within Paris, 2 sous (2 cents nearly) when the weight is under 13 grammes (not quite half an ounce), 4 sous if over 15 and under 30 grammes, &c.; for letters to or from other parts of France, Algeria, and Corsica, 4 sous if under 15 grammes, &c. If not prepaid, one-half is added to these rates. Newspapers must always be prepaid, but throughout France the postage is only 1 sou, and if treating on questions of political or social economy, only half that price. For foreign countries, the weight prescribed for single postage is 7½ grammes, or about ¼ oz. In 1859, the total number of French

was copied from the Germans. In the colonies a postal system was projected as early as 1692, and introduced into Virginia under Sir Edmond Andros. An act, passed shortly after his arrival, in 1693 sets forth a royal patent to Thomas Neale to establish a post in the American colonies for the transportation of letters and packets, " at such rates as the planters should agree to give," or proportionable to the rates of the English post-office. Rates of a postage were accordingly authorized, and the establishment of a post-office in each county. Similar laws being passed in Massachusetts and other colonies,—not, however, without the exhibition of some doubts and jealousy,—a colonial post-office system, though of a very limited and imperfect character, was presently established under this patent.[1] Neale's patent for colonial posts having expired, an act of parliament extended the British post-office system to America. A chief office was established at New York, to which letters were to be conveyed by regular packets across the Atlantic. The same act regulated the rates of postage to be paid in the plantations, exempted the posts from ferriage, and enabled postmasters to recover their dues by summary process. A line of posts was presently established on Neale's old routes, north to the Piscataqua, and south to Philadelphia, irregularly extended, a few years after, to Williamsburg, in Virginia, the post leaving Philadelphia for the south as often as letters enough were lodged to pay the expense. The

post-offices was 3,703; the total number of persons employed in the postal service was about 28,000. In 1821, the receipts were 24,000,000 francs ($4,732,000); in 1859, 58,308,000 francs ($11,256,444). The number of letters conveyed by post in France in 1859 was 259,450,000; 90 per cent. of the whole number being prepaid.—American Encyclopœdia.

[1] Hildreth's History of the United States, ii. 181.

postal communication subsequently established with the Carolinas was still more irregular,[1] but was not organized till 1710. By act of parliament of that year, the postmaster-general of the colonies was "to keep his chief letter office in New York, and other chief offices, at some convenient place or places, in other of her majesty's provinces or colonies in America." The revenue was of course very small. In 1753 Benjamin Franklin was appointed postmaster-general for the colonies, and was guaranteed the sum of £600 per annum for the salary of himself and his assistant.[2]

After Franklin was dismissed from his office of postmaster, by the royal government, one William Goddard seems to have traveled from colony to colony, exerting himself to get up a "constitutional post-office" in opposition to the royal mail, which, by this time was nearly broken down from failure of postages. Finally the Congress of the Confederation established a post-office system of its own, and appointed Franklin postmaster-general.[3]

In 1789, the reorganization of the general post-office was delayed till more complete information could be obtained, the establishment being, meanwhile, continued as it then stood. Franklin, the first continental postmaster-general, had been succeeded in that office by his son-in-law, Richard Bache, and he by Ebenezer Hazard, who still held it.[4] President Wash-

[1] Hildreth's Hist. of the United States, 262.

[2] Franklin's first astounding innovation was in 1760, when he startled the colonies by proposing to run a stage-wagon, to carry the mail from Philadelphia to Boston, once a week, starting from each city on Monday morning, and reaching its destination by Saturday night!

[3] Hildreth's History of the United States, iii. 89.

[4] Id. 2 ser. i. 105.

ington appointed Samuel Osgood postmaster-general upon his inauguration in 1789.

"Upon a bill," says Hildreth,[1] "for the organization of the post-office system, the same difference of opinion arose which had defeated any organization of that department by the preceding congress. The propriety of vesting in the president, or the postmaster-general, authority to designate and establish post-roads was urged, on the ground of the better knowledge of the subject likely to be possessed by an officer whose whole attention was devoted to it, and free from those local influences to which members of congress might be subjected. But in the act as passed, this authority was reserved to congress. A power, however, by way of compromise, was vested in the postmaster-general, to establish cross post-routes—the contractors undertaking to carry the mail for the postage. The postmaster-general was also authorized to appoint his assistants, and all deputy postmasters; and, after advertising for proposals, to make contracts for carrying the mail by stage-coaches or on horseback, as he might judge convenient; but the whole expenses of the department were to be paid out of the income. The postmaster-general was to settle quarterly with his deputies, and himself as often with the secretary of the treasury. The postage was fixed at rates varying from six cents, for distances of thirty miles or less, to twenty-five cents, for distances of four hundred and fifty miles or over, with like amounts for each inclosure—rates persevered in for more than fifty years, till the danger of private competition led to more moderate charges."

"Newspapers were to pay one cent each, for every hundred miles or less, and a cent and a half for greater

[1] History of the United States, 2 ser. , 485.

distances. The franking privilege was given to members of congress, during the session and twenty days afterward; also to the principal executive officers. An attempt was made to strike out this provision, but without success. Robbery of the mail, or embezzlement, by any officer of the post, of letters containing money or valuable papers, was made a capital offense; the opening, obtaining, or destroying other letters was made punishable by a fine of three thousand dollars, and six months' imprisonment. The salary of the postmaster-general was fixed at two thousand dollars, and that office, upon the resignation of Osgood, was conferred on Timothy Pickering. The deputy postmasters were to be paid, as theretofore, by a commission on their receipts; but none were to receive more than eighteen hundred dollars. Though considered, at first, as an inferior office, not entitling the holder to a seat in the cabinet, the extent to which its patronage has reached has since made the station of postmaster-general, in the eyes of politicians at least, one of the most important posts in the government. Perhaps it was a perception of the influence thus to be exerted, that made Jefferson so urgent, with the president, that the general superintendent of the post-office should be annexed to his department, rather than to Hamilton's—a request which he backed with the suggestion that the treasury department possessed already such an influence as to swallow up the whole executive powers, and to threaten to overshadow even the office of president.[1] Return J. Meigs, the governor of Ohio, was appointed postmaster-general, in the place of Granger, long distrusted as of the discontented faction, and who now provoked his dismission by giving to Leib, a conspicuous leader of the same

[1] Hildreth's History of the United States, 2 ser.

clique, the lucrative office of postmaster of Philadelphia."[1]

The postmaster-general was first made a cabinet officer, under President Jackson.

The present postal regulations of the United States provide as follows:

[1] Hildreth's History of the United States, 2 ser.

[2] Following is the act of congress approved June 23d, 1874, and sections explanatory thereof:

Sec. 5. That on and after the 1st day of January, 1875, on all newspapers and periodical publications mailed from a known office of publication or news-agency, and addressed to regular subscribers or news-agents, postage shall be charged at the following rates: On newspapers and periodical publications, issued weekly and oftener, two cents a pound or fraction thereof; less frequently three cents a pound or fraction thereof: Provided, That nothing in this act shall be held to change or amend section 99 of the act entitled, "An act to revise, consolidate, and amend the statutes relating to the post-office department," approved June 8th, 1872.

Sec. 6. That on and after the 1st day of January, 1875, upon the receipt of such newspapers and periodical publications at the office of mailing, they shall be weighed in bulk, and postage paid thereon by a special adhesive stamp, to be devised and furnished by the postmaster-general, which shall be affixed to such matter, or to the sack containing the same, or upon a memorandum of such mailing, or otherwise, as the postmaster-general may, from time to time, provide by regulation.

Sec. 7. That newspapers, one copy to each actual subscriber residing within the county where the same are printed, in whole or in part, and published, shall go free through the mails; but the same shall not be delivered at letter-carrier offices or distributed by carriers, unless postage is paid thereon as by law provided.

Sec. 8. That all mailable matter of the third class, referred to in section 133 of the act entitled "An act to revise, consolidate, and amend the statutes relating to the post-office department," approved June 8th, 1872, may weigh not exceeding four pounds for each package thereof, and postage shall be charged thereon at the rate of one cent for each ounce or fraction thereof; but nothing herein contained shall be held to

Letters in the United States cannot be carried out of the mail except in postage-stamped envelopes. One not acting as a common carrier, may carry a

change or amend section 134 of said act. (Amended by act of March 3d, 1875, making it read one cent for each ounce.)

Sec. 9. That the postmaster-general, when in his judgment it shall be necessary, may prescribe, by regulation, an affidavit in form, to be taken by each publisher of any newspaper or periodical publication sent through the mails under the provisions of this act, or news-agent who distributes any of such newspapers or periodical publications under the provisions of this act, or employee of such publisher or news-agent, stating that he will not send, or knowingly permit to be sent, through the mails, any copy or copies of such newspapers or periodical publications, except to regular subscribers thereto, or news-agents, without prepayment of the postage thereon at the rate of one cent for each two ounces or fractional part thereof; and if such publisher or news-agent, or employee of such publisher or news-agent, when required by the postmaster-general or any special agent of the post-office department to make such affidavit, shall refuse so to do, and shall thereafter, without having taken such affidavit, deposit any newspapers in the mail for transmission, he shall be deemed guilty of a misdemeanor; and, on conviction, shall be fined not exceeding one thousand dollars for each refusal; and if any such person shall knowingly and willfully mail any matter without the payment of postage as provided by this act, or procure the same to be done with the intent to avoid the prepayment of postage due thereon; or if any postmaster or post-office official shall knowingly permit any such matter to be mailed without the prepayment of postage as provided in this act, and in violation of the provisions of the same, he or they shall be deemed guilty of a misdemeanor, and, on conviction thereof, shall be fined not more than one thousand dollars, or imprisoned not exceeding one year, or both, in the discretion of the court.

Sec. 11. That the sixty-third, eightieth, eighty-first, eighty-second, eighty-third, eighty-fourth, and eighty-sixth sections of the said "act to revise, consolidate, and amend the statutes relating to the post-office department," approved June 8th, 1872, be amended to read as follows:

"Sec. 63. That the postmasters, except the postmaster at New York city, whose annual salary is hereby fixed at six thousand dollars, shall be divided into four classes, as follows: The first class shall embrace all those whose annual salaries

sealed letter, whether in a stamped envelope or not; but to continue so to do, for hire or profit, will subject to a penalty of one hundred and fifty dollars. News-

are not more than four thousand dollars nor less than three thousand dollars; the second class shall embrace all those whose annual salaries are less than three thousand dollars but not less than two thousand dollars; the third class shall embrace all those whose annual salaries are less than two thousand dollars but not less than one thousand dollars; the fourth class shall embrace all postmasters whose annual compensation, exclusive of their commissions on the money-order business of their offices, amounts to less than one thousand dollars.

"Sec. 80. That the postmaster at New York City and postmasters of the first, second, and third classes, shall be appointed and may be removed by the president, by and with the advice and consent of the senate, and shall hold their offices for four years, unless sooner removed or suspended according to law; and postmasters of the fourth class shall be appointed and may be removed by the postmaster-general, by whom all appointments and removals shall be notified to the auditor for the post-office department.

"Sec. 81. That the compensation of the postmaster at New York city shall be six thousand dollars per annum, and the respective compensations of postmasters of the first, second, and third classes shall be annual salaries, assigned in even hundreds of dollars, and payable in quarterly payments, to be ascertained and fixed, by the postmaster-general, from their respective quarterly returns to the auditor for the post-office department, or copies or duplicates thereof, for four quarters immediately preceding the adjustment or readjustment, by adding to the whole amount of box-rents, not exceeding two thousand dollars per annum, commissions also not to exceed two thousand dollars per annum on the other postal revenues of the office, at the following rates, namely: On the first one hundred dollars per quarter, fifty per centum; on all over one hundred dollars and not over four hundred dollars per quarter, forty per centum; on all over four hundred and not over two thousand four hundred dollars per quarter, thirty per centum; and on all over two thousand four hundred dollars per quarter, ten per centum. And in order to ascertain the amount of the postal receipts of each office, the postmaster-general may require postmasters to furnish duplicates of their quarterly returns to the auditor, at such times and for such periods as he

papers, magazines, and periodicals, may be carried out of the mail for sale or distribution to subscribers, but

may deem necessary in each case: provided, that whenever, by reason of the extension of free delivery of letters, the box-rents of any post-office are decreased, the postmaster-general may allow, out of the receipts of such office, a sum sufficient to maintain the salary thereof at the amount at which it had been fixed before the decrease in box-rents.

"Sec. 82. That the compensation of postmasters of the fourth class shall be the box-rents collected at their offices, and commissions on other postal revenues of their offices at the rate of sixty per centum on the first one hundred dollars or less per quarter; fifty per centum on the next three hundred dollars or less per quarter; forty per centum on the excess above four hundred dollars per quarter; the same to be ascertained and allowed by the auditor, in the settlement of the quarterly accounts of such postmasters: provided, that when the aggregate annual compensation, exclusive of commissions on money-order business of any postmaster of this class, shall amount to one thousand dollars, the auditor shall report such fact to the postmaster-general, in order that such postmaster may be assigned to his proper class, and his salary fixed as heretofore provided.

"Sec. 83. That the salaries of postmasters of the first, second, and third classes, except that of the postmaster at New York city, shall be readjusted by the postmaster-general once in two years, and in special cases as much oftener as he may deem expedient.

"Sec. 84. That the postmaster-general shall make all orders assigning or changing the salaries of postmasters in writing, and record them in his journal, and notify the change to the auditor; and any change made in such salaries shall not take effect until the first day of the quarter next following such order: provided, that in cases of not less than fifty per centum increase or decrease in the business of any post-office, the postmaster-general may adjust the salary of the postmaster at such office, to take effect from the first day of the quarter or period the returns for which form the basis of readjustment.

"Sec. 86. That the postmaster-general may designate offices at the intersection of mail routes as distributing or separating offices; and where any such office is of the third or fourth class he may make a reasonable allowance to the postmaster for the necessary cost of clerical services arising from such duties." . . . .

if put into a post-office for delivery, postage must be paid thereon.

Sec. 12. That section 245, section 246, section 247, section 251, and section 253 of the act entitled "an act to revise, consolidate, and amend the statutes relating to the post-office department," approved June 8th, 1872, be amended to read as follows:

Sec. 245. That every proposal for carrying the mail shall be accompanied by the bond of the bidder, with sureties approved by a postmaster, and in cases where the amount of the bond exceeds five thousand dollars, by a postmaster of the first, second, or third class, in a sum to be designated by the postmaster-general in the advertisement of each route; to which bond a condition shall be annexed, that if the said bidder shall, within such time after his bid is accepted as the postmaster-general shall prescribe, enter into a contract with the United States of America, with good and sufficient sureties, to be approved by the postmaster-general, to perform the service proposed in his said bid, and, further, that he shall perform the said service according to his contract, then the said obligation to be void, otherwise to be in full force and obligation in law; and in case of failure of any bidder to enter into such contract to perform the service, or, having executed a contract, in case of failure to perform the service, according to his contract, he and his sureties shall be liable for the amount of said bond as liquidated damages, to be recovered in an action of debt on the said bond. No proposal shall be considered unless it shall be accompanied by such bond, and there shall have been affixed to said proposal the oath of the bidder, taken before an officer qualified to administer oaths, that he has the ability, pecuniarily, to fulfill his obligations, and that the bid is made in good faith, and with the intention to enter into contract, and perform the service, in case his bid is accepted.

Sec. 246. That before the bond of a bidder provided for in the aforesaid section is approved, there shall be indorsed thereon the oaths of the sureties therein, taken before an officer qualified to administer oaths, that they are owners of real-estate, worth, in the aggregate, a sum double the amount of the said bond, over and above all debts due and owing by them, and all judgments, mortgages, and executions against them, after allowing all exemptions of every character whatever.

Sec. 247. That any postmaster who shall affix his signature to the approval of any bond of a bidder, or to the certificate

To insure the forwarding of a letter through the post-office, it must have not less than three cents in postage-stamps affixed. The word "paid" endorsed

of sufficiency of sureties in any contract before the said bond or contract is signed by the bidder or contractor and his sureties, or shall knowingly, or without the exercise of due diligence, approve any bond of a bidder with insufficient sureties, or shall knowingly make any false or fraudulent certificate, shall be forthwith dismissed from office, and be thereafter disqualified from holding the office of postmaster, and shall also be deemed guilty of a misdemeanor, and, on conviction thereof, be punished by a fine not exceeding five thousand dollars, or by imprisonment not exceeding one year, or both.

Sec. 251. That after any regular bidder whose bid has been accepted, shall fail to enter into contract for the transportation of the mails according to his proposal; or, having entered into contract, shall fail to commence the performance of the service stipulated in his or their contract as therein provided, the postmaster-general shall proceed to contract with the next lowest bidder for the same service, who will enter into a contract for the performance thereof, unless the postmaster-general shall consider such bid too high, in which case he shall re-advertise such service. And if any bidder whose bid has been accepted, and who has entered into a contract to perform the service according to his proposal; and, in pursuance of his contract has entered upon the performance of the service, to the satisfaction of the postmaster-general, shall subsequently fail or refuse to perform the service according to his contract, the postmaster-general shall proceed to contract with the next lowest bidder for such service, under the advertisement thereof (unless the postmaster-general shall consider such bids too high), who will enter into contract and give bond, with sureties, to be approved by the postmaster-general, for the faithful performance thereof, in the same penalty and with the same terms and conditions thereto annexed as were stated and contained in the bond which accompanied his bid; but in case each and every of the next lowest bidders for such service whose respective bids are not considered too high by the postmaster-general shall refuse to enter into contract and give bond as herein required for the faithful performance of his contract, the postmaster-general shall immediately advertise proposals to perform the service on said route. Whenever an accepted bidder shall fail to enter into contract, or a contractor on any mail route shall fail or refuse to

on a letter is not regarded at the office of delivery; letters so marked, and not having any stamp affixed, are treated as unpaid.

perform the service on said route according to his contract, or when a new route shall be established, or new service required; or when, from any other cause, there shall not be a contractor legally bound or required to perform such service, the postmaster-general may make a temporary contract for carrying the mail on such route, without advertisement, for such period as may be necessary, not in any case exceeding six months, until the service shall have commenced under a contract made according to law: Provided, however, That the postmaster-general shall not employ temporary service on any route at a higher price than that paid to the contractor who shall have performed the service during the last preceding regular contract term. And in all cases of regular contracts hereafter made, the contract may, in the discretion of the postmaster-general, be continued in force beyond its express terms for a period not exceeding six months, until a new contract with the same, or other contractors, shall be made by the postmaster-general.

Sec. 253. That hereafter all bidders upon every mail route for the transportation of the mails upon the same, where the annual compensation for the service on such route at the time exceeds the sum of five thousand dollars, shall accompany their bids with a certified check or draft, payable to the order of the postmaster-general, upon some solvent national bank, which check or draft shall not be less than five per centum on the amount of the annual pay on said route at the time such bid is made, and, in case of new or modified service, not less than five per centum of the amount of the bond of the bidder required to accompany his bid, if the amount of the said bond exceeds five thousand dollars. In case any bidder, on being awarded any such contract, shall fail to execute the same with good and sufficient sureties, according to the terms on which such bid was made and accepted, and enter upon the performance of the service to the satisfaction of the postmaster-general, such bidder shall, in addition to his liability on his bond accompanying his bid, forfeit the amount so deposited to the United States, and the same shall forthwith be paid into the treasury for the use of the post-office department; but if such contract shall be duly executed and the service entered upon as aforesaid, such draft or check so deposited, and the checks or drafts deposited by all other

A double rate of six cents for each half ounce or fraction thereof, is chargeable on letters reaching their destination which have not had one full rate

bidders, on the same route, shall be returned to the respective bidders making such deposits. No proposals for the transportation of the mails where the amount of the bond required to accompany the same shall exceed five thousand dollars shall be considered, unless accompanied with the check or draft herein required, together with the bond required by a preceding section: Provided, That nothing in this act shall be construed or intended to affect any penalties or forfeitures which may have heretofore accrued under the provisions of the sections hereby amended.

Sec. 14. That hereafter the postage on public documents mailed by any member of congress, the president, or head of any executive department, shall be ten cents for each bound volume, and on unbound documents the same rate as that on newspapers mailed from a known office of publication to regular subscribers, and the words "public document," written or printed thereon, or on the wrapper thereof, and certified by the signature of any member of congress, or by that of the president, or head of any executive department shall be deemed a sufficient certificate that the same is a public document; and the term "public document" is hereby defined to be all publications printed by order of congress, or either house thereof: Provided, That the postage on each copy of the "Daily Congressional Record" mailed from the city of Washington as transient matter shall be one cent.

The following additional sections and parts of sections of an act approved March 3rd, 1875, making appropriations for the service of the post-office department, &c., relate to the franking privilege, and other matters necessary to be noticed:

Sec. 3. . . . . That the provisions of section thirteen of the act of June 23rd, 1874, entitled "an act making appropriations for the service of the post-office department for the fiscal year ending June 30th, 1875, and for other purposes," shall apply to ex-members of congress and ex-delegates for the period of nine months after the expiration of their terms as members and delegates, and postage on public documents mailed by such persons shall be as provided in said section.

Sec. 5. That from and after the passage of this act, the "Congressional Record," or any part thereof, or speeches or reports therein contained, shall, under the frank of a member of congress or delegate, to be written by himself

prepaid at the mailing office. If a one or two cent stamp has been affixed at the mailing office the amount will be deducted, and the rest charged.

After a letter has passed from the mailing office the delivering of it cannot be delayed or prevented by an alleged writer; but if the writer thereof request the return of a letter placed in a post-office which has not left in the mail, the postmaster must deliver it, provided he is furnished with proper evidence that the party applying is the writer; and, if the application be made before the stamp is canceled it may be returned without canceling the stamp. But a request to return, on a drop-letter, will only be regarded, however, when the address, to which it is to be returned, is within the delivery of the office into which such letter has been dropped. For instance, if a letter prepaid at the drop rate is deposited in the New York post-office, having indorsed thereon a request if not delivered in ten days to be returned to some address in Boston, such request cannot be regarded.

When a letter-carrier delivers a letter at a designated address, in the absence of instructions to

be carried in the mail free of postage, under such regulations as the postmaster-general may prescribe; and that public documents already printed, or ordered to be printed, for the use of either house of congress may pass free through the mails upon the frank of any member or delegate of the present congress, written by himself, until the 1st day of December, A. D. 1875.

Sec. 7. That seeds transmitted by the commissioner of agriculture, or by any member of congress or delegate receiving seeds for distribution from said department, together with agricultural reports emanating from that department, and so transmitted, shall, under such regulations as the postmaster-general shall prescribe, pass through the mails free of charge, and the provisions of this section shall apply to ex-members of congress and ex-delegates, for the period of nine months after the expiration of the terms of members and delegates.

the postmaster to the contrary, it is a legal delivery, and such letter cannot be remailed unless prepaid anew; but parties may insure their letters being forwarded without additional charge, by advising the postmaster in writing. To leave word with a janitor, landlord, or clerk, or any person upon the premises except the postmaster, will not be considered a notice to him.

A letter received by mail, may, in the absence of the principal person named in the address, be delivered to any person to whose care it is directed, who in that case becomes in the nature of an agent of the writer in its delivery. All connection with and responsibility for such letter, on the part of the post-office department, cease and determine upon its passage into the possession of either of the persons named in the address; and the department has no jurisdiction in any questions arising, between the parties, as to the opening or other use of such letter, or of its contents. Delivery of a letter at a designated address, in the absence of any instructions to the postmaster to the contrary, is a legal delivery, and such letter cannot be remailed unless prepaid anew.

Postmasters are not obliged to accept in payment for postage stamps or stamped envelopes, wrappers, &c., any currency so mutilated as to be uncurrent, or the genuineness of which is at all questionable, nor to receive more than twenty-five cents in copper or nickel coins, nor to affix stamps to letters, nor to make change, except as a matter of courtesy, or to give credit for postage.

Cut postage stamps, stamps cut from stamped envelopes, mutilated postage stamps, and internal revenue stamps cannot be accepted in payment of postage. Letters deposited in a post-office having such matter affixed will be held for postage; and the use or attempted use, in payment of postage, of a postage stamp or stamped envelope, or any stamp cut from such stamped envelope, which has been before used in payment of postage, is punishable with a fine of fifty dollars.

Postal cards are cards issued by the post-office department,[1] having one blank side upon which messages may be written, for transportation any distance through the mails. These cards are to be treated by the mail service as sealed letters; with the exception only that, if remaining uncalled for by the person to whom they are directed for sixty days, they will not be sent to the dead letter office, or returned upon request, but will be burned by postmasters. In using postal cards care should be taken to write or print nothing upon the side reserved for the address; as, if anything but the address be inscribed upon that side, they are unmailable. They are unmailable likewise if anything be pinned, pasted, gummed, or otherwise attached to them, or if two postal cards be pinned or pasted together. No card is a postal card except such as are issued by the post-office department. Cards issued by private parties, containing anything written besides the address, are ratable as letters, and will be sent subject to letter postage.

The postal regulations prohibit the mailing of postal cards containing writing of an indecent character, or scurrilous epithets, but there is nothing to prohibit the mailing of a postal card containing a bill or notice of indebtedness; and such communications on postal cards may be written or printed, or both.[2]

Postmasters have the right to read communications on postal cards, and to exclude them from the

[1] U. S. Postal Laws, § 170, p. 77.

[2] *Post*, page 510.

mail when they contain obscene, scurrilous, or abusive epithets, but they should not disclose information obtained by reason of such perusal.

A postal card reaching its destination, and having been delivered to the person named in the address, has performed its functions as a postal card. In order to again pass in the mails it must be prepaid at letter rates of postage.

A postal card with one address erased and another substituted, is mailable at letter rates only; and a postal card on which anything is written, printed, or attached for the purpose of concealing the message, or any part thereof, is mailable only at letter rates.

The post-office department has no authority to issue postal cards of any other denomination than one cent. For all other purposes of correspondence postage stamps are issued.

All postage stamps of the department issues of 1861, and subsequent dates, are still available for the payment of postage. Stamps issued prior to 1861 have been declared obsolete, and will not be received in payment of postage.

Postmasters are not allowed to exchange postage stamps for goods, or to traffic in them in any manner whatever; nor has the post-office department facilities for the redemption or exchange of postage stamps in the hands of private parties.

Under the present regulations nothing is allowed to pass through the mail without stamps; and the post-office officials themselves, writing upon public business, are required to employ the stamps now issued for the particular department to which they are attached.

In printed matter sent through the mails, no written matter is permitted to be inclosed, with the exception that bills or receipts for subscription to regular subscribers to a newspaper, may be covered within them. A regular subscriber to a periodical has been pronounced to be one who regularly receives—through a designated and certain post-office, mailed from a known publication office or news agency, and at the post-office for the district in which such office is situated, or the nearest thereto, and at stated intervals—a newspaper, magazine, or other periodical, for which he has paid or undertaken to pay a subscription price, or for whom some other person has paid or undertaken so to pay. But, in the latter case, such payment must have been made or undertaken to be made, with the previous consent or request of the receiver. One to whom a publication is sent without his request or consent is not understood to be a "regular subscriber" within the meaning of the regulation. Matter printed for gratuitous circulation, or specimen copies of newspapers, will not be received at regular subscription rates.

"Should a postmaster suspect that a publisher is in the habit of mailing his periodicals to persons who are not regular subscribers thereto, without prepayment of postage as for transient printed matter, he should require such publisher to take and subscribe the oath in the form set forth in the 9th section, act of June 23, 1874.[1] If the publisher, after having been requested to take the oath, shall, either by himself or any of his agents, repeat the offense, the postmaster should present a written statement of all the facts of the case to the United States attorney for the judicial district in which his office is situated, in order that the offender may be prosecuted for the penalty named in the law—$1,000. Upon receipt of newspapers or other periodicals at a post-office, addressed

[1] *Ante*, p. 488.

to persons who disclaim being subscribers thereto, and upon which postage has not been paid by stamps, as required for transient printed matter, the fact should be promptly reported to the postmaster at the mailing office, giving the name and date of the periodical, the place of its publication, name of the publisher and of the person who denied being a subscriber thereto, with a request that such publisher be required to take the oath referred to in section 9, act of June 23, 1874. Should the offense be repeated by the same publisher, after notice given to the mailing office, the case should be fully reported to the post-office department."[1]

Any concealment or inclosure of written within printed matter, will subject the sender to a fine of five dollars; unless the party to whom it is addressed consent to pay letter postage thereon. If he decline so to do, the matter must be returned to the sending office in order that the sending postmaster may cause the offender to be prosecuted for the penalty.

Anything written upon the envelope or wrapper which covers the printed matter, more than is absolutely necessary to insure its accurate delivery—even such a request to return as is allowable in the case of letters—subjects the printed matter to letter postage. But a professional card imprinted upon the wrapper, or pen marks upon the inclosed printed matter;—designed to call attention to a portion thereof or to correct a typographical error—is permissible. The rule seems to be that no information, additional to that printed in the printed matter, shall be conveyed with a pen. A mark calling attention to a portion of the print or correcting a typographical error therein, it appears, is not considered additional matter—though

[1] United States Official Postal Guide, p. 23.

if the price of an article mentioned in the print, or if signs which conveyed any meaning to the writer or receiver, were added with a pen, such pen marks would be. The wrapper of this printed matter may be transparent and sealed; or open at the ends; or secured by a rubber band, or twine, or it may be of any such other character, form or condition, as to permit the examination of its contents by the post-office officials; the regulation being that the wrapper must be such an one as to allow of the examination without being destroyed. Postmasters are not at liberty to destroy a wrapper; therefore, if the scrutiny is not facilitated without, the matter must pay letter postage.

Publishers of newspapers are allowed to fold within their newspapers any printed supplement thereto—that is to say, any matter crowded out of the paper itself, or that, from want of time, or for greater convenience, is separately printed. Such a supplement is considered and required to be a genuine accompaniment of the paper; printed with the intent and purpose of supplying an omission in the particular issue of the paper which it accompanies, and not for any distinct purpose, without which the newspaper itself would be complete (such as a tradesman's advertisement, a postal card, or the like). A package of papers from a publishing-office sent to any one address, cannot be considered as being sent in the course of regular subscription. Newspaper-dealers, however, may return surplus papers to the publication-office at pound rates. When a subscriber to a newspaper or periodical changes his post-office, he cannot have his publications forwarded from the old office to the new, free of postage. A request to forward printed matter should be accompanied with an amount sufficient to prepay the postage at third-class rates. Publications borrowing the name, and having some of the characteristics of a newspaper, printed for gratuitous circulation, and depending on their advertisements for support, cannot be sent by mail, gratuitously,—to persons not actual and *bona fide* subscribers,—upon the footing of newspapers sent from a known office of publication and to regular subscribers.

Publications printed in weekly parts, but not offered for mailing until bound in monthly parts, must be prepaid at the rate of three cents per pound, or fraction thereof, and will be classed with publications issued less frequently than once a week. There is no law authorizing the free exchange of publications between publishers. Such exchanges may, however, be included with the bulk mail, and be prepaid at the pound rates of two or three cents, according to frequency of issue.

Ready printed outsides ("patent outsides") can only be sent in the mails at the rate of postage, and under the rules, governing third-class matter, and will not be considered as newspapers.

The delivery, in the United States, of postal matter, is not controlled by acts of congress, or by statutes, but by the rules and regulations of the post-office department. The object of the department being to facilitate, by every means in its power, the delivery of mailed matter to the persons for whom it is intended. Where a mail arrives at a post-office after closing, on Saturday night, a postmaster is not obliged to keep the office open on Sunday, except for an hour or more, if public convenience seem to require it. In the case of registered letters and money-orders, postmasters are expected to exercise a sound discretion, and require such proofs of identity of persons unknown to them, who claim the money, as are ordinarily required in banking institutions, from persons presenting checks or drafts. And in the case of advertised letters, parties should be interrogated as to from whence they are expecting correspondence, &c., &c.

Each post-office box or drawer, in all post-offices, is restricted to the use of one family, firm, or company, and the rent therefor must be paid at least one quarter in advance. A person hiring a post-office box may have the letters of his family, firm, or company, or letters addressed to his friends stopping temporarily with him—if directed to his care or to the number of the box—put into it. But letters addressed to other persons residing in the same place, and living and doing business separate and apart from a box-holder, will not be placed therein.

In every case of loss by mail, the department should be notified of the particulars, as the name of the office in which the letter was posted, and the date of mailing, and by whom; the names of the writer and the person addressed; the amount and a description of the inclosure; the office to which addressed; whether mailed direct or for distribution—if the latter, to what distributing office it was mailed, and whether registered or unregistered, with any other particulars that may aid in making a thorough investigation. Communications on this subject are to be addressed: "Second Assistant Postmaster-General, Division of Mail Depredations."

Printed matter, merchandise, and other third-class[1] matter cannot be forwarded from the office

[1] Mailable matter in the United States is divided into three classes, for convenience of regulation. The first class consists of letters: *i.e.*, all correspondence wholly or partly in writing, excepting book-manuscript, and corrected proof-sheets sent between publishers and authors; all local or "drop" letters,

to which it is addressed, unless the postmaster is furnished with postage at the rate of one cent for each ounce, or fraction thereof, for such purpose. Neither can a postmaster regard a request to return indorsed on such matter, except he is furnished with postage as above.

Only matter subject to letter postage will be registered by the department. Packages of mutilated currency sent for redemption to the treasurer of the United States may be registered free of charge, but postage must be paid at letter rates, and so copyright matter for the librarian of congress must be now prepaid at regular post-office rates.

Letters addressed to initials or fictitious names are not deliverable, unless the address contains a desig-

and postal-cards issued by the department, written visiting-cards, music-manuscript, and architects' drawings; though it has been held that photographs of such drawings are third-class matter. The second class consists of matter exclusively in print, regularly issued, at known intervals, from a fixed office of publication, bearing no written addition of writing, sign, or mark. The third class includes all pamphlets, occasional publications, magazines, transient newspapers, handbills, posters, prospectuses, books, book-manuscript (By U. S. O. P. G. No. 1, manuscript for publication in newspapers, magazines, or periodicals are subject to letter-postage; and any notation made on corrected proof of book-matter, asking for, conveying, or giving information will be subject to letter-postage), proof-sheets, corrected proof-sheets, unsealed circulars, maps, engravings, prints, blanks, flexible patterns, articles of merchandise, phonographic paper, sample-cards, letter-envelopes, postal envelopes, and wrappers, cards, plain and ornamental paper, photographic representations of different types, seeds, cuttings, bulbs, roots, scions, merchandise, almanacs, and all other matter which may be declared mailable by law, and all other articles not above the weight prescribed by law, which are not, from their form or nature, liable to destroy, deface, or otherwise injure the contents of the mail-bag, or the person of any one engaged in the postal-service; but no written matter, or request to return must be written upon matter of this class.

nated place of delivery, for example: Letters addressed A B, station G, New York, are not deliverable; but a letter addressed A B, stating street and number, or a box number, is deliverable.

Packages containing liquids, poisons, glass, live animals, sharp-pointed instruments, sugar, explosive chemicals, or any other matter liable to deface or destroy the contents of the mail, or injure the person of any one connected with the service, must be rigidly excluded from the mails. If such matter be found in any post-office, or in any mail pouch or sack, it must be retained by the postmaster, and the department (third assistant postmaster-general) notified of the fact, when instructions will be given as to its disposition. If found by a postal clerk or route agent, it must be delivered to the post-office at the end of the route, where it will be treated as above directed,

All books, pamphlets, circulars, prints, &c., of an obscene, lewd, lascivious, vulgar, or indecent character; all letters, or circulars concerning illegal lotteries (though lottery schemes, sanctioned by enactments of state legislatures, are held to be legal, and letters and circulars concerning such will be transported through the mails); so-called gift concerts, or other similar enterprise offering prizes, or concerning schemes devised and intended to deceive and defraud the public, for the purpose of obtaining money under false pretenses; letters upon the envelope of which, or postal card upon which, scurrilous epithets have been written or printed, or disloyal devices printed or engraved, must be withdrawn from the mails by postmasters at either the mailing or the delivery office, marked unmailable, and sent to the dead-letter office. Postmasters will promptly notice violations of this section, and where the party by whom such matter is mailed is known, the attention of the United States attorney for the district must be called to the case, and the evidence necessary for conviction, including the matter in question, placed in his hands.[1] The case must also be reported to the special agent of the department for the district, and all the facts at once communicated to the department (second assistant postmaster-general, division of mail depredations and special agents). If the party sending be unknown, the matter must be sent to the third assistant postmaster-general, in a securely-sealed package, with a letter advising him of the transmission of the package, sent by the same mail, but in a separate envelope. The weight of any package to be sent in the mail must not exceed four pounds, except second-class matter, documents printed by order of congress, or emanating from any of the executive departments.[2]

[1] Sections 148, 149. See United States Official Postal Guide: New York, Hurd & Houghton.

[2] The present postage rates of the United States are as follows:

A single rate of three cents is uniformly established on domestic letters: *i.e.*, letters within the various states and territories of the United States, not exceeding half an ounce; double rate if exceeding half an ounce, but not exceeding an ounce; treble rate if exceeding an ounce, but not exceeding an ounce and a half; and so on, charging an additional rate for every additional half ounce, or fraction of half an ounce.

At the post-office where letters brought by vessels or steamboats not employed in carrying the mail from any domestic or foreign port are deposited, they will be charged with double rates of postage, to be collected at the office of delivery—that is to say, six cents for the single weight if mailed, and four cents the single weight if delivered at the office; but if such letter has been prepaid by United States stamps at such double rate of postage, no additional charge will be made. If only partly prepaid by stamps, the unpaid balance will be charged and collected on delivery.

On first-class matter (letters, sealed packages, mail-matter

The post-office is a department of the general government, created by statute, and its officers are paid by the government, and cannot be understood

wholly or partly in writing, except book-manuscript and corrected proofs passing between authors and publishers, and except local or drop-letters, or United States postal-cards; all printed matter so marked as to convey any other or further information than is conveyed by the original print, except the correction of mere typographical errors; all matter otherwise chargeable with letter-postage, but which is so wrapped or secured that it cannot be conveniently examined by postmasters without destroying the wrapper or envelope; all packages containing matter not in itself chargeable with letter-postage, but in which is inclosed or concealed any letter, memorandum, or other thing chargeable with letter-postage, or upon which is any writing or memorandum; all matter to which no specific rate of postage is assigned; and manuscript for publication in newspapers, magazines, or periodicals), three cents for each half ounce, or fraction thereof.

On local or drop-letters, at offices where free delivery by carriers is established, two cents for each half ounce, or fraction thereof.

On local or drop letters at all offices where there is no free delivery by carriers, one cent for each half ounce or fraction thereof.

On all second-class matter the postage is as follows: On all newspapers and periodicals, mailed under the definition above given, to regular subscribers or news agents, which are issued weekly or oftener, two cents for each pound or fraction of a pound; and on all such issued less frequently than once a week, five cents for each pound or fraction of a pound. The 6th section of the act of June 23d, 1874, which provided that the above regulations should take effect on and after the first day of January, 1875, also provided "that on and after the said first day of January, upon the receipt of such newspapers and periodical publications at the office of mailing, they shall be weighed in bulk, and postage paid thereon by a special adhesive stamp, to be devised and furnished by the postmaster-general, which shall be affixed to such matter, or the sack containing the same, or upon a memorandum of such mailing, or otherwise, as the postmaster-general may, from time to time, provide by regulation. Under this regulation, publishers and news dealers must present their newspapers and periodicals at the post-office, sorted into the

as entering into any contract with the community or with individuals. The postmaster-general is therefore responsible only to the government of which he is an agent, and all contracts made by him are made by and binding upon the government, and not by or upon himself personally.[1] But—while the postmaster-general is not responsible either for his own default or for the default of his deputies[2]—yet his deputies themselves have been held liable, for want of diligence, or for fraud of their subordinates, when they themselves have not exercised a reasonable caution and discretion in their selection of agents.[3] Generally mail contractors will be held to make no personal contracts with the senders of letters, and to be responsible only to the government from which they receive their remuneration;[4] but it has been held otherwise.[5] No law of the United States, in reference to the postal service, makes it a legal channel of

above indicated classes, that they may be separately weighed, and the adhesive stamps above indicated must be affixed either by the department or by the proprietors. Ordinary postage stamps cannot be used for the purpose, nor can these special newspaper stamps be used for any other purpose.—U. S. Official Postal Guide.

[1] Rowning v. Goodchild, 3 Wills. 443; Whitfield v. Le Despencer, Cowp. 754; Story on Cont. § 979; on Agency, §§ 302–307; on Bailments, §§ 462, 463, 464; 1 Bell Comm. § 468; Dunlop v. Munroe, 7 Cranch, 242; Bolan v. Williamson, 2 Bay, 551; Schroyer v. Linch, 8 Watts, 632.

[2] Story on Cont. § 970; Wiggins v. Hathaway, 6 Barb. (N. Y.) 632.

[3] Maxwell v. McIlroy, 2 Bibb. 211; Bishop v. Williamson, 2 Fairf. 495; Dunlop v. Munroe, 7 Cranch, 242; Bolan v. Williamson, 2 Bay, 551; Dox v. Postmaster, 1 Pet. 318; Christy v. Smith, 23 Vt. (8 Wast.) 663; Teall v. Felton, 3 Barb. (N. Y.) 512; 1 Comst. (N. Y.) 537; Coleman v. Frazier, 4 Rich. 146; Fitzgerald v. Burrill, 106 Mass. 446.

[4] Conwell v. Voorhies, 13 Ohio, 523; Hutchins v. Brackett 2 Fost. (11) 252.

[5] Sawyer v. Coral, 17 Gratt. 230.

communication, which a party may adopt as compulsory upon his correspondent.[1] When a letter is placed in a post-office, it is within the legal custody of the officers of the government, and no one has the authority to open it, even though it comes from a criminal and is suspected of containing improper information,[2] but it is the duty of the postmaster, if the person to whom it is directed live in the same place where his office is situated (or if his office be the nearest post-office) to deliver it to that person.[3]

The postmaster is the only judge of the fact as to which paper has the largest circulation; under the act of congress of March 3, 1845, obliging him to advertise a list of letters non-called for in such a paper, and he is not responsible in a state court for the results of his judgment.[4] Nor will an action lie against a postmaster by publishers for refusing their proofs as to the circulation of their newspaper.[5]

[1] Tanner v. Hughes, 53 Pa. St. 289.

[2] United States v. Eddy, 1 Bess. 527; Id. v. Pond, 2 Curris C. C. 265.

[3] Nevins v. Bank, 10 Mich. 547.

[4] Foster v. McKibben, 4 Pa. L. J. Rep. 303: 14 Pa. St. (2 Harris) 168.

[5] Strong v. Campbell, 11 Barb. (N. Y.) 135. And see besides generally as to post-office and postmasters, U. S. v. Bank of Necropolis, 15 Pet. 378; Postmaster-General v. Rice, Gilpin, 544; U. S. v. Hart, Pet. C. C. 390; Trafton v. U. S., 3 Story, 646; Boody v. U. S., 1 W. & M. 150; U. S. v. Davis, Deady, 294; Foster v. McKibben, 4 Pa. L. J. Rep. 303; Fitzgerald v. Burrill, 106 Mass. 46; U. S. v. Driscoll, 1 Low. 303; U. S. v. Crow, 1 Bond. 51; Farnam v. U. S., 1 Col. T. 309; Chouteau v. Steamboat St. Anthony, 1 Miss. 226; U. S. v. Hedges, 13 How. (U. S.) 478; Ware v. U. S., 4 Wal. (Id.) 617; Trafton v. U. S. 3 Story, 646; U. S. v. Brown, 9 How. (U. S.) 487; Id. v. Roberts, Id. 501; Id. v. Rice, 9 Gilpin, 554; Id. v. Foye, 1 Curtis C. C. 364; Id. v. Fisher, 5 McLean, 23; Id. v. Kean, 5 Id. 509; Id. v. Tanner, 6 Id. 128; Id. v. Whitaker, Id. 343; Id. v. Emerson, Id. 406: Id. v. Sander, Id.

We have already seen that the doctrine of innocence will be insisted upon by the United States postal department, and that no scurrilous, obscene, or libelous matter will be allowed in the mails. The offense of sending scurrilous postal cards through the mails will be prosecuted by government, and heavy penalties visited upon offenders. One Chamberlin, who was indicted in the United States circuit court for the southern district of New York, for sending such postal cards, was found guilty and sentenced by the court to pay a fine of five thousand dollars.[1]

598; Id. v. Beatty, 1 Hemp. (U. S.) 487; Id. v. Parsons, 2 Blatchf. 104; Id. v. Marselis, Id. 108; Id. v. Collingham, Id. 470; Id. 4. Mulvaney, 4 Parker (N. Y.) 164; Id. v. Collins, 4 Blatchf. 142; Id. v. Kirby, 7 Wall. (U. S.) 482; Tanner v. Hughes, 53 Pa. St. 289; Sawyer v. Corse, 17 Gratt. (Va.) 230; Wingate v. McNamar, 28 Ind. 481. As to what is mailable matter, see U. S. v. Bromley, 12 How. (U. S.) 88; Teal v. Felton, Id. 284.

A common carrier cannot on the ground of its employment by government set up that it is an agent of the government, so as to escape liabilities for the negligence of its own servants. Truex v. Erie Ry. Co., 4 Lans. (N. Y.) 198.

[1] This case is as yet unreported. The indictment was filed June 30th, 1875. The trial began December 15th, 1874, and lasted nine days. The indictment contained fourteen different counts (four of which were afterwards consolidated); upon one of which counts, the jury finding the defendant guilty, he was sentenced to pay the above fine. See New York Times, December 15–24, 1874. And the offense of writing defamatory matter on a postal-card is also one civilly cognizable, and sounding in damages. In Crane v. Walker, in the Marine Court of the city of New York, the plaintiff, a collector of past-due claims, applied to the defendant, a tailor, on Fifth-avenue, in 1871, with a letter of introduction, for employment. A number of bills were given him, upon which a percentage was to be paid in case of collection, rising to thirty per cent. if suit had to be brought, the plaintiff, however, to pay all expenses. Two or three bills were collected and returned, the plaintiff in the meantime ordering and receiving a pair of pants, which remain unpaid for, although defendant claimed that pay-

The same rule will be applied to the sending of messages by private telegraph companies. A telegraph company would have the right to decline the transmission of all messages of an illegal or immoral character, or such as were in furtherance of fraud or against public policy; or where the message was for the purpose of aiding or concealing crime, or would in any other way tend to thwart the course of public justice. If this were not so, the agents of the company would, in some cases, become *particeps criminis;* and would, in all such cases, be lending their aid, for a reward, to purposes not sanctioned by the law. The same moral and legal obligation rests upon the company as upon individuals, in reference to their contracts and dealings with each other; and whatever the law would not compel it to perform, it has the

ment was promised within a month. Among the claims was one against a person named Salmonson, against whom suit was brought, judgment obtained, and examination on supplementary proceedings had, the plaintiff in the end getting forty dollars from Salmonson, not in reduction of the judgment, but in payment of referee's fees, costs, &c. This collection coming to Mr. Walker's ears, and supposing it to have been a payment on account of the bill, of which no return was made to him, and, as he says, being unable to get an explanation, he wrote the following words on a postal-card, and sent it to the plaintiff through the mail:—"It seems to me you are acting like a regular fraud in your treatment of me. You admit of having collected forty dollars from Salmonson, and yet you have made no return to me, and not on your own account which you got on false pretenses. It is more than thieving to do as you have done, and if it is possible I'll have you put in jail for collecting my money without making any return." It was shown that this was read by several parties while lying on the plaintiff's desk before his arrival at his office. The court charged the jury that a publication was established, and that the amount of their verdict would be governed by the injury done and the intent of the defendant in writing it.

A verdict was rendered for the plaintiff for three hundred dollars.—N. Y. Herald, May 19th, 1875.

right to refuse. In some of the American states the transmission of such messages is expressly prohibited by statute, and in some of them it is made a criminal offense so to do.[1] By the California statute[2] it is provided: "If any agent or operator in any telegraph office shall knowingly send by telegraph any false or forged message, purporting to be from such officer (or telegraph company), or any other person, or if any other person or persons shall furnish, or conspire to furnish, to such operator, to be so sent any such message knowing the same to be false or forged, with the intent to deceive and injure, or defraud any individual or corporation, or the public, such agent, operator, or persons, shall be deemed guilty of a misdemeanor and shall be punished by fine not exceeding five hundred dollars, or imprisonment, not to exceed six months, or both, such fine and imprisonment, in the discretion of the court."

There is a similar provision in Pennsylvania[3] and in Oregon.[4] In Ohio,[5] it is provided that if any agent officer, or manager of any telegraph line, operating in this state, or any other person, shall knowingly transmit, by such telegraph line, any false communication or intelligence, with intent to injure any one, or to speculate in any article of merchandise, commerce, or trade, or with intent that another may do so, or shall knowingly send or deliver any dispatch that is thereto, he shall, on conviction, pay a fine not exceeding five hundred dollars. By the California act of April 18, 1862, sec. 4, it is provided that nothing in the act

[1] Scott & Jarnagin on the Law of Telegraphs, § 119.
[2] Act of April 22, 1850.
[3] Purdons's Digest, 1861, Crimes, 185.
[4] Compilation of 1866, ch. 54, § 19.
[5] Act of March 31, 1865.

contained shall require the sending, receiving, or delivering of any message counseling, aiding, abetting, or encouraging treason against the government of the United States or of this state, or other resistance to the lawful authority, or any message calculated to further any fraudulent plan or purpose, o to instigate or encourage the perpetration of any unlawful act, or to fac''tate the escape of any criminal or person accused of crime. By the Revised Statutes of Kentucky,[1] "If an agent, officer, or manager of a telegraph line, constructed in this state, or other person, shall knowingly transmit, on or through the same, any false communication or intelligence, with intention to injure any one, or to speculate on any article of merchandise, commerce, or to trade, or with intent that another may do so; or if any agent, officer, manager of a telegraph line, from corrupt or improper motives, or willful negligence, shall withhold the transmission of messages or intelligence, for which the customary charges have been paid or tendered, he shall be fined not less than ten, nor more than five hundred dollars."

[1] 1860, vol. 1, pp. 394, 395; and other states have enacted to the same effect.

END OF VOL. I.

www.ingramcontent.com/pod-product-compliance
Lightning Source LLC
LaVergne TN
LVHW021305110826
845150LV00003B/488

* 9 7 8 1 4 2 5 5 5 9 6 8 7 *